MUST GLOBAL POLITICS CONSTRAIN DEMOCRACY?

The empire was something with which the French people had nothing whatever to do, and its story was that of machinations of high finance, the Church, and the military caste, which tirelessly reerected overseas the Bastilles which had been overthrown in France.

(Herbert Lüthy, *France against Herself*)

Exhortations to disregard domestic usurpation [President Adams's attempt to outlaw the Republican Party after the XYZ affair], until foreign danger shall have passed, is an artifice which may be forever used; because the possessors of power, who are the advocates of its extension, can ever create national embarrassments, to be successively employed to soothe people into sleep, whilst that power is swelling silently, secretly and fatally. Of the same character are insinuations of a foreign influence, which seize upon a laudable enthusiasm against danger from abroad and distort it by an unnatural application, so as to blind your eyes to danger at home.

(James Madison)

Pablo Picasso (1881–1973), *Guernica*. Copyright © ARS, NY. Museo Nacional Centro de Arte Reina Sofia, Madrid, Spain. Photo. Art Resource, NY.

Doch wir haben die Heimat nicht verloren,
Unsre Heimat ist heute vor Madrid.

[Yet we have not lost our homeland.
Our homeland is today in front of Madrid.]
(Erick Weinert's "Song of the International Brigades")

and governments that told me NO,
YOU CANNOT GO!
I came.
(Langston Hughes, "Hero—International Brigade")

The peasants who worked the earth where our dead
lie know what those dead died for. There was time
during the war for them to learn these things, and
there is forever for them to remember them in.
    (Ernest Hemingway, eulogy for members of the
    Lincoln Brigade who died in the four and one-
    half month battle along the heights of Jarama,
                February 14, 1939)[1]

MUST GLOBAL POLITICS CONSTRAIN DEMOCRACY?

GREAT-POWER REALISM,
DEMOCRATIC PEACE, AND
DEMOCRATIC INTERNATIONALISM

Alan Gilbert

PRINCETON UNIVERSITY PRESS   PRINCETON, NEW JERSEY

Library of Congress Cataloging-in-Publication Data
Gilbert Alan
Must global politics constrain democracy? : great-power realism,
democratic peace, and democratic internationalism /
Alan Gilbert.
p.   cm.
Includes bibliographical references and index.
ISBN 0-691-00181-2 (cl. : alk. paper) —
ISBN 0-691-00182-0 (pbk. : alk. paper)
1. International relations.   2. World politics—1945–
3. Democracy.   I. Title.
JZ1242.B54   1999
327.1′01—dc21   99-12203

This book has been composed in Sabon

The paper used in this publication meets the minimum requirements
of ANSI/NISO Z39.48-1992 (R1997) (*Permanence of Paper*)

http://pup.princeton.edu

Printed in the United States of America

1   3   5   7   9   10   8   6   4   2

1   3   5   7   9   10   8   6   4   2
(Pbk.)

For I. F. Stone

NOT QUITE RELATIVE, RADICAL, AND
STUDENT OF ATHENIAN DEMOCRACY, WHO
EXEMPLIFIES MULTIPLE HUMAN CAPACITIES
AND ADVENTURE IN THE STAGES OF LIFE

Contents

Acknowledgments

GEORGE DOWNS offered uniquely helpful suggestions for framing the argument. I have also benefited from discussions of democracy and international politics with John Rawls, and of neorealism with Stephen Krasner, Robert Keohane, and Robert Gilpin.

Jack Donnelly criticized several chapters and recommended that I look into Niebuhr. Jim Cole was an invaluable source on CIA depredations. Nikhil Hemmady and Anthony Lott tracked information about the U.N. boycott of Iraq. Paula Bard made suggestions about paintings.

Steering this manuscript between unfortunately rocky, cross-subdisciplinary shoals, Ann Wald has been a wonderful editor. I would also like to thank Kristin Gager and Layla Asali of Princeton University Press and Richard Isomaki.

A democratic internationalist theory—an internal critique of all the leading versions of realism and neorealism as well as 1990s arguments about interdemocratic peace—speaks to today's audience, but I also mean to honor the anti–Vietnam War movement, in which I participated, and other insurgencies, for instance opposition to the U.S. war on Mexico or support for the Spanish republic (the Abraham Lincoln Brigade), now neglected or forgotten. The internationalism of democrats, anarchists, socialists, and communists in World War II arose dialectically out of the heroism of fallen Spain. Thus, joining anti-Fascists in Spain, Italians emerged from the exile of Parisian cafes and sparked resistance to Mussolini at home. Picasso's *Guernica* was a sign of, and spurred international revulsion at, Franco and Hitler. Despite governmental and academic harassment, democratic action, in times of international crisis, often exerts important counterweight.

I would also like to thank Terence Ball, Benjamin Barber, Asma Barlas, David Blaney, Stephen Bronner, Hauke Brunkhorst, Wendy Brown, Gerald Chapman, Christine Chawaszcza, Jim Cowperthwaite, George DeMartino, Amy Eckert, Karen Feste, Rainer Forst, David Goldfischer, Claudio Gonzalez, Vincent Harding, Robert Hazan, Marcelo de Arau Hoffman, Brenda Horrigan, Micheline Ishay, Paul Kan, Sudarshan Kapur, Haider Ali Khan, Hong-Myong Kim, Jacek Lubicki, Sakah Mahmud, Kathleen Mahoney-Norris, John McCamant, Manoo Mofidi, Joao Nogueira, Bhikhu Parekh, Mustapha Pasha, Dan Ritchie, Tom Rowe, Alan Ryan, Mary Luke Tobin, Barbara Traudt, Doug Vaughan, Ritu Vij, Dana Villa, Michael Walzer, Lucy Ware, Matthew

Weinert, Albrecht Wellmar, Dan Wessner, and Dana Wilbanks for help-ful discussions.

I worked on this project for a year at the Institute for Advanced Study in Princeton, an environment idyllic enough to call forth academic con-flict and yet, wonderfully, to sustain scholarship. I am especially grateful to Lucille Allsden, Walter Jackson, Jim Rule, Yuval Yonay, and many others I encountered there. I would also like to thank the University of Denver and the Graduate School of International Studies—in particular Dan Ritchie, Bill Zaranka, and Tom Farer—for a congenial atmosphere and generous support.

I delivered versions of "Must Global Politics Constrain Democracy?" to Parliamentarians for Global Democracy at the Hague in the Nether-lands, January 1994; in honor of the fiftieth anniversary of the founding of Chosun University, Kwangju, South Korea, November 1996; at the conference "The Global Transformation of International Law, Human Rights, and Democracy," Kulturwissenschaftliches Institut, Essen, Ger-many, December 1996; and at the International Relations colloquium at Princeton University, April 1998. I spoke on a panel "Realism: For and Against," with Michael Doyle, Stephen Krasner, and John Mearsheimer, sponsored by both the International Security and Political Theory sec-tions, at the American Political Science Association, September 1993. I also delivered "Athenian Imperialism and Internal Corruption" at Am-herst College, November 1995, and at the Graduate School of Interna-tional Studies, April 1996; "Crossing of the Ways: The Vietnam War and Morgenthau's Realism," to the Institute for Advanced Study, February 1993, the Society for the Study of European Ideas at Graz, Austria, Au-gust 1994, the Graduate School of International Studies, April 1995, and the International Relations Colloquium at American University in Febru-ary 1996. I spoke on "Marx on Internationalism and War" at the APSA in September 1977.

Permission to reproduce *Guernica* was granted by the Museo Nacional Centro de Arte Reina Sofia, Madrid.

I am grateful for permission to print a revised version of "Must Global Politics Constrain Democracy? Realism, Regimes and Democratic Inter-nationalism," *Political Theory* 20, no. 1 (February 1992): 8–37, copy-right © 1992 by Sage Publications, and a reply to Stephen Krasner, "Power Rivalry–Motivated Democracy" 20, no. 3 (November 1992): 681–89, copyright © 1992 by Sage Publications—an exchange that prompted the 1993 APSA panel—as well as to *Philosophy and Public Affairs* for "Marx on Internationalism and War" (summer 1978), re-printed in *Marx, Justice, and History,* edited by Marshall Cohen, Thomas Nagel, and Thomas Scanlon (Princeton: Princeton University Press, 1980).

In 1998, Wolfgang Kerstring and Christine Chwaszcza, editors of *Philosophie der Internationalen Beziehungen* (Frankfurt am Main: Suhrkamp Verlag), included the first chapter. The introduction will appear in a collection edited by Hauke Brunkhorst and Gertrud Koch at Fischer Verlag in Frankfurt, forthcoming.

MUST GLOBAL POLITICS CONSTRAIN DEMOCRACY?

Power Politics, Antiradical Ideology, and the Constriction of Democracy

> A polis should not be considered happy or a legislator praised, when its citizens are trained for victory in war and the subjection of neighboring regimes. Such a policy . . . implies that any citizen who can do so, should make it his object to capture the government of his own city.
>
> (Aristotle, *Politics*, 1333b29–33)

> Therefore my Harry
> Be it thy course to busy giddy minds
> With foreign quarrels.
> (The dying king's counsel to his son,
> Shakespeare, *2 Henry IV*)[1]

> Nations troubled with civil dissension gain internal peace as a result of wars with their external enemies.
> (G. W. F. Hegel, *Elements of a Philosophy of Right*, addition to par. 324)

1. REALISM, DEMOCRATIC PEACE, AND DEMOCRATIC INTERNATIONALISM

Many Cold War investigators of international relations have attempted to forge a science of politics from classic works in political theory and history, notably those of Thucydides and Hobbes. They have translated these long-standing arguments—allegedly without residue—into an up-to-date realist and neorealist idiom. In doing this, they have ordinarily ignored the importance of democratic regimes or, when challenged, seen them at most as a secondary characteristic of international relations.[2] They have sought to extricate idiom from value, to trade in a putative currency of power, not "soft" moral rhetoric.

With the end of the Cold War, however, an underlying interest in democracy—especially in the thesis that democracies do not go to war with one another—has emerged to challenge realism. In the early 1980s,

Michael Doyle's essays about interdemocratic peace were exiled to a philosophy journal, *Philosophy and Public Affairs*.[3] Today, however, controversy over the absence of war between industrially developed European and American democracies guides the research of many investigators in the field. This controversy diametrically contrasts a view espousing the transformative, causal impact of *domestic* regimes on international politics against a view stressing *external* determination of national interests through great-power rivalry, in abstraction from domestic regime structure.[4] However welcome, this debate has so far left questions about the potential *feedback* of power rivalry on democracy unasked.

In particular, neorealists have long ignored any notion of democratic internationalism, the idea that citizens often have common interests against their own power-state, and in alliance with those of citizens elsewhere. As we will see, this critique comes from a different, much more internal, direction than the democratic-peace hypothesis[5] (I will occasionally refer to my view as democratic internationalism from below to contrast it with the latter—a democratic internationalism from above). By internal, I mean that the critique starts from the same core premise as neorealism—the autonomy of great-power rivalry—but shows that such rivalry has, contra neorealism, often devastating effects on democracy at home. While my argument focuses on the interests and sometimes the organizing of citizens on a transnational scale—and is, hence, internationalist—the democracy to which it refers is a regime that realizes a common good among citizens *within* each country. To prevent misunderstanding, I will now sketch the comparatively subtle debate between sophisticated realism and democratic internationalism and then flesh it out in the bulk of the book.

Neorealists affirm a sharp distinction between national interests—allegedly solely determined by global-power rivalry—and domestic regime structures. They set each state in a hierarchy of powers, ranked by relative, abstract, regime-neutral measures of strength: GNP, geographic location, size and technological sophistication of military, and the like. Measures of power are thus *apolitical*, politics reduced to other, allegedly more significant, fungible terms.

Though neorealism sees itself as more scientific than earlier conceptions, it strives to retain central realist insights into power-rivalry against "legalism" and "moralism" (as chapter 1 argues, neorealists often translate what were once *specific*, controversial claims about international politics into disparately justified, *epistemological* terms, which are implausible in their own right). Historically, realists stigmatized "idealists," those who imagined that international agreements, organizations, or the Melian magistrates' and Nicias's future "hopes," as described by Thucydides, would just by themselves check power-state criminality. Following Hobbes, a realist might even suggest that "diffidence" will drive those who seek to check the perhaps rare leader who engages in the "perpetual and restless search of power after power which ceaseth only in death." Herz names this feature of international politics the security dilemma. In the main, realists, neorealists, and Marxians win that debate with "idealists." But my argument *begins* only at this point.

In a jujitsu-like rhetorical figure, democratic internationalism grants, for the sake of argument, the initial neorealist claim about the autonomy of international jostling for power (realist and internationalist thesis 1) and asks: *what impact does a system of global power-rivalry have on democracy at home?*[6] This question undermines a misguided positivist doctrine, stressing differing "levels of analysis" and sanctioning an ostensibly rigid separation of the international from the domestic sphere.[7]

If realism is right, then given the threat of security-competition and the need to retain power in inegalitarian societies, leaders will have some psychological inclination as well as Machiavellian incentive to make enemies of the "other" (internationalist thesis 2).[8] Particular national traditions and ideologies buoy such inclinations. As we shall see, neorealists have often criticized such "crusading ideologies"—Stephen Krasner on "anticommunism," John Mearsheimer on "hypernationalism"—without seeing how they issue from international competition or tracing their devastating impact on *democracy*. In fact, *crusade* is a favored term of abuse for American realists and neorealists.[9]

Although such realists have often seen an analogy between power internationally and domestically,[10] they have long sought to disengage international from domestic politics, to shield "professional diplomacy" from "popular diplomacy," or, as they see it, democracy (realist thesis 2).[11] The initial neorealist assertion (realist thesis 1) reinforces this isolation by making it an assumption, perhaps implausible, rather than an argument.

During the Vietnam War, however, when anticommunist ideology committed the United States to a protracted, losing cause, Hans J. Morgenthau came to identify with the antiwar movement against the elite (in conversation, Krasner also acknowledged that "the antiwar movement represented the national interest"); others, such as George Kennan, identified "our military-industrial addiction" and the sorry electoral impact of red-baiting as primarily elite, not citizen, phenomena. As chapters 1 and 2 show, that sea-change undercuts standard realist disdain for democracy and supports a different, internationalist account of the dangers of ideological zealotry.

Perhaps more than any other twentieth-century event, the Vietnam War illustrates the *destructive feedback of international rivalry* on democracy at home.[12] Morgenthau, for example, served as an adviser on Vietnam and counseled President Johnson to withdraw American troops. As a rejoinder, LBJ launched "Project Morgenthau," stigmatizing critics of the war as "traitors." Though privately opposed to the war, Morgenthau's colleagues maintained public silence. In response, Morgenthau named an "academic-political complex," which threatens dissidents with denial of prestige, invitations to speak, promotion, and the like; he and Reinhold Niebuhr also stressed the secret CIA corruption of the National Student Association. Thus, the antiwar movement came initially, and mainly, from students and, only gradually, from a minority of faculty members outside of political science.[13] In the context of insidious governmental and university pressures on behalf of an unjust war, the attempt of neorealists to construct an intellectual wall between international and domestic politics collapses.

Concurring with Morgenthau, Krasner's *Defending the National Interest* envisions internal regimes, parallel to international powers, as predatory. He sees statism or structural Marxism as the best explanation of American politics.[14] In that case, however, an internationalist might insist, a governmental and capitalist oligarchy can, once again, use fear of enemies—Madison's "insinuation of foreign influence"—to check democratic opposition and pursue policies harmful to most citizens (internationalist and realist thesis 3).

Even with occasional concessions to workers, such oligarchic policies could not be thought to realize a common good. As in the Iran-Contra affair, they subvert equal-liberty-based, constitutional government and augment centralized secret police forces, surveillance, and stigmatization of criticism and difference.[15] Further, they tie the "loyal" opposition to international belligerence—military and police aid and training as well as CIA "intervention" to sustain oligarchies in the less developed countries—and domestic victimization. Outside of periods of popular revolt, Democrats as well as Republicans have furthered racism, undermined strikes, and suppressed radicals. In addition, through an institutional structure designed, in the *Federalist Papers*, to blunt popular demands,[16] as well as through divisions among the people, the American elite has succeeded in maintaining even more unjust policies than European ones.[17] Such claims explain, for instance, the comparative weakness, among industrial countries, of American social policies with regard to health care, employment, and the like.[18]

Moreover, recent political science has linked foreign interventions with economic and presidential electoral cycles more than external causes.[19] Thus, the *antidemocratic feedback* of global rivalry in a presidential system works as strikingly in peacetime as in war (internationalist thesis 2). In addition, special incentives to intervene may characterize such a regime compared to parliamentary ones—what Downs and Rocke call "gambling for resurrection." A directly elected chief executive may wonder if she might save a losing cause—and, hence, her job—or more likely, in appearing to save the cause, drum up support at election time and bait opponents as "unpatriotic," by escalation (realist and internationalist thesis 3).[20] Though based on international politics and democratic theory, democratic internationalism also draws on comparative politics. To demonstrate the antidemocratic-feedback effect, I offer historical evidence from President Adams's and Hamilton's attempt to pillory Jefferson and Madison as "Gallomen" and "wild Irish" and pass the Alien and Sedition Acts, to the "L" word and "card-carrying ACLU members" of the Reagan-Bush era. We might call this third, realist and internationalist thesis about electoral politics the *constriction of political alternatives, public-corruption argument* (I refer to the ancient, republican sense of "corruption": the absence of any concern for a common good).[21]

As chapter 1 maintains, Gilpin's argument on militarism and dependence emphasizes the recent U.S. slide compared to Japan, its excess of "commitments" over "capabilities," at the expense of most Americans.[22] The militarized economy after World War II and what Fulbright rightly calls "paranoid anti-communism" have ultimately exacted the "price of empire": a decline of American industry and of living standards for most workers (realist and internationalist thesis 4).

As chapter 1 also shows, Keohane underlines the impact of contemporary international *economic regimes* in stifling reforms. Now Keohane seeks to demonstrate genuine—common-good-serving—international cooperation to counter realism and Marxism. Yet his insistence that today's regimes ordinarily benefit the most advantaged at the expense of the least[23] supports the latter arguments against his own. As Keohane notes, the election of social democrats, such as Mitterand in France, leads to capital flight, slowed economic growth, and a halt in promised reforms, for instance, in health care or education, which are part of a common good; voter discontent then facilitates the resurgence of conservativism. In an oligarchic setting, the election of a (social) democratic government already occurs against domestic odds. Current international economic regimes thus serve as a "safety net" for oligarchy[24] and, in the rare instances when democrats overcome these odds, defeat reforms: a distinct kind of *antidemocratic feedback* (realist and internationalist thesis 5). (Though this argument stresses the type of antidemocratic feedback addressed in theses 2 and 3, I will also underline other forms of antidemocratic as well as democratic feedback.)

If the initial thesis of neorealism is right, then what contemporary philosophers call an *inductive* "inference to the best explanation" explains the consequent, oligarchic corruption of a common good at home (realist and internationalist theses 3–5).[25] Now realists have long exaggerated opposition to moralism that they rightly see as a misguided attempt to substitute ethical values for insight into political relationships. Yet they have mistakenly seen their own insights as, somehow, not moral; instead, they have sought a nonmoral idiom in which to criticize moralism. From Morgenthau's definition of power as "the domination of man over man"—one that, however, would make every regime a tyranny[26]—to Krasner's confusion of a national interest with the long-term interests of state institutions, realists and neorealists eschew any conception of a common good. But to oppose moralism is not to oppose any moral verdict. For in criticizing bad ethical judgments, one might argue for *better* ones rather than, peculiarly, *no* such judgments. In fact, in contrast to "legalist" or "pacifist" conceptions, realists typically commend policies that, on their conception, will save lives and stop aggression: serve a genuine common good.

In place of the mistaken realist inference from this initial verdict to an idiom of undifferentiated power to be contrasted with specific, moralistic views, neorealism offers a differently implausible, *epistemological* defense of "value-freedom" and "reductionism." It thus camouflages a theoretical error *within* international relations with an epistemological one. In contrast, democratic internationalism breaks down the artificial separation between international relations and domestic politics as well as "empirical" political science and "normative" theory. It reinterprets what is plausible in realist views and shows that an argument that defines itself rigidly as criticizing popular "zeal"[27] on behalf of "professional diplomacy" has, in the changed circumstances of more evident elite aggression, *unexpected* democratic consequences.

For if the national interest is a common good, an internationalist might note, then (neo)realist theses 3–5 contradict the elitism of (neo)realist thesis 2—that defense of a national interest must, putatively, be removed from popular influence—and explain the shift, with the Vietnam War, in the character of realist explanations. Realists now see an elite as responsible for harmful American policies (Morgenthau's "academic-political," conjoined with Eisenhower's "military-industrial complex"), democratic resistance from below as a useful alternative (realist and internationalist thesis 6).

Further, neorealists rightly warn of the danger of democratic—or socialist—"crusades" for conquest from above. They focus as a *touchstone* on Woodrow Wilson, the zealously punitive Versailles Treaty, and resultant German grievances (realist thesis 7).[28] Democratic internationalism, however, proposes no such crusades, only the reversal from below of harmful external interventions (internationalist thesis 7). Inferences 3, 4, 5, 6, and 7 are common to realism and internationalism; they undercut central realist thesis 2: that judicious statespersons must shield diplomacy from democracy. For especially in an oligarchy, a common good can often be achieved only through democratic protest from below.[29]

Ironically, democratic internationalism strengthens the original realist skepticism of power, stressing the special incentives to belligerence in the elite. For realists have sometimes checked their initial skepticism with a hope that wise advisers could help statespersons ward off "popular" crusades (realist thesis 7).[30] But as President Johnson's stigmatization of Morgenthau and others shows, only democratic *counter*power, embodied in movements from below, can check unjust power (internationalist thesis 7). Further, the Vietnamese resistance broadly inspired an American antiwar movement, an unusual example of the *democratic feedback of international rivalry*. Similarly, chapter 1 stresses organizing by immigrants for basic rights throughout Europe in the 1980s, and the international influence of 1995 and 1996 French workers' revolts against European Community–mandated cutbacks in social programs.

To save their account against this unexpected challenge, realists would *at least* have to show that the American regime is not an oligarchy that serves a particular interest rather than a common good (I do not suggest that oligarchy "causes" realism, but rather that, in an uncomplicated, official form, realism serves oligarchy, and that, even in a sophisticated version, the existence of oligarchy challenges realists to show that major governmental policies uphold a common good).[31] Upon reflection, however, one might find it hard to deny that the American government is an oligarchy with parliamentary forms. In the early United States, a commercial elite barred a majority of the population, for instance, slaves and women, from voting, set about killing off Native Americans, and suppressed rebellious farmers.[32] Historically, struggles from below—the abolitionist movement, early union efforts, the battle for women's suffrage, the CIO, the civil rights movement and "riots" in American cities,[33] the American Indian Movement, La Raza Unida, and the like—have forced concessions and expanded the participatory basis for a modern, decent—nonpredatory—democracy.[34]

Yet even today, the special influence of the rich on politics is startling. One need only consider who serves in Congress—lawyers and a few other professionals, but no industrial workers, poor people, or even members of the lower middle class—or the dramatic increase in income inequality beginning in the Reagan-Bush era.[35]

Now the causation of American oligarchy—as well as the degree of its advantage—is multifaceted, overdetermined. Nonetheless, I will argue that presidential interventions in the international arena—for instance, the XYZ affair, "Remember the Maine!" and the Gulf of Tonkin incident—have blunted social movements from below. Causally reversing the democratic-peace argument that emphasizes the impact of the structure of the domestic regime on international politics, this internal critique of realism broadens renewed interest by political scientists in democracy and reveals the startling, *antidemocratic feedback* of global rivalry (internationalist theses 2 and 3).[36]

Further, weaknesses in realist and neorealist formulations also lead to errors in foreign policy. For instance, most citizens, I will suggest, have a common interest in opposing realist advocacy of moderate imperial "reach" into Mexico, Brazil, and the Middle East (realist thesis 8).[37] Such interventions have little to do with the moral core of realism: defense of national *survival*, the life of each citizen—against aggression; they also strengthen an apparatus of domestic repression (internationalist thesis 8). As we see in chapter 5, to curtail elite belligerence, citizens have an interest in furthering institutional openness, say, referenda on war where possible, the barring of covert "operations," and the like.[38]

But neorealists have rightly criticized the interdemocratic-peace hypothesis, noting a pattern of American aggression against democracies. For instance, during the Cold War, American "democracy" destroyed elected regimes in Guatemala, Iran, Brazil, Indonesia, Chile, and Guyana; it murdered the president, Lumumba, in the Congo, undermined Juan Bosch, and then overthrew Camano-Deño by direct invasion in the Dominican Republic. It violated the Geneva Accords that mandated elections for 1956 in Vietnam and, covertly as well as overtly, organized to dismantle the Sandinistas, even during the *democratic* elections of 1984, featuring competition of eight parties with equal airtime and public funding.[39] In many less developed countries, the United States armed dictators against democratic opposition and trained their military and police officers. Despite participating in the 1991 overthrow of the elected Aristide government in Haiti, however, the United States has slowly begun to favor parliamentary regimes—what are sometimes called, following Dahl, (elitist) "polyarchies"—as the best defenders of oligarchy.[40]

Behaviorist advocates of the "democratic peace" hypothesis have often—in later versions, perhaps, without reexamination—adopted an implausible "data set," differentiating "a war," in which each side loses a thousand soldiers, from an "intervention," even when a great power destroys democracy in another country. But that criterion makes the *pattern* of U.S. intervention disappear from an allegedly empirical count of "wars."[41] This definition is thus a misguided, ideological way of making the American regime appear peaceful toward other democracies, whereas it has, in fact, *only* been less belligerent toward European, mainly powerful ones.

In response to this criticism, Bruce Russett has recently discussed the U.S.-sponsored overthrow of six parliamentary regimes.[42] Though his criteria for democracy do not require maintenance of a "free market," he implausibly suggests that, say, an elected Guatemalan regime's national- ization of the United Fruit Company disqualifies it:[43] "[T]he targeted gov- ernments could plausibly be seen [by U.S. policymakers] as *unstably dem- ocratic* with a leader either unwilling or unable to resist radical pressures for reform employing authoritarian methods."[44] Now Russett celebrates the American public's resistance to "overt" wars. Yet "covert" overturn- ing of parliamentary regimes apparently does not qualify the *U.S. govern- ment* as "unstably democratic,"[45] nor does this pattern of belligerence present, for Russett, an anomaly for "democratic peace." Since even he concludes on a critical note, however, it may simply not have occurred to him to apply his criteria to the American executive:[46]

> Whatever legal and moral responsibility the U.S. government bears for these acts [covert interventions] must not obscure the fact that American military units did not fight in an organized fashion in any of these cases. They were covert, and American participation could be denied with varying degrees of plausibility. The Nicaraguan operation—the most protracted, expensive and bloody [*sic*—the coup against Sukarno in Indonesia resulted in the slaughter of at least half a million people] of the group—illustrates the point most clearly. These operations were covert, and denied, because as overt activi- ties, support for them in the U.S. political system would have been dubious at best. . . . The normative restraints of democracy were sufficient to drive operations underground amid circumstances when the administration other- wise might well have undertaken an overt intervention. . . . The constraints could and did prevent an interstate war, but could not preserve the United States from deep culpability in initiating and sustaining one side in a for- mally 'civil' war.[47]

Like other proponents of "democratic peace," Russett also disregards the deeper pattern of U.S. aggression against ordinary citizens in the less developed countries. For example, he might have considered the correla- tions suggested by Chomsky and Hermann's table presenting post–World War II U.S. military and police aid to regimes that practice torture.[48] This evidence would have strengthened his point about democratic peace as a concern of most citizens rather than an often bellicose elite.

In contrast, both democratic internationalism and neorealism stress the pattern of American aggression.[49] Yet, a proponent of internation- alism might also note, advocates of realism and interdemocratic peace share, ironically, an underlying, statist thesis: in evaluating foreign pol- icy, both start from the *assumption* that a state represents its citizens.[50] In this context, Russett's account of covert action, highlighting the *non- belligerence* of a democratic public, supports internationalism against his own statist version of interparliamentary peace.

As opposed to today's main alternatives, internationalism stresses how often democratic regimes—in reality, oligarchies with parliamentary forms—do *not* represent the fundamental interests of their citizens, how often such interests are aligned with those of ordinary people in other regimes. Yet oligarchies are powerful; unsurprisingly, as chapters 1, 2, and 5 suggest, the citizen concerns, which cohere with democratic internationalism, can often today be realized, *if* they are to be realized, only through struggle from below.

In the setting of this novel theoretical debate, a realist critique of democratic peace, ironically, gives little comfort to realists and neorealists. For that claim underlines *antidemocratic feedback*: the interconnection between power-rivalry, the ideologies of antiradicalism and racism that make "enemies" of, at most, international and domestic rivals and, more likely, innocents, antidemocratic interventions abroad, and the constriction of democratic options at home (internationalist theses 2 and 3). Democratic internationalism is thus an unexpected, *internal* critique of realism, linking, as we see in chapters 1 and 2, explicit claims about a common good with the harms of great-power rivalry. The transformed vision of realism that it hopes to articulate differs dramatically from the power-serving views sometimes advanced in the name of what I will call official realism. For the latter extirpate the moral roots of realism and dissociate a national interest—seen as whatever serves the state—from a common good.[51]

Thus, the emergence of diverse democracies strongly influenced by the interests of ordinary citizens—nondomineering regimes, domestically—would contribute to the existence of nonaggressive norms and regimes internationally.[52] In this respect, the antidemocratic-feedback hypothesis offers support—through the possibility of a democratic internationalist response *from below* in the relevant countries—for the idea that a society of genuinely democratic states would be more peaceful than current regimes. To the realist question, *must* global politics constrain democracy? it responds cautiously but negatively.

2. THE ANCIENT CRITIQUE OF PRIDE AND MODERN DEMOCRATIC INTERNATIONALISM

Contrary to neorealism and, to some extent, earlier American realism, I will argue, ancient realism was centrally a moral and political point of view. It aimed to avoid the hubris or pride that crazed politicians and destroyed them and their causes. "Pride," however, misleadingly translates an ancient Greek word, *hubris*, which meant wantonness, exceeding human bounds, viewing oneself as godlike.[53] Not just Sophocles and

Thucydides, but, perhaps surprisingly, Socrates exemplify opposition to hubris. In the *Apology*, for example, Socrates maintains that his philosophical "ignorance" about exactly what piety, justice, virtue, goodness, and the like are, is a merely "human" wisdom:

> But very likely, Gentlemen, it is really the God who is wise, and by his oracle [the Pythia at Delphi told Chaerophon that no man was wiser than Socrates], he means to say that "human nature is a thing of little worth or none." It appears that he does not mean this fellow Socrates, but uses my name to offer an example, as if he were saying "he among you is wisest, Gentleman, who, like Socrates, realizes that he is truly worth nothing in respect to wisdom." That is why I still go about even now on behalf of the God, searching and inquiring among both citizens and strangers, should I think some one of them is wise; and when it seems he is not, I help the God and prove it.[54]

Those who puff themselves up and "pretend to know," predominantly in politics, kill others; thus, the trial of Socrates and the murderous Greek civil wars of which Thucydides and Plato warn serve as paradigms. For the Greeks, moderation or restraint—*sophrosune*—contrasts with hubris; later Christian interpretations stress humility.[55]

Thucydides' explanation of the defeat of Athens by democratic Syracuse traces the dangers, to a *democracy*, of hubris in public life, consequent corruption, and, what is called by today's neorealists, imperial "overexpansion."[56] For Pericles had warned the Athenians not to fight a war on two fronts, not to seek enlarged empire. In opposition to that counsel, however, post-Periclean demagogues swayed Athenian citizens to commit aggression against largely unknown Sicily. Athenians ended up, helpless and cowardly, dying, in Syracusan quarries. A Corinthian ambassador in book 1 and Pericles' funeral oration emphasize the Athenians' restless character as opposed to the stolid, cautious Spartans. Perhaps that untamed striving, combined with greed—*pleonexia*[57]—and hubris doomed them.[58] Yet Thucydides also stresses the political choices—the contrary advice of Pericles—that might have spared Athenian democracy.[59]

In ancient political science, Plato and Aristotle took up Thucydides' critique and gave it a philosophical form. When Athenians spoke of a common good—at least one of preserving the existence of, but also, in Pericles, the equal public freedom of and a "noncensorious" private life for each citizen—they named a genuine good.[60] Despite a widespread, misleading, absolute contrast between "modern" notions of "the right" and "ancient" notions of "the good," liberals consider basic rights—freedoms of conscience, speech, and association, the right to vote, and the like—as equally applicable to each person, and, thus, when realized, a common good.[61] This book will stress a fairly uncontroversial conception of such a good—for instance, of a regime that upholds the life, well-being, and, perhaps, equal liberty of each—similar to those central in ancient political theory.[62] It will invite a novel conversation of political theory and political science, one that refines an account of ancient realism to overcome the arbitrary separation of today's international-relations and democratic theory, and articulate a modern, democratic realism.

Now Pericles stresses community more than a modern theorist would. Furthermore, in contrast to today's liberals, he praises imperial grandeur. Yet his funeral oration also foreshadows the modern defense of individuality. Unlike modern liberals, however, he does not see the furthering of individuality as the justification of political and social institutions, but rather, as an adjunct to glory. In the idiom of my *Democratic Individuality*, given the ancient failure to recognize slaves, women, and other humans as equals, Pericles defends not the intrinsic good of modern democratic *individuality*, but the mainly instrumental one of ancient, imperial, *partly democratic* individuality.[63]

All thinking about politics needs to start from possible commonalities between citizens, ones constituted by core ethical goods such as the life of each and equal liberty. A regime that facilitates such goods is clearly superior to a tyranny that ravages them. The rhetoric of mere threatening power, for instance that of Thrasymachus, Callicles, Anytus, and Meletus in Plato, echoing, as chapter 4 shows, the nameless Athenian spokesmen at Melos, excludes such distinctions, but only at the cost of incoherence and, in action, horror. Further, though Morgenthau misguidedly strives, theoretically, to abstract from relevant distinctions, he, too, contrasts a regime "disciplined by moral ends and controlled by constitutional safeguards" to an "untamed and barbaric" one.[64] Krasner and other neorealists vacillate even more sharply, underlining this distinction when they seek some *justification* for their account, eschewing it, when they wish to speak in an official "realist" idiom.[65]

Like Thucydides and Pericles, Plato and Aristotle reject imperial "overexpansion"; in contrast, however, they oppose democracy.[66] In the ancient world, democracy, a short-lived though glorious regime, had no theoretical defenders.[67] Yet these philosophers concur with and elaborate many central points in Thucydides. They see class dissension—*stasis*—as a danger to any regime, exposing it to external enemies in the context of unrelieved international ferocity. They fear the lethalness of oligarchy as well as democracy.

As chapter 4 emphasizes, Greek history, philosophy, and tragedy point to a common framework. Given the ordinary danger of class war between oligarchs and democrats, as well as international clashes, Greek theorists admired the—perhaps rare—regime that sustains a common good. Among Greek philosophers, however, only Socrates, in the *Republic*'s "city in speech," opposed slavery; ancient democracies degraded the humanity of many.[68] In addition, as I have emphasized, Pericles, and, to some extent, Thucydides, sought imperial dominion. That these Greek figures should have articulated central insights into politics, notably democracy, overlooked by many "value-free" accounts, produced in more inclusive "democracies," is a striking anomaly. Subtle judgments about hubris and corruption, a philosophical discussion of a common good, and a prefiguring of democratic individuality all characterize Greek democratic realism. Modern liberal theory dialectically transforms, yet retains, these themes.

3. THE TRAJECTORY OF THE ARGUMENT

Through an internal, democratic internationalist critique of leading realist and neorealist arguments, chapters 1 and 2 stress the theoretical implausibility and moral thinness of current political science. In contrast, they present—and the next two chapters work through—a range of "normative" alternatives, for instance, those of Thucydides, Aristotle, Hobbes, Marx, and Kant. Taken in tandem, this critique and internationalist counterargument illustrate a striking hypothesis. If much contemporary political "science" has peculiarly thinned itself, then perhaps a need for mainstream debate to license or conceal imperial policies, to serve the powers-that-be, particularly during the Cold War, has been an important cause. The political history of the natural sciences, for instance, the execution of Giordano Bruno, the persecution of Galileo, the Scopes trial, and the like, underlines the baneful effects of power on the search for truth. Even more sharply, a sophisticated realist might note, power constrains the social sciences. As we have seen, Morgenthau names the latter as, mainly, part of an "academic-political complex."

Part 1 of this book, "Democratic Internationalism as an Internal Critique of Neorealism and Realism," focuses on the main American and European émigré exponents of the latter views. The first chapter—"Must Global Politics Constrain Democracy?"—explores innovative neorealist studies, those of Stephen Krasner, Robert Gilpin, and Robert Keohane about U.S. intervention to secure raw materials in less developed countries, renewed great-power, American-Japanese rivalry, and the possibility of genuine, citizen-benefiting cooperation between governments. Keohane's search for cooperation, oddly, omits democracy. The chapter thus also constructs, and answers, a different, internal critique of realism, a Doyle-Keohane version of the democratic-peace hypothesis.

If "official realism" and neorealism are right, one would think that coalitions of great powers can only occur at the expense of others. On these views, democracies in each country could not unite to acknowledge the voices and concerns of ordinary people on a world scale. To capture this core point, I have entitled the chapter with a realist question: *must* global politics constrain democracy? Surprisingly, however, these leading neo-"realists" undercut official realism's core thesis: that a state's international policies serve citizen interests. An internal critique of each argument reveals the common interests of citizens—democratic internationalism from below—against their own state(s) and across national boundaries.

Although neorealists have spoken in the idiom of empiricism or behaviorism, they have, also, ironically, defended an ambiguous, doubtfully empirical concept of power. When they speak of military "power," for instance, do they refer simply to means of dominion over others, or to a democratic resistance to oppression? One might think here of Soviet and other resistances to Nazism; the Chinese rebellion against Japanese aggression; Vietnamese uprisings against French, Japanese, and American conquests; and the like. We need an idea of a common good to account for the latter examples. Yet neorealist *reductionism* misguidedly attempts to excise such a conception from political "science." By power, do neorealists mean primarily economic or political might?[69]

Chapter 2, "Crossing of the Ways: The Vietnam War and Realism in Morgenthau, Niebuhr, and Kennan," focuses on Hans Morgenthau's theory of power-rivalry, which founded the American "science of international relations," in the light of his comparatively clear, originally persecuted, now largely unread indictment of American policy in Vietnam. It underlines a fundamental shift in Morgenthau's, Niebuhr's, and Kennan's versions of American realism. For instance, Kennan endorsed the standard realist critique of the democratic zealousness of the Treaty of Versailles, which embedded the seeds of World War II into the slaughter ground of World War I, and then of citizen pacifism, confronted by the dangers of Nazism, before World War II. As I have noted, he gave two lectures after the Vietnam War to underline a new danger: the influence of a primarily elite ideology of anticommunism or antiradicalism that had triggered unnecessary, murderous intervention, and had accompanied corruption—in Kennan's memorable phrase, "our military-industrial addiction"—at home. Roughly, this ideology sees outside agitators as the diabolical cause of protests against the ostensibly harmless privileged. As high school history texts in California put it even in the late 1960s, slaves were "happy, singing, down on the plantation," till "Northern" abolitionists like John Brown and Harriet Tubman "stirred them up."[70] Similarly, according to the State Department "white paper," the Vietnam uprising occurred as a result of "Northern" agitation—as if a U.S.-instigated violation of the Geneva Accords had not artificially solidified the North/South division, and the Americans, not the (North) Vietnamese, defended an indigenous cause.[71]

In John Locke's words, however, ordinary people do not rebel against a prevailing power for slight cause:

> [S]uch revolutions happen not upon every little mismanagement in public affairs. Great mistakes in the ruling part, many wrong and inconvenient laws, and all the slips of human frailty will be borne by the people without mutiny or murmur. But if a long train of abuses, prevarications, and artifices, all tending the same way, make the design visible to the people, and they cannot but feel what they lie under and see whither they are going, it is not to be wondered that they should then rouse themselves and endeavour to put the rule into such hands which may secure to them the ends for which government was at first erected.[72]

Many have offered serious criticisms of "Communist" dictatorships, and of massive state intervention in constricting the liberties of citizens. I refer here *only* to a not widely recognized antiradical ideology, though one with sharply identifiable characteristics. Further, to stigmatize, as anticommunist ideologues do, participants in such rebellions as "dupes" highlights this view's oligarchic thoughtlessness.[73] In contrast, attentive to harms to citizens, post-Vietnam realism in Morgenthau, Niebuhr, and Kennan highlights an elite, easily deterred neither from genocidal policies abroad nor oppression at home.[74]

As chapter 2 also argues, Niebuhr articulated the core moral standard of a common good as a starting point in realist theory. He saw differences, not only with idealists but between insightful and ideological realists, as centering around "contingent facts," or what I call social theoretical, psychological, and empirical claims. Thus, sophisticated realism concurs with Marxian or democratic internationalist themes and distances itself from official realist contentions, for instance, that a state's foreign policy, most likely, serves the interests of its citizens.

The second part of the book, "Forgotten Sources of Democratic Internationalism," restores two worked-out versions of this vision—the one unacknowledged (Marx), the other miscast as founding "realism" (Thucydides). In tandem with the internal critique of the main versions of neorealism and realism, these chapters articulate a democratic internationalist alternative to today's neorealism and the democratic-peace hypothesis.

The third chapter, "'Workers of the World, Unite!': The Possibility of Democratic Feedback," shows that Marx's defense of the solidarity of democratic and radical movements inherits and develops liberal themes. For instance, he stressed the startling opposition of English workers to American slavery, despite unemployment due to the shortage of cotton, and a belligerent, upper-class campaign to intervene on the side of the

South. These workers not only sympathized with slaves, but also feared the potential antidemocratic impact on their own destiny of a slave-holders' victory. Their resistance exemplified the international *democratic feedback of the abolitionist movement.*

Marx also emphasized that foreign interventions, particularly colonialism, reinforce a repressive regime against democratic movements at home—a persistent, antidemocratic feedback of great-power politics. In 1848, for example, he highlighted the surprisingly reactionary role of the English elite, faced with the first working-class movement, the Chartists. The most powerful parliamentary regime in Europe allied with the Prussian monarch and the czar to crush democratic resistance internationally and domestically. In contrast, Marx looked to the common interests of democratic and social republican movements—once again, the *democratic feedback of revolutionary example.* During the Cold War, the American government often intervened against democracy in the less developed countries. In the case of Vietnam, the United States provides a striking analogy to England in 1848. Correspondingly, broadly inspired by Vietnamese struggles against various aggressors, the American antiwar movement illustrates democratic feedback.

Based on subsequent practical experience, the Sepoy mutiny in India in 1857 and the movement for Irish independence of the 1860s, Marx refined his initial theory. Colonialism in Ireland, he now contended, not only victimized a people, but also facilitated the dissemination of racism among the colonizer's lower classes and kept English workers from uniting with Irish immigrants against their common oppressors. Colonialism and racism thus embodied the "secret of the impotence of the English working class, despite its high level of [union] organization."[75] Marx's new theory shows that the obstacles to democratic internationalism are far greater even than the powers aligned against union movements.[76]

Democratic internationalism from below, in the *Manifesto's* idiom, "defends the common interests of the working class, regardless of nationality" and speaks out on behalf of—ultimately, in the voices of—the most oppressed. Thus, surprisingly from a nationalist standpoint, racism harms most workers even of the dominant nationality (despite striking, econometric evidence about the contemporary United States, that conclusion is surprising still).[77] Socialist revolution in England, Marx concluded, could only follow Irish emancipation—a potential democratic feedback of anticolonialism. Generalizing Marx's insight, Lenin subsequently insisted that a radical movement in an imperialist country must oppose all acts of colonial oppression and racism.

Chapter 3 employs Marx's insights to illuminate the unexpected redistributive effects of modern anticolonial movements as well as immigration into advanced capitalist regimes.[78] Many of the world's people now hope for a single meal a day. Contemporary theories of justice focus on arbitrary inequalities between the rich and poor internationally—inequalities so large that the term *inequality* barely does them justice. For instance, as Honderich points out, "The average lifetime of males and females taken together in all the less-developed societies, by one common definition of the latter [Kuznets's], is about 42 years. The average lifetime of males and females together in developed countries, again with the latter defined in one common way is about 71." He then suggests that those in the developed countries get to live, as it were, two lives for each life lived in the less developed countries.[79]

As in the case of Rawls's *Theory of Justice*, however, moral theorists do not give serious attention to social theory; they simply hope that some support for their favored redistributive proposal can be found.[80] But such theories, I will argue, require the transnational or democratic internationalist solidarities that Marx highlighted, to achieve the redistribution they mandate. Put differently, the *sharper* the moral justification for such redistribution, the *greater* the—usually unstated—obstacles to redistribution that are likely to be indicated by social theory, and hence, the need for *democratic internationalism* from below to overcome them.[81] Marxian strategy thus names—and provides some basis for achieving—*liberal* moral insights.

Now conservative and liberal economists, today, question a Marxian thesis about the necessity of increasing inequality in the less developed countries[82] and see possible benefits to all from capitalist growth. Their argument, however, ignores important evidence—for instance, about augmenting inequality in the U.N. development decade—and the effect of such inequality in corrupting regimes and producing oligarchy. Further, International Monetary Fund loans have required drastic cutbacks in social programs for the poor. Clinton adviser Anthony Lake's slogan about "market democracy" is an oxymoron, not a conception of decent economic and political development.[83] Such phenomena are comparatively easily explained by some version of radical theory. Nonetheless, this book does not advance a hard Marxian or dependency argument—one requiring that capitalist growth inevitably produce suffering for the majority of people in the less developed countries. With organizing from below in the latter, and decent social policies—initiated, especially, by a more democratically inspired, American regime—much current suffering might be curtailed. That possibility is, however, not thus far a reality.

The fourth chapter, "Democratic Imperialism and Internal Corruption," focuses on Thucydides' history of the downfall of Athenian democracy through aggression—a classic illustration of antidemocratic feedback. It also traces the role of his promonarchical translator, Hobbes, in winnowing justice from political theory and constraining Thucydides' themes to bare realism. From Hobbes to the architects of intervention in Vietnam, international-relations scholars have embraced Thucydides as an archetypal "realist." They have even mistakenly seen the nameless Athenian ambassadors' standpoint, in the Melian dialogue, as realism's "purest" expression.[84] Yet contemporary classicists, notably de Romilly and Connor, have shown that Thucydides strikingly indicts the long-term effects of democratic imperialism and public corruption.[85]

In contrast to today's neorealism, however, even Hobbes's theory stresses the good of preserving the life of each citizen against aggression.[86] That theory is far richer than neorealism, as well as an "operationalist"[87] purporting of U.S. "peacefulness" toward other democracies.

Finally, chapter 4 underlines the arrogance that spurred American aggression in Vietnam—a successor to French colonial and Japanese fascist efforts to conquer that country. What is not remembered must be relived. The American parliamentary regime repeated in Vietnam what Thucydides recognized about Athenian imperialism in Syracuse two thousand years ago. Contrary to neorealism and the democratic-peace hypothesis, this book offers a theoretical account of global politics that highlights the democratic and moral implications of that history and makes Vietnam central to the Cold War.

Part 3 of the book integrates this new social theory with a theory of democratic deliberation. It stresses that deliberative democracy is, centrally, a conscience-sustaining regime. Chapter 5, "Deliberation as a Medium for Internationalism," asks: given the current intensification of oligarchy and the (nearly) intractable discord about many complex ethical and political issues, what novel movements and institutional changes might make citizen participation more effective and facilitate livable, common-good-sustaining policies, domestically and globally? It sketches some practical consequences of democratic internationalism.

TABLE 1
How Realism Leads to Democracy

	Neorealist Thesis	Internationalist Thesis
Thesis 1	An autonomous competition among states in international politics conditions the national interest of each actor (*the power-competition thesis*)	Same
Thesis 2	Global politics is—and should be—separate from domestic politics. Democratic opinion hinders a sound, professional pursuit of the national interest (the *harmfulness of democracy*)	In each power (especially those with significant internal inequalities), leaders have a psychological and Machiavellian incentive to make "enemies" of the "other" and blunt internal opposition (the *antidemocratic-feedback thesis*)
Thesis 3	A statist or structural Marxian account of *oligarchy* and the ideology of "anticommunism" that serves it best explains American policies	Antiradical, racist, and sexist ideologies buoy the tendency to stigmatize "others" in capitalist oligarchies. "Democratic" opinion is often oligarchically stimulated. These trends are enhanced in presidential systems, in election years (the *threat of external enemies, constriction of democratic options*)
Thesis 4	Overemphasis on the military has led to a decline of American industry and of living standards for most workers: *the American militarism and decline* or *price of empire* thesis (Gilpin, Fulbright, Krasner)	Same
Thesis 5	If a democratic socialist government is elected in a particular country, capital flight slows economic growth and deters reforms that would realize a common good; the failure of reform, in turn, disenchants voters and leads to conservative reaction—a distinct, *antidemocratic feedback of international economic regimes* (Keohane)	Same. In Europe, immigrant organizing in varied settings has resulted in the protection of basic rights; the 1995 and 1996 French strikes upheld a domestic common good against European Community–mandated cutbacks in social programs and might inspire similar efforts elsewhere— *a democratic feedback of international politics*

continues on next page

TABLE 1 (*cont.*)

	Neorealist Thesis	Internationalist Thesis
Thesis 6	If the national interest is a common good, then neorealist theses 3–5 contradict the elitism of neorealist thesis 2 and explain the shift, with the Vietnam War, in the character of realist explanations. Methodologically operationalist definitions of the national interest, which attempt to translate a common good into the state's interest, elide harms to citizens and are implausible (*democracy as a common good*)	Democratic movements from below are needed to undo the harms to most citizens of great-power rivalry (*democracy as a common good*)
Thesis 7	Realism, however, aims, centrally, to head off ideological crusades, such as Woodrow Wilson's, that attempt to force democracy—or, perhaps, socialism—on recalcitrant others, and injure one's own citizens. It urges moderation or humility in foreign policy. Yet it sometimes relies on individual advice to statespersons as an antidote to popular "zeal"	More than realism, internationalism seeks to strengthen democratic activity *from below* against the incentives to pride and belligerence characteristic of elite public life
Thesis 8	Neorealists sometimes advocate "moderate" imperial reach into Mexico, Brazil, and the Middle East (Krasner)	Such interventions defend a common good for citizens neither against aggression nor economically; in fact, they reinforce antidemocratic feedback
Thesis 9	But liberal democracies sometimes go to war against other democracies (the U.S. in Guatemala, Iran, Brazil, Guyana, Chile, Sandinista Nicaragua, Haiti, and the like). Perhaps no common good, internal or international, is possible (*the factual overriding of a common good*)	Oligarchies with parliamentary forms do not intervene against other democracies unless the latter can be stigmatized as political and "racial" "enemies." As chapter 4 shows, more democratic, self-consciously internationalist regimes, mandating for example, referenda on war, where possible, and tolerating civil disobedience, would be less likely to engage in aggression (*a common good against "democratic" imperialism*)

Part One

DEMOCRATIC INTERNATIONALISM

AS AN INTERNAL CRITIQUE OF

NEOREALISM AND REALISM

CHAPTER ONE

Must Global Politics Constrain Democracy?

The government itself, which is the only mode which the people have chosen to execute their will, is equally liable [with the standing army] to be abused and perverted before the people can act through it. Witness the present Mexican war, the work of comparatively a few individuals using the standing government as their tool; for, in the outset, the people would not have consented to this measure.

(Henry Thoreau, "Civil Disobedience")

It is easy to say—and often is said—that we cannot have tolerable relations with the new revolutionary regimes. The problem is that our anti-communist paranoia has made it impossible to find out. We do not know whether Mao's declared interest in a relationship with the Americans in the 1940s or Ho Chi Minh's were sincere. And the reason we don't know is that we never tried to find out. Those who reported it was a possibility were hounded out of the foreign service because of our suspicion and fear of communism. The legacy of that era brings to mind Ivan the Terrible's practice of murdering the bearer of bad news. We are more civilized than that: we have been content simply to ruin people's careers.

(J. William Fulbright, *The Price of Empire*)

This poisonous thing I'm trying to describe is [a] characteristic way of dealing with criticism. It used to be enough to brand a critic as a radical or a leftist to make people turn away. Now we need only to call him a liberal. Soon "moderate" will be the M word, "conservative" will be the C word and only fascists will be in the mainstream.

(E. L. Doctorow, Brandeis commencement, May 21, 1989)

1. A NEGLECTED THEORETICAL DEBATE

Though they usually misread Thucydides' Melian dialogue, realists have rightly envisioned international politics as a realm of power clashes, characterized by the self-aggrandizement and criminality of state interests.[1] So obvious does this insight—perhaps not so pointedly formulated—seem, that Cold War international-relations theory was overwhelmingly realist. Ironically, as I have already noted, ordinary political ideas that, for example, democracy or even human rights made—or ought to make—some difference in the foreign policy of parliamentary regimes were foreign, another tongue; they fell outside prevailing paradigms.[2] The international sphere appeared not as a constraint on democracy but as its denial.

Today, however, the democratic-peace hypothesis has emerged to challenge neorealism. Yet, as the introduction emphasizes, the former stands in diametric opposition to neorealism, a proposal that stresses the causal influence of domestic politics on the international sphere and ignores the corrosive impact of global power competition on democracy.[3] In contrast, as an *internal* critique of the neorealist view, democratic internationalism highlights the constraints posed by the latter on a common good at home.

In political theory, internationalist arguments, advanced, for instance, by Thucydides, Aristotle, and modern liberals and radicals, register the long-term erosion of the justification and sometimes the practice of conquest and slaughter. Yet in a theoretically burgeoning field, international political economy, their voices are strangely silent. The first two sections of this chapter articulate a democratic internationalist alternative and reinterpret the moral and political significance of current debates. They reveal the creativity of realism as an explanation of past and, to some degree, current global politics. They highlight the moral basis *within* realism for its surprising affirmation of important Marxian economic claims and a "structural Marxian" account of the state. The next four sections, however, maintain that, ironically, today's "mainstream" neorealist views have radical implications, while a seemingly "radical" alternative—dependency theory—fails to be liberal or democratic. Exploring Krasner's, Gilpin's, Keohane's, and Doyle's arguments, they suggest that democratic internationalism has a sound human, social, and economic basis but that distinctive *political*—and organizational—obstacles have limited its impact. The eighth section shows how leading theoretical insights of classical realism, feminism, and postmodernism strengthen the case for democratic internationalism. The conclusion highlights the explanatory strength of realism, its emphasis on the so far profound historical limits, given power jostling, of the realization of human rights. In a jujitsu-like reversal, however, this section also underlines the corresponding *anomaly* for realism of the international existence and progress of human rights and democracy.

To fix the terms of this argument, I will offer at the outset a clear, if brief, view of the history, substance, and motivation of *democratic internationalism*. Theorizing a theme of Thucydides, Aristotle set Sparta's organization for war as a warning to Athenians: "[A] polis should not be considered happy or a legislator praised, when its citizens are trained for victory in war and the subjugation of neighboring regimes. Such a policy . . . implies that any citizen who can do so, should make it his object to capture the government of his own city."[4] Since conquest abroad leads to tyranny at home, citizens should oppose expansion: *the antidemocratic-feedback thesis*.

In modern times, Kant's "Perpetual Peace" suggests that while monarchs treat subjects as servants to be spent in the "pleasure party" (*Lustpartei*) of war, citizens, whose views and fundamental concerns—or interests—count, will find bellicosity "a poor game" (*ein schlimmes Spiel*):

> [I]f the consent of the citizens is required in order to decide that war should be declared, nothing is more natural than that they would be very cautious in commencing such a poor game, decreeing for themselves all the calamities of war. Among the latter would be: having to fight, having to pay the costs of war from their own resources, having painfully to repair the devastation war leaves behind, and, to fill up the measure of evils, load themselves with a heavy national debt that would embitter peace itself and that can never be liquidated on account of constant wars in the future. But in a constitution which is not republican. . . , a declaration of war is the easiest thing in the world to decide upon, because war does not require of the ruler, who is the proprietor and not a member of the state, the least sacrifice of the pleasures of his table, the chase, his country houses, his court functions, and the like. He may, therefore, resolve on war as on a pleasure party for the most trivial reasons, and with perfect indifference leave the justification which decency requires to the diplomatic corps who are ever ready to provide it.[5]

Democratic internationalism is the thesis that the basic political and moral concerns of ordinary people conflict with imperial domination, and will, through political activity from below, sometimes check the normal inclination of the powerful and advantaged to war.[6] As the introduction emphasizes, internationalism also emerges out of an *internal* critique of neorealism. For the initial neorealist assumption attempts to isolate international from domestic politics, especially regime structure (neorealist thesis 1).[7] For instance, accentuating the standard positivist insistence on "levels of analysis," Waltz's structural realism "abstract(s) from every attribute of states except their capabilities. . . . We abstract from any particular qualities of states."[8] An internationalist may, however, grant this central neorealist thesis for the sake of argument and then ask: what effect will such global power-rivalry have on democracy at home?

She may then propose the *antidemocratic-feedback thesis*: in inegalitarian societies, leaders may use international power-competition as a condition for "making enemies" and as justification for intervention or war. Such interventions can serve as a pretext to drum up "patriotic" support at home and discredit internal opposition, either as similar, racially or politically, to the "enemy," or as "soft" on this threat (internationalist thesis 2). In electoral systems, antiradical ideology and racism thus become a striking feature of presidential and other campaigns and constrict political options (internationalist thesis 3).

Curiously, even Waltz underlines the limited explanatory fruitfulness of neorealist theory: "Structurally, we can describe and understand the pressures states are subject to. We cannot predict how they will react to the pressures without knowledge of their internal dispositions."[9] Contradicting the central thesis of structural realism, this claim treats domestic politics as a central *ingredient* of explanation, but, still, as an external (to theory), isolated, vaguely specified sphere. My critique of realism, however, which asks about the interplay of global with domestic politics, is a more direct, *internal*, worked-out version of this insight.

Realists and neorealists have, historically, looked to sound policy advice by individuals—"professional diplomacy"—to discourage aggressive democratic "crusades" (realist thesis 2).[10] This classic thesis motivates the attempted neorealist banishing of regime structure as an important causal variable from the study of international relations. But an internal, internationalist critique shows that *even if* we accept the initial thesis of the neorealist argument—that great-power rivalry significantly conditions national interests independently of regime structure—leaders may still use such rivalry to curtail a common good and democracy at home. This *oligarchic feedback* justifies internationalist movements from below and undercuts central realist thesis 2. Strikingly, as we will see, contemporary neorealist arguments support this and other internationalist claims against the core realist idea that in foreign policy, a state, by and large, represents its citizens.

I use the term *democratic internationalism* to include (1) the historic liberal recognition of a *universal* human capacity for moral personality and political participation that rules out slavery, sexism, colonialism, absolute monarchy, tyranny, and, probably, constitutional monarchy;[11] (2) the justification, through that capacity, of a right to a culture of one's own and core democratic rights such as freedom of conscience, speech, association, and the vote, as well as, as a stranger, to be treated decently; (3) the Thucydidean, Socratic,[12] and Aristotelian insight that conquest abroad undermines democracy at home (*the antidemocratic-feedback thesis*); (4) the sanctioning of resistance by ordinary citizens to their own government's aggressions; and (5) some degree of empathy with democratic and radical movements in other countries. In a crucial error, realist theories often reduce the "national interest" to the security of leading state institutions (neorealist thesis 2: *a national-security-focused conception of a common good*). In contrast, internationalism holds that the *public good* in democratic regimes opposes aggression, colonialism, and neocolonialism and sustains democracy abroad (internationalist thesis 2: *a nonaggressive, democratic conception of a common good*).[13]

Now Marxians often emphasize uprisings that entertain self-consciously cooperative—communist or socialist—aims. Yet the character of power-state politics and the prevalence of realist intuitions among diplomats and academics make *even* liberal internationalism an unexpected, "radical" idea. For much radical policy, for instance that which united the anti–Vietnam War movement, checks aggression by one's own government but does not, immediately, seek revolutionary change.[14] Against realist expectations, the mainly nonviolent, democratic movements that swept Eastern Europe and the Soviet Union in the late 1980s undermined the security apparatuses of each state. Ordinary citizens checked the threat of external intervention by their own government(s) against uprisings in other states. So the term *democratic internationalism* captures a commonality of coherent liberal and radical theories.

As opposed to a widespread impression that he was an economic determinist, the hallmark of Marx's political theory and action was democratic internationalism.[15] Thus, during the German revolution of 1848, as chapter 3 explores, he led the opposition to Prussian expansion into Poland and, at the cost of half the subscribers to his newspaper, *Die Neue Rheinische Zeitung*, celebrated the Paris workers' June insurrection as "the most colossal event in the history of European civil wars." In the 1860s, as chief strategist of the International Workingmen's Association (cited hereafter as IWA), he fought for the solidarity of English and Irish workers in support of independence for Ireland and, despite personal attack, memorialized the Paris Commune. Where today's liberals look to a union of republican *governments* pursuing peaceful policies, radicals focus on democratic pressure against aggression from ordinary citizens. Such controversies pit a liberal *internationalism from above* against a radical *internationalism from below*.[16] In this context, ironically, Marxian theory is more robustly deliberative and democratic than (other) liberal arguments, since the sustenance of dissident movements, lacking state power, requires clear political argument, internal discussion, and reflection.[17]

Realists, however, frequently interpret their disagreements with liberals and radicals as matters of *social theory*. Krasner, Huntington, and Skocpol, for example, stress the *autonomy of state interests* in foreign policy in contrast to the dominance of societal ones (pluralism, "instrumental" Marxism). But a liberal or radical need not pit empirical "economic" causation against statist—"political" though not democratic—power rivalry. Instead, as I have noted, democratic internationalism reverses the realist's argumentative figure: support for reactionary—authoritarian, oligarchic—regimes abroad erodes domestic liberty. Imagined and actual enemies license national security apparatuses, surveillance, blacklisting, and judicial murder of opposition, the chilling of debate and deliberation.

Thus, to turn the embarrassingly full pages of American political history from this standpoint, the invocation of enemies—great power and other—has fueled antidemocratic policies. For instance, President Adams and Alexander Hamilton invoked French Jacobins—"Gallomen"—and the "Wild Irish" and "democratic disorganizers" of the 1798 anticolonial uprising against England to license the Alien and Sedition laws and jail the immigrant editors of republican—pro-Jefferson—newspapers.[18] Congressman Harrison Gray Otis, an ally of Hamilton, conjured "the mass of vicious and disorganizing characters who cannot live peaceably at home . . . the hordes of wild Irishmen [and] the turbulent and disorderly of all the World [who] come here with a view to disturb our tranquility, after having succeeded in the overthrow of their own governments."[19] They might, Otis continued fearfully, ally with "the Democracy."

In response, Madison denounced Adams's alleged XYZ affair[20] and administration efforts to suppress the republican party: "Exhortations to disregard domestic usurpation until foreign danger shall have passed, is an artifice which may be forever used; because the possessors of power, who are the advocates of its extension, can ever create national embarrassments to be successively employed to soothe people into sleep, whilst that power is swelling silently, secretly and fatally."[21] Similarly, Jefferson's "Draft of the Kentucky Resolution" stresses the need for unity of immigrant and citizen: "[T]he friendless alien has been selected as the safest subject of a first experiment; but the citizen will soon follow, or rather, has already followed, for already has a sedition act marked him as its prey."[22] The election of Jefferson as president in 1800 was a defeat for antiradical ideology and established, for the first time, a "legitimate" two-party system in the United States.

After the Civil War, the specter of the Paris Commune and integrated Reconstruction governments motivated the Hays-Tilden "compromise," sanctioning Klan violence and the rule of a single white party in the American South; fear of Bolshevik "agitators" and "inferior" immigrants from southern and eastern Europe spurred Woodrow Wilson's Palmer raids, eugenic laws, and the judicial murder of Sacco and Vanzetti; the Truman-McCarthy period invoked the "red menace," now variously colored, for example, the "blue ants" of China, to attack critical thought in every area of culture and murder the Rosenbergs; the Reagan-Bush era conjured "the evil empire" and "terrorism" to sanction the secret government of "Iran-Contragate" and nearly overturn the U.S. Constitution; and the like.[23] The ugly weight of state security and political and racial "respectability" has played an enormous, so far largely uncriticized role in the anemia of orthodox American democracy—the fact that "elections are not about issues" but personal "images"—and the blandness of much social science. As Herbert Lüthy's eloquent image of the French colonial republic's domination of Algeria suggests, the ruling elite has rebuilt from abroad the Bastilles torn down at home (internationalist thesis 2: the *antidemocratic-feedback thesis*).[24]

Now contemporary realism, a sophisticated, prudential standpoint, often opposes aggressive "crusades." Thus, (neo)realists question whether follies like Iran-Contragate[25] and criminalities like the Vietnam War further the "national interest." As the introduction suggests, they present their view as a *nonmoral critique of moralisms*, emphasizing social theory and ideologically concealed political interests. But their *official* critical conclusions have a moral undercurrent, for first, realists warn of unnecessary waste of life. Since ethics is, however, the discipline that focuses on preservation of life and the possibility of a good life, that concern is a moral one. To be against moralism is not to oppose every notion of ethics, for ironically, to reveal that moralisms are *harmful* requires an underlying notion of the good.[26] In fact, the democratic persuasiveness of a realist critique arises from its underlining of such harms: the waste of lives in renewed war, stemming from the punitive "idealism" of Versailles, or the destruction of moral integrity and wantonness of American aggression in Vietnam. Thus, we may best interpret the realist view as a *clearheaded, ethical critique of moralism*.

But then, the self-interpretation of neorealists is incoherent: power-based expansion, they *officially* maintain, where *necessary* for the national interest, is prudentially justified, whatever the waste of life. They thus deny the political and moral persuasiveness of (some of) their most important practical conclusions.[27] In contrast, a justifiable conception of a common good must encompass the lives and basic rights of the citizens of *each* power.[28] A coherently stated realist view of the national interest licenses (many realist) moral conclusions and undercuts "realist" imperialism. Second, since its inception, realism has also devoted itself to *truth telling*, unmasking the harmful pretensions of rulers. It has invoked the very ethical criteria belied in state rationalizations to indict prevailing policies.

Now sometimes, as in Max Weber's theory, advocacy of imperial aggrandizement erases moral clarity, for official realism does not hinder Weber's move; a power may advance any values consistent with a "national" interest. But that view is *self-refuting*: it recommends the life, liberty, and economic well-being of citizens embodied in the national interest; yet it denies, metaethically, that such moral interests are rationally defensible.[29] Epistemology aside, however, the practical realist argument cannot so easily check its ethical concerns, like a hat, at state borders. If the lives and liberties of each citizen of one's own nationality are morally important, so are the lives of the foreign-born: a well-formulated statism maintains merely that the realities of the international political sphere importantly constrain the human pursuit of a good life.[30] Thus, once again, restated realism—contra its advocates, a kind of *moral* realism—shades into the concerns of democratic internationalism. In fact, as we will see, the self-refutingness of official realism, despite its empirical attractions, yields an important explanatory advantage to a democratic internationalist alternative.

2. THE KINSHIP OF OFFICIAL REALISM AND DEPENDENCY

Given this historic conflict of theories, contemporary debates in international politics seem peculiarly misnamed, for the most common "radical" position—dependency theory—denies the basis and substance of democratic internationalism, while mainstream neorealist positions, so I will suggest, inadvertently underline the reasoning for internationalism. Dependency theory insists that workers and most others in the advanced countries benefit from the domination of people in less developed countries.[31] It thus envisions a common economic interest in the antiradical ideology and constriction of democracy emphasized earlier. But this thesis overlaps with a core contention—actually an implicit, underlying premise—of realism: most inhabitants of a power-state have common economic interests with its leaders that, sometimes, sustain an aggressive, antidemocratic conception of the national interest (the *internal bonding, harm to outsiders assumption*). At best, realism envisions the interests of states, checked by those of counterpowers, as nondemocratic even where nonexpansionary. But contemporary neorealist analyses undercut this assumption and, ironically, sustain internationalism against their own theoretical intentions.

Now the presupposition that citizens of advanced capitalist countries jointly benefit against outsiders underpins the realist contention that states, where they pursue "nonideological" policies, *represent* the common, *national* interest within their territories. The realist-democratic internationalist debate, however, reveals this claim's strikingly antidemocratic character, for a worked-out *democratic theory* must envision the possibility that uncoerced citizen deliberation, based on fundamental human concerns, can affirm basic rights domestically—for instance, freedoms of conscience, speech, and political organization—and peaceful policies externally.[32] But if a dependency or realist claim about common economic interests abroad is right, imperialist policies—even in some circumstances, extreme ones—will receive popular support.[33]

Yet to contemporary (neo)realists, the underlying claim seems attractive because it appears consistent with a domestic, "democratic" common good: preservation of freedom and augmented economic well-being. In addition, this view of a national interest provides a politically persuasive, Archimedean point to criticize ideologically motivated crusades, especially those characterized by a (temporary) domestic consensus as a "national" interest. On this realist conception, however, economic interests in exploitation abroad override the *general* human capacity for moral personality—for living with others cooperatively at least domestically. Further, the exercise of this human capacity is, by implication, always under similar threat from oligarchic or state interests at home. As a nondemocratic theory, (neo)realism renders the persistence and expansion of democracy obscure. Similarly, although dependency theorists stress harms to impoverished citizens in less-developed countries, their view eradicates the possibility of decent democratic change in the developed ones. Among the victims, they emphasize a nationalism arising from a narrow logic of putative economic interests. They thus justify local—and sometimes international—capitalist elites and provide no alternative to harms directed against the least advantaged.[34]

Dependency theorists also often present their views as a social theory- and interest-based critique of imperialist platitudes about human rights and democracy, an alternate, nonmoral indictment of moralism. Like realism, however, dependency's ethical attractions belie its self-interpretation. Nonetheless, a liberal should be wary of endorsing either theory, for both render institutions to further thoroughgoing democratic deliberation—as well as stands opposing aggression and domination—fruitless. Thus, a realist mitigates Vietnams, but cannot coherently head off Nicaraguas, Guatemalas, Salvadors, Brazils, Haitis, or an internal national-security apparatus that sometimes menaces even "balance of power" critics ("Project Morgenthau," the often brutal government response to an initially quite limited, student antiwar movement,[35] Watergate, the Truman-McCarthy persecutions, and the like). For official realism and dependency, the ideology of antiradicalism and the constriction of debate result from the *common economic interest*; on an informed popular vote, dependency expects repression to override democracy. Thus, an economic nationalist conception of the *public interest* coheres best with imperialism rather than with prudential realism, *dependencia-style* radicalism, or even minimal liberalism.[36]

3. IS KRASNER'S "NATIONAL INTEREST" DEFENSIBLE?

Stephen Krasner's *Defending the National Interest* (1978) implies a defense of the national interest in two senses: (1) that state policies or interests, not the economic interests of particular corporations, are the chief causal factor in American foreign economic policy; and (2) that the national interest, properly understood, is a genuine common good. Yet surprisingly, he directs his account only toward the first but not the second theme.

In method, Krasner's book marks an important turn in international social theory. For the past two decades in philosophy of science, critiques of empiricism have emphasized the theory-governed character of scientific advance. Contemporary neo-Kantian and especially *epistemological realist* views stress that sound research design in a domain of inquiry centrally contrasts the (usually) two leading alternative theories, or paths of development within a prevailing theory.[37] This insight opposes the still prevailing empiricist methodology of political science that stresses "testing" single hypotheses, suitably specified or "operationalized," against "[radically theory-external] data." Surveying the terrain in a new field, Krasner's commonsense approach coheres with scientific realism. Thus, to focus case studies of violent U.S. intervention to secure raw materials, he contrasts leading theories, society-centered (pluralist, instrumental Marxian) and state-centered (realist, structural Marxian) ones. Proceeding with unusual fairness, he even suggests the *theoretical indistinguishability* of his own statism and structural Marxism:

> There is a formulation offered by some working in a Marxist tradition that cannot be distinguished from the arguments offered here. Habermas, for instance, sees ideology not simply as a manifestation of a particular class structure (the position taken by Poulantzas), but as a phenomenon that can take on a life of its own. In *Legitimation Crisis*, he writes that the "evolution of morality, like the evolution of science, is dependent on truth." Once ideology [*sic*—neither ethics nor the sciences are simply "ideological," for to con-

demn a perspective as the latter requires socially based error, not truth, as the explanation for its prevalence] is accorded such an autonomous role, there is no empirical evidence that can distinguish this position from a statist one.[38]

As a positivist, however, Krasner imagines that acknowledging Marxism as, by and large, right has *no moral baggage* associated with it. Yet his core attempt to show that the U.S. government, rather than the oil companies, caused, say, the shah's overthrow of the democratic Mossadegh regime, affirms statism but does not make the American "national interest" attractive. For this change about the *causes of imperialism* merely shifts the object of ethical *indictment*: power-states degrade other peoples for autonomous political reasons rather than economic ones. Given a defective argumentative strategy, Krasner's realism ironically concedes the entire moral territory defended by democratic liberalism to radicals.[39]

Now, political theory has long emphasized the moral ambiguity of state autonomy. For as Aristotle put it, when such autonomy sustains particular domineering interests rather than a common good, it is *tyranny*. A liberal theorist with Krasner's concerns might naturally explore Woodrow Wilson's or Jimmy Carter's policies, stressing democracy or human rights: a *common good-sustaining* or *democratic autonomy*.[40] Yet Krasner might maintain: that choice is implausible. Realists have often suggested that "idealistic" administrations undercut the national interest; radicals have noted how ambivalent these leaders' commitments to democracy were: as Wilson celebrated the Ku Klux Klan's role in suppressing Reconstruction, launched the Palmer raids, and backed the White Armies in the Russian civil war, so Carter toasted the shah, just before his fall, as "beloved of his people."[41] Thus, Krasner treats examples of "democratic" autonomy peripherally because even the best cases present an *anomaly* for liberalism. Taken together, however, the natural liberal theoretical choice and empirical realism suggest that a radical political theory best explains American foreign policy. For, if true, Krasner's view morally separates the American "national interest" from democracy or human well-being elsewhere.

Domestically, Krasner strives to place the concept of a national interest in a morally favorable light. His argument vacillates, however, between a state-oriented, might-makes-right conception of the "national" interest and a defense of a common good. On the first, reductionist account—one that insists that all moral claims are vague and must be "operationalized" into some other, empirical idiom—he modifies Huntington's argument that the public interest is the interest of the governing institutions.[42] Against Huntington, he insists that the national interest must be long term; he excludes narrowly tyrannical acts like Watergate. In addition,

Krasner suggests that an array of foreign policies embodies a *national interest* only if it is prioritized—"transitively ordered"—across administrations.[43] In effect, Krasner uses a *methodological*, operationalist definition of the national interest as the state's interest to veil a distinctive realist claim, persuasively advanced only as a *specific* argument *within* international politics: that to defend a common good, professional diplomacy is always preferable to purportedly zealous, democratic influence (realist and neorealist thesis 2).

Krasner's epistemological claims are, however, morally implausible, for, on this view, the enforcement of the Fugitive Slave Law would have been the *common* good in the United States—for slaves, Quakers, and democrats as well as slaveholders—at least until the Emancipation Proclamation of 1863. Attempting to deny, by operationalist fiat, the harms to most people of *antidemocratic feedback*, his argument might mistakenly rename a victory of the CIA as a secret government, chilling domestic dissent, as a *public good* (realist thesis 2). By claiming that the distinction between tyranny and commonality is unclear, this view daubs the pallor of despotism in the colors of democracy.[44]

In contrast, however, Krasner's second conception of the national interest invokes straightforward moral goods. First, he notes that each state defends its territorial and political integrity.[45] This claim appeals to international standards about the goods of life and a culture of one's own—a culture not imposed by an invader—to each citizen. At least where the regime is democratic, this view conjures the freedom of each. As Walzer has emphasized, long-standing moral traditions about harm to innocents justify these standards.[46] But these standards are consistent only with self-defense against attack, not aggression to secure raw materials.

In addition, Krasner wants a fleshed-out view of the national interest that articulates the priority of particular foreign policies. He thus emphasizes a common economic well-being that results from control of vital materials and augmented production. In a morally self-aware formulation, he strives to differentiate his view from Marxian indictments of capitalist exploitation by insisting that justified policies further the interests of *all classes* or "promote the general wellbeing of society."[47] Prima facie, such a common interest *could* be internationally harmless. But Krasner describes the forcing of the American "national interest" on others. His view is thus ethically backbroken; it concurs with Marxians about damage abroad but sustains a quasi-moral, perhaps *national* appeal at home.

The prevention of aggression and preservation of equal (democratic) freedom—the goods that Krasner initially cites—however, have moral priority, as Rawls has argued, over securing raw materials. Thus, a democratic internationalist might point out, American interventions justify violent response by others (as a great power, whose leading rivals do not engage in war for this purpose, U.S. policymakers may ordinarily ignore this point).[48] More importantly, however, intervention legitimizes an extensive national-security apparatus to check radical "enemies" at home and poisons electoral competition. Such institutions and practices undercut the thoughtfulness and decency of every governmental policy (realist and internationalist thesis 3). Repression, ultimately, permits the kind of disaster illustrated by U.S. policy in Vietnam.

This argument highlights the ethical and political debilities of realist "antimoralism." As chapter 5 emphasizes, the legitimacy of a democracy depends on the maintenance of mutual regard among persons of differing conscientious views.[49] A regime whose "state interest" persistently violates that regard forfeits that legitimacy. Even within Krasner's argument, a liberal or radical might note, we purchase alleged economic commonality only at too great a sacrifice of moral and political—democratic—integrity; we should rule out his claims as a genuine "defense of the national interest." Further, Krasner presents no argument for common economic benefit. In fact, his leading example in repelling structural Marxians—once again, the Vietnam War—had at best a tenuous relationship to direct procurement of raw materials, let alone to the prospering of ordinary Americans. On balance, as an internationalist might stress, Vietnam took the lives of citizens and undercut their freedoms as well as, through inflation, their economic well-being.

During the Vietnam War, a majority of Americans, workers and soldiers as well as students, came to oppose government policy. Many recognized the war as aggressive. Illustrating Kant, others found it "a poor game." The moral and political concerns that underlie democratic internationalism subsequently hindered the ability of the American regime to intervene violently against popular protest movements ("the Vietnam syndrome"). An ethically coherent version of Krasner's view might justify such internationalism, regarding the antiwar movement as representing the national interest (realist and internationalist thesis 6). Further, Krasner often opposes interventions as "ideologically motivated" (realist and internationalist thesis 7). The foregoing *internal* critique of his argument makes a morally and politically explicit case for democratic resistance. Yet this criticism of Krasner raises an important question that reinforces realism: if democratic internationalism is in the interest of most people, why hasn't it had a greater impact in transforming global politics? (realist thesis 8) Alternately, why if the democratic-peace hypothesis has any merit, has the impact of democracy, in blunting aggression, been so slow?[50]

The internationalist may sketch four broad responses: the *governmental opposition; foreign enemies, external divide and rule; racist and anti-*

radical ideologies, internal divide and rule; and *greatness of scale* theses. First, if the prevailing powers have oligarchic or statist interests in war, democracy will have only a rare, blunted impact, coincident with dissident mass movements or revolution: *the governmental opposition rejoinder*. Second, a world of state competition often produces external intervention against a revolt in any power and, at least initially, divides radical movements by territory, regime, and culture. It thus weakens democratic initiatives and makes international revolution, for instance the interplay of the late 1980s East European democratic movements, unusual. In addition, even formally parliamentary regimes regularly use the image and reality of foreign enemies to divide democratic movements from one another. Consider the fate of socialist internationalism, aside from the Bolsheviks, the Italian socialist party, and the American IWW (Industrial Workers of the World) in World War I: the *foreign enemies, external divide and rule thesis*.

Third, in the case of U.S. interventions against non-European democracies—Guatemala, Iran, Brazil, Indonesia, Chile, Guyana, Nicaragua, Haiti, and the like—the ability to paint the attacked regime as an "enemy," through racist and antiradical ideology, plays a special role. Only with a large and costly U.S. war effort in Vietnam, and the emergence of a vehement antiwar movement, could these trends be limited, in *that* case.[51] In addition, however, such ideologies divide the population at home. During Vietnam, for instance, as chapter 2 emphasizes, they were used to discredit antiwar activists as "traitors" or "un-American." Fourth, these points highlight the vast objects of such movements: international cooperation and peace. To be successful even more broadly than the anti–Vietnam War movement, they need enormous energy and participation: *the greatness of scale argument*. Although large movements have come to pass, accomplishment of their full goals was, from the outset, unlikely (taken together, these claims comprise internationalist thesis 8).

To develop a thoroughgoing answer to this realist objection, however, would require a complex political and historical discussion.[52] Nonetheless, the foregoing analysis of Krasner's argument suggests that the obstacles to democratic internationalism are primarily *political and organizational*, not economic. Thus, democratic movements may hope to cancel the inevitability in the question: *must* international politics constrain democracy?

Because Krasner's version of structural Marxism fails to emphasize the common interests of citizens across national borders, it misses the central theoretical feature of radicalism. Yet Krasner's failure to prove statism superior to (even his version of) structural Marxism underlines the case for democratic internationalism. For Krasner, first, only hegemonic powers have the luxury of pursuing a misguided "ideology" in foreign affairs. In Paretian terms, he characterizes ideological policies as "non-logical"; they employ means too dear for the ends in view. In American interventions, he identifies that ideology as "anticommunism." Second, the U.S. government lost in Vietnam. On Krasner's account,

> [T]his nonlogical behavior . . . cannot be easily apprehended from a structural Marxist perspective. For structural Marxists, the central purpose of the state is to preserve the coherence of the society; the state strives to act rationally. This is not to say, however, that it will always succeed. . . . Can Vietnam be understood from a structural Marxist perspective that emphasizes ideology? Such an argument would be difficult, for American intervention in Vietnam undermined the very coherence that the dominant ideology is supposed to preserve.[53]

Now Krasner's second claim confuses Marxian with elite theory on which the powers-that-be mainly act rationally and get their way.[54] If so, however, how could socialist or communist revolution ever occur? How can U.S. defeat in Vietnam be a *counterexample* to a view that insists, in the *Manifesto*'s image, that capitalism digs its own grave?

Krasner's first claim, however, is innovative and important. It recognizes the force of antiradical ideology—remember the "Wild Irish" of the 1790s—in undermining American democracy. For anticommunist ideology, though far less recognized, is probably as pervasive a force in deterring popular movements as racism or sexism.

A modestly dialectical Marxism, however, can explain the role of this ideology that stigmatizes "outside agitators," speaking a "foreign tongue" filled with bizarre "rhetoric," who will nonetheless "dupe" otherwise happy people to oppose the government. It protects an exploitative, dishonorable elite, one that cannot straightforwardly defend its policies to citizens. As the introduction notes, however, except for the remarkably antidemocratic prejudice that ordinary citizens are likely "dupes," proponents might have trouble figuring out how such unlikely "agitators" could possibly gain a following. By contrast, democrats expect untrue opinions to dispel long term on fair discussion (perhaps, as chapter 5 argues, to ensure fairness, citizens will also have to engage in civil disobedience and/or other forms of protest, and reconstruct the public arena to check the overweening power of the rich). Yet on State Department formulations, French colonialism in Indochina, sustained by U.S. aid, or American-sponsored reversal of land reform in South Vietnam did not victimize peasants; instead, the latter were "misled" by alien forces with "other" aims in view. Establishment ideology transfigured the sole technological power raining chemicals from the sky from alien invader to indigenous defender of "democracy." It revisioned Vietnamese who had battled French and Japanese aggression as "outsiders."

For a radical, the rulers are likely to have some quasi-conscious sense of their oppressiveness, and of the danger of "democratic distemper" and revolt.[55] They need to project a mirror image on radicals. Now a Marxian might have difficulty accounting for, say, a contending feminist hypothesis about the main—or an important, additional—ideology of American intervention, one that fixed on the violent *machismo* of American leaders, their need to be "real men." A radical explanation would, if plausible, require supplemental theses to original Marxism, for instance invocations of national and international status hierarchy and theories of gender identity.[56] But if there is *an* ideology that a dialectical Marxian theory can explain, it is that "specter haunting Europe, the specter of communism."

Despite stressing this ideology, however, Krasner never defines it. Instead, he confuses reasonable objections to state socialist regimes, for instance, that they have often been dictatorial, with a bizarre view aimed to paralyze popular protest.[57]

Yet antiradical ideology has played an enormously costly role in U.S. foreign policy. For instance, as Goldfischer's *The Best Defense* argues, a non-civilian-targeted nuclear strategy may have been possible at the outset of the Cold War; Oppenheimer and Allen Dulles supported it. The air force under Secretary Forrestal as well as the Pentagon, however, used anticommunist ideology to stigmatize this decent alternative. They made adherence putatively a sign of "being a foreign agent."[58] Oppenheimer was crucified. Dulles fell silent on this issue and, subsequently, as head of the CIA, authorized the criminal subversion of democratic governments abroad, for instance, of Arbenz in Guatemala in 1953 and Mossadegh in Iran in 1954. In a less threatening nuclear environment, for instance, one not enhanced by demonology against "radicals," such interventions might have appeared unnecessary. Allegedly to enhance individual security, the nuclear arms race targeted millions of civilians—a paradigm of insecurity—and threatened extinction.[59]

But if antiradical ideology preserves capitalism against democratic "distemper," it is likely, on a Marxian thesis, to be widely influential, especially among elites. From that theoretical standpoint, the rulers would *rationally* pursue these ideas in international class conflict, even though, from a realist, balance-of-power perspective such as Krasner's, these ideas are "nonlogical." Further, Krasner's critique of the Vietnam intervention highlights the *anomaly for realism* of "ideological" failures of prudence, and creates his theoretically unmotivated need to suppose that only hegemonic states, not lesser ones, can be autonomous and ideological[60] (in fact, contra Krasner, against French, Japanese, French, and

U.S. aggression, Vietnamese resistance reflected the autonomy of politics, *and*, in terms of justice, truth). Theoretical realism, which emphasizes the (perhaps varying) autonomy of *all states* in the international system, undercuts Krasner's move. Further, the very example he urges against Marxism shows why a radical explanation, capturing the rationality of anticommunist ideology from the standpoint of capitalist interests, is superior to statism.

Readers may find these criticisms of Krasner's account surprising for two reasons. First, they highlight just how strong even a minimal Marxian rejoinder—one based solely on the *Communist Manifesto*, without further refinement—is against Krasner's neorealism. Second, they suggest that in the current state of American academia, fair-minded mainstream theorists rarely run across radicals from whom they might learn obvious rejoinders.

4. SOPHISTICATED NEOREALISM VERSUS DEMOCRATIC INTERNATIONALISM

A restatement of the debate between neorealism and democratic internationalism may help to highlight central differences. Krasner initially makes the historically grounded *induction* that each state seeks at least to defend its territorial and cultural integrity against conquest (realist thesis 1). He then suggests that specific historical traditions, bureaucratic rivalries, and the psychologies of leaders also affect the definition and pursuit of national interests.[61] But at this point, his argument bifurcates between older American realism, in which an autonomous state represents the citizens (more exactly, the state represents the quiescent majority of citizens; as we will see in Kennan, it overrides the clamor of politicians and publicists for unwise policies), and a *post-Vietnam realism*, which undercuts that claim. On the one hand, criticizing the vengeful Versailles Treaty and 1930s pacifism, Krasner joins American realists since Kennan in worrying that democratic opinion and the separation of powers—the "weak American state"—will palsy statecraft. Against internationalism, such realists have long sought normatively to insulate foreign policymaking from popular influence (realist thesis 2). They have maintained that the state somehow defends the *real* interests of citizens *against democracy*. On the other hand, Krasner notes that the Vietnam War—the most "damaging" of the Cold War era—"was probably shortened by popular discontent,"[62] or, as he put it in conversation, "*the anti–Vietnam War movement represented the national interest*." His insistence on the role of "anticommunist ideology" strengthens this second, antielitist strand in his argument. For an internationalist may often interpret ostensibly "democratic opinion" as mass opinion shaped by an oligarchically dominated media and politics (realist and internationalist thesis 3).

Thus, although Krasner avers the standard realist disdain for democracy, his own central theses about Vietnam, comparable, as chapter 2 shows, to those of Morgenthau, Niebuhr and Kennan, *undercut* this claim: most Americans were hurt by the war, and popular protest helped to curtail it.[63] Further, Krasner endorses Gilpin's argument on American militarism, deindustrialization, and the decline of living standards for most citizens (realist and internationalist thesis 4).

As I have noted, Krasner's confusion stems in part from an ambiguous conception of the national interest that wobbles between an operationalist defense of the state's interest and a reasonable conception of a common good among citizens. On Krasner's view, instrumental Marxism sees lobbying by particular capitalists as the driving force behind government violence to control foreign raw materials. In contrast, Krasner underlines an independent state role: that interest is allegedly whatever, in the long term, strengthens the government. But, this causal claim is not a defense. Krasner hopes to escape this point by appeal to the supposed "classlessness" or community of the robbers. It is enough to show, he thinks, that capitalists do not engineer state policies that harm others; hence, every American must benefit. But that conclusion does not follow. As the internationalist argument on the invocation of external enemies, constriction of political options and public corruption suggests, such policies hurt most Americans—no domestic common good is realized (realist and internationalist theses 3, 4, and 6).

Now Krasner rightly rejects ideologically motivated "crusades" and urges a largely, though not completely, noninterventionary American foreign policy. Democratic internationalism, however, rules out unilateral military interventions, even those Krasner recommends.[64] It opposes wars to extend "democracy" or "socialism" (realist and internationalist thesis 7).

Krasner concedes, however, that U.S. military and police aid to oligarchies in less developed countries serves no common interest among American citizens. But that claim highlights a striking *anomaly* for his theory. As chapter 2 emphasizes, advancing false *empirical* contentions, other, more policy-influential realists saw popular movements abroad as instigated by "outside agitators," fantasized long-term threats of "aggression" against the United States, and recommended American interventions—actual aggression—to sustain oppressive regimes.[65] On Krasner's view, those realisms were *ideological* and violated American interests. But an internationalist stress on this patterned abridgment of a common good, highlighting domestic oligarchy, the propagation of antiradical, racist, and sexist ideologies, and the constriction of political options, better accounts for what Krasner downplays as "extraneous" factors.[66]

To save realism from this internal critique, Krasner pits democracy against democracy. For instance, Michael Doyle emphasizes the absence of war among parliamentary regimes. But Krasner, following Mearsheimer, rightly stresses the United States' overturning of the democracies of Allende in Chile, Arbenz in Guatemala, and Mossadegh in Iran[67] (realist thesis 9—*a factual overriding of an otherwise desirable common good*). My argument, however, recognizes such interparliamentary rivalry.

With Doyle, I stress mass resistance to war because of the likeness of citizenries and the *public injustice* of claims to dominate other democracies[68]—the need for leaders to conjure external, "racially" and regime-different "enemies." In contrast to Doyle, however, democratic internationalism *from below* also emphasizes the reality, despite parliamentary forms, of oligarchy and the dangers of intervention against radical and/or democratic movements. This view anticipates and explains Krasner's counterexamples (internationalist thesis 9). Against regime-based claims, Krasner advances an alternate cause for post–World War II peace among parliamentary democracies: the menace of nuclear extinction. But that insight—along with the threat of a poisoned environment—reveals the novel, *transnational* dangers to citizens of today's capitalist and power-state rivalries, and reinforces an explicitly internationalist, democratic conception of a common good (realist and internationalist thesis 10).[69]

In international politics, a prevailing empiricist paradigm entrenches misguided or badly stated theory. Krasner, for instance, insists that his neorealism is, following Waltzian positivism, "deductive," as if the claim that states tend to defend themselves when attacked were not an (empirical) induction.[70] This elevated, "nomothetico-deductive" status of the core of realist theory mistakenly relegates Krasner's striking insights into "anticommunist ideology" and statist oligarchy to secondary importance. Put differently, Krasner's argument is most interesting at the second "level of analysis"—the interplay of international and domestic politics. Yet as a neorealist, he insists on the primacy as well as the analytic isolation of the international sphere. Further, Krasner's *operationalism* about a common good—his claim that the national interest is whatever strengthens the state in the long term—leads to his inability to distinguish a causal claim about harmful state action from an (ethical) extenuation.

Finally, as I note in the introduction, in attempting to achieve *value-freedom* through *reductionism*, this version of neorealism is insufficiently empirical about "power." For example, to mobilize a population to repel aggression requires political motivation, an appeal to a genuine common good.[71] Thus, Soviet resistance to Nazism, Vietnamese to French colonialism, or American and Indian to British colonialism conflict with conventional neorealist notions of "power" and require a well-stated, moral conception of a common interest to explain their surprising *counter*power.

Even in periods without direct repression, however, American academia is hierarchical and fashion-driven.[72] A government- or industry-funded behaviorism in psychology and the study of politics has sought to base a "science" not on the increasingly rich, specific theories characteristic of physics, chemistry, or biology, but on a mistaken philosophical doctrine—an empiricist picture of such theories. It has thus substituted a uniform, external standard of *method* for substantive argument: operationalism, reductionism, value-freedom, the nomothetico-deductive method, methodological individualism (the word *method* recurs in the names of empiricist doctrines), levels of analysis, econometrics, some graphs. Ignoring a commonsense obligation to supply and refute the best version of an opposing view, positivism often ignores *plausible* alternate theories.[73]

5. GILPIN'S RESTORATION OF GREAT-POWER RIVALRY

Like dependency theory, Krasner's and, as we shall see, Keohane's views focus on the relations of advanced capitalist to less developed countries. In this respect, they are less classically realist than Robert Gilpin's (1987) *Political Economy of International Relations*, for the latter emphasizes Japan's supplanting America as the world's leading economic power. Yet Gilpin concentrates not just on the erosion of American competitiveness but on the interplay of belligerence, characteristic of the Reagan years, and economic decline. Starting from a neorealist focus on global competition of states, his book, surprisingly, concludes that presidential posturing hurt most citizens: antidemocratic feedback. Ironically, his argument thus supports democratic internationalism, a theoretical alternative that he, like other neorealists, ignores.

On Gilpin's account, Reagan pursued vast military expenditures to combat the "evil empire" and make the United States "No. 1," while he also reduced taxes. To offset unheard-of deficits and yet not impose more burdens on most citizens, he borrowed over $100 billion, primarily from Japan. He thus mortgaged America's future, fueling industrial decline through huge debt repayments:

> In the words of U.S. Secretary of State George Shultz, "I think one could say that, if the world were content to let the Japanese provide a major share of the savings and wind up owning more and more, it's O.K. But that is not the

way the United States, at least, is oriented." The Secretary failed to add that it was the policies of the Reagan Administration that had created this unfortunate situation.

First, the competitive position of important sectors of the American economy has been permanently damaged, and the structure of the entire economy has been distorted. Second, repayment of the immense external debt and the associated interest payments will absorb a large share of America's productive resources for many years to come; these costs will substantially lower the standard of living for a considerable period, even if defense expenditures are considerably curtailed. And, third, the newly acquired preference of Americans for foreign goods and the expansion of productive capacity abroad have decimated many industries in which the United States once had a strong comparative advantage; America will be required to develop new products and industries if it is to regain even part of its former competitive position in world markets. The task of reversing the trends toward deindustrialization will be difficult and very costly.[74]

Gilpin presents his argument dispassionately. Yet a subdued *realist* fury flashes in his unmasking of Reagan's imperial pretenses. The latter revived grandiose illusions of U.S. hegemony while, in reality, making the American economy dependent on Japan at the expense of most Americans. In a footnote describing the views of an honest adviser aware of the emperor's new clothes, Gilpin's anger crystallizes in a single word: "Feldstein provides a *frank* appraisal of the damage to capital formation and other aspects of the American economy caused by the economic policies of the administration."[75]

Methodologically, like Krasner, Gilpin emphasizes contending theories. Invoking the empiricist claim about *theoretical indistinguishability*, he maintains, "as formulated by Lenin, Marxism has become nearly indistinguishable from the doctrine of political realism."[76] Theoretical indistinguishability suggests both that different general theories may apply, with diverse auxiliary statements, to the same "data," and, more controversially, that they explain those "data" *equally* well. The doctrine of "value-freedom," once again, improbably suggests that inability to differentiate the empirical outcomes of Marxian from neorealist theories has no ethical consequences.

In contrast to Gilpin's and Lenin's views, dependency theory concentrates on center/periphery relations at the expense of great-power/"inter-imperialist" rivalry. Yet failing to see the contrast between realism and democratic internationalism, Gilpin does not sufficiently articulate his argument *politically*; an internationalist might reinforce it.

First, *deindustrialization* victimizes ordinary Americans; Gilpin's argument depicts an *economic* underpinning for democratic internationalism.

In this context, his "(neo)realism" contrasts with a misguided strain in Lenin's *Imperialism* out of which dependency theory grows: an insistence that economic parasitism affects a large segment of workers in the advanced capitalist countries who become "an aristocracy of labor." But then, contrary to Lenin, those workers would be unlikely to make revolution. Gilpin nicely captures this tension in Lenin's view but fails to see its importance for his own critique: "The workers or the labor aristocracy in the developed capitalist countries temporarily shared in the exploitation of colonial peoples but ultimately would pay for these gains on the battlefield."[77]

Gilpin's argument thus highlights the side of Lenin's view that stresses the common interests underlying potential democratic internationalism, not the putative economic sources of reactionary division. Further, sophisticated radical arguments suggest a complex political causation for the failures—or successes—of revolutionary movements, not a mainly economic one.[78] But Gilpin's argument, concurring with such radical ones, undermines the *central presupposition of realism* that the interests of ordinary people align with major foreign policies. To make his argument at all consistent with official realism, Gilpin needed to maintain that Reagan's militarism was arbitrary, not an expression of "transitively ordered," transadministration interests. His critique is thus an *anomaly* for his realism.

Second, under the spell of the prevailing paradigm that emphasizes political *economy*, Gilpin fails to see the *political* element in his thesis. For internationalism focuses on checking the belligerent policies of one's own—democratic or, more accurately, parliamentary—government. Now Reagan directed his *militarism* mainly at asserting American power against the weak, bombing Libya and sponsoring the Contras in Nicaragua. In the Libyan case, Reagan's answer to terrorists, whom he rightly condemned for killing innocents, was to bomb innocents. In Nicaragua, the president mobilized remnants of the former U.S.-client Somoza dictatorship[79] along with others discontented with Sandinista policy. The American government flouted international law, mining Nicaraguan harbors, and the Contras largely marauded against civilians. Measured by the actual commitment of American citizens, these activities were comparatively low-cost ways of projecting power and undermining "the Vietnam syndrome." They created an ideological aura for the renewed use of U.S. citizens in unjust wars as in Panama,[80] for the enormous arms-driven deficit with concomitant dependence on Japan, for the elimination of any "peace dividend," and for deindustrialization and economic injury to most Americans (realist and internationalist thesis 4).

To criticize this internationalist reformulation of Gilpin's view, a liberal might argue for more flexible possibilities of American growth, diminished dependence on Japan, and lessened *economic* harm. But internationalism yields a further *political*-economic response: the Reagan years saw a vast increase in CIA and FBI surveillance of ordinary Americans, an augmented chilling of the democratic process that culminated in the attempted subversion of the Constitution, Iran-Contragate, and a resuscitation of antiradical ideology against moderate "liberalism" (the "L" word and "card-carrying ACLU member" leveled even at the Democrats' technocratic nominee, Michael Dukakis). If defense of freedom of conscience and speech are characteristic of well-stated conservatism,[81] then Reagan and Bush were, because they were not liberals, not conservatives. A liberal view aims for uncoerced patriotism, not rote and propaganda. It thus contrasts with Bush's use of the Pledge of Allegiance in the 1988 campaign. From a democratic point of view, the Reagan-Bush years *undermined* political and civil freedom. Independently of economic interest arguments, these *political* claims show why most Americans have an interest in opposing elite belligerence (internationalist theses 3 and 4). They add a distinctive *militarism and decline* or *price of empire claim* to the undermining of mistaken realist thesis 2: that in an international regime, ostensibly independent from domestic regime structures, a state (by and large) represents the interests of its citizens.

This internationalist reformulation makes Gilpin's argument a fully political economy. He fails to see these implications because he shares today's overly economic, "beneficial market" paradigm of liberalism—his other leading theoretical rival to realism. Now, Gilpin distances himself from the common view that "there is no such thing as a liberal theory of political economy because liberalism separates economics and politics from one another." Yet he does not articulate the core features of a well worked out liberal theory.[82]

One can justify the free market, however, only insofar as it coincides with the extension of individual freedoms, particularly for political liberals, those of conscience, speech, and participation (suffrage). Without these primary liberties, one reduces liberalism to Friedman's "Chicago boys," advisers to the Chilean dictator Pinochet, linking the realities of the body count of "disappeared" individuals to vapidities about economic "freedom." A democratic internationalist critique internally strengthens Gilpin's view. Once again, an explicit liberal democratic political theory, conjoined with Gilpin's realism, leads to *radical* conclusions.

Since this chapter emphasizes issues of philosophy of science, I want to underline Gilpin's conflicting epistemological claims. First, he advances the scientific realist argument that theory contrasts can give rise, in the light of the evidence, to claims of greater explanatory capability: "a [power state] realist interpretation I believe, is far superior to that of

Marxism in explaining the relationship of uneven growth and political conflict"; second, a neo-Kantian thesis that since these theories allegedly start from different premises, they must be incommensurable, and, hence, that no overall comparison is possible: "although particular ideas or theories associated with one position or another may be shown to be false or questionable, these perspectives can be neither proved nor disproved through logical argument or the presentation of contrary empirical evidence"; and third, the empiricist claim that good theories must be predictive, not explanatory: "[radical theories of state autonomy,] like Lenin's theory of imperialism, are best regarded as ad hoc hypotheses that seek to explain away the predictive failures of Marxist theory rather than as extensions of the theory."[83]

Now, his second claim contradicts the first: if sophisticated comparisons of theories as contending explanations of relevant data were impossible, then the point of Gilpin's—and, for that matter, Krasner's or Keohane's—arguments would be lost. In addition, as Thomas Kuhn's argument reveals, it is strange for a theorist to give us a vivid comparative tour of two intellectual "worlds"—pre-Copernican and Copernican astronomy, realism and Marxism—and then suggest, as an epistemological gloss, that no such travel back and forth between them is possible. Through an internal critique of realist notions of a common good, this chapter and the next show that it is possible to compare liberal, radical, and realist theories of international relations. Gilpin's third claim—that a good theory cannot employ auxiliary statements (factual claims, relevant abstractions, and the like)—is a Popperian prejudice, criticized today even by many empiricists and Popperians. We can determine if modifications of a theory are ad hoc only by *comparison* with sophisticated explanations offered by an alternative.[84] Further, the suggestion that a good social scientific theory must be predictive makes Darwin's explanatory account of the origin of species "nonscientific." If true, it would exclude all interest in Gilpin's argument that explains the trend of U.S. decline but makes no exact predictions. Of Gilpin's three epistemological intuitions, the scientific realist one is best illustrated in his actual political economy.

Against a *democratic internationalist* refinement, Gilpin's argument suggests some objections. He maintains that Lenin's Marxism underestimates the role of states and sees war as the inevitable outcome of economic rivalry.[85] His realist counterargument makes the debilities of American policy more contingent—a pursuit of personal glory at the expense of the national interest—than, he supposes, a radical view may allow. Yet a sophisticated radical theory can, as Krasner notes, emphasize the dialectical role of politics and make war a tendency rather than an inevitability. It then has two advantages over Gilpin's statism: first, a straightforward emphasis on common citizen interests against militarism, and second, an ability to redescribe such political contingencies as an *oligarchic* distortion of—-and defeat for—-democracy.

6. KEOHANE'S LIBERALISM: ARE CONTEMPORARY REGIMES COOPERATIVE?

Robert Keohane's *After Hegemony* (1984) imports game theory and neo-classical arguments about market failure into international-relations theory to turn realist premises in a liberal direction. Let us imagine, he suggests, a competition of actors—states—who are purely self-interested. Iterated prisoner's dilemmas and Akerlof's insistence on the need for reliable information—finding a trustworthy secondhand car dealership to avoid "lemons"—show that international economic cooperation is possible.[86] For in important arenas of global interaction, regimes have emerged, characterized by norms and sometimes organizations, such as the International Monetary Fund, that allow secure, informed state cooperation.

Keohane defines such *regimes* as "sets of implicit or explicit principles, norms, rules and decision-making procedures around which an actor's expectations converge in a given area of international relations." He sees norms, in a nonmoralistic vein, "simply as standards of behavior, whether adopted on grounds of self-interest or otherwise."[87] If governments violate regime norms wherever the latter oppose particular "national" interests, their other important aims may be frustrated. Thus, Keohane suggests, current international regimes embody cooperation to some degree. We may envision future reforms, coherent with state interests, to make them fully cooperative.

On a realist theory, however, coordination will occur only in the presence of overarching power. Yet given the decline of American hegemony, Keohane maintains, the persistence of regimes reveals—contra statism—unexpected possibilities of multilateral cooperation.

Moreover, in a liberal thought startling to realists, he notes the "empathetic interdependence" of nongovernmental actors such as Oxfam. That interdependence includes the good of others in one's self-conception or "interest," and might, he imagines, contribute to the reshaping of international politics.[88] Following Keohane, a radical might think of the IWA and the Socialist and Communist internationals as prototypical regimes, characterized by democratic solidarity or empathetic interdependence.

In addition, in contrast to empiricism in today's political science, Keohane's argument is well formulated in ethics and consistent with the foregoing internal critique of realism. Thus, his last chapter invokes

Rawlsian and utilitarian criteria to evaluate contemporary regimes and concludes that they harm—or at least do not much benefit—the least advantaged both in Europe and the less developed countries:

> It is not clear that any of the international regimes discussed in this book would be regarded as good on the basis of either utilitarianism or Rawls' difference principle, even if only effects on people in advanced industrialized countries were considered. Utilitarians could argue that aggregate human welfare gains would be made by using these regimes to transfer resources from advantaged to disadvantaged people within these societies. Likewise, adherents of the difference principle would demand to know whether these regimes really help the least well-off people. . . . Would it not be possible for the IMF to demand greater contribution from banks and less from taxpayers. . . ? Why should the IEA not press for national policies to subsidize the fuel bills of the poor. . . ?
>
> . . . The principles on which current patterns of cooperation are based show insufficient sensitivity to the interests of disadvantaged people in the Third World. This suggests, however, not that there is too much cooperation, but that its *orientation towards the interests of the rich* is morally questionable. . . . They [regimes] *create some benefits for poor countries* but these are small compared to what would be needed to correct gross violations of basic human rights that take place when people die of hunger or are continually miserable because of lack of clean water, adequate health care, or decent shelter.[89]

To justify contemporary regimes, Keohane sometimes asserts that the worst off gain from their current situation in comparison to all-out state rivalry. But this hypothetical claim that *even worse is possible* can justify extremes of victimization. As Rousseau says, of Hobbes's comparable endorsement of (temporary) physical security, Odysseus and his companions were "tranquil" in the cave of the Cyclops, waiting to be devoured, but this tranquility was "itself one of their miseries."[90] Further, Keohane advances no argument that regimes benefit the least advantaged; even the preceding formulation is not promising, since "some benefits for poor *countries*" may accrue to oppressive elites.

Thus, his chapter on ethics subverts his earlier game-theoretic account of seeming interstate "cooperation" and underlines the *antidemocratic feedback of contemporary international regimes.* Further, a radical critic might note, this argument suggests not liberal coordination from above but democratic internationalism from below, that of the least advantaged across national boundaries, to press their governments and international regimes for decent policies. Like Krasner's, Keohane's alternative suffers from a lack of appropriate *theoretical setting* in the realism/democratic internationalism debate.

As a striking example of solidarity from below, Ireland notes that diverse forms of immigrant organizing have influenced the policies of the European Union. For immigrant activity in one country—accompanied by formal Community recognition of immigrant rights—stimulates organizing in others, and illustrates an unusual *global feedback of democratic example* (internationalist theses 6–8).[91] Given social and political differences in national setting and attempted learning by successor movements and their enemies from their predecessors' strengths and weaknesses, democratic feedback is, however, at best, limited. These facts underline the irrationality of the American government's domino theory: if Vietnam "fell" to Communism, Burma, Japan, the Philippines, and the West Coast "must" also "fall." Yet some striking influence, say of the American on the French Revolution, the Russian on Chinese "New Democracy," or Gandhian nonviolence on Martin Luther King's, occurs, as do less significant cases (say, the impact of diverse revolutions on Communist movements in India).

Now, Keohane acknowledges many Marxian claims about current regimes—for instance, "their orientation towards the interests of the rich"—suggesting, once again, the *theoretical indistinguishability* of a Marxian view and (neo)realism.[92] Further, in a fundamental insight that sustains realist and internationalist emphases on the tyrannical power of oligarchy and undercuts his own claims about beneficial cooperation, he argues that in advanced countries, capital flight often frustrates liberal or social-democratic efforts to enact reforms:

> The restraints imposed by an open world economy[93] are likely to be particularly severe for socialist governments seeking to pursue stimulative policies. . . . the adverse effects on the value of its currency are likely to be accentuated by capital flight and low levels of private investment. The French socialist government of François Mitterand experienced such difficulties during 1981–82.
>
> . . . Where international liberalism prevails, citizens may be reluctant to vote socialist governments into office, even if they regard socialism as superior to capitalism as a system, for fear of these economic disruptions. Furthermore, socialist governments in power and socialist or communist movements seeking power may be constrained by fear of capital flight, as the experiences of the British Labor Party, the Italian communists, and most recently the French socialists illustrated. The road to socialism may be blocked by liberal international regimes, constructed by conservative predecessors in conjunction with their capitalist allies.[94]

Contrary to Keohane's central thesis about cooperation, this claim—what I will call realist and internationalist thesis 5—underlines further global obstacles to democratic reform posed by current regimes. In addition, Keohane emphasizes only the constricting effect of such an environment on domestic economic growth—"stimulative policies"—which would, however, benefit capitalists more than the poor (realist thesis 5). But such global limitations also constrict social programs that uphold the *basic rights* of citizens—for instance, to feed otherwise hungry children, to guarantee a fair trial (say, through public funding of lawyers for the poor), to provide medical care, to expand educational opportunity, and the like. As an Aristotelian might stress, in a capitalist regime, such rights are central to maintaining a *common good* (internationalist thesis 6). Instead, due to global capitalist hostility, capital flight, the decline of domestic investment, and the like, economic growth slows. Elected socialist governments fail to live up to their promises and incur popular disfavor. The *capitalist* "cooperation" of current international regimes constricts domestic political options.

As a further example, the 1995 workers' rebellion in France—a movement from below to defend the rights of those whom the European "Union"'s policies would impoverish—opposed supranational influence. As Ignacio Ramonet puts it,

> The stunning French revolt of December, 1995 was the first collective refusal of a society founded on economism, ultra-liberalism, the supremacy of the market and the tyranny of globalization ["openness," indeed]—and a reminder to the French leaders of an old republican principle: the people prefer chaos to injustice. . . . the crisis called government, democracy and the elites into question, . . . [elites] which slavishly eulogize "one-track thought," refusing all critical analysis, using "modernization," "realism" and "responsibility" as their justification . . . which reject as irrational all those who refuse to accept that "the market is the natural state of society." In this regard, the French revolt may mark the end of one of the most reactionary periods in recent history, a period which, from 1983 to 1993, saw socialist leaders and intellectuals abandon all hope of changing the world, proposing instead . . . a simple formula drawn from the Darwinian terminology so dear to the ultraliberals: to adapt—that is, to renounce, abdicate and submit.
>
> . . . Even at the blackest hours of the Great Depression of 1929, there was less human flotsam. If one adds all those excluded for one reason or another to the 3.5 million unemployed, there is a total of 6 million people on the margins of society—half of them below the poverty line, on less than 60 francs ($12/£7.50) a day. . . . Such a misery is contrary to basic human rights, and, consequently, to the whole conception of the Republic.[95]

Thus, the oligarchic rule of current regimes conflicts with "the whole conception of the Republic" and is now being challenged from below. In 1996, the French oil workers' strike won a retirement age of fifty-five years.

European Union and government efforts to trim a comparatively high level of wages and social services have also affected German workers:

> Surprisingly, some business executives have questioned efforts to cut wages and social security entitlements, saying the cuts could produce damaging friction between labor and management. . . . Strikes have become more frequent.
>
> Cologne economist Joachim Stulz said that business executives "are worried that an all-out assault on [Germany's] wages and benefits system, however justified from an economic standpoint [*sic*--a putatively "value-free" economics, which ignores a common good, rather plainly serves capitalist interests] would lead to political turmoil. Germany has been a tranquil country for 50 years. There is fear, in view of our history, of even the slightest spread of unrest."[96]

German unemployment is 11 percent. Strikes in France help to stimulate solidarity among German workers. Further, the American media nearly did not cover the French rebellion, stifling *democratic feedback*. For trends similar to those that harm French or German workers injure most Americans.[97] These facts are a sign of capitalist control of the media, as we see in chapter 2's exploration of Morgenthau and Niebuhr and in chapter 5.

Despite his radical insights, however, Keohane pits his view only against a mainly economic version of Marxism that putatively invokes a "the worse, the better" argument: the collapse of current regimes would allegedly, just by itself, be a good. But again, Keohane's characterization may make oppressive regimes "positive" solely by comparison to imagined worse alternatives. It allows radical theorists only negativity without imagination.[98]

To correct the abuses of current regimes, Keohane adopts the moral stance of the Bishops' letter on deterrence: such regimes are *conditionally acceptable* only "if people relying on [them] seek to find a better way to manage their relations."[99] As a glaring internal weakness, however, he provides no recommendations for reform. Yet responding to the threat of nuclear war, Gene Sharp's proposal of nonviolent, civilian defense for Europe might realize Keohane's condition. Sharp's notion seems especially promising in the post–Cold War era because it proposes the mobilization of diverse, democratic populations on its behalf and illustrates democratic internationalism.[100] But revolts like the 1995 and 1996 French strikes to defend basic rights might also realize Keohane's condition. Finally, as chapter 5 explores, in the post–Cold War era, a number of treaties, for example banning land mines or the use of children as soldiers, instigated by pressure from below, illustrate moral cooperation. In the past, so did international agreements, largely provoked by democratic movements, against enslavement.[101] But at the time when Keohane wrote, no such treaties were prominent. Further, unlike the IMF, antislavery was, by then, a long established regime that no longer required significant international activity.[102]

Keohane's last chapter illustrates the problems raised within international-relations theory by *liberal* moral clarity. For imagine conversations between Keohane and, first, a realist, then, a radical. The statist notes: "Your moral critique of current regimes shows that realism is basically right. Such regimes serve the interests of the advanced capitalist powers, notably the United States and increasingly Japan, at the expense of poor people. But we realists have always recognized exploitative *alliances against others*: that's all regime cooperation is." For the realist, Keohane's failure to articulate meaningful reforms is not a fault; on a more clearheaded view, it testifies to the sad reality of the state system, revealing how derisory talk of empathetic cooperation is. Thus, this critic argues: "Granting your moral clarity as an improvement on earlier realist accounts like Krasner's and your counter against Marxian objections, I maintain that nonhegemony—great-power rivalry and war—would be even worse. With your argument, what realism asserts is that contemporary regimes are conditionally acceptable, though in many respects, exploitative, and against your view, that little change is possible."

7. AN INTERNAL, DOYLE-KEOHANE VERSION OF THE DEMOCRATIC-PEACE HYPOTHESIS

As a critique of *After Hegemony*, this realist rejoinder is effective. A refined version of Keohane's view, however, underlining potential reforms, might answer this objection. In addition, one might modify Keohane's view in an explicitly democratic direction. For his starting point, an economic liberalism based on the self-interested cooperation of *capitalist* powers, is not promising.

On the contrary, Keohane might have invoked Doyle's neo-Kantian argument and pointed out that liberal democracies, except in their early phases or in the pattern of American belligerence against parliamentary regimes in less developed countries, have not gone to war against each other.[103] In fact, Doyle turns realist critiques of liberal "crusades" against realism. Those crusades, he maintains, just show how serious—not merely hypocritical or ideological—these regimes are about *their* liberalism, suggesting that their legitimacy requires a "pacific union of republics." Thus, Doyle takes seriously precisely what realists respond to, centrally, with aversion. We might read his argument as an *internal* critique of realism.

In that case, Doyle might note, earlier American realism emphasizes the dangers of democratic zeal from below. But citizen aversion to war—a justified form of such "zeal"—can sometimes check the aggression of the powerful, at least against other, parliamentary regimes. This version of the democratic-peace argument criticizes realism more effectively than the currently popular one, which presents itself, causally, as the introduction emphasizes, in diametric opposition to neorealism.

Following Kant and the fourth *Federalist Paper*, an advocate of the Doyle-Keohane argument might suggest, actual and potential citizen resistance, bringing into play the state's need for democratic legitimacy, has, at least with regard to war, mitigated some nationalist rivalries.[104] But this argument accords with democratic internationalism. For instance, Sharp envisions cross-cultural citizen cooperation, with significant governmental support, to realize a nonviolent, civilian-based defense for Europe. In addition, this Doyle-Keohane argument might envision a political basis for greater economic cooperation, benefiting the least advantaged. DeMartino and Cullenberg, for example, think of international, union-based solidarity to enact their proposal for an antisexist, proenvironmental trade regime.

In fact, Keohane's own social theoretical argument morally requires *democratic internationalism*. For, on that view, not only the interests of the least advantaged in the advanced countries but, a radical would add, those of the great majority, hurt in income and social policy by internal division, are potentially allied with comparable majorities in the less developed countries.[105] A politically organized internationalism, deepening democracy in each setting, could force the changed policies required by Keohane's *conditional acceptability*. Properly understood, Keohane's liberal appraisal of current economic regimes is a restatement of the classic Marxian argument for democratic internationalism from below.

In addition, undercutting a nonradical version of their argument, Keohane and Doyle recognize that parliamentary regimes, in supposedly "nonliberal" circumstances, often intervene harmfully. For instance, Keohane mocks the CIA overthrow of the elected Mossadegh regime to secure the interests of American oil companies:

> The AngloIranian Oil Company remained intransigent. . . . The U.S. Central Intelligence Agency put into action a plan designed to overthrow Mossadegh and put the Shah, who had been deprived of all effective influence on the government, back into power. Aided by thugs whose services were secured with CIA funds, the Iranian army deposed Mossadegh. . . .
>
> The Iranian episode illustrates the variety of instruments at the disposal of the U.S. government. . . . The United States was able through political intervention and its links with the Iranian military, to bring about a revolution in Iranian politics. It then secured the establishment of a new oil consortium

that provided American companies with 40 per cent of Iranian production for a relatively small outlay of funds. Political, military and economic resources were used in combination with one another. . . . The remarkable part *of the trick* was that the American government and American firms, profited immensely while appearing reluctant to become involved and only to be doing so to aid in reconciliation, economic development, and the provision of public order.[106]

As the introduction's critique of Russett emphasizes, that intervention was part of the American regime's pattern of overthrowing democracies in the less developed countries.

A sophisticated radical counter to Doyle-Keohane liberalism would insist on two additional themes. First, even with the collapse of the Cold War, the antidemocratic apparatus of American intervention is highly developed and unlikely to be easily set aside. For instance, as chapter 5 shows, in 1991, the U.S. government intervened against Haitian president Jean-Bertrand Aristide. That apparatus includes military and police aid and training to the officers of repressive, allied regimes, CIA creation and subsidy of news "disinformation" as in Guatemala, covert aid to antidemocratic "popular" movements as in Allende's Chile, and the like.[107] Thus, *extensive, repressive, interventionary politics* sustain what Keohane recognizes as anticooperative international economics.

Second, as Keohane suggests, oligarchic policies, sanctioned by the IMF and World Bank and supported by the United States, undercut the promise of liberal democratic internationalism. Thus, the American government undermines new democracies allied with it since they undergo a "democratic distemper." The American media, mainstream political process, and "responsible" policy advisers legitimize such interventions (internationalist thesis 2).

In a classic, official realist argument, Huntington rewords this oppression: institutionalization in less developed countries—more exactly, American-influenced "state building"—requires that the poor "not overburden government with their demands," namely, against hunger, lack of medical care, and the like for the majority of citizens. Sheldon Wolin criticizes Ithiel de Sola Pool's similar assertion that "[i]n the Congo, in Vietnam, in the Dominican Republic, it is clear that order depends on *somehow compelling* newly mobilized strata to return to a measure of passivity and defeatism from which they have recently been aroused by the process of modernization."[108]

Further, in normal as well as repressive periods, restriction of political and cultural options in the United States stems from such reactionary global policies (realist and internationalist thesis 3). Thus, without vigorous *radical democratic* movements in both the advanced and less developed countries, we can expect little *liberal* internationalist progress. Since the recent democratic movements in Eastern Europe, the USSR, and China have undercut the militarization of Europe and diminished the threat of nuclear war, they also highlight the case for—antigovernment—democratic internationalism. In today's political circumstances, coherently stated liberal arguments turn out to be radical.

8. INTERNATIONALISM, FEMINISM, AND POSTMODERNISM VERSUS PREDATORY REALISM

Three further theoretical considerations strengthen the case for democratic internationalism. First, the central neorealist project of separating international from domestic politics is a contemporary eccentricity. Classical realist arguments often defended republican or democratic regimes instrumentally, on great-power grounds, as successful imperialists. Thus, in contrast to Sparta and Venice, Machiavelli celebrated Rome's novel combination of a citizen-army and recruitment of foreigners. For Weber, "heroic" statesmen, nurtured by English parliamentary institutions, enabled "a minute but prudent minority to bring a quarter of mankind under its sway." Given the dangers of oligarchy and tyranny, Thucydides, Socrates, Plato, Aristotle, Montesquieu, Kant, Marx, and today's democratic internationalism doubt that such *predatory republican realisms*[109] achieve a common good; so do well-formulated versions of neorealism (realist theses 3–5). This contrast highlights the controversy over realist thesis 2 that pits democracy as an intrinsic good, to be defended against *antidemocratic feedback* from the global arena (internationalism), against democracy as an instrument (classical realism), and democracy as a supposed obstacle to the national interest (American realism and neorealism). It underlines the distinctiveness, coherence, and plausibility of a *power-rivalry cognizant* Kantian interpretation.

Second, feminist theory stresses that the splitting off and suppression of feminine characteristics as "other" also contributes to needless violence.[110] Thus, a satiric petition about President Bush during the 1991 Middle East confrontation announced: "George, we know you're not a wimp. Bring the troops home now!" This feminist thesis reinforces the *external enemies—constriction of domestic political options* argument (internationalist theses 2 and 3).

Third, postmodernism also focuses on the contributions of denigrated "other" to the formation of "self" (internationalist thesis 2).[111] Whatever differences arise from the denial of the distinction between genuine individualities and other pluralities of self, this core postmodernist argument supports an internationalist account.

9. DEMOCRACY AS AN ANOMALY FOR REALISM

Realists may grant that great-power rivalry significantly corrupts domestic freedom—the *antidemocratic-feedback* thesis; nonetheless, they might insist, the testimony of modern history is that it *must* do so. As I have shown, the reason why realists have resisted a clear liberal political formulation of a common good is, schematically, that *liberalism plus realism equals radicalism*. Nonetheless, in a jujitsu-like reversal of this argumentative figure, the best realist objection maintains that the equation only works because statism so powerfully captures central features of current interstate rivalry.

The internationalist, however, may respond that the realist neglects the considerable impact of democratic internationalism in the modern era. Democratic and socialist revolutions, anticolonialism, opposition to Nazism and genocide, and the movements that recently swept Eastern Europe have generated standards condemning aggression, affirming peace, and advancing some basic human rights (those sustaining personal physical and moral security). Those standards, however, also reveal the horror of "ethnic cleansing" within and between the fledgling parliamentary regimes in the former Yugoslavia and, thus, underline a weakness in the democratic-peace hypothesis.[112] Yet though often belied in practice, such standards have become critical tools available globally to citizens and theorists.[113] Further, as a view capable of endorsing *any effective* pursuit of a purported national interest, including fascist ones, official realism has difficulty *explaining* as opposed to debunking this democratic trend. Realism does best in conversations that ignore the long-term influence of democracy and basic rights.[114] Moreover, while internally coherent realism undermines Doyle's and Keohane's initial *internationalism from above*, that critique inadvertently testifies to the impact of democratic internationalism *from below*, for the latter has made the vision of a decent international politics articulate and, to some extent, a force.

Five major examples may suggest the historic importance of that internationalism. First, even more than the American, the French Revolution triggered what Kant called "disinterested" republican sympathies among observers and democratic movements from Toussaint-Louverture's slave revolt in Haiti[115] and the Revolutions of 1848 to the Russian (1905 and 1917) and Chinese "New Democratic" Revolutions. These broadly democratic movements received significant international support—consider, though in a losing cause, German democrats' resistance to Prussian intervention in Poland in 1848, the English workers' support for abolitionism that checked a potential pro-South intervention in the

American Civil War, and the first International's campaign on behalf of the Paris Commune. Second, radical solidarity, displayed in three international organizations of millions of workers, peasants, intellectuals, and soldiers (the IWA, the Second—Social Democratic—and Third—Communist—internationals) has had an enormous, sometimes liberal as well as radical impact. Not only Waltz but even Marxians, such as Cohen,[116] too easily dismiss these movements for their failure to accomplish unheard-of feats: for instance, stopping world wars. Such requirements, as a criterion of significance, seem exaggerated. For example, several socialist movements opposed World War I. Afterward, the Kiel revolt of German sailors and the November Revolution put an end to the kaiser's Treaty of Brest-Litovsk and massive seizure of Russian territory.[117] Further, most participants in partisan movements against fascism were democratic internationalists. Whatever the problems of their leaderships and vision, those movements gained influence or power in many countries—the French and Italian resistance, Yugoslavia, China, Albania, and the like.

Third, in the United States, consider the defeat of the Alien and Sedition Acts and the safeguarding of a "loyal" opposition in the election of 1800;[118] the resistance of Lincoln, Thoreau, and others to Polk's conquests in Mexico in 1846–48; internationalist opposition to the McKinley-Theodore Roosevelt expansion of 1898; IWW- and socialist-led organizing that kept the United States out of World War I until 1917; the "premature antifascism" of the Lincoln brigades that violated the Roosevelt administration's "neutrality" in the Spanish Civil War;[119] and the movement to check U.S. aggression in Vietnam. Fourth, because they take the lives and harm the well-being of so many citizens, long (neo)colonial wars often engender significant domestic opposition: for instance, as chapter 3 stresses, the democratic overthrow of Portuguese fascism and the movements against French colonialism in Algeria and the American War in Vietnam. Fifth, responding to the danger of nuclear war, a peace movement emerged on both sides of the Atlantic and behind the Iron Curtain.[120] The democratic revolutions in Eastern Europe have undermined the standard official realist objection that peace movements weaken democracies against their authoritarian opponents (internationalist thesis 10). Further, while realism has always debunked moralistic crusades *from above*, a morally reformulated realist view maintains that *protest movements from below*—the anti–Vietnam War movement, contemporary peace movements—represent the national interest.

Taken together in the modern era, these movements have changed the idiom of international discourse, the realm of political possibility. Following Kant, they have made peace, democracy, and human rights, if often less than a palpable reality, more than a dream. Divisions among nations, characteristic of global politics, render democratic internationalism an always threatened project to be undertaken against obvious odds; sophisticated, morally coherent realism is a fruitful theory of many state interactions. Nonetheless, the historic impact of democratic internationalism and, ironically for official realism, the concerns so well captured in recent neorealist analyses suggest that the renewal and development of this resistant citizen project is worthwhile.

TABLE 2
A Modification of Table 1: Neorealism versus Democratic Internationalism

	Neorealist Thesis	*Internationalist Thesis*
Thesis 1	An autonomous competition among states in international politics conditions the national interest of each actor (*the power-competition thesis*)	Same
Thesis 2	Global politics is—and should be—separate from domestic politics. Democratic opinion hinders pursuit of the national interest (the *harmfulness* of democracy). [Neorealists implausibly *reword* this thesis within international politics as an epistemological matter: on an operationalist, value-free account, the national interest is, putatively, the state's interest]	In each power (especially those with significant internal inequalities), leaders have a psychological as well as a Machiavellian incentive to make enemies of the "other" and blunt internal opposition (the *antidemocratic feedback* thesis)
Thesis 3	A statist or structural Marxian account of oligarchy and the ideology of "anticommunism" best explain American policies	Antiradical, racist, and sexist ideologies buoy the tendency to stigmatize "others" in capitalist oligarchies. "Democratic" opinion is often oligarchically stimulated (the *threat of external enemies, constriction of political options*)
Thesis 4	Exacerbated military spending has led to a decline of American industry and of living standards for most workers: the *American militarism and decline* or *price of empire* thesis (Gilpin, Fulbright, Krasner)	Same
Thesis 5	The policies of international economic regimes often harm the least advantaged—and, perhaps, majorities—in the advanced and less developed countries. Through capital flight, depleted domestic investment, and disenchantment with reform, such regimes serve as an	Same. In addition, democratic movements in one country—for instance, immigrant organizing in Europe, the 1995 and 1996 French strikes—inspire, to some extent, movements in others (the *international power of democratic example*)

continues on next page

TABLE 2 (cont.)

	Neorealist Thesis	Internationalist Thesis
Thesis 5 (cont.)	international "safety net" for oligarchy against elected governments—democratic socialist ones such as Mitterand's, for example—whose proposed reforms often sustain a common good (the *antidemocratic feedback of contemporary regimes*)	
Thesis 6	If the national interest is a common good, then realist theses 3–5 contradict the elitism of realist thesis 2. In the case of Vietnam, the antiwar movement defended the American national interest (*democracy as a common good*)	Democratic movements from below are needed to undo the harms to most citizens of great-power rivalry (*democracy as a common good*)
Thesis 7	But realism aims to head off ideological crusades, such as Woodrow Wilson's, to force democracy—or, perhaps, socialism—on unwilling others and harm one's own citizens. In general, realists urge caution in international politics	Same. More explicitly than realism, internationalism strengthens democratic resistance *from below* against the incentives to power and belligerence characteristic of elite political life. It challenges the realist stereotype that sound individual advice to statespersons is the main corrective to crusades
Thesis 8	Some interventions, for instance, in Mexico, Brazil, and Argentina, might still be justified	In addition to their harms to others, such interventions serve a common good neither in terms of combating aggression nor economically; they legitimize antidemocratic feedback
Thesis 9	But liberal democracies sometimes go to war against other democracies (U.S. in Guatemala, Iran, Brazil, Chile, Sandinista Nicaragua, Haiti, and the like); perhaps no common good is possible (*the factual overriding of an otherwise desirable common good*)	Oligarchies with parliamentary forms do not intervene against other democracies unless the latter can be stigmatized as political and "racial" enemies. The obstacles of *governmental opposition; foreign enemies, external divide and rule policies; racist and antiradical ideologies, internal divide and rule*; and the

TABLE 2 (*cont.*)

	Neorealist Thesis	Internationalist Thesis
		need for transnational *greatness of scale* undercut democratic resistance. Nonetheless, as chapter 5 shows, self-consciously internationalist regimes, mandating, for instance, referenda on war, where possible, and tolerating civil disobedience, would be less likely to intervene (*a common good against "democratic" imperialism*)
Thesis 10	The threat of nuclear war has also, contingently, deterred interdemocratic wars. But peace movements weaken their own states	The threat of nuclear war, as well as potential destruction of the environment, *underline* novel, transnational common goods. As the revolutions in Eastern Europe show, peace movements had an important, internationalist impact in diminishing the nuclear threat

TABLE 3
A Keohane-Doyle Version of the Democratic-Peace Hypothesis, Realism, and Democratic Internationalism from Below

Keohane's Institutionalism, Realism, and Democratic Internationalism			
	Keohane Thesis	*Realist Rejoinder*	*Democratic Internationalist Rejoinder*
Thesis 1	International regimes can provide scarce information and establish mutually beneficial cooperation		
Thesis 2	Actual regimes, like the IMF and the IEA, however, often harm the least advantaged in Europe, most obviously in the setting of an elected reform government, as well as in the less developed countries (the *antidemocratic feedback of current regimes*)	Keohane's thesis 2 shows that today's predatory international regimes operate on behalf of the rich and powerful. An explicit moral picture of cooperation—Keohane's thesis 2—undermines Keohane's thesis 1	Realism and liberal institutionalism concur that the least advantaged and, in fact, most citizens, are mainly hurt by the policies of today's international regimes (the 1995 and 1996 French workers' revolts highlight this point). The policies of such regimes are, thus, inconsistent with a common good internally or internationally; only an internationalist movement from below can uphold such a good (Sharp, Goldfischer, DeMartino)

An Internal Doyle-Keohane Critique of Realism			
	Realism	*Doyle-Keohane*	*Refined Realism and Internationalism*
Thesis 1	Democratic crusades undermine the national interest, which is best upheld by professional diplomats	Since ordinary citizens have common interests against war, democratic "zeal" for peace often upholds a common good. Advanced capitalist oligarchies with parliamentary forms do	Powerful oligarchies with parliamentary forms have, however, widely "intervened" against democracies, for instance, the U.S. overthrow of the Arbenz regime in Guatemala,

TABLE 3 (*cont.*)

	An Internal Doyle-Keohane Critique of Realism		
	Realism	*Doyle-Keohane*	*Refined Realism and Internationalism*
		not go to war with one another. Further, such citizen influence suggests other potentials for beneficial, transnational cooperation	Mossadegh in Iran, Goulart in Brazil, Allende in Chile, and the like
Thesis 2			Using Doyle-Keohane thesis 1 against a standard realist argument, we can see that democratic movements from below, such as the anti–Vietnam War movement, sometimes secure a common good both domestically and internationally. Further, the likelihood of citizen protest probably accounts for the failure of comparatively stable, European and American democracies to go to war with one another (the American elite can more easily use racist and anti-radical ideology to crush smaller democracies, in less developed countries)
Thesis 3			In fact, the realist response to Doyle's internal critique undermines the central official realist claim that a state's policies, by and large, represent the common good of its own citizens. Moreover, democratic internationalism suggests some truth in the democratic-peace hypothesis *if* current oligarchies with parliamentary forms were to become more democratic

CHAPTER TWO

Crossing of the Ways:
The Vietnam War and Realism in
Morgenthau, Niebuhr, and Kennan

One could write the history of our involvement in
Vietnam in terms of self-deception and deception of
others.
> (Hans J. Morgenthau, "The Shadow and
> Substance of Power," 1965)

Even Reinhold Niebuhr signs petitions and editorials
as if Reinhold Niebuhr had never existed.
> (Paul Ramsey, cited in John C. Bennett, "From
> Supporter of War in 1941 to Critic in 1966,"
> *Christianity and Crisis,* February 7, 1966)

Let me be clear that realism means particularly one
thing, that you establish the common good not purely
by unselfishness but by the restraint of selfishness.
That's realism. Now, on the basis of realism, you
have all kinds of contingent facts.
> (Reinhold Niebuhr, interview, *Christianity and
> Crisis,* March 17, 1969)

Woe to those who lie on beds of ivory, and stretch
themselves on their couches and eat lambs from the
flock ... who sing idle songs to the sound of the
harp.
> (Amos 6:4–5)

1. FORGETFULNESS ABOUT MORGENTHAU

Professor Hans J. Morgenthau was the leading practitioner of international-relations theory in the Cold War era; he was also a skilled and
trusted policy adviser. In the Vietnam War, those roles came into conflict.

The Eisenhower administration invited Morgenthau to counsel it on
Vietnam and sent him, in 1954, on the first of his three tours. In the war

of independence against French colonialism, he concluded, the Vietnamese people had chosen its own, Communist leadership. This leadership had widespread support among peasants, whom it had benefited through land reform. No Marshall Plan strategy of aid to a stable non-Communist regime in Vietnam was possible, because no procapitalist leadership enjoyed even limited support.[1] Wishful thinking would not make the Vietnamese Communists more to the U.S. government's liking. But that leadership was not Russian or Chinese; it did not share the priorities of America's leading enemies. Thus, he insisted, the U.S. government could negotiate with the Vietnamese as an independent force.

At first, Morgenthau's differences with American policy appeared minor. Over time, however, the disparity became fundamental. President after president decided to seek anti-Communist leadership in the south. Thus, Eisenhower and Kennedy created and then shored up the corrupt Diem regime. They relied on physical power, an attempt to reverse the Vietminh land reform and restore the landlords, and inept racism, to cover up their own likely defeat, about the alleged military inadequacy of the Vietnamese. They lied, to others and themselves, about the nature of the war; the habitual American avenues of politics and publicity broadcast these lies as "justifications" for policy. "One could write the history of our involvement in Vietnam," Morgenthau suggested, "in terms of self-deception and deception of others."[2] At first, presidents brushed him aside.

But a third trip in 1964 confirmed Morgenthau's basic position. Even more fiercely, he strove to place his views before President Johnson. After many presidential evasions, Morgenthau, finally, forced LBJ to consider them. LBJ excoriated his counselor as a fool and potential traitor. The president set out publicly to discredit Morgenthau.

Leading realist though he was, Morgenthau no longer found power on his side. Furthermore, other critics of the war—ones even less powerful than he—could not be regarded as "strong" allies. Here was a choice between "realism," as many understand it,[3] and Morgenthau's realism.

Bemusedly and forthrightly, he opposed Johnson: "I remember with wry amusement my strenuous and ultimately successful efforts in 1965 to bring my views on the Vietnam war to the attention of President Johnson—efforts undertaken in the naive assumption that if power were only made to see the truth, it would follow that lead." Here Morgenthau ironically criticizes his own "naive," realist commitment to truth from the standpoint of his—also realist—insights into the arrogance of power. As an undertone, we can also hear Morgenthau's hurt—he had given advice that could have prevented U.S. genocide in Vietnam; he had also been the leading American theorist of international relations: "President Johnson's political reaction to this kind of responsible criticism is a matter of public record. His personal reaction was a systematic attempt, making full use of the informal powers of his office, to discredit and silence the voice of the dissenter. In that latter undertaking, he had the voluntary and sometimes enthusiastic assistance of eminent academic and institutional [for instance, Freedom House] supporters of his policy."[4]

Johnson entitled his campaign against the Chicago professor "Project Morgenthau," a many-sided governmental effort to discredit all opposition as the creature of that "German." LBJ's slander, unfortunately, succeeded among many—silent—international-relations professors,[5] but it could not bend the truth. Morgenthau, however, sadly recognized his colleagues' timorousness: "Academics in particular, that is, intellectuals, who are professionally committed to the pursuit of truth, are not immune from aspirations for power, academic and political. . . . [Such an] intellectual deals with "safe" issues in a "safe" manner. On the great issues of political life, which are controversial by definition, he [sic—or she] must remain silent. He does not need to be silenced; he silences himself."[6]

Students, however, and, ultimately, many faculty—though mainly scholars from other disciplines—came to oppose the war. In this, they were, in part, joined, in part even, unwillingly, led by Professor Morgenthau. But his insight into the "utopianism" of liberal hopes for American power underlines a weakness of sophisticated realism. For only a democratic countermovement from below, not just sound advice to statespersons by individuals, could halt an unjust war.

Today, orthodox international-relations theorists routinely criticize American intervention in Vietnam—a now past episode—but have forgotten Morgenthau's isolation as an opponent during the war. At most, teachers assign only the first chapter of his influential theoretical book, *Politics among Nations*. Yet, registered in the short essays of the now unread *Truth and Power*, the courage and clarity of Morgenthau's criticism of the war, I will argue, reveal the truth of his realism. For reinterpreted to fill in an initial, moral step in the argument—a plausible view of a national interest as, at least in part, a common good for citizens—realism leads to democratic internationalism: the view that citizens often have *common interests* against their own state(s) across national boundaries.[7] In contrast, the current, *official* interpretation of realism holds to the abstract, frequently self-contradictory formulations of *Politics among Nations* and mistakenly discards Morgenthau's clearer formulations during the antiwar movement, his immediately costly but, in the long term, heroic political stands. Perhaps (sophisticated) realism is not so friendly to prevailing power as is often thought.

The next four sections trace the specific theses in Morgenthau's conflicting realist arguments. Part 2 will explore his erroneous view of human nature and reductionist account of power, which might—perhaps stretching a point—sanction Kissingerian policies. Yet such claims do not even explain Morgenthau's fierce stand against the Vietnam War. The third section, however, examines the repeated theoretical contradictions that highlight the implausibility of an amoral account of power. In contrast, sections 4 and 5 sketch a realism consistent with Morgenthau's opposition to the war and novel critique of American democracy as dominated by an "academic-political" as well as "military-industrial complex." As an opponent of American aggression, Morgenthau offered a not very controversial moral account of a common good (for instance, proponents disagreed with Morgenthau over whether the war as a *matter of fact* realized such a good, not about the nature of the good itself). Such an account is central to sophisticated realism. Part 6 explores Morgenthau's mistaken admiration for Lincoln's statism. The latter temporarily overrode Lincoln's opposition to slavery and its link to a public good.

The seventh section traces Niebuhr's social theoretical emphasis on global and class conflict that limit possibilities for individual "transcendence" and a common good. In contrast to Morgenthau, Niebuhr also stressed Lincoln's mercy, which stemmed from "a broken spirit and a contrite heart." Section 8 explores Niebuhr's creation of a democratic forum—*Christianity and Crisis*—to deliberate about and combat the Vietnam War. It highlights *antidemocratic feedback* as well as the common interests of the Vietnamese and American people. In addition, Niebuhr delineated the moral and social theoretical structure of well-stated realist views as opposed to "conforming" ones.

The ninth section examines Kennan's changed realism in response to Vietnam, his emphases on "our military-industrial addiction" and the central role of anticommunist ideology in U.S. presidential elections. Following Weber, realists often see the state as an organization that monopolizes the legitimate use of *force* in a territory. This section, however, explores Kennan's surprising affirmation, in response to the threat of nuclear war, of a nonviolent, civilian defense for Europe. The conclusion stresses the common, underlying moral standards that characterize the debate between sophisticated realism and democratic internationalism. It then highlights the social theoretical and empirical disputes that motivate complex ethical clashes and alternative visions of policy.

2. HOW TO EXTRACT KISSINGER FROM MORGENTHAU

Sometimes, apologists reword prevailing ideologies in realist terms. For instance, in 1965 State Department officials believed that Dominican leader Juan Bosch and the subsequent regime of Camano-Deño endorsed a radicalism dangerous to American power. They seized on Ambassador Bennett's charge that he had "a list of 53 Communists" to apologize for a U.S. invasion that reversed democratic reform. Sophisticated realists like Morgenthau, however, oppose such ideologies, which phrase, in a "realist" idiom, implausible *empirical* charges.[8]

A difference between well-stated realist arguments and trivial, ideological ones arises from an attempt by proponents of the former to understand questions of fact and explanation—theory—dispassionately rather than chauvinistically. Further, if right, the views of sophisticated realists diverge from those of ideological realists not only about empirical issues, but also in complex political and moral judgments. Sophisticated realists oppose antidemocratic interventions of the sort favored by Ambassador Bennett. The latter, they might note, tricked up "a list" of radicals to undergird a fantasy of "aggression"—the danger of all Latin America becoming Communist, and then . . . Despite the nonmoral rhetoric in which they are phrased, both serious and fantastic "realist" arguments appeal to the same *underlying* moral standards. Proponents of the former concurred that aggression is evil, but doubted that the threat of future Latin aggression against the United States justified actual American aggression against the Dominican Republic.

If there is, however, a distorted reading of *Politics among Nations* that opposes Morgenthau's subsequent stands and legitimizes antidemocratic U.S. interventions, it might look like this:

> **Thesis 1:** Every regime aims, if possible, to achieve preeminent power internationally—"power," in Morgenthau's notorious phrase, "is the domination of man [*sic*] over man."
>
> **Thesis 2:** It uses incentives to draw all internal forces, "men" as well as economic and military capacity, into its orbit.
>
> **Thesis 3:** "Men" aim to achieve power—to dominate—and act selfishly to do so (Morgenthau attributes this supposed drive to human nature).
>
> **Thesis 4:** "Men" thus initiate aggrandizing projects or, to protect themselves, become (selfish) servants of power. They may offer sound advice to the powerful, but only from the standpoint of furthering *domineering* interests.[9]
>
> **Thesis 5:** Nationalism will, very likely, hold unchallenged sway, so long as a power is dominant.

This argument, however, pivots on whether advisers must inevitably become purveyors—and citizens, supporters—of "the emperor's new clothes." By an unfortunate sociobiology, Morgenthau himself partly sanctions this view: "The situation is different when we deal not with social arrangements and institutions created by men, but with those elemental bio-psychological drives by which in turn society is created. The drives to live, to propagate, to dominate are common to all men."[10]

Morgenthau thinks that this argument—which relies on an extraordinarily general, hard to substantiate, one-sided claim about human nature—sustains realism. He does not invoke a much less psychological realist reading, one contingent on the actual shape of international politics, namely, that political insecurity or uncertainty will force even the "diffident" (Hobbes) to seek power and advantage. For even the nonoffensively minded cannot know, with certainty, when the rare, bellicose policymaker will win out in a powerful opponent. But given that possibility, trust is a risk that no self-aware statesperson can run. Secret armaments in a hostile power could, by surprise attack, lay waste one's own citizens. Herz names this central feature of sophisticated realism "the security dilemma."[11]

In addition, Morgenthau's affirmation of a "biology of man"—once again, he leaves out women[12]—is a contradiction in his argument (realist theses 3 and 4). For if we believe that all "men" will be inclined, by biology, to become dominators, or, to achieve security, servants, for example, as "realist" advisers, then, evidently, none—at least within the sphere of power—will be motivated to oppose injustice by appeals to a *common* good. But Morgenthau is himself a counterexample to this false generalization. Without notable self-doubt, he denounced LBJ's war on Vietnam. (In various historical contexts, at the cost of advancement or career, realists have stood out against prevailing policies.) Further, contrary to supposedly realist thesis 5 about citizen nationalism, a vigorous movement, ultimately supported by a majority of the American people, emerged to oppose the war.

In concluding his essay, "Truth and Power," Morgenthau avowed a startling, *seemingly* paradoxical—for a realist—reliance on Kant:

> On January 22, 1967, about thirty people demonstrated in Pushkin Square in Moscow against the trial of four persons who had transcribed the court records in the trial against Andrei Sinyavsky and Yuri Daniel. One of the organizers of the protest, Khaustov, who was sentenced to three years of hard labor, admitted at his trial that he had read Kant and Hegel and that his reading of Kant "made me see a lot of things in a new light." The experience of the 1960's has dispelled the illusion that truth can show power the way in direct confrontation. But historical experience reassures us that truth can indeed make people "see a lot of things in a new light." And when people see things in a new light, they might act in a new way.[13]

Morgenthau also praised the initially isolated but increasingly widespread resistance of American soldiers in Vietnam: "[M]embers of the

Armed Forces who would rather be relieved of their command or court-martialed than be responsible for indiscriminately killing civilians . . . are the real moral heroes of this war, even though they will never get the Congressional Medal of Honor."[14]

"Never" for two such soldiers turned out to be thirty years. At My Lai, helicopter pilot Hugh Thompson

> spotted villagers crowded in a hut—an old woman standing in the doorway, a baby in her arms, a child clutching her legs. U.S. soldiers were approaching.
>
> "These people were looking at me for help, and there was no way I could turn my back on them."

Thompson landed between the Americans—who screamed, in response to his request for help, that the only thing the villagers would get from them was "a grenade"—and twelve innocents. He ordered Lawrence Colburn, his gunner, to train his M-60 on the troops, climbed out of the helicopter, and, until help arrived, stood—unarmed—between soldiers and villagers.[15] Glenn Andreotta, Thompson's other crewmate, spotted a two-year-old boy, lying in a ditch beside his dead mother, and rescued him.

Though Thompson's testimony helped convict Lieutenant William Calley,[16] the Pentagon covered up the former's heroism. Only a BBC film about My Lai ten years ago, which interviewed Thompson, sparked citizen interest in the United States.[17] Only now, to send honorable American representatives to a thirty-year Vietnamese commemoration for those murdered at My Lai, have Thompson, Colburn and Andreotta finally been recognized.

As Morgenthau's vision of Thompson-like heroism illustrates, whatever the isolation or public harassment, truth, for a realist, requires following one's own course.[18] Niebuhr would name this *prophetic* realism.

In contrast, unsophisticated realist appeals to an allegedly uniform, domineering power—"realist" thesis 1—cannot even discriminate between resistance and Nazism. A proponent of that argument could say only that the Nazis were more "powerful." But undercutting thesis 1, democracies, for instance, sometimes pursue peace, just war, and other policies affirming a common good. In addition, such a "realism" cannot explain Morgenthau's Kantian adherence to truth.

For women and men do not inevitably act selfishly. At great personal cost, they sometimes follow truth and adhere to a common good against their regime's attempts to silence them. In opposition, realists, genuine patriots, and internationalists often speak in a similar voice. They stand for unpopular policies, regardless of immediate outcome. As in the anti–

Vietnam War movement, they can become political heroes. But even if their voices are defeated, as the Nazis crushed the student resistance, the White Rose, others who look back, with dispassion, will find them admirable. Realism needs a sound, abstract formulation—one that envisions policies that serve a perhaps rare, common good—to clarify the basis for profound opposition to horrifying policies.

This book contrasts well-stated or sophisticated realism—one that affirms a common good—and what I call official realism.[19] The latter insists on power at the expense of morality rather than drawing a plausible distinction, frequently averred by Morgenthau, between consistent, limited ethical judgment and ideological moralism. A reductionist emphasis on power has contributed to realism's current, unsavory reputation; so have Kissinger's crimes. For example, defending the CIA's central role in the overthrow of the democratically elected Allende regime in Chile, the then secretary of state asserted: "I don't see why the United States should let a country go Marxist just because its people is irresponsible."[20] But U.S. intervention harmed democracy, though it may temporarily have advanced capitalism.

3. ETHICAL CONTRADICTIONS ABOUT "POWER"

This section explores the repeated contradictions in Morgenthau's power-reductionism. These contradictions highlight a misguided aim of official realism: to strip "power" of ethical content. In contrast, as the subsequent two sections will argue, these tensions reveal the comparative clarity and force of Morgenthau's argument on Vietnam. Abstract theoretical formulation was not Morgenthau's strength; yet he was an erudite, often unusually thoughtful scholar.[21] Recognizing this difficulty, he even, in the words of Montesquieu, asked the reader's indulgence: "I beg one favor of my readers which I fear will not be granted me; that is, that they will not judge by a few hours' reading the labor of twenty years; that they will approve or condemn the book entire, and not a few particular phrases. If they would search into the design of the author, they can do it in no other way so completely as by searching into the design of his work."[22]

In revising *Politics among Nations*'s five editions, Morgenthau moved from an implausibly stripped down account of power to one increasingly aware of moral issues and the history of prophetic and tragic realism. For instance, the 1950 version briefly defines power as "control over the minds and bodies of others" and lacks the famous six principles of realism that are the centerpiece of later editions. Over time, he articulated what he already believed, though often, perhaps striving to found an "autonomous" science of politics, inconsistently. Thus, during Vietnam, the fifth edition (1973) defends the thesis that power may be "disciplined by moral ends and controlled by constitutional safeguards."[23] But this thesis contradicts Morgenthau's assertion, earlier in this same sentence, that "power is the domination of man over man."[24]

Further, though repeating the latter view, Morgenthau did not treat his distinction between power "disciplined by moral ends" and an "untamed and barbaric force" as controversial. On the contrary, as he recognized, it serves as an underlying ethical standard.[25] For although power is present in both just and unjust uses, *official realism* cannot wish away this distinction without becoming an apology. In addition, in the preface to the second edition, Morgenthau noted that "the influence domestic politics exerts on foreign policy has been greatly stressed. In recognition of its importance, the *quality of government* has been introduced as a new element of national power."[26] But a definition of power merely as domineering cannot capture diverse "qualities" of regime.

Thus, Morgenthau's emphasis on a common good has a plausibility that his account of abstract hunger for power lacks. Even Morgenthau's moral formulation, however, mistakenly envisions domineering power as an *underlying* force, one to be "disciplined" or "controlled" from outside. Yet, a critic might note, power sometimes realizes a common good. Morgenthau's error here echoes that of a more influential realist, Max Weber, on forms of legitimate "domination."[27] Now realism rightly emphasizes the *empirical* importance of international power-competition and the threat of aggression—the danger that foreign invasion will waste the lives of one's citizens. Without this underlying ethical standard, however, the realist critique, for example, of scholarly fealty to international law for endangering lives in the 1930s,[28] would be incoherent.

Further, to infer *general*, amoral principles from this specific dispute with "legalists"—Morgenthau grandiosely invoked "eternal laws"—is a mistake.[29] Ironically, such appeals betray a theoretical hubris that cuts against the very moderation—*sophrosune*—central to realism.[30] The subordinate clause of his famous later definition of power, cited above, implies a common good; so do the "universal moral principles," which, as we shall see, Morgenthau frequently affirmed. But outside of his writings on Vietnam, Morgenthau failed to define such a good or mistakenly treated it as the state's interest.

Now Morgenthau maintained that public action always involves moral choices: "To say that a political action has no moral purpose is absurd; for political action can be defined as an attempt to realize moral values through the medium of politics, that is power."[31] In Morgenthau's terms, however, this seemingly reasonable statement is actually a contradition: a political action tries to realize moral—genuinely public—purposes through a medium geared to the "domination of man over man," the opposite of such purposes. Given any coherent definition of moral and political, however, for instance, a liberal one, such as Morgenthau affirmed, that a good society facilitates the individuality of *each* so long as (s)he does not harm others, power cannot be solely "the domination of man over man."[32]

Similarly, in *Politics among Nations*, Morgenthau maintains that "a man who was nothing but a 'political man' would be a beast, for he would be completely lacking in moral restraints."[33] Yet Morgenthau's abstract insistence, two pages earlier—that statesmen "cannot but subordinate these other standards to the political one"—requires a rapacious foreign policy.[34] In addition, he sought a categorical "autonomy" of politics.[35] But he also insisted on "the curious dialectic of ethics and politics, which prevents the latter, in spite of itself, from escaping the former's judgment and normative direction."[36] Instead, he might have noted, more consistently, that, given the special dangers of aggression, each statesperson must include preparation for defense, among reasonable motives, in formulating a broader foreign policy.

Morgenthau argued: "By making power its central concept, a theory of power does not presume that none but power relations control actions";[37] moreover, he avowed, "I have always maintained that the actions of states are subject to universal moral principles."[38] One might then, however, invoke such underlying ethical standards to judge conflicts between states. Yet he occasionally undercut these plausible claims: "universal moral principles cannot be applied to the actions of states."[39] To avoid this contradiction, he might have insisted—as he sometimes did—that core ethical standards, for instance, those ruling out wanton killing, influence statespersons in international affairs: "Nations recognize a moral obligation to refrain from the infliction of death and suffering under certain conditions despite the possibility of justifying such conduct in the light of . . . the national interest."[40]

In such cases, on a realist argument, the *empirical* character of power-rivalry and the threat of aggression limit but do not rule out the application of clear moral principles in international politics. Thus, the *complex ethical debates* that affect policy arise from the conjunction of core underlying moral standards with empirical or social theoretical disputes.[41]

Now the idea that "men" mainly strive to dominate others undergirds official realism. To support it, Morgenthau misreads Aristotle's famous thesis that "man is a political animal":

> The desire for power . . . concerns itself not with the individual's survival but with his position among his fellows once his survival has been secured.

Consequently, the selfishness of man [*sic*] has limits; his will to power has none. For while man's vital needs are capable of satisfaction, his lust for power would be satisfied only if the last man became an object of his domination, there being nobody above or beside him, that is, if he became like God. "The fact is," as Aristotle put it, "that the greatest crimes are caused by excess and not by necessity. Men do not become tyrants that they may not suffer cold."[42]

Morgenthau, oddly, projects domineering onto God.

Aristotle's thesis, however, that tyrants are not driven to great crimes by poverty, does not suggest, as Morgenthau misguidedly averred, that *every* man or woman, positioned as leader, would strive to become a tyrant. For instance, Aristotle and Morgenthau are counterexamples to that claim. The former might have encapsulated it in the phrase, "man is a *tyrannical animal*." In contrast, Aristotle's thesis that "man is a *political* animal" foresees forms of a common good—vital to Morgenthau's *liberal realism*—as well as the tyrannical rule of particular interests.[43]

4. A REALISM CONSISTENT WITH MORGENTHAU'S STAND ON VIETNAM

Let us consider Morgenthau's second, *democratic* paradigm, which recognizes a limited common good and conflicts with official realism:

Realist thesis 1: power may be "disciplined by moral ends and controlled by constitutional safeguards."[44]

Realist thesis 2: tyrannical power, even in a democracy, may become a "coherent system of irrationality."[45] It may violate a common good for citizens and the *substance* of a regime's interest.

To characterize the horror of transadministration, American war in Vietnam, Morgenthau added this insight to the 1973 edition of *Politics among Nations*. He wondered if "modern psychology and psychiatry" might provide a "counter-theory of irrational politics, a kind of pathology of international politics," and underlined the insights from which such a psychology would start:

The experience of the Indochina War suggests five factors such a theory might encompass: the imposition upon the empirical world of a simplistic and *a priori* picture of the world derived from folklore and ideological assumption, that is, the replacement of experience with superstition; the refusal to correct this picture of the world in the light of experience; the persistence in a foreign policy derived from misperception of reality and the use of intelligence for the purpose not of adapting policy to reality but of re-interpreting reality to fit policy; the egotism of the policy makers widening the gap between perception and policy, on the one hand, and reality, on the other; finally, the urge to close the gap at least subjectively by action, any kind of action, that creates the illusion of mastery over a recalcitrant reality.[46]

Morgenthau meant to describe a corrupt system of power, not an incidental manifestation, which violated a common good. Under fierce governmental attack, he insisted, however, that public policies may sometimes serve as a source of common empowerment.[47]

Realist thesis 3: even in capitalist societies that are otherwise exploitative, a common good includes at least preventing aggression and protecting citizens' lives. Such a good may conflict with (temporarily) prevailing state or citizen nationalism.

In *Truth and Power*, Morgenthau contended, "Even where that justification [talk of a democratic common good] masked special interests or served as an ideology for a particular class identifying its interests with those of the community, the claim has, in the past, a certain plausibility. For even a democratic government that only served the pursuit of happiness of some of its citizens, sought to preserve the life and liberty of most of them."[48] Here, revealing the overlap between realism and an adequate, ethically stated Marxian theory,[49] Morgenthau rightly stressed the core moral standard of preserving the lives and, sometimes, elevating—though unequally—the economic wellbeing of members of a democratic regime. But he also wrongly suggested that a capitalist regime may realize the liberty, and perhaps the economic advancement, of each. For that regime's restriction of the liberties of the many—the near inverse relation between formal and *substantive* liberty—to advance the few permits the latter to rule and violate a common good.[50] We can see that truncation of liberty vividly in the persecution of Morgenthau.

As opposed to *Politics among Nations*, Morgenthau also contrasted attention to democracy—"the interests of the nation"—with catering to a (tyrannical) state's interest: "This patriotism [of a 1966 Freedom House advertisement that equated dissidence with treason, signed by many of Morgenthau's colleagues and former students] deems it its duty to support the policies of the government in times of crisis, thus identifying the government with the nation, and in the process sacrifices the interests of the nation upon the altar of conformity."[51]

Realist thesis 4: moderation as well as humility are leading political virtues.

Here, as we shall see, Morgenthau relied on a Greek tragic or, alternately, Augustinian version of realism. Moderation or self-restraint—*sophrosune*—and humility are, for realists, virtues that stand outside the conventions and cliches of normal, power-aggrandizing politics, and reveal its hubris, its wanton brutality and murderousness.[52] The Greek term *sophrosune*, which means not exceeding human limits, differs, as we will see in Niebuhr, from the later Christian conception.

Yet concerning theory, Morgenthau was rarely "humble." In contrast, Kennan and Niebuhr insisted on humility as a primary virtue in thinking about as well as enacting a decent foreign policy.[53] Nonetheless, in *Politics among Nations*, Morgenthau invoked moderation with the voice of a prophet: "As political realism distinguishes between truth and opinion, so it distinguishes between truth and idolatry. The lighthearted equation between a particular nationalism and the counsels of Providence is morally indefensible, for it is that *very sin of pride* against which the Greek tragedians and the Biblical prophets have warned."[54]

Realist thesis 5: realists are disinterested truth-seekers, not clever sycophants.

Vital to all realist critiques of "crusades," as I have stressed, this thesis celebrates the realist aim to speak the truth in contrast to power-hungry ideologues.[55] For, with Thucydides, to conform to a *realist* sense of power is to see *beyond the power*, however dazzling, temporarily represented by one's nation. As Niebuhr emphasized, sophisticated realism foresees the possibility, even the inevitability, of the decline of the powerful.[56] Despite their weaknesses, American (or émigré American) realisms—those of Morgenthau, Niebuhr, and Kennan, for instance—are more coherent on this moral theme, one opposing imperial crusades and urging self-restraint, than the arguments of today's neorealists.

In fact, to speak the truth, especially when confronted with repudiation by the powerful, is one of the oldest themes of realism. Yet today's empiricist, "value-neutral" neorealism implausibly covers up and contradicts this motivation (once again, scholars cannot coherently affirm "value-neutrality" between truth and falsehood). Before his lonely opposition to the Vietnam War, Morgenthau spoke out on Columbia's firing of Charles Van Doren, who had lied for money:

> The moral law is not a utilitarian construct aimed at the protection of society, even though its observation has this effect. The arguments of the good teacher and of teaching not being concerned with truth [which anonymous student letters had advanced on Van Doren's behalf] go together. You as-

sume that the teacher is a kind of intellectual mechanic who fills your head with conventionally approved and required knowledge, as a filling station attendant fills a tank with gas. . . . You recognize no relation between a teacher's general attitude toward the truth and the way of transmitting knowledge because you do not recognize an organic relation between transmitted knowledge and objective, impersonal truth.[57]

5. DEMOCRATIC CRITICISM, OLIGARCHIC PERSECUTION

Morgenthau's most sophisticated realist formulations about Vietnam highlight the inextricable importance of a moral thesis about a common good. Contrary to a common view of realism as recommending individual advice to the powerful—"professional diplomacy"—Morgenthau's argument, and, as we will see, Niebuhr's, justify a democratic internationalist movement from below.

Realist thesis 1: The U.S. government waged war against a civilian, peasant-based, nationalist revolution. It therefore risked genocide:[58]

A war fought against indigenous guerillas, either supported by the population or to whom the population is indifferent, is bound to obliterate traditional distinctions between combatants and noncombatants, soldiers and civilians.

That practice betrayed America's democratic principles. In Morgenthau's words, "This [Vietnam] is a counterrevolutionary war waged by a revolutionary nation. It is Metternich's war waged by the nation of Jefferson and Lincoln."[59] Further, American racism transformed counterrevolution against civilians into war against a people: "To the Vietnamese we appear as the successors to the French—whose ranks, by the way, also included non-white soldiers. . . . We can argue that the Vietnamese ought not to hate us as the white destroyers of their country. But they have begun to hate us as such and it is this fact that counts."[60]. American power betrayed a common good internationally, and as we shall see, internally. As Morgenthau put it, this war undercut the *democratic substance* of American power to chase its murderous, ultimately losing, "shadow."[61]

As his analysis of Vietnam underlines, Morgenthau did not regard power—though he often tried, mistakenly, to theorize it, in a reductionist vein, as one thing—uncritically. He had fled Nazi Germany. In contrast to that and other tyrannical regimes, the United States stood, in his mind, for the human possibility of achieving a common good. Morgenthau's political affection for the American regime has three aspects. First, negatively, it reveals, a realist might note, an almost uncritical, ahistorical allegiance to early American leaders. In an unintended irony, Morgenthau ignored the initial American regime's slaveholding, its genocide toward Native Americans, and the like.

But, second, as a German exile, Morgenthau contrasted America's sense of isolation as a key to domestic freedom with the European elite's inevitable wariness of proximity and the accompanying likelihood of war:

> Throughout the nation's history, the national destiny of the United States has been understood in anti-militaristic, libertarian terms. . . . When the United States, in the wake of the Spanish-American war, seemed to desert this anti-imperialist and democratic ideal [in the corruption of "Manifest Destiny"], William Graham Sumner restated its essence: "Expansion and imperialism are a grand onslaught on democracy. . . . expansion and imperialism are at war with the best traditions, principles and interests of the American people."[62]

Morgenthau stressed early America's anti-(external) imperialist isolationism to highlight the (further) profound corruption required to wage war in Vietnam.

Third, Morgenthau exemplified an extraordinary—though, still, realist—willingness to confront *specific*, contemporary features of the regime, notably its (somewhat) democratic character, its willingness to debate policies, which would otherwise have been adopted as a matter of course. That willingness strengthens the *substance* of its power. Concurring with Niebuhr, Morgenthau's critique stresses formal democracy and its deliberative consequences, not just power. It, thus, rightly deviates from official, abstract realist formulations.

Now, as Krasner later put it, a realist sees power rivalry only as a long-term, *underlying* force. Given an initial reduction to power-capabilities, realists, he then argued, still need, as a second stage in the argument, to take regime-differences into account. But even this attempt to "save" realism misinterprets the sequence of argumentative steps. For although initial realist skepticism about power is sound, reduction of all moral and political claims to underlying, domineering "power" is false. In fact, the very notion of such a uniform power is, actually, the doubtful *moral* claim that power is always exploitative. But for instance, as in Vietnamese resistance, the just support of a people can sometimes shape a different kind of "power."[63]

Occasionally, Morgenthau's invocation of the democratic *substance* of American power seems to be mainly historical: "The war is not only politically aimless and militarily unwinnable in terms of the administration's professed aims [the standard realist, seemingly amoral critique], but it also violates the very principles on which this nation was founded and for which it has stood both in the eyes of its citizens and of the world."[64]

But even in evaluating America's democratic isolation at the founding, would Morgenthau have extenuated genocidal policies against Native Americans and blacks—the horrifying shadow of power? Concluding "Truth and Power," Morgenthau united his affection for the *substance* of American tradition with truth:

> What makes this deformation of the relationship between intellectuals and the political sphere tragic for the intellectuals is that what is true in general is true with particular poignancy for Americans: that power needs truth to be wise and great. This nation owes its very existence, its institutions, and its ethos to a rare conjunction of truth and power.... For America was founded not upon power blindly and unrestrainedly pursued, but upon power informed and restrained by truth.[65]

Truth "informs" power, a democratic realist might note, when power flows from a common good. In insisting that truth "restrains" domineering power, Morgenthau retained the misguided conception of *Politics among Nations*. In the insight that truth can inform power, however, he saw a different possibility. The latter claim elucidates Morgenthau's central distinction between the *substance* and *shadow* of power.

Now, Morgenthau also defended American liberty in a historical guise because of a misguided metaethical relativism: "It is a relativism in time ... when certain principles are applicable in one period of history, and not applicable in another period of history, and it is a relativism in terms of culture—of contemporary culture—in that certain principles are obeyed by certain political civilizations and are not obeyed by others."[66] Yet Morgenthau stressed the central realist theme that America's historical accomplishments—its (limited) liberty—should serve as an *example* to others, not be imposed by force.[67] But this distinction is moral. For it condemns the American war in Vietnam as the *shadow* of that liberty. Morgenthau would better have spoken of the relativity—rather than the relativism—of ethical principles.

Morgenthau and Herz, however, both recognized the central realism/ idealism distinction as "frankly inadequate in the realm of more refined political theory."[68] The same caveat, however, applies to Morgenthau's remarks about ethics. That humans have not yet *discovered* certain features of a decent social life does not license metaethical conventionalism: for instance, slavery existed for a historical epoch, but is no part of the human good. Similarly, that people disagree intensely about what is true, morally speaking, does not mean no truth is to be had, for example, that the Vietnam War was, just as likely, benevolent.[69]

Realist thesis 2: to cover up its crimes, the government accused its ever increasing number of moral critics of treason, as in, for example, Project Morgenthau.

LBJ's striking out at critics underlines the *antidemocratic feedback* of international politics on domestic politics. Thus, Johnson's official spokesperson among intellectuals, John Roche, signaled the press—willing, influential columnists like Jimmy Breslin, largely dependent on the White House for news—to attack:

> The term intellectual has been batted about loosely. When you mention intellectuals today, who do you mean? There is a large group. The ones we talk about when we mention the President's relations with them are only a small body of self-appointed people who live in affluent alienation on Cape Cod and fire off salvos against the vulgarity of the masses. But this is a well-orchestrated outfit with fine Madison Avenue techniques. They live in their old highly fashionable apartment houses which tower over the Hudson River [the sniping at putative lifestyles on the Cape and on the Hudson seeks—obviously and falsely—to mobilize a certain resentment. . .]. And they send out a flow of words against the war in Vietnam and against Lyndon Johnson. Their out-of-town copy comes from Cambridge and Berkeley and in the Midwest from Professor Hans Morgenthau of the University of Chicago.

The latter, Roche continued in the *New York Times Magazine* in October 1965, "is a scholarly, urbane European intellectual; his major premise is that Americans cannot be trusted with power and since Johnson (like Kennedy . . .) is an American, there is little more to say."[70] In highlighting the decadence of the Vietnam War, Morgenthau celebrated "the nation of Jefferson and Lincoln." As he put it, "[T]his summary of my political position is pure fabrication, and it cannot be lost even on an obtuse reader that here an attempt is being made to exploit a residual American xenophobia in order to question my credentials."[71]

Recently, former secretary of defense Robert McNamara has stressed the "ignorance," caused by the exiling of Asian specialists by McCarthyism, as central to American policy.[72] He unawaredly echoes Thucydides' insight, artfully half-hidden in the long, opening sentence of book 6, about the causes of Athenian defeat in Syracuse. But McNamara leaves aside the government's—and his own—role in creating such ignorance, for instance, in hounding expert, outspoken critics like Morgenthau, whom it had hired for advice on Vietnam

As columnists Germond and Witcover note:

> Officialdom equated pursuit of the war with loyalty and patriotism and criticism of it as disloyalty and even treason. The voice then of a key figure in the

conduct of the war questioning its core, would have been explosive and have given the protest a credibility it lacked with many Americans. Instead, Mc-Namara's voice now sounds more like a whisper. . . . It will be of little solace to the Americans who served and died in Vietnam [some mention of the Vietnamese would have been fitting, here], and to the thousands more at home who were vilified for saying then what he has finally said now.[73]

With anguish, McNamara records that in 1966, Jackie Kennedy beat his chest and demanded that he "do something to stop the slaughter." In contrast to Morgenthau's integrity, McNamara, sadly, does not understand that his public silence—his loyalty to an Ahab-like president—was criminal.[74]

Realist thesis 3: the U.S. government sought to infiltrate and undermine pluralism and resistance, committing the "totalitarian" mistake of reducing freely given loyalty to manipulation and semblance. Thus, the CIA suborned presidents of the National Student Association.

This perversion of private associations to serve hidden government purposes threatened democracy—what we might call Morgenthau's central versions of the *antidemocratic feedback* and *public-corruption theses*:[75]

It testifies to the vigor of our democratic habits that the scrutiny of public opinion has been able to uncover governmental deception. . . . The pity of it is that, had the government had more confidence in the strength of a free democracy than in the efficiency of pseudo-totalitarian methods, it could have served the national interest without paying so heavy a price. Internationally, all individuals and organizations, speaking on behalf of the United States, will from now on be suspect as secret agents of the government. Even if they speak the truth as free agents, they will risk not being believed. Thus, the unique and precious asset of a free society, the intellectual and moral autonomy of its members vis-a-vis the government, will go to waste.[76]

Against such corruption, citizens have no defense except radical opposition. But as Morgenthau stressed, the U.S. government does not—so far—have the full "benefits" of totalitarianism, for it does not relentlessly control voluntary organizations (he sometimes referred to a "pseudo-totalitarianism"). Morgenthau did not think, however, that the government would become more successful through being more totalitarian. Instead, he recognized that the latter course would make "counterproductive," even genocidal, policies, like the Vietnam War, more likely.

Though the Cold War has ended, the U.S. government continues corrupt policies. For instance, in 1995, Jennifer Harbury—an American lawyer—conducted a seven-week hunger strike in Guatemala City to seek out the fate of her Mayan husband, a guerilla leader, Efrain Bamaca Velasquez. The Guatemalan military, under the command of a CIA "informer," Colonel Alpirez, murdered him in 1993. The CIA kept silent about it. So did Congress. Finally, Robert A. Torricelli, a conservative Democrat who served on the Congressional Oversight Committee, spoke out: "The direct involvement of the Central Intelligence Agency in the murder of these individuals [an American, Michael Devine, an innkeeper in the rain forest, who stumbled onto army drug smuggling, as well as Velasquez] leads me to the extraordinary conclusion that the agency is simply out of control and that it contains what can only be called a criminal element."[77]

Fortified by U.S. military and covert support, the Guatemalan regime has murdered "110,000 people, mostly Mayan Indians, razing hundreds of villages . . . over the last three decades."[78]

House Republicans initially sought the removal of Torricelli from the Oversight Committee for telling the truth, though they were eventually defeated.[79] Further, Richard Nuccio, a State Department official, who released the—now admitted by the CIA—information about the murders to Torricelli, was denied a security clearance by CIA director Deutsch in an attempt to ruin his career.

A government commission has recently admitted the routine employment by the CIA of murderers in Guatemala.[80] During and since the Cold War, agency chiefs were evaluated mainly on the numbers of agents recruited. In early 1997, the CIA fired its one hundred worst torturers, mainly Latin American officers.[81] As chapter 5 suggests, a decent regime would bar covert activities.

Realist thesis 4: teachers are, by and large, no longer committed to the truth.

Today, Morgenthau insisted, an "academic-political complex" matches Eisenhower's "military-industrial" one: "As the integrity and independence of the government have been subverted by the 'military-industrial complex,' so the integrity and independence of the educational community have been impaired by the academic-political complex. The educational community has in large measure become *the handmaiden of government*, while maintaining its pretence to independence."[82] Morgenthau also named universities a "gigantic and indispensable *service station* for the powers-that-be, both public and private."[83]

In Marxian terms, the pressure of an unjust war, including a mass antiwar movement, forced the ruling group, previously more effective in setting limits to dissent in official circles, to emerge as a self-conscious ruling class.[84] Yet, as Morgenthau also stressed, such a class conducts foreign policy *less effectively*. The existence of an *academic-political complex* means that fewer intellectuals will stand out for truth because their pay and, perhaps more importantly, their prestige depend upon governmental solicitude.[85] Prestige gives the intellectual his (seeming) importance, his privilege of being heard as the "one and only" authority—or at least, one of a few—in a field. To remove prestige is, thus, to remove air, to reduce the "intellectual" to an unimportant figure, merely one of the democratic crowd, in an oligarchy.

Given the burgeoning antiwar movement, however, Morgenthau could have his views recorded at teach-ins and become a different kind of public figure, a *democratic* intellectual. A democratic public in Dewey's terms, one, in part, created by Morgenthau's insights as well as by student protest from below, brought criticism to the fore. It held the government to the democratic standard that it must justify military policies to ordinary soldiers and their families. But this criterion the Johnson administration, faced with an increasingly informed public, could not meet.[86]

Through sit-ins and demonstrations as well as teach-ins, extralegal as well as legal protest, the antiwar movement created and engaged this public. Hans Morgenthau, along with I. F. Stone and Senator Fulbright, articulated defining criticisms of the war[87] (so, often, did the, now as well as then "officially" disregarded, student movement). Though Stone, an independent journalist, was never part of the elite, Morgenthau's criticisms—for instance, in affirming the desirability of revolution, if possible—were more radical.[88] Further, elite stigmatization meant *the beginning* of democratic influence for Morgenthau. Despite isolation from colleagues and former friends, it underlined the *democratic resonance* of his realism.

> **Realist thesis 5**: the prevalence of democracies in the world might, ultimately, make peace possible. A common interest among regimes in preventing nuclear war reinforces this possibility.

Morgenthau concurred with the Kantian argument according to which democracies—in Kant, republics—are capable of relative stability and peaceful conflict. Thus, as *Politics among Nations* maintains,

> Political realism does not assume that the contemporary conditions under which foreign policy operates, with their extreme instability and the ever present threat of large-scale violence, cannot be changed. The balance of power, for instance, is indeed a perennial element of all pluralistic societies, as the authors of *The Federalist* papers well knew; yet it is capable of operating, as it does in the United States, under the conditions of relative stability and peaceful conflict. If the factors that have given rise to these conditions can be duplicated on the international scene, similar conditions of stability and peace will then prevail there, as they have over long stretches of history among certain nations.

Thus, Morgenthau's realism coincides with a cautiously stated version of the "democratic peace" hypothesis, for instance, that industrialized, European and American democracies do not war with one another.[89]

In addition, like Herz, Morgenthau saw the novel dangers and possibilities of the nuclear era: "[U]ntil the advent of that age, a nation could use its diplomacy to purchase its security at the expense of another nation. Today short of a radical change in the atomic balance of power in favor of a particular nation, diplomacy, in order to make one nation secure from nuclear destruction, must make them all secure."[90] As the *antidemocratic-feedback* hypothesis underlines, however, an internationalist might wonder whether within nations, prenuclear policies mainly served the security of a ruling class rather than all classes. For citizens have always had a common interest in peace that conflicted with the interests of leaders or elite classes. The danger of nuclear extinction, however, eliminates prospective *particular* gains for the elite. This novel strategic interest conjoins with citizen influence to hinder interdemocratic war.

Yet in the post–World War II era, power in the United States had swollen. Its structure corrupted relative stability and undermined the possibility of peace. That structure enabled the rich to reinforce their prestige without attention to dissent and escalate the Vietnam War. Further, the academic-political complex created a clamor of approval for any government policy, no matter how irrational and brutal.

> **Realist thesis 6:** a mass, antiwar movement was needed to stop American aggression in Vietnam and (in future) other unjust policies *(democratic internationalism)*.

Exemplifying an official realist paradigm that stresses sound advice to the powerful, *Politics among Nations* insists: "Diplomacy must be divested of the crusading spirit," that is, the influence of transient, popular passions.[91] Confronted with the Vietnam War, however, Morgenthau contended, "We came to realize now, through political experience, what some of us had concluded before by way of philosophic reflection, that power positions do not yield to arguments, however rationally and morally valid, but only to superior power. We also came to realize that the distribution of power in America favors the continuation of policies that we regard to be indefensible on rational and moral grounds."[92]

The antiwar movement of which Morgenthau became a part exerted just *counter*power. At this point, realism transforms into democratic internationalism. For the decisive claim about a democratic public follows on a sophisticated—one attentive to a common good—realist account.

> **Realist thesis 7:** real American relations of power sustain oligarchy and make (democratic) revolution desirable, though not possible.[93]

Morgenthau now saw a single industrial-military-political-academic complex—a ruling class—in which "the interests of the government are inextricably intertwined with the interests of large groups of academics. These ties are both formal and informal, and the latter are the more dangerous to intellectual freedom, as they consist in the intellectuals' unconscious adaptation to imperceptible social and political pressures."[94] Morgenthau's insistence on such informal ties as status, income, and the avoidance of subtle harassment (secret sanction by administrators, for example), ones harder to characterize but decisive in the unwillingness of many to break with outrageous policies, highlights an oligarchic check on the *democratic* (free) expression of opinion in the contemporary United States.[95]

6. MORGENTHAU'S MISTAKEN CELEBRATION OF LINCOLN'S STATISM

Realists, however, do not err in the claim that zealous affection often leads to folly. Ironically, however, this realist insight applies to Morgenthau's stress on Lincoln's preservation of the Union at the expense of the latter's gradual, ultimately decisive critique of slavery. Morgenthau misread Lincoln's downplaying of servitude as a classic realist move, an adherence to *official duty* as opposed to *personal morality*. His interpretation highlights a central, seemingly realist emphasis on statism at the expense of a core liberal notion of a common good that, as we will see, separates his argument from Niebuhr's. Further, it reveals a prototypical difference between official realism and democratic internationalism.

Morgenthau repeatedly invoked one citation, endorsing consequentialism, from Lincoln's speeches: "There can be no political morality without prudence. . . . [As] Lincoln said: 'I do the very best I know how, the very best I can, and I mean to keep doing so until the end. If the end brings me out all right, what is said against me won't amount to anything. If the end brings me out wrong, ten angels swearing I was right would make no difference.'"[96]

To put Morgenthau's claim in formal terms:

> **Realist thesis 1:** state defense against external aggression is a good.
> **Realist thesis 2:** Lincoln's prudence in preserving the United States overrode the evil of slavery.

Thesis 2, however, does not follow from thesis 1. For, as a liberal or democratic internationalist might insist: aggression is committed by an internal power, slaveowners, against slaves; slavery is inconsistent with a common good.

The 1860s United States both opposed external expansion, compared to Europe—Morgenthau's idealization—and, as a *slaveholding* nation, horrifyingly illustrated such imperialism. Thus, slavery might have justified an unusual, "external aggression" against the American regime—what Michael Walzer rightly calls humanitarian intervention by outsiders.[97] Further, once Lincoln issued the Emancipation Proclamation, defeating the evil of slavery *sanctioned* internal American revolution, the Civil War, on the Northern side.[98] But Lincoln waited to free the slaves until 1863, two years after the war began. Until then, John Brown and the abolitionists, not Lincoln, represented the cause of justice—and of sophisticated realism. Put differently, the internationalist critique emphasizes: we can defend Lincoln's upholding of the Union *only* insofar as the North waged an *abolitionist* war. Today, we rightly see the president as an Emancipator—consider the Lincoln Memorial. But if Lincoln had not been forced to save the Union by ending slavery, mere preservation of an exploitative system would not have seemed, in moral perspective, so remarkable a political accomplishment.[99]

Morgenthau's mistake here illustrates, once again, the unreflective influence of *official realism*. In criticizing American policy, as I have noted, he invoked an idealized, semi*historical* picture of the American past rather than thinking through an ethical one. But only his moral insistence on a common good—a linking of the *substance* of power to truth—makes the historical critique work. A clear, ethical insistence that "the national interest" requires commonality, not merely consistent benefits to a prevailing, often genocidal elite, characterizes well-stated realism.[100]

In his theoretical arguments, however, as I have also stressed, Morgenthau assumed rather than articulated a conception of the national interest. Thus, *Politics among Nations* works only with a generalized conception of interest as power. In contrast, Krasner's *Defending the National Interest* strives to identify what is specific to a common interest among citizens in foreign policy. Despite ambiguities in Krasner's account—for instance, his mistaken attempt to abstract such an "interest" from domestic politics—his explicit theoretical wrestling with this conception is an improvement.[101] For even Morgenthau's 1952 *In Defense of the National Interest* alleges imperial, U.S. domineering in Latin America to be a common good. But that claim is false and undercuts Morgenthau's otherwise sophisticated—democratic—realism.[102]

In his *American Political Science Review* rejoinder to Tucker in that year, Morgenthau finally, mentioned, inter alia, that a national interest requires the "survival" of each of its citizens, that is, defense against aggression.[103] Reliance on this core conception might have helped Morgenthau to see the aggression toward slaves in—rather than the praiseworthiness of—Lincoln's original policy of preserving the Union.

7. "THINGS THAT ARE NOT" AND "THINGS THAT ARE"

As a theologian of public issues, Reinhold Niebuhr's Christianity helped him to see not only the prevailing darkness of social and international conflict, but a realm of moral possibility. Niebuhr identified human self-ishness and hunger for power with original sin. Unlike the Greeks, how-ever, he drew no distinction between love of self and mere selfishness. Yet in contrast to most American realists and neorealists, he dialectically rec-ognized a rarer human capacity to "transcend" this natural condition. Thus, he saw realism as prophetic, following a God who brings the new into being: "Yea, and things which are not [hath God chosen] to put to nought things that are" (1 Cor. 1:28).[104] Envisioning transformation through struggle from below, Niebuhr's conception counters the static insistence of neorealism on like, abstract "powers." His realism recalls Marx's insight that history proceeds by the "bad side" of oppression and struggle rather than the good side of noble intentions and kind deeds.[105]

Niebuhr's view also resembles those of the Syracusan Hermocrates (to whom I return in chapter 4) as well as democratic internationalists:

> The conclusion . . . is that equality, or to be a little more qualified, that equal justice is the most rational ultimate objective for society.[106] If this conclusion is correct, a social conflict which aims at greater equality has a moral justifi-cation which must be denied to efforts which aim at the perpetuation of privilege. A war for the emancipation of a nation, a race or a class is thus placed in a different moral category from the use of power for the perpetua-tion of imperial rule or class dominance. The oppressed, whether they be the Indians in the British Empire, or the Negroes in our own country,[107] or the industrial workers in every nation, have a higher moral right to challenge their oppressors than these have to maintain their rule by force. . . . equality is a higher social goal than peace.[108]

Neorealism's reductionist emphasis on "power" cannot explain, for instance, anticolonial struggles, the appearance of fascism, or the emer-gence and decline of socialist regimes.[109] If, however, like Niebuhr's, a realist view of internal and external power-struggle can accommodate notions of a perhaps rare common good and even the possible emergence of "things that are not," it can illuminate such changes. Concerned with the sources of "power," a realist may, nonetheless, stand aside from pre-vailing power.

Articulating a transformative realism, Niebuhr adhered to the Jewish and Christian *prophetic* tradition and indicted a *conforming* religion that truckles to the rich and powerful. In response to Billy Graham's sermon in Nixon's White House, he invoked Amos: "I hate, I despise your feasts, and I take no delight in your solemn assemblies. . . . Take away from me the noise of your songs; to the melody of your harps I will not listen.[110] But let justice roll down like waters, and righteousness like an everflowing stream."[111] Illuminating Morgenthau's stigmatization by an "academic-political complex," Niebuhr recognized the class consequences of religiously sanctified, secular dominion: "the rulers of Israel . . . trample upon the needy and bring the poor of the land to an end" (Amos 8:4).

In fact, Niebuhr identified the paradigmatic, official realist stance of advising statespersons with Amaziah, who banished Amos: "O thou seer, go, flee thee away from the land of Judah, and there eat bread and prophesy there. But prophesy not again any more at Bethel: for it is the king's chapel and the king's court."[112] On the contrary, Niebuhr sided with social movements from below (this prophetic aspect, however, diminishes in his writing and activity between World War II and Vietnam). *Moral Man* and *Reflections on the End of an Era* thus work out a form of (prophetic) realism close to democratic internationalism.

For realists need not dramatically contrast international and domestic "power."[113] In a Marxian as well as realist vein, Niebuhr's "Life and Death of Civilizations" highlights the split between a capitalist's profit- and power-driven activity and "personal" morality: "The modern oligarch conducts a bank or a factory. He [*sic*] 'serves' mankind. All bloodshed is abhorrent to him. . . . The lust of power and the imperial impulse may prompt his actions but they express themselves subconsciously rather than consciously. He may tenderly send his family to escape the winter's cold on the sands of Palm Beach while his workers starve to death amid the social confusion of an economic depression." This division or what we might call *alienation* of social from personal morality—though alienation often distorts even the latter—generally affects the privileged: "His cities are filled with humanitarians who eat meat but regard the killing of animals with repulsion. His institutions of learning boast of academics, supported by rather generous crumbs which fall from the rich man's table, who invent schemes for saving modern civilization by transmuting it into a rational and moral accommodation of interest to interest in which all coercion and conflict will be avoided."[114] In a central realist insight, he maintained, such ideal harmonies emerge as an ideological "unconscious," out of startling moral difference—consider an average congressional representative, a homeless child—and a "terrific conflict of power." In this context, Niebuhr regarded prophetic religion as "bound to speak a special word of warning and condemnation to those who are firmly established in history, whether individuals or classes, because they are particularly tempted to imagine themselves the authors and sole protectors of what is good."[115]

Thus, thematically, Niebuhr ferreted out "illusions"—perhaps his favorite word—about social harmony. Moralists "do not recognize that when collective power, whether in the form of imperialism or class domination exploits weakness, it can never be dislodged unless power is raised against it."[116] His "Life and Death of Civilizations" mocks the "mechanical" insistence that somehow—in the early 1930s—war and depression can be averted, progress triumph: "It is a strange irony of history that a commercial and industrial civilization, which might have had special reasons for being anxious about its vitality and longevity, should have been particularly optimistic."[117] A later review by Morgenthau of Niebuhr's *Structure of Nations and Empires* suggests that he "lays bare the mechanism by which morality clothes politics with undeserved dignity and politics transforms morality into an instrument of political domination. It is particularly fascinating to observe how this mechanism operates in the relations between great imperial and religious structures. The religious structures become imperial in performance and the imperial structures become religious in pretence."[118]

In *Moral Man*, Niebuhr even criticized Dewey's notion of social experiments as idealist. Underlining affinities between prophetic realism and Marxism, he averred that only comparatively justly organized power can secure a common good, and counseled the proletariat: "No class of industrial workers will ever win freedom from the dominant classes if they give themselves completely to the 'experimental techniques' of modern education."[119] He did not spell out his conception of a balance between "educational experiments" and political struggle. Yet some experience in the former might encourage participation in the clashes needed for emancipation (fighting prevailing teaching might, however, be more direct). Niebuhr's "Prophecy of Doom" stresses the inverted relationship between (fantasies of) harmony and oligarchy: "To invite the oligarchies which rule every society to live by the law of justice is equivalent to requesting the oligarchs to abdicate."[120]

On Niebuhr's account, such "illusions" stem from "pride": "The mighty stand under the judgment of God in a special sense. They are, of all men, most tempted to transgress the bounds of human creatureliness and to imagine themselves God. . . . The perennial sin of man is his rebellion against God, his inclination to make himself God."[121] In this context, he invoked the Greek conception of hubris—striving to exceed merely human stature.[122] Illuminating Morgenthau's account of the "academic-political complex," Niebuhr saw such pride not only in politics and economics, but in churches and universities as well:

> The genuine achievements of mind and conscience may also be new occasions for expressing the pride of sinful man: "If any man stand, let him take

heed lest he fall" is a warning which is as relevant to bishops, professors, artists, saints and holy men as to capitalists, dictators and all men of power. Every one who has achieved a high form of culture imagines that it is a necessary and final form of culture. It is the man [sic] who stands, who has achieved, who is honored and approved by his fellows who mistakes the relative achievement and approval of history for a final and ultimate approval.[123]

To criticize religious and social tendencies with which Niebuhr disagreed—for instance, "a misguided Hellenistic denunciation of sensuality"—he frequently spoke rhetorically: "*Without question*, Biblical religion defines sin as primarily pride and self-love."[124] His emphasis on humility, however, underlines his own arrogant, apparently unselfconscious dismissal—"without question," they counter "inevitable" trends—of alternate views.

According to Niebuhr, such illusions even affect philosophers, for instance Hegel and Marx,[125] who discern "things that are not." But Hegel maintained only that philosophy lives with the negative: "the owl of Minerva takes flight at dusk." His *Phenomenology of Spirit* makes death's transforming power a central theme. As in the Crucifixion, such changes move in no predictable way. His insight is thus more profoundly Christian and less stricken with "illusion" than Niebuhr recognized.

Niebuhr also missed Marx's self-critical idiom—his willingness to learn from practice and caution about prescribing, beyond broad guidelines, what the future may suggest to a revolutionary movement. Thus, Marx's critique of utopianism deepens Niebuhr's—and realism's—indictment of moralism. Nonetheless, Niebuhr's psychology of pride, reminiscent, as chapter 4 argues, of Hobbes's, explains the transfixing appeal of small incentives in the "academic-political complex."

In *Moral Man* and *Reflections*, Niebuhr invoked capitalism's "moribundness." Yet he rightly underlined the indignation that motivated Marx's and Engels's mistaken optimism that blatant oppression would lead swiftly to revolution: "The error in these predictions is usually derived from a moral passion which imagines that social injustice will not survive because it ought not to. It does not recognize that history is as lenient as it is inexorable in its processes and is as slow in executing judgment as it is certain to pass negative judgment on predatory life."[126] Ironically, however, Niebuhr's more cautious judgment about "inexorability" does not escape his insight into Marx and Engels.

In forging a prophetic realism, Niebuhr combined a Marxian insistence on class war—and a realist one on international clashes—with spiritual pessimism: "In my opinion adequate spiritual guidance can come only through a more radical political orientation and more conservative religious convictions than are comprehended in the culture of our era. It will satisfy neither the liberals in politics and religion, nor the political radicals nor the devotees of traditional Christianity."[127]

Moral Man's most famous formulation, however, downplays any transformative possibility of social conflict. Individuals, Niebuhr maintained, transcend selfishness more easily than groups or states. Policies appropriate to the latter might seem outrageous in relations among the former:

> Individual men [*sic*] may be moral in the sense that they are able to consider interests other than their own in determining problems of conduct, and are capable, on occasion, of preferring the advantages of others to their own. They are endowed by nature with a measure of sympathy and consideration for their kind, the breadth of which may be extended by an astute social pedagogy. Their rational faculty prompts them to a sense of justice which educational discipline may refine and purge of egoistic elements until they are able to view a social situation, in which their own interests are involved with a fair amount of objectivity. But all these achievements are more difficult, if not impossible, for human societies and social groups [influenced by its earlier tradition of nonviolence, the policies of the postapartheid, ANC government in South Africa, particularly the Truth Commission, and the attempt to heal without vengeance, are, however, a counterexample]. In every human group there is less reason to guide and to check impulse, less capacity for self-transcendence, less ability to comprehend the ends of others, and therefore more unrestrained egoism than the individuals, who compose the group, reveal in their personal relationships.[128]

On one level, Niebuhr's distinction between groups and particular persons lacks psychological sophistication, either in understanding the relation of one individual to others—Reinhold's brother, Richard, commented, "I hate to look at my brotherly love for you to see how it is compounded with personal pride—taking some kind of credit for the things you do and basking in reflected glory—and selfish ambition—trying to stand on my own feet, trying to live up to you, being jealous of you, to use a harsh and brutal term"—or in comprehending a transference of projections from individuals, for instance fathers and mothers, onto groups.[129] On another level, on his own theory, Niebuhr's formulation underestimates the moral potential of the oppressed, their ability, as Marx puts it, to realize "a universal" or *common* good, at least in comparison to older regimes (as uncontroversial examples, consider anticolonial or democratic revolutions). Nonetheless, with these qualifications, Niebuhr's point is well taken.

Attempting to differentiate individual conduct from manifestations of group power, however, Niebuhr took an individualist ideology in the

middle classes—one that routinely accompanies domineering, the opposite of individuality—too easily for its realization, and considered proletarians—in an anti–working class stereotype—as merely loyal to class:

> The differences between proletarian and middle-class morality are on the
> whole differences between men [sic] who regard themselves as primarily in-
> dividuals and those who feel themselves primarily members of a social
> group. . . . Insofar as this [middle-class morality] represents an honest effort
> to make the ideals of personal morality norms for the conduct of human
> groups, it is a legitimate moral attitude which must never be completely
> abandoned. Insofar as it represents the illusions and deceptions of middle-
> class people, who never conform their own group conduct to their individual
> ideals, it deserves the cynical reaction of the proletarian.[130]

But this comment misunderstands the effect of social circumstances on
individual conduct. For a political response by workers, for example,
joining a union or a leftist party, may be a sign of their individuality. A
theory of individuality[131] may justify participation in many activities and
relationships for their own sakes, even when the participants do not
speak of such loyalty as a personal commitment. Further, Niebuhr elsewhere suggested, the oppressed need to form resistant groups. Such commitment is morally justified.[132] Inverting this image, capitalists and professionals often lead *predatory* public—and even private—lives. It takes
a, to some extent, examined life to counter this tendency.

As a socialist, Niebuhr could imagine a decent regime that would check
the tendencies of "immoral society."[133] Yet he also saw sharp limits to
transformation, interpreting Soviet use of wage differentials as a dramatic
concession to capitalist practices, though, on his view, an "inevitable"
one. Even before the introduction of such differentials within the Communist Party in 1934, Niebuhr maintained:

> They have tried to hide the fact that this is a concession to, and compro-
> mise with, an inevitable weakness in human nature by insisting that it is
> merely a concession to a vestigial remnant of capitalist psychology. . . .
> Waldo Frank[134] reports the following interesting conversation with a com-
> munist factory director: " 'Is there then no danger,' I said at last, 'to your
> communist ideal? . . . here you are, remunerating inventions with money,
> paying superior sums of money to the more capable men . . . planning your
> new hierarchy of merit by the old hated symbol of money. . . . When has
> education been according to an ideal superior to the practiced way of
> life?' "[135]

Niebuhr, however, also influenced the transformation of the Fellowship
of Socialist Christians into an activist movement, which supported the
organizing of black and white sharecroppers in the Southern Tenant
Farmers Union.[136]

Following Weber, *official* realism—and contemporary political science—define a state as holding a "legitimate monopoly of the use of force in a territory." In contrast, Niebuhr looked to nonviolent as well as violent movements (if the latter attend to likely moral consequences) as central political possibilities. His realism, as we will see, prefigures Kennan's. Criticizing "mechanical" capitalist societies, Niebuhr's "Christian and Bourgeois Individualism" remarks:

> Gandhi will extend the power of the spirit over the world of nature in collective life as far as it can be extended at any time in this century [foreclosing the future, the tone is, once again, prideful]. . . . His fast for the sake of abolishing untouchability suggests that he will end his days as a religious saint rather than a political leader. . . . But ultimately, the Indian will must be implemented by something more than Gandhi's technique if it to conquer the British will, symbolized by men like Winston Churchill. The cynical and realistic Churchill, with his unyielding imperial ambition, is the perfect symbol of the inertia of nature in politics.[137]

Gandhi, however, proved an abler politician than Niebuhr imagined. In "The King's Chapel and the King's Court," Niebuhr relied on the same passage from Amos as Martin Luther King's "I Have a Dream" speech.[138]

From 1920 to 1934, Niebuhr led the nonviolent Fellowship of Reconciliation. Yet he subsequently rejected pacifism as being insufficiently aware of the political role of sin.[139] Nonviolence, he thought, must appeal to the generalizing of individual good will into the public arena and overlook the problematic character—the harmful consequences to others—of all politics. It tends, therefore, to abstain from a necessary resistance to tyranny, paradigmatically, as Niebuhr emphasized, Nazism.

Thus, Niebuhr's realism rests on fundamental psychological claims, for instance, about the human capacity for selfishness extending into pride and evil. His Christianity shares in—is, in Rawlsian language, a more comprehensive version of—what I call *moral* realism, which stresses an equally sufficient human *capacity for moral personality* to understand and obey reasonable, public laws.[140] Discerning an "overlapping consensus" of more comprehensive views, moral realism is a self-standing, political conception, one that requires neither a Christian framework nor thinking about whether a divinity exists, and, if so, of what sort.[141]

In addition, Niebuhr's Christianity stresses a psychological insight vital both to sophisticated realism and democratic internationalism. In the context even of just struggles, he emphasized mercy. Where Morgenthau assimilated Lincoln to a misguided statism, Niebuhr affirmed the latter's insight into the justice of emancipation: "Slavery was to be condemned even if it claimed divine sanction, for [in Lincoln's words] 'It may seem strange that any men should dare ask a just God's assistance in wringing their bread from the sweat of other men's faces.'"[142] Niebuhr also rightly saw Lincoln's misguided affection for the Union as flowing from a nonvengeful, spiritual, deeply political sense of compassion:

"[H]is brooding sense of charity was derived from a religious awareness of another dimension of meaning than that of the immediate political conflict. "Both sides," he declared, "read the same Bible and pray to the same God. The prayers of both could not be answered—that of neither has been answered fully."[143]

Lincoln's forgiveness—"with malice toward none, with charity for all"—embodies a central realist insight: a critique of the pretence and vengefulness in the idealism of *both* sides. In Niebuhr, this critique draws on a transcendent Providence. In ordinary psychological terms, however, even a fight against slavery, that paradigm of injustice, does not erase the human limitations of the fighters. As Niebuhr's coeditor of *Christianity and Crisis*, John Bennett, noted: "Lincoln exemplified, as hardly any other political leader has done, the commitment to the cause he was called upon to defend without identifying that cause with the will of God in absolute terms. He was . . . resolute without self-righteousness."[144]

Transforming an initial realist emphasis on selfishness, such mercy, Niebuhr maintained, flows "from a *broken spirit and a contrite heart*." For each experiences the death or disappearance of those close to us. Compassion is a possibility in every life. A sophisticated realism thus joins the "original sin" of pride to the experience of mercy; a narrower, reductionist realism sees only "the domination of man by man."[145]

By the height of the Cold War, Niebuhr, however, had moved away from his initial radicalism to support American power. He was now a celebrated theologian—a dangerous position, as his warning, "If a man stand, let him take heed lest he fall," testifies. He even served on the State Department's Policy Planning Board, headed by George Kennan, while the FBI, under the influence of Truman-McCarthyism, expanded its file on him.[146] Belying his onetime stress on struggle from below, he now, misguidedly, urged American blacks to go slow in resisting racism. Yet while many prestigious American "liberals" actively persecuted or informed against their fellow citizens, Niebuhr supported Junius Scales and others under attack.[147] As with Morgenthau, the Vietnam War would bring *democratic* themes in his realism to the fore.

8. EXILE FROM THE "KING'S CHAPEL"

While international-relations specialists neglect Morgenthau's essays on Vietnam, Niebuhr's five years of passionate protest against the war in *Christianity and Crisis* have not even been reprinted. Niebuhr edited

Christianity and Crisis along with his fellow Christian realist John Bennett. Deepening Morgenthau's adherence to the "nation of Jefferson and Lincoln," his conduct of a forum for diverse views—though centered in the Protestant churches—exemplifies, to a considerable extent, the democratic deliberations that chapter 5 explores theoretically. Over time, *Christianity and Crisis* came to emphasize the violation of a *common good*, internationally—for the Vietnamese—and domestically, as part of a well-stated realism. Niebuhr's opposition to the war, however, bewildered official realists. As Paul Ramsey put it, "Even Reinhold Niebuhr signs petitions and editorials as if Reinhold Niebuhr had never existed."[148]

Like American democracy at its best, *Christianity and Crisis* represented only a limited spectrum of opinion: those of almost no women (in the 1970s, the editorial board finally appointed Rosemary Radford Reuther; Ursula Niebuhr coauthored an article with Reinhold), only two students in 1969, and nearly no pointed opponents of the U.S. government. In celebrating *Christianity and Crisis*'s twenty-fifth anniversary,[149] Vice President Hubert Humphrey joined with Morgenthau to praise Niebuhr. The latter's movement into "treachery" to the administration and official realism, while courageous, was not as forceful as Morgenthau's.

Initially, Niebuhr linked opposition to the war's horrors for the Vietnamese and the corruption of American institutions, notably by the CIA, with balance-of-power considerations: that, for example, "we" were driving the Vietnamese into the arms of China. Over time, however, he became increasingly aware of the war's *antidemocratic feedback*. He also condemned a court religion that perfumed odious policies. Nonetheless, during his editorship, the voices of others sometimes render his own conclusions more dramatically. This section will invoke both his own words and the words of those *Christianity and Crisis* published.[150]

To instigate debate, in 1964, the editors printed clashing portraits of Vietnam's future. Senator Wayne Morse's "The US Must Withdraw" traces American backing of French colonialism—"we put over $1¼ billion into that futile struggle"—and invokes FDR's unheeded warning: "Each case must, of course, stand on its own feet, but the case of Indochina is perfectly clear. France has milked it for 100 years. The people of Indochina are entitled to something better than that."[151] For Morse, the war expresses "our interests, not theirs": "Since 1954, we have been a provocateur of military conflict in Southeast Asia and marched away from our obligations under the UN Charter."[152] In contrast, Frank N. Trager called for an expanded war on Laos, Cambodia, and North Vietnam; Alan Geyer hoped to instill American values in the Vietnamese.[153]

In March 1966, however, the board issued an appeal: "We Protest the National Policy in Vietnam." In an epigraph, it cites Herbert Butterfield: "The hardest strokes of heaven fall in history upon those who imagine that they can *control things in a sovereign manner* as though they were *kings of the earth*, playing Providence not only for themselves but for the far future."[154] The editors argued that "our nation is becoming increasingly lonely in the world . . . building a legacy of hatred and resentment for 'neo-colonialism.' " They still softened the crime—which they put in scare quotes—of the United States siding with and then supplanting French colonialism, of fighting a "white man's" war in Asia. Nonetheless, they emphasized the pride involved in a step-by-step escalation of an initially small belligerence: "Nobody planned the war. Neither brute malice nor innocent miscalculation brought it about. It is the result of a series of fateful decisions in which human fallibility, accentuated by moral insensitivity and *pretension*, turned a brush-fire war into a major conflict. In the process, the nature of the initial U.S. commitments has changed beyond recognition."[155]

The editors' criticisms, however, fuse principled and pragmatic considerations. American military policy ravaged Vietnam—the war "is *destructive* of the people whom we claim to help": "The burning of villages, the killing and maiming of civilians, area bombing and the use of napalm and chemical destruction of crops inflict immediate human suffering that makes incredible the official promises of pacification and remote benefits. Repeatedly, such tactics alienate and harm the very people we purport to save."[156] This "arrogant inhumanity" in the conservative, Peter Berger's, words, or near genocide in Morgenthau's, eroded the substance of U.S. power. It made people think of nonprotesting Americans as "good Germans."[157] The war threatened the interests of other regimes and most Americans.

The editors had yet to recognize that the government *lied* to the American people about Vietnam. They already, however, saw harms to democracy to home, the

> deep confusion in our government's aims. . . . Sometimes the stated policy is to prevent any gain for communism. At other times, it is to give the people of Vietnam their free choice of a government—and that, everybody knows, may be a Communist government. Talk of unconditional readiness to negotiate is mixed with adamant unwillingness to concede anything. These contradictions may not be confusing the enemy, but *they are certainly confusing the American public and our allies.*[158]

Between 1966 and 1969, nearly half the articles in *Christianity and Crisis* link U.S. foreign policy and domestic oppression.[159]

For instance, Niebuhr, among others, underlined the destructive impact of the war on private organizations—the NSA,[160] unions[161], the press and universities—and, thus, on pluralism at home. Invoking Morgenthau's idiom, Niebuhr stressed the "corruption of truth by power," the destruction of the integrity of institutions and leaders by CIA covert activity, and, thus, the violation of trust between a people and its "private" as well as electoral representatives necessary in a democracy: "While the public was properly shocked by the disclosure of CIA undercover dishonesties, the official reactions were as disquieting as the CIA policies themselves. . . . patriotic justifications of dishonesties are always dangerous, particularly in a free democratic society, which must assume integrity as a bond of trust."[162] In addition, journalist Morley Safer described an unsettling meeting in Vietnam with Arthur Sylvester, assistant secretary of defense for public affairs:

> "Surely, Arthur, you don't expect the American press to be the *handmaiden of government*."
> "That's exactly what I expect," came the reply.
> ". . . Look [he continued] if you think any American official is going to tell you the truth, then you're stupid. Did you hear that?—*stupid*."
> ". . . Look I don't have to talk to you people. I know how to deal with you through your editors and publishers back in the States."[163]

One might amend Morgenthau's formulation to speak of an "academic-political-*media* complex."

Like Morgenthau, Safer was subject to racist rumors. Belittling, claims of "treachery," and antiradical ideology did not suffice:

> It's no secret that the former President of CBS News, Fred W. Friendly, was informed that I was married to an Asian and therefore presumably had some kind of bias in favor of Asians, and therefore was not one hundred per cent American in my thinking. The fact that I'm not married at all makes the whole thing ludicrous.
> The pressure can take less subtle forms: 'Unless you get Safer out of there, he's liable to end up with a bullet in his back."[164]

University protests had become the driving force of the antiwar movement. By May 1969, Michael Novak's "Hypocrisies Unmasked" stresses the service to corporations, not search for truth, central to university life, and subtly criticizes academic emphases. Conservative professors and administrators at Cornell

> have been shocked by the resistance of blacks to the peculiar patterns of "reasonable discourse," "objectivity" and "democratic procedures" selected by great American universities; they have been less shocked by the exclusion from universities of values, perceptions, attitudes and methods dear to most people of most cultures in human history. Feeling, fantasy, impulse, ritual, prehistoric emotional signals, subtle perceptions in human relations, and the like are systematically excluded from universities in favor

of highly developed and economically productive powers of analytic reason. The universities function to sort out those human types that manifest qualities along one small range of the human spectrum.[165]

An interview with Paul Bernstein, a graduate student in political science at Stanford, underlines the corruption of prevailing university culture:

> Yet the way these questions were examined [in the Majority Report on the Stanford Research Institute] shows very much the faults in our assumptions about whether or not we are working in a democracy here. Professor Solomon from the Business School . . . said something about Viet Nam war research, chemical and biological research, telling us it should be judged— warfare research—by the fact that it's 1% of what SRI does. . . . Similarly, he spoke about research which is related to the war in Viet Nam, and the war against the peoples in Laos and Thailand, and he said that was something about 10% of SRI's funds.
>
> Ten percent of SRI's funds is not necessarily all one needs to know about that research in order to understand how to make a moral decision upon it. . . . the consequences of that research are monstrous.[166]

The Harvard strike (April 1969) had provoked Novak's editorial. By that time, Students for a Democratic Society had swelled to over one hundred thousand members and led hundreds of thousands of others to protest the war. Yet until militant actions occurred on university campuses, no writing from this movement's participants appeared *even* in the pages of *Christianity and Crisis*.[167] By 1969, however, administrative squelching of reasonable questions that threatened university ties to the military or anticommunity activity, coupled with truckling to university presidents, had become clear to students as well as a wider public. Novak ironically referred to a "dean of the highest stature" at Harvard[168] who belittled even a *faculty* resolution against ROTC:

> At Harvard, a dean of the highest stature wrote to President Pusey last February that major resolutions taken by his faculty regarding the ROTC were "very badly framed, gratuitously unpleasant and basically confused." He reviewed the President's options and recommended that the Faculty be asked to re-write its decision. He describes whatever dissent might arise from the faculty as "loud squeals." He expresses sorrow that the Harvard faculty obliged him to transmit "the quickly formulated product of public debate."[169]

In addition, Pusey's sole speech about protest in 1968 had suggested that students who sat-in against the Dow Chemical Corporation, manufacturer of napalm, weren't upset about the burning of children, but wanted "to tear down centers of higher learning and dance in the rubble."[170]

During the occupation of University Hall, a striker had lifted the dean's letter from the files and gave it to a reporter. As Novak noted, however, the press did not honor such a person: "Deplorable actions which observers daily expect from adults shock them in students."[171] He concluded: "The liberal, reasonable men who lead universities and who teach in them, must take swift steps to overcome their fey revulsion and to open their eyes to a world they are unaccustomed to seeing. Their tactics of close conversation; prolonged openness; hard, honest public debate; and a willingness to confess the partiality and relativity of one's own methods, are more proper to universities than swift, 15-minute assaults by club swinging police."[172]

As *Christianity and Crisis* also reports, in the spring of 1969, in Berkeley, hippies took over a vacant lot—previously used for a year for "unofficial" parking—and "planted flowers." The University of California then fenced it. Demonstrators tore down the fence. The University called in the police from nine counties and the National Guard. One student was murdered, a bystander blinded, and scores injured. Nonetheless, though met with "a spiral of terror," People's Park, as Mark Juergensmeyer, a Berkeley graduate student in political science, stressed, had been a creative, yet mild act: "an impromptu sign captured the mood: 'Welcome to Prague.' "[173]

As chapter 5 argues, we might imagine contrasting democratic authorities who would welcome civil disobedience. But the stonewalling of officials—even "progressive" ones—about murder outraged students:

> Hundreds of appeals were made to the Berkeley City Council but the Mayor . . . claimed the police were temporarily under control of the country sheriff, and the county supervisors could not discuss the matter since it had not been put on the weekly agenda. Local doctors, attempting to determine whether certain chemical repellents were harmful, were refused the list of ingredients by police and by the National Guard. A news reporter trying to trace the decision for the helicopter tear gas bombing, ended up speaking with a Brigadier General in Sacramento. The chairman of the Biology Department and a Nobel laureate physicist confronted the Governor, and together accused him of having made the campus a political pawn, and in the process destroy[ed] the University. Reagan called them "liars," and claimed that People's Park was a "phony issue" trumped up by radicals.[174]

As students manifested striking diversity and deliberativeness, public reasonableness declined among university administrators and other authorities: a telling example of *antidemocratic feedback*.[175]

Among politicians like Johnson, Humphrey, and Nixon, *Christianity and Crisis* notes the use of a formula—hailing "freedom of speech, *but* . . ."—to silence opposition. The war drove many to protest; Robert McAfee Brown urged "escalation of dissent."[176]

Yet though a majority of the American population opposed the war by 1968,[177] the United States withdrew only in 1975. Official denial, severe punishment, and the war's prolongation intensified resistance. In 1968, *Christianity and Crisis* published Phillip Berrigan's "Letter from a Baltimore Jail": "Our society can absorb almost anything, you know—nearly two decades of debacle in Southeast Asia, the fourth costliest in our history; self-immolations by war protestors (mostly unreported),[178] troop rebellions at several Army posts; war profiteering; credibility gap— almost anything."[179]

As another example of antidemocratic feedback, conscription menaced the young.[180] In "Justice and the Selective Service," Roger Shinn maintained that "some of the protestors complain specifically about irregularities of the draft. They are serious enough to be willing to jeopardize their own interests. That is, they are objecting to their own privileged status as students enabling them to avoid military service."[181]

Yet the trial of the "Boston Four" for instigating draft resistance focused on older movement advisers, notably William Sloane Coffin and Benjamin Spock. The judge suppressed "the main substantive issues":

> The defendants were not allowed to challenge the legality of the war under the United States Constitution, nor were they allowed to challenge its morality or legality in the context of the Nuremberg judgment. Two witnesses were brought by the defense to present a case for selective conscientious objection based upon the "just war" tradition . . . but neither was allowed to say a word about that subject. Yet this is relevant to the issues at stake for most of those who have resisted the draft might have become selective conscientious objectors if that had been a legal alternative.[182]

In a Socratic reflection, John C. Bennett wondered about the quality of laws that could underpin such a trial: "[W]hen our laws, whether through clear intent or through a one-sided or even forced technical interpretation of them cause our government to prosecute and seek to imprison some our most conscientious and respected citizens, there is great fault with the laws themselves."[183]

Six hundred of Coffin's colleagues signed a statement of support, Bennett noted. The Yale Corporation appointed Coffin university chaplain for an unlimited term: "The picture of our county as one in which its most creative and loved citizens are assassinated by private persons [1968 was marked by the murders of Martin Luther King Jr. and Robert F. Kennedy] would be supplemented by the picture of our nation as one in which the Government, through the legal process, imprisons others of its finest citizens."[184]

Underlining antidemocratic feedback, Tom Driver's "Near the Point of No Return" links this still undeclared war to violation of the Constitution: "The constitutional aspect of the Vietnam crisis has not occasioned much debate, although it contains a very grave threat to American democracy. History affords many examples of people who have lost freedom at home while 'defending' it abroad, either because their leaders deliberately employed foreign expenditures to achieve tyrannical power over the nation, or because of the undesired but inevitable stress that warfare places upon the civil liberties of those who wage it."[185] Bayard Rustin insisted on Vietnam's class consequences: "[T]he burden of carrying on the war [falls] on poor people in our ghettoes and in Appalachia."[186]

In "Our Schizoid Vietnam Policy," Niebuhr underlined the domestic harms of an imperial enterprise: "[W]e cannot conduct two wars at the same time, the one to eliminate the ghettoes in our urban centers, and the other to vindicate the right of self-determination in Asia. The first war is bound to suffer from our unrealistic imperial venture in Asia. We are a rich nation but not rich enough to combine a necessary domestic venture for racial justice with a foreign quixotic adventure."[187] The undercutting of the struggle for civil rights and the "War on Poverty"—each a striking harm of the Vietnam War—illustrates Niebuhr's earlier insights into the uses of "patriotism" against common-good-sustaining, moderate Social Democratic movements.[188]

In *Moral Man*, Niebuhr had noted that "the British socialists, who seemed for a time to be winning the middle class to a degree which the continental socialists found impossible, saw in the election of 1931 how the middle class will inevitably turn against socialism in a crisis when national patriotism can be arrayed against the policy of the working class."[189] Once again, Niebuhr asserted too easily the "inevitable" victory of patriotism. Nonetheless, "war scares" have characterized monarchical regimes faced with strong socialist movements, notably in Germany, even more than the United States.[190] As chapter 1 emphasizes, however, American appeals to nationalism and antiradical ideology combine with the antidemocratic feedback of international economic regimes to sustain oligarchic domination, despite parliamentary forms.

Ironically, by the 1960s, Niebuhr, the former radical, was less explicit than Morgenthau, or even some of his coauthors in *Christianity and Crisis*, on the class structure of American society.[191] For example, the former's "The President on the 'Arrogance of Power,'" insists that professors like himself have a greater "disinterestedness than powerful politicians." For LBJ had arrogantly "warn[ed] the scholars that their search for truth in the complexities of foreign affairs might be corrupted by 'prejudice.' The admonition was most revealing because it betrayed how unconscious the President was of the corruption of prejudice among powerful and responsible statesmen. Scholars are not saints, but they have a much greater degree of disinterestedness than powerful politicians."[192] Though the comparison of academics with politicians is apt, Niebuhr's argument, peculiarly for a realist, sees mainly the "good side"—the few, outspoken, tenured professors. In contrast to Morgenthau and his own earlier insights into professorial pride, he downplayed place-seeking, corruption, and a comparatively timid majority who only gradually came to sign moderate statements of protest.[193]

In "Beyond Discreet Silence," Harvey Cox stressed our "guilt for the wanton genocidal destruction of Vietnam."[194] In contrast, in an interview conducted by Ronald H. Stone, Niebuhr hoped that Nixon would make peace: "I think this was a tragic mistake in Vietnam, only an opposition party can correct the mistake. . . . peace can never be effected without a united front with the communists and the terrorist communists at that. So the peace we all desire will result in a Communist-united Vietnam."[195]

In 1965, a new, contributing editor to *Christianity and Crisis*, Vincent Harding, stressed the role of a racist "Anglo-Saxon tendency to pride," coupled with the ideology of "paranoid anti-communism," which sustained American ignorance of the long history of Vietnamese struggle against oppression:[196]

> History is very important here, whether it be the 2,500-year history of the Vietnamese people, the history of centuries of foreign oppression, the history of French failure (which we repeat step by escalated step), or our own tawdry, dishonest and bloody annals in Vietnam. . . . It [American ignorance] reveals our Anglo-Saxon tendency to fear and *pride* in the face of Asia, our lack of sympathy with the oppressed, our still *paranoid anti-communism*, our failure to face the *realities of the world of the have-nots*. It reveals our willingness to continue participating in neo-colonialist adventures and suggests that we have no honor to defend in Vietnam.
>   . . . The universal family [Christianity] must not kill for national honor or die for a negative creed.[197]

Harding articulated a sometimes buried, yet central moral theme of realism that defends just wars against aggression and scorns the idol of "national honor."[198]

John David McGuire's "Martin Luther King and Vietnam" notes the way "the war diverts funds and efforts from social programs at home, 'directing away money like some *demonic suction pump*.'" In a suggestion relevant to the contemporary Republican "revolution," King prophesied: "a nation that continues year after year to spend more money on military defense than on programs of social uplift is approaching spiritual death."[199] Harding also insisted on the mockery that the Vietnam War made of even "limited anti-poverty programs": American victims were temporarily fed so that they could fight in an unjust war in Asia. Prophetically, he underlined the link between sophisticated realism and democratic internationalism:

> Is it possible for us to continue watching with great lethargy as a minimal anti-poverty program is eviscerated by a war that rains death on the Asian poor? Do we sense no horror as our own unemployed are swept off the streets—like so much debris—into the furnace of a fight that promises them only free food, free clothes and death?
>
> Shall we go on living our lives and eating our meals as if no one had burned himself, no one had vomited to death under our gas, no one were fasting to the limit of life? Shall we dance our prosperous national jig as though God's in his heaven—or in his grave—and all's right with American action in Vietnam?[200]

To protest the persecution of the Vietnamese majority by U.S. client-regimes, saffron-robed Buddhist monks sat still in meditation in the fire of self-immolation—*akshobya*. Their sacrifice moved many Americans.

Like Morgenthau and other dissidents, King suffered antiradical stigmatization: "[I]t was one thing for King to carry on a human rights campaign mainly in the South and another to criticize his nation's actions overseas. When he began speaking out against this country's military role in Vietnam, he was called a traitor, attacked by friends and enemies, disparaged by President Johnson, and labeled a liar by J. Edgar Hoover, then head of the FBI."[201]

In 1969, Ronald Stone asked Niebuhr what the central differences were between anti-Vietnam realists—he and Morgenthau, for example—and the war's realist supporters. Stone suggested that perhaps "political realism is not immediately relevant to policy." In response, Niebuhr delineated realism's moral and empirical structure and prefigured a central theme of this book: "[L]et me be clear that realism means particularly one thing, that you establish the *common good* not purely by unselfishness but by the restraint of selfishness. That's realism. Now, on the basis of this realism, you have all kinds of contingent acts."[202] For this particular psychological formulation stresses the core moral insight that defines realism and rightly suggests that controversies over "contingent fact"—as well as, one might add, of social and psychological theory—motivate more complex ethical disputes. To combat moralism—the politics of good will—does not mean, as Niebuhr emphasized, to abandon ethics: "[R]ealism is applicable if you admit that justice, particularly collective justice, in any society depends not on pure love or on pure self-sacrifice but upon an equilibrium of power and perhaps on a conflict of power."[203]

In 1969, Niebuhr's "The King's Chapel and the King's Court" reaffirms the prophetic tradition of Amos.[204] In response, Nixon's aide,

John Ehrlichman, requested the FBI file on Niebuhr. As an invalid who could no longer write, Niebuhr continued to use the telephone to urge friends to protest the war.[205]

9. "OUR MILITARY-INDUSTRIAL ADDICTION": KENNAN'S 1984 REFORMULATION OF *AMERICAN DIPLOMACY*

The Vietnam War has proven almost as formative a political experience for contemporary scholars—and citizens—as the Spanish Civil War for World War II. Today, almost no academic realist affirms the reasonableness—or even the decency—of administration policies during Vietnam. Yet, with the exception of Morgenthau, Niebuhr, and Stanley Hoffmann, most were silent during the war itself.[206]

George Kennan, however, testified before the Fulbright committee in 1966.[207] While his criticism does not match Morgenthau's or Niebuhr's courageous opposition—Kennan is not, as a matter of temperament, a *public* dissident—he introduces other realist features of *moral criticism* of Vietnam. His critique changes the theme of *American Diplomacy*. Read by every diplomat-in-training and student of American foreign policy, Kennan's initial lectures, reprinted in that volume, had established the realist paradigm in American scholarship and the foreign service: a tendency to criticize *nongovernmental*—that is, democratic—opinion as the leading source of foreign-policy blundering. Even here, however, Kennan routinely rendered moral verdicts as part of his realism: "It may be true, and I suspect it is, that the mass of people everywhere are normally peace-loving and would accept many restraints and sacrifices in preference to the monstrous calamities of war."

He, thus, aimed to help ordinary people avoid such "monstrous calamities"; that initial, *ethical* concern is what motivates sophisticated realism. That realism is, once again, *a moral critique of moralisms*[208]: a less intelligent, non-power-oriented view, such as a pacifist or legalist one, so sophisticated realism maintains, will, most likely, lead to war, *and* on unfavorable, hideously wasteful terms.

Further, Kennan scathingly indicted publicists or ideological zealots who would "die" if they lost the public spotlight:

> But I also suspect that what purports to be public opinion in most countries that consider themselves to have popular government is often not really the consensus of feelings of the mass of people at all but rather the expression of the interests of special highly vocal minorities—politicians, commentators and publicity-seekers of all sorts: people who live by their ability to draw attention to themselves and die, like fish out of water, if they are compelled to remain silent.[209]

Still, the initial version of *American Diplomacy* stresses only the comparatively random, *nongovernmental* "politicians, commentators and publicity-seekers," whose ideas distort presidential policy. In contrast, the two post-Vietnam lectures emphasize *"our military-industrial addiction"*[210] and move toward Morgenthau (and Marxism). For instance, Kennan indicted a nuclear policy that threatens cities and millions of civilians.[211] Such a policy violates the moral, not just the prevailing legal, rules of international engagement: it menaces *innocents*.[212] But realism is the *moral* argument that aggression wantonly sacrifices the lives of one's fellow citizens, and only a state can resist it. In contrast, the prevailing, *official realist* but intellectually indefensible view that every state, large or small, must strive inexorably to aggrandize its power misunderstands the core realist critique of "idealist" views.

Kennan had long been aware of the problem he eventually named "our military-industrial addiction." As author of the famous "X" memorandum on containing the Soviet Union, he knew how fortuitous it was, as a policy adviser, to be heard. Thus, in 1948, President Truman, Secretary of the Air Force James Forrestal, and Secretary of State George Marshall exaggerated Soviet troop capabilities to trump up a "war scare" that the USSR would invade Western Europe.[213] Celebrating antidemocratic feedback, Truman's campaign adviser, Clark Clifford, hoped that this "scare" would bolster the former's standing in the polls: "The worse matters get . . . the more there is a sense of crisis. In times of crisis, the American citizen tends to back up his President."[214] War hysteria spurred not only congressional acceptance of the Marshall Plan, but also sanctioned a massive arms competition and the *first American peacetime draft*. In addition, as Goldfischer shows, it triggered the antiradical persecution of Oppenheimer and Allen Dulles, who had, unsuccessfully, proposed an alternative to a civilian-targeted, nuclear arms race.

In contrast, Kennan suggested that indigenous Communist victory in Czechoslovakia and a new pact with Finland did not indicate aggressive Soviet intentions toward Western Europe. Like Morgenthau, he, too, though in a less vigorous form, encountered "the King's Chapel":

> The greatest mystery of my own role in Washington in those years, as I see it today, was why so much attention was paid in certain instances . . . to what I had to say, and so little in others. The only answer could be that Washington's reactions were deeply subjective, influenced more *by domestic-political moods and institutional interests than by any theoretical considerations of our international position*. It was I who was naive—naive in the assumption that the mere statement on a single occasion of a sound analysis . . . had any appreciable effect on the *vast, turgid, self-centered, and highly emotional process* by which the views and reactions of official Washington were finally evolved.[215]

Responding to the unprecedented dangers of nuclear war, Kennan would introduce Gene Sharp's book (1986) on a nonviolent, civilian defense for Europe.

> It is inescapably clear that in the two great European wars of the century there were, in reality, no victors. These were, in effect, *simply senseless orgies of destruction*. The damages they inflicted, on the nominal victor, and the defeated alike, were far greater and more insidious than people were even aware of at the time, reaching as they did into the spiritual and genetic, as well as the purely military and physical realms. It is idle for the independent European country of this day to suppose that by entering into a new and even more horrible round of such carnage it could protect anything worth protecting.[216]

The *citizens* of each power, he maintained, had lost; civilian disaster would be the appropriate name for any future nuclear—or massive conventional—war. Ironically for a prototypical American realist, Kennan endorsed Sharp's proposal and suggested some additional, centralized, secret preparations for nonviolent resistance. Like Niebuhr, he moved away from Weber's realist claim about the centrality and necessity of state violence.[217] In dealing with the nature of power in a novel setting, Kennan demonstrated the contrasting imaginativeness of democratic realism. Further, as an adherent to violence in the case of some past, just wars (though note his reservations even about World War II),[218] he could still ally with Gandhi.

Nonetheless, Kennan warned that this proposal

> goes against the grain of all established strategic thinking. The professional military establishments will brush it off with incredulity, if not with contempt. It will arouse in many circles the same skepticism, and perhaps the same derision, that this reviewer brought down upon himself when he had the temerity to advance somewhat similar ideas in a widely publicized radio lecture delivered over the facilities of the BBC many years ago.[219]

As a sophisticated realist, Kennan underlined the difficulty of proposing new ideas to "power." Yet, endorsing Sharp, he foresaw the potential, society-transforming effects of disciplined nonviolence: "'With effort, risks, and cost, it is possible for Europeans—and all peoples—to make themselves politically indigestible to would-be tyrants.' Perhaps these words overstate the case; but if so, not greatly. One ends the reading of the book wondering whether, if this change of political philosophy were to take place, it might not have wider effects than just those that relate to the concepts of national security—whether many other things might not also change and, in the main, usefully so."[220]

Deepening the democratic insights of Morgenthau and Niebuhr, Kennan thus justified internal, nonviolent resistance. As chapter 5 argues, even a less oligarchic "democracy" than the United States would need to tolerate wider civil disobedience to raise basic issues unaddressed in elections. A policy of nonviolent civilian defense in interstate relations, as Kennan suggested, might encourage militant, nonmurderous forms of domestic protest: a novel *democratic feedback* of international affairs.

For Kennan, as the 1984 version of *American Diplomacy* emphasizes, the American government's conduct of the Vietnam War reflected an irrational, anticommunist ideology.[221] Morgenthau saw sustained political interests behind this "bipartisan" policy. Hence, he endorsed fundamental political change. Kennan, however, made this ideology's roots in the structure of U.S. politics explicit. It imputes to electoral competitors a "softness" on "foreign" radicalism, which is responsible for all "our" problems (or at least the central ones). More than any economic stake, this elite *political* interest helps to explain the otherwise startling role of anticommunist or antiradical ideology in American elections.[222] Thus, in 1960, a Democrat, Kennedy, ironically, beat the notorious anticommunist, Nixon, by making false claims about Soviet missile superiority. Nixon subsequently defeated Humphrey, and Reagan triumphed over Carter, by means of similar antiradical belittling.[223] A certain sexism—the fabrication of one's opponent as less of a "man"—also plays a role here. Ironically, such antiradical and sexist ideologies are of service to the ruling class not only as a weapon against ordinary people, but also at the expense of particular candidates who have dutifully striven to uphold its interests.

As Kennan put it,

> These attacks [claims that the United States "lost China"] were an early part of the wave of anti-communist hysteria which was to become known as McCarthyism—an episode of our public life so disgraceful that one blushes today to think about it.[224] . . . Because of the failure of successive administrations to challenge head-on these outrageous imputations, these administrations repeatedly became the victims of them. And so it was in Vietnam. Not only did no administration feel that it could afford to be seen as unwilling to make the effort to oppose a communist takeover in Vietnam, but no administration, down to that of Mr. Nixon, having once engaged itself in such an effort and having been obliged to recognize that the effort was hopeless, dared to try to extract itself from the involvement at all, for fear of being pilloried by the silly charge that it had "lost Vietnam."[225]

This constriction of political alternatives through antiradical ideology, notably the role of such ideas in shaping electoral competition even between moderates and sustaining, across parties and administrations, an aggressive, losing war strikingly exemplifies the antidemocratic feedback of international politics.

Now, Kennan did not participate in the extracongressional, antiwar movement and sometimes attacked it.[226] Buoyed by this movement, however, his argument also reveals new confidence in political leaders who could challenge popular stereotypes rather than become "victims of them." Furthermore, contrary to his thematic warnings against "popular" as opposed to "professional diplomacy," his account betrays fresh insight into the rationality of the American people. Given forthright leadership, a popular movement could grasp a common good. It would see through the initially plausible, but false claims of antiradical ideology.[227] In this insight, Kennan's realism resembles Morgenthau's and Niebuhr's. For realists as well as radicals, the experience of Vietnam protest underlines the importance of popular resistance—ultimately, of democratic internationalism from below—to tyrannical, ruling class wars.

10. SOCIAL SCIENCE AND MORAL ARGUMENT

International-relations theory during the Cold War mistakenly emphasized science at the expense of ethics; it also sought a misguided reduction of a common good to *power* and denied the *potential* peacefulness of democracy. It occasionally apologized for criminal interventions and caricatured realist moderation, the latter's aversion to hunger for power. This chapter, however, restores to sophisticated realism contrasting critical, democratic emphases. The latter realism stresses a *limited* common good—at least in the sense of defending the lives of citizens against aggression—and, thus, affirms a moral, rather than solely historical, conception of democracy. That conception also values the liberty of each citizen.

As Niebuhr recognized, sophisticated realism *starts* from underlying ethical judgments about a common good. It then provides a comparatively elaborate, empirical—and social theoretical—critique of the oligarchic structure of contemporary "democracies" that can lead to unjust, even genocidal wars.[228] Its indictment of such tyrannical wars is a *complex* moral and political judgment that rests both on core, initial moral standards—concealed by official realism—and subsequent empirical and theoretical argument. Controversies over the latter, which motivate complex political and ethical differences, have, however, obscured underlying agreement on the former. Thus, chapters 1 and 2 newly illustrate a central theme of *Democratic Individuality* and prefigure the theory of deliberative democracy in chapter 5.[229]

In addition, as empiricists rightly note, social science should not be swayed by prejudice. Yet, whatever turns out to be true in the social sciences will have an impact on the kind of society one can hope—decently—to achieve. Suppose, for instance, that contemporary criticisms of state-centered regimes prove to be true, and that no alternative, decentralized socialism or communism is possible. Then, one could hope, at most, to mitigate the harms of capitalism.[230] Thus, the empiricist desire to create a "value-free" social science is an illusion and leads, in practice, to bizarre results (for instance, "sanctioning" Kissingerian service to unjust power as opposed to Morgenthau's, Niebuhr's, or Kennan's moral critique).[231]

Official realism also ignores a central feature of contemporary philosophy of science, underlined by scientific realists[232] and accepted by today's empiricists and neo-Kantians. They concur that scientific advance occurs only through sophisticated contrasts of contending theories, not through an attempt to "prove" a single theory against the "evidence" or reduce otherwise diverse opponents to a unique straw "man," for instance, "idealism." Thus, as my internal critique of realism and neorealism has shown, sophisticated realism needs to contrast itself to a long-standing, but long-ignored alternative, democratic internationalism. Yet, ironically, most American realists have made an anomaly of democracy, just as they have failed to learn from the initial unpopularity, in elite circles, of Morgenthau's critique of Vietnam. They have even forgotten Morgenthau's endorsement, in *Politics among Nations*, of Kant's thesis about the *potential* peacefulness of democracies. But Morgenthau's claim requires a reformulation of today's central debate between realism and idealism, since it appears that a sophisticated realist may be a *contingent* idealist.[233] It stresses the moral insight that drives Morgenthau's praise of the *substance* of democratic power. If this argument is right, official realism is not scientific.

Even in fields distant from international relations, however, truth, as Morgenthau emphasized, is usually far removed from power. Further, hierarchical, academic power is far from congenial to a morally clear, well-formulated social science. This book joins Morgenthau and others in resisting unjust policies. It hopes to restore clarity about international politics so that, in an era of spurious "value-free social science," similar wars and campaigns of public vilification will prove harder for an elite—despite initial academic support—to entertain.

TABLE 4
Morgenthau's, Niebuhr's, and Kennan's Realisms and
Democratic Internationalism

	Realist Thesis	Democratic Internationalist Critique or Thesis
	Morgenthau's Misguided Universal-Domination Paradigm	
Thesis 1	Every regime aims, if possible, to achieve preeminent power internationally—"power is the domination of man over man," in Morgenthau's famous phrase	This version of "realism" implausibly excludes any notion of a common good or empowerment nationally or internationally
Thesis 2	It uses incentives to draw all internal forces, human beings as well as economic and military capacity, into its orbit	
Thesis 3	Human beings aim to dominate and act selfishly to do so (Morgenthau attributes a drive to dominate to human nature)	
Thesis 4	Human beings thus become leaders in aggrandizing projects, or, to protect themselves, (selfish) servants of power. The latter give sound advice only from the standpoint of furthering *domineering* interests	
Thesis 5	Nationalism will hold unchallenged sway so long as a power is dominant	
	Morgenthau's Conflicting Democratic Paradigm	
Thesis 1	Power may be "disciplined by moral ends and controlled by constitutional safeguards"	Same
Thesis 2	Tyrannical power, even in a democracy, may be a "coherent system of irrationality," violating a common good for citizens and the *substance* of a regime's interest	

TABLE 4 *(cont.)*

	Realist Thesis	Democratic Internationalist Critique or Thesis
	Morgenthau's Conflicting Democratic Paradigm	
Thesis 3	A common good includes at least preventing aggression and defending citizens' lives, even in capitalist societies that are otherwise exploitative. Such a good may conflict with prevailing nationalism	
Thesis 4	Moderation or humility are leading political virtues	
Thesis 5	Realists are disinterested truth-seekers, not clever sycophants	
	Morgenthau's Democratic Critique of U.S. Aggression in Vietnam	
Thesis 1	The U.S. government waged war against a civilian, peasant, nationalist revolution. It therefore betrayed its democratic principles and risked genocide	Concurs with theses 1–5, highlights the harms to a common good of theses 2–4, and underlines the role of democratic internationalism from below in defeating genocidal war. It differs, however, on whether revolution, if necessary, is possible (thesis 6)
Thesis 2	It accused critics of treason as in "Project Morgenthau" (the *antidemocratic feedback of global rivalry* thesis	
Thesis 3	It sought to infiltrate and destroy pluralism and resistance, committing the "totalitarian" error of reducing freely-given loyalty to manipulation and semblance—the CIA in the NSA (the *external enemies, constriction of political options*)	
Thesis 4	Teachers are, by and large, no longer committed to truth. An "academic-political(-media) complex" now reinforces the "military-industrial complex" (one might also call claims 2–4 the *public-corruption thesis*)	

continues on next page

TABLE 4 (*cont.*)

	Realist Thesis	Democratic Internationalist Critique or Thesis

Morgenthau's Democratic Critique of U.S. Aggression in Vietnam

Thesis 5	Nonetheless, a mass, democratic, antiwar movement from below, not just sound individual advice ("professional diplomacy"), was needed to drive American power from Vietnam (*democratic internationalism*)	
Thesis 6	The real relations of power in the United States sustain oligarchy and make revolution in principle desirable, though not, in practice, possible	

Morgenthau's Misinterpretation of Aristotle

Thesis 1	"Man" strives to dominate other "men" and is, in this sense, a "political animal."	Morgenthau mistakenly maintains that "man is a *tyrannical animal*." But "man is a *political animal*," one capable of creating forms of a *common good* as well as tyranny (the rule of particular interests)
Thesis 2	The fact, Aristotle suggests, that tyrants seek excessive power and wealth, not merely to escape poverty, underlines this claim	

Morgenthau's Mistaken Celebration of Lincoln's Statism

Thesis 1	State defense against external aggression is a good	Defense against aggression requires a domestic common good. Slavery is inconsistent with such a good; thesis 2 does not follow from thesis 1. Lincoln's defense of the Union is justified only insofar as the North waged an *abolitionist* war
Thesis 2	Lincoln's prudence in preserving the American nation overrides the evil of slavery	

Niebuhr's Prophetic Realism

Thesis 1	While individuals are sometimes capable of moral conduct, especially those characterized by "a broken spirit and a contrite heart," collective organizations, especially classes and states, (mainly) are not	Same, although some advocates of internationalism would extend the argument for nonviolent resistance universally

TABLE 4 (*cont.*)

	Realist Thesis	Democratic Internationalist Critique or Thesis
	Niebuhr's Prophetic Realism	
Thesis 2	For (sophisticated) realism, oppression justifies resistance and fundamental change, say, for workers in general, blacks in the United States, and the colonized in India	
Thesis 3	Gandhi's leadership exemplifies admirable possibilities of spirit in combating the realities of political "nature" (Churchill)	
Thesis 4	Ideological "illusions," however, arise from pride. They mislead both the powerful and the oppressed	
Thesis 5	Sometimes, as in the case of Nazism, violent opposition to oppression is necessary. In both international and domestic relations, (exploitative) force must be opposed by (nonviolent or violent) force from below	
Thesis 6	Capitalist powers can use interventions or wars to bolster "patriotism" at home and divide workers both among themselves and from other oppressed groups (the *antidemocratic feedback* of international politics)	
Thesis 7	As in the case of anticolonial movements or antiracism in the United States, "things that are not" ultimately overturn the "things that are"	
	Niebuhr's Account of Lincoln's Mercy	
Thesis 1	Slavery is a great evil	Same
Thesis 2	Nonetheless, even in the Civil War, both sides displayed pride, or, in Niebuhr's terms, "idealism"	

continues on next page

TABLE 4 (*cont.*)

	Realist Thesis	Democratic Internationalist Critique or Thesis
	Niebuhr's Account of Lincoln's Mercy	
Thesis 3	Recognition of the humanity of one's opponents and mercy, where possible, are central political virtues	
Thesis 4	The possibilities of political reconciliation and individual healing stem from "a broken spirit and a contrite heart"	
	Niebuhr's Critique of the Vietnam War	
Thesis 1	Détente was possible between the United States and the USSR. Further, the Sino-Soviet split underlined cleavages in a superficially "monolithic Communist bloc"	Same, though with a sharper class characterization of systemic American intervention
Thesis 2	Contrary to the Johnson administration, a civil war divided South Vietnam	
Thesis 3	The use of such weapons as napalm, indiscriminate military sweeps against civilians, and resettlement of peasants in "strategic hamlets" made the U.S. effort a war against a people. Protection of the elite of a Catholic minority while persecuting Buddhists exacerbated these harms	
Thesis 4	*Antidemocratic feedback* from the war—government belittling of dissent, the corruption through covert CIA activity of the National Student Association, faculty professionalism, unions, and the media, the attempted crushing of selective conscientious resistance, the disproportionate drafting of poor people and especially blacks, and diversion from civil rights	

TABLE 4 (*cont.*)

Realist Thesis	Democratic Internationalist Critique or Thesis
Niebuhr's Critique of the Vietnam War	

	Realist Thesis	
	and antipoverty programs—drove most Americans into opposition (*democratic internationalism*)	
Thesis 5	Prophetic realism affirms just *counter*power: an antiwar movement	

Niebuhr's Account of the Moral and Empirical Structure of Realist Argument	

Thesis 1	A common good exists in any society, though one shaped by human selfishness, not individual "goodness"	Niebuhr's first thesis fuses a controversial psychological insight with an uncontroversial moral one. The reign of selfishness and the possibility of transcendence is a further empirical and social theoretical thesis, limiting the application of moral concurrence on, say, the good of defending the lives of citizens against aggression. Thus, we might restate thesis 1: a common good exists in any society and thesis 2: human selfishness as well as great-power rivalry limit the realization of such a good, both domestically and internationally. We might then offer an internationalist (as well as realist) thesis 3: disagreement about empirical questions shapes complex ethical disputes
Thesis 2	Disagreements over "contingent facts," however, motivate complex political and moral clashes	

Kennan's 1984 Critique of Vietnam	

Thesis 1	"Professional diplomacy" comprehends great-power rivalry; "popular diplomacy" is dangerous	Something near a ruling class and a harmful ideology that serves its interests, across administrations and parties, overrides the national interest and renders "professional diplomacy" ineffective. Realist thesis 2 contradicts thesis 1

continues on next page

TABLE 4 (*cont.*)

	Realist Thesis	Democratic Internationalist Critique or Thesis
	Kennan's 1984 Critique of Vietnam	
Thesis 2	In contemporary America, however, a "military-industrial addiction" has emerged. That addiction, coupled with the special role of anticommunist ideology in electoral politics, maintained destructive, losing efforts like Vietnam or initiated the 1948 "war scare" and an escalating military buildup, across administrations and parties	Only democratic movements from below—a form of "popular diplomacy"—can defend the national interest

	Kennan's and Sharp's Internationalist Rejection of Statist Violence	
	Statist Thesis	Kennan's and Sharp's Thesis
Thesis 1	Interstate relations are governed by the threat of force. Following Weber, a state controls the monopoly of the legitimate use of violence in a territory. That force is at the disposal of a military and political elite	In the nuclear age, Europe is likely to be sacrificed to the interests of other powers
Thesis 2		To avoid nuclear carnage, European regimes should rely on nonviolent, civilian defense against aggression. This claim highlights a democratic aspect of defense: the motivation and non-violent resistance of citizens. It thus conflicts with a seemingly defining characteristic of realism and affirms democratic internationalism

Part Two

FORGOTTEN SOURCES OF

DEMOCRATIC INTERNATIONALISM

CHAPTER THREE

"Workers of the World, Unite!": The Possibility of Democratic Feedback

> I have lived for the last month—and I think that every man in Massachusetts capable of the sentiment of patriotism must have had a similar experience—with the sense of having suffered a vast and indefinite loss. I did not know at first what ailed me. At last it occurred to me that what I had lost was a country. I had never respected the government near to which I lived, but I had foolishly thought that I might manage to live here, minding my private affairs, and forget it. . . . I feel that my investment in life here is worth many per cent less since Massachusetts last deliberately sent back an innocent man, Anthony Burns, to slavery.
> (Henry David Thoreau, "Slavery in Massachusetts")

> Labor cannot be free in the white skin where in the black it is branded.
>   (Karl Marx, *Capital*)

> No more tradition's chains shall bind us
> Arise ye slaves no more in thrall . . .
> let each stand in her place
> The international working class
> shall be the human race.
>   (Eugene Pottier, "The Internationale")

1. GLOBAL INEQUALITIES AND DOMESTIC REPRESSION

Part 1 provided an internal critique of the leading forms of American neorealism and realism and showed that, properly stated, these views lead to democratic internationalism. But in today's universities, internationalism is not a well-recognized position. Further, while an only recently rediscovered Kant foresaw citizen resistance to unjust, interdemocratic wars, a forgotten Marx offers a theory of internationalism, one central to his political activity and that of subsequent radical movements. On his account, democratic and socialist movements—in Marx's time, the French Revolution, Chartism, the Paris Commune, and the like— stimulate rebellion by the oppressed in other countries: *a distinctive democratic feedback of international politics*.[1] Contrary to neorealism, such feedback—variably—inspires movements within each country for a common good. Marx's argument and practice embody novel possibilities of solidarity, defending a common good within each society *and* internationally.

Now, across dramatic changes, Marx's theory maintains that imperialism harms not only the colonized, but also the workers—and other oppressed people—in the colonial power. But the dominant viewpoint in American universities—pluralism—doubts that the least advantaged have common interests across group boundaries, and thus, ironically, that genuine democracy—which upholds the basic rights of each person, and, thus, members of minorities—is possible.[2] For pluralists, Marx's conclusion is surprising. But if Marx's argument on the international as well as domestic impact of democratic and socialist example is, as I will show, with minor fleshing out, straightforward, its unexpectedness is, as a Popperian might stress, a scientific virtue. In chapter 5, I defend a refined pluralism that incorporates this internationalist insight.

Many scholars still adhere, however, sometimes inadvertently, to an economic determinist notion of Marx's politics, according to which the development of capitalist productive forces in each country, taken separately, will inevitably produce proletarian revolution with minimal organizing.[3] For instance, in Hunt, Avineri, and Cohen,[4] this view overlooks the central role of politics in Marx's social theory and especially his advocacy of internationalism—the hallmark of his political activity—and the dramatic effect of the global setting on radical revolt in each country.[5] It misses the centrality of democratic as well as antidemocratic feedback in Marx's general theory, historical explanations, and political strategies.

Now Marx sought to further the mass rebellions of "the present" (democratic revolutions, unions). Yet, dialectically, he argued that communists must simultaneously take care of the "future" of the movement: advocate the overall politics, especially internationalism, abolition of private property, and, after 1871, formation of a state modeled on the Paris Commune, which would lead to proletarian revolution.[6]

Marx's defense of internationalism drew fierce attacks. For his support of the Paris insurrection of June 1848, Cologne's leading newspaper, *Die Kölnische Zeitung*, stigmatized his journal, *Die Neue Rheinische Zeitung*, as an organ of "red riot." As a result, Marx lost half the financial backing for his paper. His support for the Paris Commune, he wrote happily to Kugelmann in 1871, had made "the devil of a noise, and I have the honour to be at this moment the best calumniated and most menaced man in London."[7]

This chapter shows that the international dimension of Marx's theory and activity strengthens *democratic internationalism*: an international-ism from below that defends liberal values about institutions, and radical values as a subset of liberal values. Democratic internationalism affirms those arrangements that further the individuality of each person;[8] it fo-cuses on the wellbeing—or capabilities[9]—of each. To affirm a common good, internationalism not only opposes unjust or imperial wars, but also seeks to further justice in global distribution. I first examine Marx's argu-ments and then explore unexpected, contemporary redistributive possi-bilities, including those created by opposition to neocolonial wars, illus-trative of Marx's theory.

Today, the problem of international justice is apparent in the contrast between life expectancy in rich capitalist nations and nations so poor that large numbers verge on starvation. As the introduction underlines, individuals born in advanced capitalist regimes live on average nearly two lifetimes (death age: seventy-one) compared to each life (death age: forty-two) lived in the less developed countries. In addition, during the United Nations' first "Development Decade," inequality of income shares, within poor countries, worsened.[10] This situation has caused phi-losophers such as Peter Singer to advocate a natural duty of individuals in rich nations to help the starving elsewhere. Others, such as Charles Beitz, stressing international relations of dependency, have applied Rawls's dif-ference principle to international affairs. Yet the actual social and politi-cal connections between at least the elites in the rich countries and the citizens of the poor countries offer little hope that such obligations will be fulfilled. If the conventional dichotomy between rich and poor nations holds, most citizens of the rich nations should benefit from the impover-ishment of most citizens in poor ones. The more accurately one depicts exploitative international relations of dependency, the weightier the moral obligations of citizens of the rich nations to those of the poor will appear. But as social theory becomes more specific and empirical, the less likely these obligations are to be honored.[11] That conclusion, as chap-ter 1 suggests, also follows from a morally well stated dependency theory as well as Keohane's critique of contemporary international economic "cooperation."

In contrast, Marx maintained that the interests of most people—at least those of working people—in the rich nations coincide with those of the majority of people in the poor nations, and not with the elite of their own state. For this elite benefits from international oppression and utilizes that setting—for instance, through the making of "enemies"—to justify repression at home: the antidemocratic-feedback effect. In this context, a Marxian argument envisions important alternative strategies.

2. MARX'S FIRST VERSION OF DEMOCRATIC INTERNATIONALISM: THE REVOLUTION OF 1848

In the *Communist Manifesto*, Marx argued that advocacy of internationalism distinguishes communists from other working-class parties: "In the national struggles of the proletarians of the different countries, they point out and bring to the front the common interests of the entire proletariat independently of all nationality."[12]

In the *Manifesto*'s opening sections, Marx drew a general picture of the capitalist transformation of the world that he thought might lead to "common interests" among workers of different nationalities. As capitalism develops within nations, it produces proletarians who "know no country." Concentrated in large factories, these people have only their own labor-power to sell. As capitalism expands internationally, it "batters down all Chinese walls" with the low prices of its commodities, seeks out raw materials in the "remotest zones," and, finally, "creates a world after its own image."[13] Yet the *Manifesto* does not fully explain either the nature of these common interests or how radicals may pursue them in different situations.

In other writings, Marx argued that proletarians have common enemies. He saw the suppression of the Paris Commune of 1871 as a leading example. In that case, fresh from fighting a war against each other, the French and Prussian ruling classes put aside their differences and joined to crush a revolutionary government—the antidemocratic feedback of international politics. In Marx's critique of German Social Democracy's *Gotha Program* (1875), he attacked the influence of Lassallean patriotism, which had de-emphasized the bourgeoisie's hostility toward a proletarian movement as well as the former's international connections: "Not a word . . . about the international functions of the German working class! And it is thus [on the basis of a political development limited to Germany alone] that it is to challenge its own bourgeoisie—which is already linked up in brotherhood against it with the bourgeoisie of all other countries."[14]

These common enemies, irrespective of domestic regime structure, create a common interest in international unity among proletarians of different countries. Marx innovatively urged mutual support—the novel instigation of what I call *democratic feedback*—among radical working-class or "red republican" movements. For instance, he and his followers in

Germany backed the Paris insurrection of June 1848, and the IWA supported the Paris Commune of 1871. Such solidarity did not depend upon an advanced level of productive forces within countries, let alone a great degree of capitalist penetration into a foreign economy. Rather, it rested on a political factor—the likelihood of a common response by European bourgeoisies to a revolutionary threat affecting any one of them. Further, the structure—parliamentary or monarchical—of diverse capitalist regimes was not a decisive factor; the English parliament and the czar joined to oppose both democracy and communism. Radicals could only counter this common threat, Marx emphasized, by breaking down all divisions—internal and international—among the working classes. As Marx's "General Rules of the IWA" state, "[A]ll efforts aiming at that great end [the economic emancipation of the working class] have hitherto failed from want of solidarity between the manifold divisions of labor in each country, and from the absence of a fraternal bond of union between the working classes of the different countries."[15]

The previous argument clarifies the common interests between socialist movements, but how would these interests be pursued in differing situations? The fourth section of the *Manifesto* attempts to apply Marx's general theory, sketched in the opening section, to the specific, international setting of 1848. Here he advocates mutual support, not only among incipient communist movements but also among democratic movements (taken together, these positions comprise a *radical* version of democratic internationalism). The *Manifesto*'s opening arguments stress the rapid breakdown of national boundaries and the dissolution of national attachments, while the later section emphasizes the pivotal role of "national emancipation" in Poland in 1848. Though the first sections picture the dispossession of small property-holding classes, particularly the peasantry, and characterize these classes as "reactionary *insofar* as they try to hold back the wheel of history," the latter supports Polish "agrarian revolution."[16] How did Marx reconcile these seemingly paradoxical conclusions?

To be applied in a particular historical situation, Marx's theory requires auxiliary statements that specify the international as well as the national historical context.[17] Attention to the political setting in 1848 will clarify Marx's reasoning. Democratic revolutions loomed in many Europeans countries, including Germany and Poland. These mutually strengthening revolutions endangered the absolutist powers, especially czarist Russia. Parliamentary capitalism in England also feared the shock of European democratic revolution—once again, *democratic feedback*—which would spur on its own working-class movement, Chartism, just then at its peak. Since Chartism advocated universal suffrage for (male) workers,[18] participants in the movement strongly sympathized with democracy on the Continent. While contemporary liberal politicians spoke of democracy, only radicals acted to achieve *liberal* democratic internationalism: the solidarity of republican or democratic political movements. Thus, successful revolutions in Europe would also strengthen Chartism in England.

A political link, Marx argued, existed between the interests of different oppressive social and political systems—czarist Russia, the most backward, and capitalist, parliamentary England, the most advanced; they would attempt to crush the incipient European democratic revolution. Correspondingly, democratic and proletarian, "social republican" movements would have to unite in order to succeed.[19] In this context, Poland, previously divided between Prussia and Russia, would play a pivotal role. An independence movement there would cause revolutionary tremors throughout Europe.

In 1792, the duke of Brunswick's threat to raze revolutionary Paris triggered the Jacobin Convention's *levée en masse*.[20] For Marx, renewed democratic revolution in 1848 might, similarly, result in a counterrevolutionary invasion. The latter would force democratic movements to mobilize their populations for war against absolutism and parliamentary capitalism. If these movements internally weakened or failed to support each other internationally, their common enemies could divide and crush them one by one. The latter experience of *antidemocratic feedback*, more or less, actually occurred.

Marx's analysis of the need for democratic internationalism in 1848 rested on a specific global configuration of reactionary powers—a setting of war and revolution—and not mainly on the development of productive forces, or on capitalist crisis, in a single country. In this sense, his argument foreshadows the development of successful revolutions in the twentieth century in the context of world war. The Chinese and Vietnamese Communist movements against Japanese imperialism during World War II provide the closest parallel to what Marx hoped radicals could achieve in 1848.[21]

As Marx contended, wars of conquest waged by monarchies play a vital role in maintaining their domination at home.[22] *Antidemocratic feedback* is thus, for Marx as well as Hegel, a decisive mechanism for maintaining power in monarchical or authoritarian regimes, not just in parliamentary ones. As Hegel identified the decisive, initiatory role for the slave in the freeing of the master, so he articulated an emancipatory dialectic in which the struggle of the colonized would also, ultimately, liberate the colonizer. Thus, he admired the Venezuelan independence movement against Spain in the early nineteenth century.[23]

To stem revolution at home in 1848, Marx noted, the Prussian government intervened against democratic movements in Poland, Czechoslovakia, and Italy. To divert the revolutionary movement, it sought to rouse patriotic fervor. At the same time, Prussia built up its army to crush democracy.

Marx named these striking examples of antidemocratic feedback "*wars of restoration.*" Comparable to later cases, the Prussian government sought to legitimize such expeditions with a wave of racist propaganda, in the words of chapter 1, to make their objects of conquest "enemies." Through *Die Neue Rheinische Zeitung*, Marx and Engels waged an unremitting campaign against Prussian justifications for expansion. As Engels argued, "a nation which throughout its history allowed itself to be used as a tool of oppression against all other nations must first of all [proclaim] the freedom of the nations hitherto suppressed by her."[24] Without opposing Prussian war efforts, Marx and Engels maintained, the German democratic movement could not defeat absolutism.

3. THE HEROISM OF THE ENGLISH WORKERS: ABOLITION VERSUS COTTON

English working-class support for the antislavery cause in the American Civil War provides another arresting example of the role of war in Marx's thinking on internationalism, of the democratic feedback of one emancipatory movement on others, and of the difficult choices faced by workers in defending "the common interests of the proletariat independently of all nationality."

In *Democratic Individuality*, I argued that the abolition of slavery underpins *liberal* political theory; Montesquieu's satire of the slave trade marks the emergence of mature liberalism.[25] But theorists who were only partially liberal, such as Locke, and supposedly liberal regimes, like the United States, justified or practiced slavery. In *Emancipation and Independence*, I show how Britain freed blacks who fought for it, nearly defeated the American Revolution, and crippled the latter's democratic dynamism. But imperial Britain was only an emancipator where such policies supported its otherwise exploitative interests. During the American Civil War, for example, its rulers sided with the South. In contrast to earlier monarchical emancipation, only English workers, in a paradigm of liberal and radical democratic internationalism, fought for abolition. Their solidarity with slaves underlines the feedback of robust democratic politics in one country—American abolitionism, black revolt and escape—on citizens in others. This case also highlights the way genuine radicalism often fulfills the promises of liberalism.

Yet, ironically, even after 135 years, the American regime little honors John Brown, leader of a militant, multiracial movement against slavery whose hanging triggered the Civil War. At rallies following Brown's capture at Harper's Ferry, however, proponents of democratic individuality like Thoreau and Emerson extolled him as a modern hero. In 1881, invoking Brown as a "great soul," Frederick Douglass said: "It [his hatred of slavery] was as the burning sun to my taper light; mine was bounded by time, his stretched away to the boundless shores of eternity."[26]

Marx saw the antislavery movement in the United States and the struggle to abolish serfdom in Russia as the two decisive political developments of the 1860s. At that time, the United States possessed "the only popular government" in existence.[27] If the South successfully seceded, he prophesied, it would impose slavery in the border states, and, in a paradigm of antidemocratic feedback, influence the entire future development of North America and Europe in a profoundly conservative direction:

> In the northern states, where Negro slavery is unworkable in practice, the white working class would be gradually depressed to the level of helotry. This would be in accord with the loudly proclaimed principle that only certain races are capable of freedom, and that as in the South real labor is the lot of the Negro, so in the North it is the lot of the German and the Irishman, or their direct descendants.[28]

The defeat of slavery would, however, strengthen the working-class movement throughout the country, potentially unite black and white laborers, and give an important impetus to a revived working-class movement internationally (democratic feedback). Within the United States, Marx maintained, "labor cannot be free in the white skin where in the black it is branded."[29] Abolition would, he insisted, trigger further radical developments. The historic struggle of American workers for shorter working hours culminating in 1886, as well as the existence and protracted, violent suppression of Reconstruction, reveal these potentials.[30]

During the Civil War, due to the need for American cotton in textile production, the English capitalists and press favored the South. Until the North took two Confederate diplomats, Slidell and Mason, from the British ship HMS *Trent*, workers remained largely silent. A major rift then emerged between the United States and Britain, where proslavery agitation intensified.

If English workers had followed their narrowly conceived economic interests, they might have become prowar. In a newspaper dispatch, Marx vividly depicted their misery:

> The distress among workers in the northern manufacturing districts, motivated by the blockade of the slave states which closed the factories or shortened the working hours, is unbelievable and increases daily. The other portions of the working class do not suffer to the same degree, but they suffer keenly from the repercussion of the crisis in the cotton industry on other

branches of industry, from the reduction of exports of their own products to North America as result of the Morrill Tariff and the destruction of exports from the southern United States as a result of the blockade. At the present moment, English intervention in America has therefore become a bread and butter question for the working class.

Despite the ruling class's proslavery political campaign as well as economic distress, however, *no* pressure to go to war emerged from below. Moreover, workers held mass, antiwar meetings in Manchester, Sheffield, and London. Marx cited the resolution passed by the London gathering:

> Therefore this meeting considers it the particular duty of the workers since they are not represented in the senate of the nation, to declare their sympathy with the United States in its gigantic struggle for maintenance of the Union, to denounce the base dishonesty and advocacy of slaveholding indulged in by the *Times* and kindred aristocratic journals, to express themselves most emphatically in favor of a policy of strictest nonintervention in the affairs of the United States, and to manifest the warmest sympathy with the endeavors of the Abolitionists to bring about a final solution to the question of slavery.[31]

Though some prowar sentiment existed in the English labor movement, abolitionism predominated. As Royden Harrison notes, "The Sheffield workmen told [the union leader] Roebuck—who wanted to recognize the South: 'Never! We should have a Civil War in England.'"[32]

In his 1864 "Inaugural Address of the IWA," Marx maintained, "It was not the wisdom of the ruling classes but the heroic resistance to their criminal folly by the working classes of England that saved the West of Europe from plunging headlong into an infamous crusade for the perpetuation and propagation of slavery on the other side of the Atlantic."[33]

This example raises two theoretical issues. First, internationalism involves a conflict of interest, and, thus, a choice for the worker. On the one hand, the English textile laborer who supported the war against slavery and the U.S. blockade of the South suffered for it, to some extent. Economic considerations gave him—or her—at least some interest in war (though slavery is a paradigm of oppression, comparable economic losses, however, hardly rule out strikes of solidarity, as, for instance, when one group of workers, at a giant corporation, walks out to support another).[34] On the other hand, through antidemocratic feedback, the international impact of a victorious slave republic would worsen a laborer's own economic and social conditions. In addition, the English government would conscript him—or her relatives—to fight in any war effort. Therefore, Marx argued, the worker's main interest lay in opposing slavery. His decision for the "common interest" against the narrow interest rested on understanding the war's larger political and economic consequences.

Given this conflict of interests affecting workers, however, no guarantee existed that democratic internationalism would win out. Only a political movement could defend the long-range, common interests of the proletariat—democratic feedback—against short-lived economic gain.

Second, under exceptional circumstances, internationalism may lead to redistribution of the means of production. The workers prevented British intervention to aid an emblematic unjust cause and, thus, supported a fundamental redistribution in the South as former slaves gained property in their own persons. English resistance defended a core *liberal* insight. Marx's theory affirms redistribution of the means of production through democratic as well as communist revolution. Within a given mode of production, however, he believed that no basic redistribution could occur.[35]

4. INTERNATIONAL STRIKE SUPPORT

As another important example of internationalism, Marx built the IWA around forms of solidarity specific to capitalism—strike support across national boundaries and the fight for the shorter work week. Such strike support consisted of stopping the importation of scabs from the Continent to England, and collecting funds for and publicizing European strikes among British workers.[36] Marx's strategy, once again, furthers democratic feedback and sustains today's liberal democratic internationalism.

In the strike wave between 1864 and 1868, the IWA grew rapidly into a mass movement in Europe. In 1868, the Rouen manufacturers hoped to drive down wages and undersell their international competitors; the workers walked out. During the IWA's support of the Rouen strike, Marx formulated the principle of solidarity: "This was a great opportunity to show the capitalists that their international industrial warfare, carried on by screwing wages down now in this country, now in that would be checked at last by the international union of the working classes."[37] In a paradigm of democratic feedback, this consciousness and organization among workers around union issues internationally, Marx argued, could lead to support for such critical political developments as the U.S. abolition of slavery, the movement for an eight-hour day, independence for Ireland, and the Paris Commune. Marx looked mainly to international solidarity in the settings of socialist revolution or independence movements. He regarded union solidarity, though important, as secondary.

With today's multinational corporations, however, novel possibilities exist for mutual support among unions in different countries. Thus, in the 1970s, the Colgate-Palmolive local in Oakland made the rehiring of ten black workers, fired for union organizing at Colgate in Boksburg, South Africa, a central contract demand. The Convention of the International Boilermakers' Union voted to refuse work on ships contracted by South African companies so long as apartheid continued.[38] As a delegate, Dwight Threepersons organized "unofficial" showings of the film *Last Grave at Dimbaza* in the hallway outside the convention, with startling effects on the rank and file.

5. THE SEPOY REBELLION AND ENGLISH DISSENSIONS

A critic, however, might object that Marx's analysis of British rule in India and the historical role of colonialism is an important exception to his views on internationalism. As many scholars have noted, Marx "extenuated" English intervention in India. He suggested that British transformation of the "stagnant" Indian village and introduction of railways and capitalist production would prepare the way for eventual independence and socialism. Today's liberals, however, see colonialism mainly as an exploitative, harmful episode in international politics[39] and condemn Marx's temporary extenuation of it.

Such interpreters, however, do not consider the changes in Marx's view on the political role of colonialism within the context of his internationalism.[40] A comparison of Marx's analysis of English rule in India with his later views on colonialism in Ireland will illustrate this metamorphosis. Further, the Third International generalized Marx's opposition to colonialism. Its radicalism prefigures the subsequent liberal repudiation of empire and suggests, once again, novel political activities to forge international democratic solidarity.

In 1853, Marx contended that a "sordid passion" for individual gain at the expense of the Indian population accompanied even the positive side of British rule in India, its breaking down of the old social forms and introduction of a measure of capitalism:

> All the English bourgeoisie may be forced to do will neither emancipate nor materially mend the social condition of the mass of the people, depending not only on the development of the productive powers, but on their appropriation by the people. But what they will not fail to do is to lay down the natural premises for both. Has the bourgeoisie ever done more? Has it ever affected a progress without dragging individuals and peoples through blood and dirt, through misery and degradation?

At this time, Marx imagined, liberation of India would come either from a proletarian revolution in England or from an independence movement in India itself: "The Indians will not reap the fruits of the new elements of society scattered among them by the British bourgeoisie, till in Great Britain itself the now ruling classes shall have been supplanted by the industrial proletariat, or till the Hindoos [*sic*—and Moslems] themselves shall have grown strong enough to throw off the English yoke altogether."[41]

Far from extolling British paternalism as Mill did, Marx saw the main positive role of colonialism as breaking down rural isolation and uniting the Indian people *to rebel* against the Raj. If a strong Indian independence movement emerged, Marx suggested, in an example of democratic feedback, English socialism, then at a low ebb, should support it.

In 1857, the Sepoy Rebellion erupted among Indian soldiers in the British army. The monarch based her rule in India, Marx contended, on the Roman imperial precept, divide and rule.[42] Yet in forging a nationwide army, composed largely of Indian soldiers, the British had created a "general center of resistance" against themselves. The mutiny broke down political divisions that provided the foundation of the Raj: "Mussulmans and Hindoos, renouncing their mutual antipathies, have combined against their common masters" in a genuine "national revolt." For Marx, the rebellion appeared all the more threatening to English rule because, unlike previous mutinies, it spread beyond isolated localities; a movement, beginning with Hindus, sought to restore a Moslem emperor in Delhi; sepoy regiments, for the first time, executed European officers; and Indian resistance to English supremacy coincided with resistance in China—the seventeen-year Taiping rebellion—and Persia.[43] At this time, Marx may have overestimated the likely success of Asian resistance. Yet from his point of view, the development of British colonialism had undermined its own power.

Citing Indian reports of the "universal existence of torture as a financial institution" (to extort newly imposed taxes), Marx even extenuated supposed Indian atrocities against the colonialists: "In view of such facts, dispassionate and thoughtful men may perhaps be led to ask whether a people are not justified in attempting to expel the foreign conquerors who have so abused their subjects. And if the English could do these things in cold blood, is it surprising that the insurgent Hindoos should be guilty, in the fury of revolt and conflict, of the crimes and cruelties alleged against them?"[44] Referring to the London *Times*' outcry against revolutionary "atrocities," Marx commented sardonically:

> The outrages committed by the revolted Sepoys in India are indeed appalling, hideous, ineffable—such as one is prepared to meet only in wars of insurrection, of nationalities, of races and above all of religion; in one word, such as respectable England used to applaud when perpetuated by the Vendeans on the "Blues," by the Spanish guerrillas on the infidel Frenchmen, by

Serbians on their German and Hungarian neighbors, by Croats on Viennese rebels, by Cavaignac's Garde Mobile or Bonaparte's Decemberists on the sons and daughters of proletarian France.[45]

In addition, Marx argued, the bourgeoisie augmented economic and social pressure on English workers by raising taxes to maintain an army and by wars to defend the empire—striking examples of antidemocratic feedback. He estimated that the costs of the Raj might outstrip the revenues. The English people, however, paid the costs; the benefits went to the East India Company, aristocratic military officers, and civil servants.[46] As chapter 4 also emphasizes for Thucydides, empire weakened democracy. In this context, Marx saw the Indian revolt as a source of increasing tension among English social classes, and, hence, as an impetus for the reemergence of a radical working-class movement. This proletarian movement would share interests with rebellious Indians. In January 1858, underlining the possibility of democratic feedback, he wrote to Engels that "with the drain of men and bullion which it must cost the English, India is now our best ally."[47]

6. MARX'S SECOND VERSION OF DEMOCRATIC INTERNATIONALISM: IRELAND AS THE KEY TO ENGLISH RADICALISM

Marx's sympathy for the Sepoy Rebellion foreshadowed the fundamental transformation of his views on English colonialism in Ireland. It made initially unpopular anticolonialism central to the building of democratic movements. Consider, for example, how those directly oppressed by colonialism might respond to "radicals" in imperial countries who are indifferent to large independence movements as opposed to internationalists who challenge chauvinist policies at every turn and support anticolonial movements even when they are weak.

In 1867, the Fenian movement made Irish liberation a central issue in British politics. Further, famine drove large numbers of emigrants into English cities, dividing the working class between English and Irish laborers.

In the 1840s and 1850s, Marx had believed that British socialism would liberate the colonies. Though he stressed internationalism, he saw it mainly as a political necessity among the democratic or socialist revolutionary movements in relatively advanced capitalist countries. His strategy restricted radical revolt to Europe and the United States. But Marx's political experience in the IWA and the evident difficulties of winning English workers from a trade union perspective—even an internationalist one—to socialism caused him to reverse his earlier estimate. He now became convinced that only a movement to support Irish independence among British workers could lay the foundation for a strong revolutionary movement in England.[48] Marx thus extended the sphere of concern for socialist movements: "For a long time I believed that it would be possible to overthrow the Irish regime by English working-class ascendance. I always expressed this point of view in the *New York Tribune*. Deeper study has now convinced me of the opposite. The English working class will *never accomplish anything* until it has got rid of Ireland. The lever must be applied in Ireland."

In Marx's analysis of the international situation in the 1860s, the "material conditions for revolution," particularly a large proletariat that "had developed up to a certain degree of maturity," existed in England. A successful struggle there could spur the socialist revolution internationally.[49] Yet further economic development—even an economic crisis—in England alone would not produce revolution, for colonialism in Ireland permitted the dissemination of racist political attitudes among English workers—a classic illustration of antidemocratic feedback.

As Marx put it in 1870:

> Every industrial and commercial centre in England now possesses a working class *divided* into two *hostile* camps, English proletarians and Irish proletarians. The ordinary English worker hates the Irish worker as a competitor who lowers his standard of life. In relation to the Irish worker he feels himself a member of the *ruling* nation and so turns himself into a tool of the aristocrats and capitalists of his country against *Ireland*, thus strengthening their domination *over himself*.[50]

The religious, social, and national prejudices the English worker harbored against the Irish paralleled those of poor whites against blacks in the American South.[51] The Irish worker responded by seeing the English worker as "at once the accomplice and the stupid tool of *English rule in Ireland*." The ruling class, Marx argued, directed all of its ideological means to maintain this artificial antagonism, including "the press, the pulpit, the comic papers." The old political tactic of divide and rule bolstered the political and economic power of English capitalism:

> This antagonism is the secret of the impotence of the English working class, despite its organization.[52]
>
> It is the secret by which the capitalist class maintains its power. And that class is fully aware of it.[53]

During this period, Marx reevaluated the historical role of English colonialism of Ireland, starting with the Puritan Revolution. "By engaging in the conquest of Ireland, Cromwell threw the English republic out the window. Thence the Irish mistrust of the English People's party." Once again, empire is the talisman of (capitalist) oligarchy. Based on his new theory, Marx campaigned for the First International to support Irish independence as its foremost political objective.

The development of a strong working-class movement in England, concurrent with an Irish independence movement, would, as Marx pictured it, force the British government to withdraw. An agrarian revolution of the starving peasantry in Ireland would then dispossess both English and Irish landlords. The power of the aristocracy in England rested, however, according to Marx, on its holdings in Ireland. Consequently, the liberation of the latter, based on the unity of English and Irish workers, would destroy the influence of the landed aristocracy in England itself. In addition, Irish independence would remove an essential justification "for retaining a big standing army." The diminution of that army and the threat of its use "against the English workers after having done its military training in Ireland," would make a proletarian revolution much more likely. These possibilities all pointedly suggest democratic feedback. A revolutionary government in England and a democratic Ireland, possibly with a strong socialist movement, might federate on a nonexploitative basis.

In estimating the potential for internationalism among English workers, Marx again saw their interests as divided. The English proletarian, typically holding a slightly better job, feared the Irish worker "as a competitor who lowers his standard of life." On this fear rested the capacity of the bourgeoisie to exploit the English proletarian and to render unions "impotent" (today, Proposition 187 has a similar, debilitating effect on unions and the living standards of ordinary Californians). Marx argued that the International could win these workers to support the Irish.

Marx saw this solidarity as arising mainly from common interests and not from "humanitarian sentiment" or concern for "international justice." In debates with moralistic radicals resembling those of realists with "idealists" that chapters 1 and 2 explore, he refused to base his social theory or political strategies on appeals to justice. Nonetheless, Marx often used categories—exploitation, solidarity among workers, democracy, and the like—loaded with at least a rough moral conception. Further, as I argue in *Democratic Individuality*, Marx and Engels were more often confused about the metaethical status of claims of justice than they were about their own indignation, stemming from "crying contrasts of rich and poor, luxury and starvation."[54]

Marx's social theoretical analysis echoes his previous understanding of the *complex* interests of English workers with regard to slavery and suggests a more complicated picture than an economic determinist interpretation allows. On Marx's conception, workers always have *some* interest in remaining quiescent—keeping a job, for instance, or avoiding the threat of imprisonment. Thus, the common interests that emerge in social movements—to end diverse forms of exploitation, defeat slavery or colonialism, create a cooperative regime, and the like—must override these other interests. Further, some individuals—scabs, the apathetic, and the like—adhere to lesser interests. Only a political movement can realize the "common interests of the proletariat, independently of all nationality." In addition, the most general statements of Marx's theory are insufficient to interpret actual history; rather, he invoked complex, often *international*, auxiliary statements to explain the specific prospects of radical movements.[55]

An economic determinist misinterpretation of Marx's theory oddly prefigures the split invoked by neorealism between domestic and international politics traced in the introduction and chapter 1. On a determinist account, even if proletarian revolution were to occur in a number of countries at once, that eventuality would be motivated solely by productive development in each one. In contrast to both perspectives, Marx's conception of revolutionary politics as well as of capitalist economics was always *international*, expecting democratic as well as antidemocratic feedback.[56]

For example, the cause of the Fenian prisoners evoked considerable English and other international support for the Irish cause. However, German and French ruling-class suppression of the Paris Commune and a subsequent repression of the IWA all over Europe provided an unfavorable global context for the Irish agitation. Given antidemocratic feedback, that campaign ended without major success.

Marx's new argument that the emancipation of Ireland provided the lever for a socialist movement in England, however, represented a fundamental change in his theory, in his political strategy for proletarian revolution, and in his estimate of colonialism. In 1848, he had maintained that no nation could be free if it oppressed another. As a modern, Marx transformed Thucydidean insights into the dangers of imperialism for democracy, recognizing, with Hegel, that all persons are (potentially) free. Yet he did not fully apply this analysis to the implications of colonialism for socialist movements in advanced capitalist countries. As we have seen, he thought such movements could come to power before colonies had been liberated from the prevailing regime. Now, however, Marx no longer believed this possible—at least, for Ireland—and pursued his internationalism of 1848 to a novel conclusion: only national revolt in Ireland, supported by the British workers, would permit the full development of socialism in England.

An economic determinist view would make this later political argument incomprehensible. A determinist might conclude that English workers in the 1860s would not join a revolutionary movement because their economic conditions had improved. If they were still impoverished, however, determinism suggests, they would certainly have rebelled. Yet Marx knew that English workers' economic conditions had *not* improved. Instead, he stressed the politics of racism and patriotism as an explanation for the post-1848 weakness of British radicalism.

Nonetheless, emphasis on the possibilities of socialism in less developed countries, recurring to Marx's views on Germany in 1848, would await Lenin and Mao.[57] It seems but a short step, however, from Marx's argument to the notion that colonialism, patriotism, and racism flourish together, and that any socialist or radical democratic movement should oppose them.

In an 1881 letter to the Russian N. F. Danielson, Marx commented, once more, on Indian independence. The English "bleeding" of India, he argued, would probably produce a national revolt. In 1882, Engels's letter to Kautsky combined elements of Marx's old and new arguments. Following the 1848 style of analysis, Engels suggested that a socialist revolution in an advanced country would have to free the colonies as rapidly as possible. Yet on the new argument, he also expected revolution in India and pointed out that the "victorious proletariat can force no blessings of any kind upon any foreign nation without undermining its own victory by so doing." Here, in recommending *only* socialist example, Engels exhibited a political caution, comparable to that of sophisticated realists.[58] On obtaining power, democrats and communists should not to attempt to impose "emancipation" on others by force. Recognizing the reactionary feedback of international conquests, Lenin extended Marx's later view. He insisted that revolutionary movements in advanced countries must oppose all colonial enterprises and support the right of self-determination.[59]

7. CONTEMPORARY IMPLICATIONS I: ALGERIA, MOZAMBIQUE, AND REBELLION INSIDE THE COLONIAL POWER

Turning to today's international affairs, Marx's framework highlights certain unusual but important possibilities for redistribution to which most discussions have paid little attention. I would like to explore two of them: (1) cases of colonial—and by implication neocolonial—wars waged by capitalist countries against independence or radical social movements, and (2) immigration of individuals from poor countries to rich ones. I will then consider briefly the relevance of Marx's argument to contemporary discussions of unequal distribution between individuals in rich and poor nations.

In discussing colonial wars, I will concentrate on two examples of great international impact—the French war in Algeria and the Portuguese wars in Mozambique, Angola, and Guinea-Bissau. My argument, however, also applies to the French and American wars in Indochina.

In a style reminiscent of Marx's, Herbert Lüthy has described the feedback of colonialism and war in Algeria on the internal conflicts that raged in French society: "The empire was something with which the French people had nothing whatever to do, and its story was that of machinations of high finance, the Church and the military caste, which tirelessly re-erected overseas the Bastilles which had been overthrown in France."[60] Similarly, empire in Africa sustained fascism in Portugal. When serious resistance movements emerged in Algeria and the Portuguese colonies, the costs to the French and Portuguese people, in lives, freedoms, and taxes, rose enormously. The impact of war, both in the colonies and on the population at home, underlined Marx's point about the common interests of workers and peasants against oppressive or inegalitarian regimes and policies.[61] In response to antidemocratic feedback in Portugal, various forms of resistance emerged, ranging from massive emigration— one-third of the population, including many men of draft age, left the country—and desertion, to the halting by resistance from below of all fighting months before the formal end of the wars in Mozambique and Guinea-Bissau. An officer in the Armed Forces Movement summarized an attitude that became widespread during campaigns abroad: "[T]he armed forces began to understand that the arms they had to defend the people were being used to destroy the people. Angola, Mozambique and Guinea were places where people had gone to get rich, and it was only a certain class who got anything from it."[62]

Even without a Marxian movement, the oppressed as well as military officers—who saw that colonialism and economic stagnation held back their country and perverted their ostensible role—recognized class divisions. In addition, contacts between soldiers including officers and the African independence movements may have had a radical or internationalist impact. Eventually, the Armed Forces Movement, composed mainly of officers, overthrew the Portuguese fascist regime and stopped these wars. As the turbulent postcoup period showed, this movement had considerable popular support. In this case, even more strikingly than in Algeria, the internal costs of a war against independence—the oppressive feedback of international policy—drove an important part of the population of the exploiting power into opposition. This resistance restricted the government's maneuverability, and, ultimately, overthrew it.

Portuguese workers, soldiers, and peasants, however, displayed only a limited degree of conscious international working-class or democratic solidarity, and the Armed Forces Movement did not neatly fit a Marxian framework.[63] In Marxian terms, the officers belonged to the old ruling class. That argument more easily explains French officers' militant efforts to maintain colonialism than the left-wing Portuguese movement to overthrow it. But in the latter case, a Marxian might stress the international setting: the uneven development of Portugal in relation to the rest of Europe.[64] Portugal—the last empire—fought to hold on after stronger colonial powers had met defeat. In an era when fascism had been discredited, Portugal was nearly the last fascist power; simultaneously, it was also the most economically backward country in Europe.[65] Under the impact of a long, costly, and losing war, many officers decided that only democratic socialism would enable Portugal to rid itself of unjust colonial slaughters and leap ahead of the rest of Europe.

The interconnected resistances in Africa and Portugal, however, strikingly confirm Marx's internationalism: colonialism and fascism fell together (similarly, the Vietnamese resistance to American aggression inspired the antiwar movement in the United States and generated a "Vietnam syndrome" against other interventions). Thus, the independence and revolutionary movements, both in the colonies and the advanced country, created circumstances where new regimes, once they assumed power, might achieve a certain degree of internal redistribution. (Whether they do so depends upon decisions taken after the movements come to power.)[66] Further, one might underline how liberal, by today's standards, such emancipatory and redistributive movements often are. In conditions of capitalist oppression, radicals are, once again, instigators of liberalism.

8. CONTEMPORARY IMPLICATIONS II: IMMIGRATION IN CALIFORNIA AND EUROPE, AND INTERNATIONAL REDISTRIBUTION

Let us now consider a second possibility for redistribution. Since World War II, Western Europe and the United States have experienced an increasing immigration from the poorer nations of Europe, Africa, and Latin America. In most West European countries, immigrants account for 10 percent of the industrial workforce. Though not always the poorest individuals, many come from the "least advantaged" backgrounds, and their remittances contribute directly to the support of the poorest people in their country of origin—an example of unintended, democratic feedback. This case focuses on individual responses to *economic* oppression. It thus differs from examples that stress great-power rivalry or trade and investment regimes.

According to one study, in the 1970s, two million rural inhabitants of Algeria received income remitted from immigrants in France. In some villages, such remittances amounted to 80 percent of total money income (in the late 1970s, Mexican immigrants to the United States remitted an estimated three billion dollars per year).[67] In terms of the relations between the advanced countries and, as Rawls would emphasize, the least advantaged individuals internationally, the policies adopted toward immigrants represent an interesting test case. Similarly, for Keohane, this example might promise some cooperation through global or regional immigration regimes. Yet most of the philosophical and social-science literature on redistribution ignores this issue.[68]

For states regarded as mainly self-sufficient, current international law entitles immigrants to be treated in accordance with "ordinary standards of civilization."[69] Rawls rightly argues that today, such "ordinary [international] standards" include basic human rights.[70] Adopting the perspective of a natural duty to mutual aid or of Rawls's difference principle, one might look upon the presence of such individuals in the advanced countries—and the incomes they remit—as an important vehicle to further international redistribution. Given the fact that elites in poor nations benefit from increasingly unequal income distribution and do not use intergovernmental aid to improve the conditions of the poor, the existence of immigrants provides a special opportunity for the advanced countries— dealing with individuals under their direct jurisdiction—to guarantee fair treatment and a certain amount of economic support.

Except for satire, however, current policies and international regimes have nothing to do with redistribution. Immigration serves to recruit cheap labor; democratic feedback is, from the standpoint of capitalism, accidental. Castles and Kosack have aptly characterized current immigration policies as a form of development aid from the poor countries to the advanced ones.[71]

Some European governments—for example, Germany—restrict legal immigration to "unmarried workers," tolerated only for a limited period. Immigrants can thus expect a high rate of turnover in the hardest and lowest-paying jobs, with considerable harassment, in return for temporary improvement in their living standards. In cases of recession, as in 1967, the (West) German government can require them to return to their countries of origin. Where many immigrants are "illegal," as in France or in the United States, employers and the government subject them to even worse conditions on the job than citizens as well as to harassment and threat of deportation, whether or not they organize to improve their conditions. As Marx suggested, the press often pillories "foreigners." Reactionary groups also subject them to legal and extralegal campaigns of harassment, for instance, the wave of murders of immigrants in Marseilles in the early 1970s, the Schwarzenbach Initiative in Switzerland, or the recent Proposition 187 in California.[72] Led by Governor Pete Wilson, the California elite seeks to deny health care to immigrants while taking special advantage of them. Despite greater recognition of immigrant rights by the European Union, government, capitalist, and media policies toward immigrants will probably not shift in a decisively cosmopolitan, redistributive direction.

As in the case of the Irish in the nineteenth century, a Marxian framework considers the impact of immigration on the working classes in the advanced countries. On one side—the one most played up by the press and by some union leaders as well[73]—immigration, as Marx put it, "lower(s) the standard of life" of citizen workers through competition. Taking the given conditions between classes as fixed, the ruling classes depict what is available to workers themselves as a zero-sum game. On the other side, however, the workers might organize an internationalist effort for better conditions either as a greater share of growth or a cut in profits. Many immigrants work in the same factories as citizen workers, though at lower pay and in worse jobs. For example, in the early 1970s, 46 percent of semiskilled autoworkers in France were immigrants. In Europe, immigrants have frequently gone on strike or attempted to organize against repressive conditions. They have also joined larger strike movements, such as the May 1968 revolt in France. Though some European union federations have expressed sympathy with immigrant efforts, only the French CFDT (Confédération Française Démocratique du Travail) has seriously and successfully organized them.

In a Marxian framework, organizing immigrants would benefit citizen workers whose living standards—relative to the capitalists—would otherwise decline (antidemocratic feedback). In addition, immigrants have successfully and diversely organized themselves. They have pressured not only city governments and individual states, but the European Union, for recognition. As Ireland has shown, in an important example of democratic feedback, the Community has granted important rights—a formal, liberal mutual recognition or adherence to international conventions on human rights—to immigrants.[74] In contrast to Keohane's argument in *After Hegemony*, which provides no actual examples, Ireland's analysis illustrates the Union's realization of morally desirable features in Keohane's conception of regimes. Conversely, in a paradigm of feedback of antidemocratic example, the revival of European fascism—Le Pen in France, murderous neo-Nazi gangs in Germany, and the like—and attacks against immigrants threaten all workers and other oppressed people.[75] Thus, the case of immigration highlights the sharp economic and political *connection* between inequalities in the poor nations and inequalities in the advanced ones.[76]

The economist Michael Reich has studied the impact of racism toward blacks in the United States on the living standards of white workers. His work reveals that where the income of, and social services available to, black workers are the lowest, the income of and social services available to white workers are also, relatively, the lowest, and the income differential between most whites and the top 1 percent of income-gainers is at its highest.[77] If the relationship between the incomes of citizen and immigrant workers is comparable to the one Reich traces between blacks and whites, however, then despite elite propagation of racism among citizens, Marx's point about common interests would be well taken.

Reich's *Racial Inequality: A Political-Economic Analysis* was published in paperback by Princeton in 1983. A state-of-the-art work both econometrically and in terms of contrasting theories—he received tenure in the Department of Economics at Berkeley based on it—his findings have been met, mainly, by silence, which, one might suggest, is likely to greet radical—and liberal—arguments published by mainstream presses, *if* they are true, and the countertheories are, intellectually as well as morally, unappealing. For dominant conceptions of, for instance, intransigent status hierarchy—that majorities have an interest in victimizing minorities—make the upholding of the equal basic rights of each person and, hence, the substantive realization of democracy, unlikely.[78]

9. THE ECONOMIC, SOCIAL, AND POLITICAL CONSEQUENCES OF EXPLOITATION

A Marxian argument can thus justify cooperation among working-class democratic or socialist movements of different nations, regardless of the degree of economic interconnection of their respective ruling classes. Does this theory provide any special insight into the current relationships between rich and poor nations?

International economic interconnection, especially through the investment of multinational corporations, has grown greatly since the mid–nineteenth century, when Marx examined it. On Marx's theory of surplus value, foreign corporations would benefit from processes of unequal exchange. In addition, they would take advantage of what Marx called the special "moral" or "historical" conditions of subsistence in these countries—until the past few years, say, the breaking of unions in Brazil or race laws in South Africa—that would increase the rate of exploitation.[79] At this point, however, a critic might object that under some conditions, the capital-intensive multinational firm pays a relatively small number of workers higher wages than do other, more labor-intensive firms with domestic ownership. International exploitation may exist, such an argument might suggest; multinational firms may even openly or tacitly—by their presence—support regimes that have race laws or destroy unions, but they are not the worst exploiters. In fact, this critic continues, they contribute strongly to economic growth.

To assess this conservative argument, one would have to look—as Marx himself did—at the broader social, political, and economic consequences of exploitation. The Marxian critique of an exploitative class system rests not simply on an analysis of the relationship of the non-producers, who extract unpaid labor, and the producers, but also on the larger social and political consequences of this relationship. Under capitalism, for example, Marx indicted the alienation of the worker in production, the capitalist's control of the government and corruption of formal political equality, the propagation of racism and divisions among workers, the recruitment of workers to fight in and pay the other costs of wars to maintain despotism or exploitation, economic crises and massive unemployment, and so forth. As chapter 5 shows, this criticism presses strongly on supposed Rawlsian defenses of capitalisms that adhere to a difference principle; those oligarchies with parliamentary forms, nonetheless, harm workers and others. Such regimes fail to assure to each person what Rawls calls the "fair value" of liberty. Thus, the priority of the equal liberty principle—the barring of oligarchy—overrides any economic benefits to the least advantaged, even in those rare cases where the difference principle is upheld.

In many dependent countries, however, to give a rough typical sketch, narrow growth in production of raw materials and manufacturing occurs mainly through highly technological, multinational firms, which discourage more labor-intensive, local industry.[80] Meanwhile the spread of capitalism to the countryside has undermined the old comparatively reciprocal social relationships and replaced them with more exploitative ones.[81] Increasing numbers of unemployed agricultural laborers either hang on in the villages or migrate to the cities to join a large, unemployed proletariat. Population growth magnifies this process. As a result, a highly skewed system of income distribution develops, in which the relationship of the wealthy to the urban and rural poor grows more unequal as economic growth occurs. Even capitalist growth in the Southeast Asian "NICs" and China, despite important political differences, exacerbates inequalities.

The political system, especially a dictatorship or a limited party competition regime growing out of repression and relying on foreign military and economic aid, maintains this unequal development (as chapter 5 emphasizes, in most cases, one refers to U.S. military and police aid and training and CIA oversight of torture).[82] The broader consequences of exploitation impose a variety of severe economic, social, and political costs on the majority of the people. These hardships may amount to what

Marx once referred to, characterizing British rule in India, as "a bleeding process with a vengeance." For instance, though South Africans have freed themselves from apartheid in a forgiving, heroic struggle, most still suffer the consequences of the exploitative system described here.

As Marx maintained, the increasingly intertwined political and now economic interests of two elites—the ruling class of the country itself and the multinational corporations and governments of the advanced countries—reinforce this process. Although the interests of these elites may sometimes conflict, investment by multinationals creates an additional foreign interest in maintaining the stability of broad exploitative relationships, at least against radical social movements aiming at redistribution.[83] The intervention of ITT, the CIA, and international monetary institutions to undermine the Allende regime in Chile provides a vivid example of mutual support among elites given a radical threat.[84]

Such common interests in exploitation conflict with the spread of democracy. The American empire allows the establishment, in less developed countries, of formally parliamentary regimes, coupled with continuing military and police aid. A modest reform of the CIA, such as President Clinton's, may stop, say, the murder of an American innkeeper in Guatemala—for stumbling across army drug smuggling—or American nuns in Salvador but will not, without cessation of covert operations, prevent continuing U.S. crimes. Nonetheless, as the NICs illustrate, some capitalist economic development—in a highly inegalitarian form, with oligarchic domination of the state—is possible under these circumstances.

Would a contemporary Marxian examination of international distribution conclude that the workers of the advanced countries and the exploited populations in the poor nations share significant common interests? Unjust war, as in the case of Portuguese colonialism in Africa, provides the best example. Given class divisions within the advanced nations, the government will send those who least benefit from the exploitation of the poor nations to fight. Because of the costs in lives, freedoms,[85] taxes, and inflation—once again, antidemocratic feedback—these situations provide the strongest basis for overriding narrow interests and producing internationalist activity. In other cases, such as the energy crisis or the slowdown in economic growth, the structure of advanced capitalism imposes differential costs that hurt mainly workers and the middle classes (though with "downsizing," even some executives are affected). Whether, aside from defeat in war, such inequalities can generate a sufficiently strong radical movement to ally with comparable movements in the poor nations is unclear. In the context of such a movement, however, one of Marx's basic points about internationalism—that the elite of the advanced country would appeal to foreign expansion in order to restore the nation's onetime power and deflect a radical movement—might reappear. Marx's internationalism highlights antidemocratic feedback. To create a genuine democracy, respecting the human rights of each person, minority as well as majority, an anti-imperial movement would have to unite diverse groups. To succeed, Marx's argument suggests, an egalitarian movement in an advanced capitalist country would have to be internationalist.[86]

TABLE 5
A Contrast of Democratic and Antidemocratic Feedback

Internationalist Thesis

In the Revolution of 1848

Thesis 1	Internationalism is a response to an elite strategy of divide and rule internally and internationally. In general, democrats, as well as working class and radical movements, have common interests against their state(s) internationally and in breaking down major social—"status"—divisions internally
Thesis 2	Monarchical or authoritarian powers will join forces with capitalist parliamentary regimes—oligarchies—to suppress even moderate, democratic movements (consider England in 1848, and the U.S. in the Cold War). Thus, *antidemocratic feedback* stems from the foreign policies of formally democratic powers

---

Marx's Theoretical Shift on Ireland

Thesis 3	Workers—and other oppressed groups—have complex, somewhat divided interests. For example, in the 1860s, English workers feared competition of Irish immigrants for jobs. Their misguided support for colonialism, however, eroded their overall political and social freedoms and powers (antidemocratic feedback)
Thesis 4	Between 1848 and the 1860s, the income and wellbeing of the English working class declined. Yet no radical movement emerged. No economic determinist account explains this fact
Thesis 5	As a consequence of divide and rule, racism toward the Irish imposed political, social and economic burdens on both Irish and English workers (antidemocratic feedback)
Thesis 6	The English elite furthered racism through "press, pulpit and comic paper"
Thesis 7	An English socialist movement must oppose racism toward the Irish and support the liberation of Ireland—the *democratic feedback of radical example*. Through political organizing, that movement could overcome divisions between citizen and immigrant
Thesis 8	Citizens should oppose all (neo)imperial policies—as well as all instances of antidemocratic feedback—promoted by their own power (Lenin)
Thesis 9	A democracy, organized around a common good of mutual regard among persons with diverse comprehensive views,[a] is possible

TABLE 5 (*cont.*)

Some Contemporary Examples

Anti(neo)colonial revolutions, as in Angola, Mozambique, and Guinea-Bissau, produce democratic changes in the colonial power. Responding to Vietnamese revolt, the American antiwar movement and the subsequent "Vietnam syndrome" also illustrate this paradigm

Immigrants in advanced capitalist countries remit part of their income to the least advantaged in their home countries—an unintended (on the part of citizens of the advanced countries) and unorganized form of democratic feedback

Immigrant organizing in Europe has stimulated the European Community's promulgation of basic rights. Community recognition has, in turn, sparked immigrant organizing (a democratic feedback of radical example)

Anti-immigrant organizing including murders by states and local, neo-Nazi groups has also occurred throughout Europe and the United States—the dictatorial feedback of reactionary example. California is an American center for such activity. This example—fortunately still pallidly—recalls international elite support for fascism in response to the Russian Revolution

[a] Rawls, *Political Liberalism*, chap. 1.

CHAPTER FOUR

Democratic Imperialism and Internal Corruption

> We have lived with violence for seven years
> It was not worth one single life
> But the patriot's fist is at her throat
> Her voice is in mortal danger.
> (Adrienne Rich, "Natural Resources")

> How many wars do we see undertaken in the history of Rome, how much bloodshed, how many people destroyed, how many great actions. . . . But how did this project for invading all nations end—a project so well planned, carried out, and completed—except by satiating five or six monsters?
> (Montesquieu, *Considérations sur la grandeur et décadence des romains*)

> And this was the greatest action that had happened in all this war, or at all, that we have heard of amongst the Grecians, being to the victors most glorious and most calamitous to the vanquished. For being wholly overcome in every kind and receiving small loss in nothing, the army and fleet and all perished (as they used to say) with an universal destruction. Few of many returned home. And thus passed the business concerning Syracuse.
> (Thucydides, *The History of the Peloponnesian War*)

1. AMERICAN POLITICAL "SCIENCE" AND ATHENIAN DEMOCRACY

This chapter highlights the initial recognition by Greek historians—notably Thucydides—tragedians, and philosophers of the dangers of imperialism to a *democratic* common good. Many contemporary investigators of international relations have overlooked this central argument.[1] Gilpin's study of hegemony, for example, envisions Thucydides' *History* as a story of uneven economic and military growth in which Athens threatened Sparta, of power-rivalry, and of prodigious international conflict. On this account, power displaces power; democracy is at best secondary, a characteristic of regimes that falls outside the basic parameters—those of power-growth and decline—of international politics.[2] Gilpin also ignores Athenian defeat by democratic Syracuse, even though he, anachronistically, idealizes Athens as a democracy—not, as it was, a despotism toward slaves—in contrast to Sparta, a "slavocracy" (call these theorists *realist nondemocrats*). In addition, proponents of the alternate, democratic-peace hypothesis have neglected this startling counterexample to their view.[3] Thus, this chapter stresses Thucydides' account of the public *corruption* that accompanies empire, the initial, and in many ways still fresh and unrepeated, *antidemocratic-feedback argument*.

Contrary to international-relations specialists, classicists like Jacqueline de Romilly and Walter Connor, ironically, see Thucydides mainly as a defender of *Athenian* democracy.[4] They envision that democracy, however, as gradually overwhelmed by economic growth, hunger for power, and imperialism. While neorealist scholars often ignore democracy to study "power," classicists have studied power in the context of democracy (call these theorists *democratic realists or internationalists*). As they emphasize, the defeat of imperial Athenian democracy occurred, not in the Peloponnesian War with Sparta, but in its clash with little-known (to Athenians), democratic Syracuse.

Today's neorealists, however, stop reading the *History* at the Athenian slaughter of the citizens of Melos (the end of book 5). Surprisingly, even in the debate over interdemocratic peace, the war with Syracuse goes largely unmentioned. In contrast, classicists depict the gradual degeneration from articulate attention to honor and a democratic common good, under Pericles, to a concern with interest and advantage. American realists and neorealists, however, ignore Athenian democracy and concentrate only on imperial decadence. Like Hobbes, neorealists deny, where Thucydides strikingly affirms, justice as the outset and driving force of realism (unlike neorealists, Hobbes, however, rightly stresses the common good of preserving the life of each citizen). Strengthening Niebuhr's insights, de Romilly maintains that "Thucydides' realism ultimately consists, then, in showing that what counts more than anything in the preservation of power is morality—both for individuals and the state, both in particular decisions and in the deepest aspirations of the citizens as such."[5] For Thucydides, the gradual thematic deterioration of the words that signify "commonality" and "justice" measures the decline of Athenian democracy.

During the Cold War, American international-relations theory studied presidents who invoked, as slogans, human rights (Carter) or democracy (Reagan), though their policies undermined these putative goals. On the surface, as chapter 1 stresses, this discipline ought to be profoundly concerned with democracy. Yet neorealism makes a theoretical point of ignoring democratic regimes and other domestic political structures as important variables in international conflict. In addition, even the alternate thesis that democracies do not go to war with one another omits not only the defeat of democratic Athens by democratic Syracuse, but also the pattern of American belligerence against democracies in the less developed countries.[6]

In contrast, classicists concentrate only on the initial, slaveholding democracies. Ironically, they focus on the famed theoretical opponents of these democracies. Even Thucydides criticized many aspects of the Athenian regime. Thus, until anticolonial or antiimperial wars broke out against the French in Indochina and then the United States in Vietnam, classicists tended to be skeptical, conservative, antidemocratic.[7] De Romilly and, as we will see, Connor, however, came to see parallels between Athenian imperialism and the Algerian and Vietnamese conflicts.

That classicists should now focus on the corruption caused by democratic imperialism and that many international-relations theorists should ignore it, even in discussing Thucydides, is, however, a striking anomaly (one might say, perhaps more charitably, such international-relations theorists have only cursorily read at the *History*). Further, participants in today's debates have not seen the *problematic* relationship of foreign policy to a domestic common good. Thus, even advocates of the "democratic peace" hypothesis have so far failed to consider how antidemocratic *belligerence* abroad strengthens oligarchy at home.

As I have noted, Gilpin and other neorealists criticize the Vietnam War as an "overexpansion" of American power. In Krasner's peculiarly neutral words, U.S. presidents revealed an inability to align commitments with capabilities.[8] Neorealists, thus, gesture at the original Thucydidean insight that democratic zeal to conquer others ultimately undermines a common good at home and leads, over time, to tyranny. Except for an implausible separation of international and domestic politics and a denial of any common good through endorsement of the empiricist doctrines of "value-freedom" and "reductionism," this critique of "overexpansion" might encourage neorealists to recognize democratic themes in Thucydides. Stressing the internal costs of aggression, the pressure put on the lives and livelihoods of either subjects or citizens, they note, instead, that even imperial, "totalitarian" regimes may decline, as, for example, the USSR did through waging war on Afghanistan.

Nonetheless, neorealists sometimes invoke harms to democracy and human rights stemming from American foreign policy. During or after the Vietnam War, as chapters 1 and 2 show, neorealists and realists often became stern critics of the "paranoid" or "obsessive anti-communism" (Fulbright) that has haunted American interventions.[9] Stigmatizing even moderate opponents of Cold War dictatorships as "Communists," the American government has provided—and continues to provide—aid and training to the military and police as an apparatus of torture in the less developed countries[10] and shores up elites through covert activity. For instance, between 1984 and 1991, the Institute of the Americas in Panama used a manual in Spanish that graphically explained how to "neutralize" dissidents. Since the end of the Cold War, the U.S. government has tried to recall all the copies.

In Aristotelian terms, the American regime is a capitalist oligarchy with parliamentary forms, not, as chapter 5 emphasizes, a democracy in which the voice of each citizen counts equally. Given the cruelty of U.S. interventions, academic realists have rarely praised the practices underlying presidential ideologies that aver democracy or human rights. The reactionary character of American foreign policy, thus, helps to explain both the theoretical choice by neorealists to emphasize power over democracy, and the more ironic decision, among those who have restored a concern for democracy in international relations, to distinguish rigidly between antidemocratic "interventions" and "wars."

But political science, this chapter argues, skirts moral judgment, along with an accompanying, core democratic theory, at great risk. It must then ignore Thucydides' themes of the decline of a democratic common good in Athens, the role of class strife in decadence, the defeat of imperial democracy by democracy both in Athens, and, with qualifications, in modern America,[11] and the like. Starting with Thucydides, the ancient Greek focus, by historians, tragedians, and philosophers, on a common good and its abridgement provides a framework for an apt political science. Following Aristotle, that political science would integrate *Ethics* with *Politics*.[12] Shaped by repressive American policy and a sometimes plausible, but misguided, philosophy of science—logical positivism and, in social science, behaviorism—however, neorealism as well as that version of the democratic-peace hypothesis that ignores American "interventions" against other democracies, offers ideology, not science.

Section 2 of this chapter explores Thucydides' account of the nobility, desire for imperial grandeur, and defeat of Athenian democracy and its widely influential "realist," more exactly, *monarchical* misinterpretation by Hobbes. Section 3 distinguishes the criticisms of hubris offered by Socrates, Thucydides, and Hobbes. The fourth section highlights the identity, for Thucydides, of official "realism"—zealous hunger for power—and public corruption. Hobbes, misguidedly, fails to distinguish between a common good and tyranny; this section traces the subtle, Hobbesian sources of realist misreadings. Section 5 stresses that official realism misunderstands the Melian dialogue, empathizing with the Athenian ambassadors' praise of the "law of the stronger," in contrast to Thucydides, who cautiously sympathizes with the courageous, doomed Melians. The sixth section attempts to reformulate today's "democracies do not war on other democracies" thesis in the light of the Athenian-Syracusan conflict and U.S. foreign policy during the Cold War. The seventh emphasizes the horror of the American War in Vietnam, which brought home to classicists, notably Connor, a parallel with Athens at Syracuse, and, thus, a comparatively apt reading of the *History*.

2. INTEGRITY AND DEMOCRACY: THUCYDIDES
VERSUS HOBBES I

Perhaps no two figures in political theory and history deserve to be so associated—though, often, commentators have neglected both their connection and their distinctness—than Thucydides and his antidemocratic translator, Hobbes. An absolutist in the Puritan Revolution, Hobbes sneered at "democraticals."[13] Later antidemocratic interpretation of Thucydides echoes—though it lacks the power of—Hobbes's translation and political theory. Ironically, American realism has often been *antidemocratic* realism. As the change in Morgenthau illustrates, democratic understandings of realism and Thucydides have emerged only since Vietnam.[14] Nonetheless, even in Hobbes's idiom, traced in, say, the words and actions of Pericles, as well as the destiny of Athenian imperialism, Thucydides' democratic concerns shine through.

In the history of Athens, Pericles stands out, among politicians, as a paradigm of moral character. He leads because of his superiority to base concerns. Most notably, he is not for sale:

> [B]eing a man of great power both for his dignity and wisdom, and for bribes manifestly the most incorrupt, he freely controlled the multitude and was not so much led by them as he led them. Because having gotten his power by no evil arts, he would not humour them in his speeches but out of his authority durst anger them with contradiction. Therefore, whensoever he saw them out of season insolently bold, he would with orations put them into a fear; and again, when they were afraid without reason, he would likewise erect their spirits and embolden them.[15]

Among Athenians, Pericles also stands apart as an aristocrat, with startling rhetorical skill.

His strategy invokes Athenian democratic forethought and daring to overcome Spartan caution. First, he sought to maintain but not expand

Athens' empire: "For he told them that if they would be quiet and look to their navy, and during this war seek no further dominion nor hazard the city itself, they should then have the upper hand. But they did contrary in all,[16] and in such other things besides as seemed not to concern the war managed the state [sic—city] according to their private ambition and covetousness, perniciously both for themselves and their confederates."[17] Faced with defeat by the Athenians at Pylos in book 4, the Spartans offered the very peace that Pericles had envisioned. But Cleon sought to humiliate their representatives, to force them to speak before the assembly; they withdrew the offer.[18] Prefiguring Melos and Syracuse, the Spartan speech of surrender called for "moderate terms": "And naturally to those that relent of their own accord, men give reciprocally with content, but against the *arrogant*, they will hazard all, even when in their own judgment, they are too weak."[19]

Second, through boldness, Pericles sought to strike terror into Spartan hearts. For instance, he suggested that Athenians should not grieve the burning of their properties. On the contrary, if they heeded his counsel, they would destroy outlying houses themselves to show how little such possessions constrained them:

> We must therefore, drawing as near as can be to that imagination [of Athens as predominantly a naval power], lay aside the care of fields and villages, and not for the loss of them, give battle to the Peloponnesians, far more in number than ourselves. . . . Nor bewail ye the loss of fields or houses but of men's bodies; for men may acquire these, but cannot acquire men. And if I thought I should prevail, I would advise you to go out and destroy them yourselves and show the Peloponnesians that you will never sooner obey them for such things as these.[20]

In a parallel invocation in book 6, Hermocrates suggests that Syracuse should, unexpectedly, attack the Athenians at Tarentum across the sea. Athens would then be struck by fear and never invade Syracuse: "But if they should see us once bolder than they looked for, they would be terrified more with the unexpectedness than with the truth of our power itself."[21]

Daring and pride in Athenian greatness, both democratic and imperial, provide the public motivation for Thucydides rather than insight into an ethical good. Predominantly, he stressed democracy as an *instrument* to Athenian greatness. Yet the funeral oration also defends that regime as an *intrinsic good*, one that secures a common interest among citizens and tolerates diverse individual ways of life. Pericles' adherence to these opposed goals runs through his account like intertwined, diversely colored threads. In retrospect, however, Athenian nobility arises from intrinsic goods, not domination over others.

In a passage in book 1 that prefigures Pericles' funeral oration, the Corinthian ambassador, an enemy, praises the restless, innovative character of the Athenians, which he sees as bound to their democratic regime:

> For they love innovation and are swift to devise and also to execute what they resolve on. But you [the Spartans], on the contrary, are only apt to save your own, not to devise anything new, nor scarce to attain what is necessary. They again are bold beyond their strength, adventurous above their own reason, and in danger hope still the best whereas your actions are ever beneath your power. They are stirrers, you studiers; they love to be abroad, and you at home the most of any.[22]

This speech shows that Pericles did not idly boast about Athenian character, but invoked well-known characteristics. Athenian greatness, so he suggested, focuses not only on the supposed good of limited empire,[23] but on freedom, creativity, openness, and toleration.

Marked by poetic structure, Thucydides' *History* self-consciously weaves—without commenting on—telling parallels. Thus, Thucydides' emphasis on Athenian *polypragmosune*—innovativeness—and resilient "hopes" for the future, reads better backward, in the daring of just war against Persian Empire, than forward, to Melos, where the magistrates' "hopes" prove idle against Athenian murderousness, or Syracuse, where Athenians are "adventurous above their own reason, and in danger hope still the best," and are destroyed.

The Spartan regime, as Pericles suggested, terrorizes the young, who must shed any trace of particularity and focus their lives upon the city. In contrast, Athenians allow their children to grow up freely and scorn "bad looks" at those who are eccentric in "private" life: "And we live not only free in the administration of the state but also with one another void of jealousy touching each other's daily course of life, not offended at any man for following his own humour, nor casting on any man censorious looks, which though they be no punishment, yet they grieve."[24] Such toleration distinguishes Athenian democrats from the Hobbesian children of pride (the human psychological capacity for tolerating differences of habit and conscience also makes a modern regime, characterized by democratic individuality, possible). Further, in opposition to Sparta as well as the contemporary American security state, which, during the Cold War, forbade visas to "radical" foreigners and passports to domestic "enemies," Athenians disdain secrecy:

> We leave our city open to all men; nor was it ever seen that by banishing of strangers we denied them the learning or sight of any of those things which, if not hidden, an enemy might reap advantage by, nor relying on secret preparation and deceit but upon our own courage in the action.[25]

Pericles celebrated the natural, rather than studied, quality of Athenian life:

And yet when, from ease rather than studious labour and upon natural rather than doctrinal valour,[26] we come to undertake any danger, we have the odds by it that we shall not faint beforehand with meditation on future trouble and in the action we shall appear no less confident than they that are ever toiling.[27]

Reflecting on Athenian defeat, Thucydides imagines that democratic Syracuse might supplant Athenian greatness. Echoing Pericles, he sees democracy as *instrumental* to imperial dominion:

Knowing that this city hath a great name amongst all people for not yielding to adversity and for the mighty power it yet hath after the expense of so many lives and so much labour in war, the memory whereof, though we should now at length miscarry (for all things are made with this law, to decay again), will remain with posterity forever. How that being Grecians, most of the Grecians were our subjects; that we have abided the greatest wars against them, both universally and singly, and have inhabited the greatest and wealthiest city. Now this he with the quiet life will condemn, the active man will emulate, and they that have not attained to the like will envy. But to be hated and to displease is a thing that happeneth for the time to whatsoever he be that hath the command of others; and he does well, that undergoeth hatred for matters of great consequence. For the hatred lasteth not and is recompensed both with a present splendour and an immortal glory hereafter.[28]

Though the ancients had no conception of progress, Thucydides' and Pericles' sense of the transitoriness of glory—"all things are made with this law to decay again"—prefigures Niebuhr's realism. Ironically, in envisioning the supplanting of Athens by Syracuse, Thucydides ignores the former's unique social, public, and aesthetic character, which he had earlier celebrated. That character made Athenian democracy legendary, while its absence denied fame, though not justice and victory, to the Syracusans.

Pericles analyzed Athenian character, and its role, as chapter 5 shows, in a deliberative democracy:

[W]e also give ourselves to bravery and yet with thrift; and to philosophy, and yet without mollification of mind. And we use riches rather for opportunities of action than for verbal ostentation, and hold it not a shame to confess poverty but not to have avoided it. . . . We likewise weigh what we undertake and apprehend it perfectly in our minds, not accounting words for a hindrance of action but that it is rather a hindrance to action to come to it without instruction of words before.[29]

"The city," so Pericles noted, "is in general a school for the Grecians," both in its way of life—an intrinsic good—and in imperial grandeur.

Though democratic, Athens practiced the nobility of Aristotle's magnanimous *(megalopsuche)* man. One might note a certain arrogance here, for it, condescendingly, made friends by offering benefits. The city never entered into—as psychologically beneath it—debt to others:

> And he that bestoweth a good turn is ever the most constant friend because he will not lose the thanks due unto him from him whom he bestowed it on. Whereas the friendship of him that oweth a benefit is dull and flat, as knowing his benefit not to be taken for a favour but for a debt. So we only do good to others not upon computation of profit but freeness of trust.[30]

Yet the rapacity of Athenian empire would, ultimately, overturn this characteristic. As imperialism developed, tribute flowed primarily to Athens and paid for citizen participation in the assemblies.[31] In contrast, in the contemporary United States, an oligarchy with parliamentary forms, an elite mainly gets the benefit. Yet as Pericles, and, especially, Thucydides stress, Athenian expansion would, ultimately, doom its citizens. Brutal Athenian leaders at Melos consider only the "use"—only the "computation of profit"—that Pericles and Thucydides disdain.

3. SOCRATES', THUCYDIDES', AND HOBBES'S DIFFERING RESPONSES TO HUBRIS

The Greek tragic and, later, the Christian prophetic tradition focus on hubris that leads to political domineering. With importantly differing emphases, this theme figures in Socrates, Thucydides and Hobbes. Contrasted to official versions, it reveals the depth of sophisticated realisms.

In *Gorgias*, Socrates questions Pericles' fine words: "[T]hey [Athenians] were corrupted by him. . . . that's what I myself heard said, that Pericles has made the Athenians idlers and cowards, chatterers and spongers, by starting them on drawing pay."[32] Although Pericles originally tried to make the Athenians noble, Socrates maintains, the citizens still sought, after the plague and the initial hardships of the war, to indict him. Had Pericles' policies been genuinely good, Socrates suggests, Athenians would have become better, not, as shown by the injustice of the indictment, worse. Though Socrates criticizes imperialism, he overlooks the fact that Athenians rejected Pericles' advice, neither to undertake further expansion nor to open up a second front against Sicily. This omission makes Socrates' criticism of Athenian imperialism less telling.[33] Now he might have suggested, with Thucydides, that the very characteristics that Pericles articulated, in particular desire for grandeur, meant, given

Athenian restlessness, that Pericles' anti-imperial advice could not hold sway. For Socrates not only shares Thucydides' critique of pride; he extends it to capture an egotistical holding of philosophical opinions linked to politics—those who pretend to know what they do not[34]—as well as the murderousness of Greek public life. Ironically for the stereotype of Plato as an "idealist," in the portrayals of Callicles, Thrasymachus, Anytus, and Meletus, Socrates is, perhaps, the sharpest Athenian *realist* about politicians.[35] In particular, Callicles and Thrasymachus belligerently invoke the phrase of the Athenian delegates at Melos about the "law of the stronger."

To Socrates, moderation or awareness of merely human limits about large claims *(sophrosune)*, as opposed to puffing oneself up in imitation divinity, requires living an examined life. One must not, Socrates suggests, commit particular injustices, be impious. He does not know, however, *in general*, what the ideas of justice, virtue, goodness, and piety are. Socrates' questioning about knowledge avoids hubris and differentiates him from Sophists as well as politicians. It deepens the central realist critique of ordinary philosophical and political opinion—of the way views are held—as what we would call ideologies. Nonetheless, when Socrates questioned the literal faith of many Athenians, they accused him of impiety.

In contrast, a liberal understanding of equal freedom of conscience—a precondition of modern democracy—would bar the monstrous crime of putting someone to death simply for his beliefs.[36] Yet Socrates, who stripped himself of worldly goods[37] and would die for his convictions about justice, is, on Plato's account, profoundly pious. The *Apology* and the *Crito* end with invocations of "the god"; the *Laws* begins with one. By ignoring Pericles' anti-imperialist advice, however, Plato loses the chance to link dynamism, wantonness—hubris—and imperial disaster, to integrate Thucydides' specific account of Athenian character with a more general vision of the debilities of political life and philosophy.

A less spiritual realist, Hobbes focuses more favorably on Pericles: "That which gives to human action the relish of Justice, is a certain noblenesse or gallantnesse of courage, rarely to be found, by which a man scorns to be beholding for the contentment of his life to fraud or breach of promise."[38] Hobbes maintains, however, that Pericles illustrates the antidemocratic rule—"rarely to be found"—of the "best man." In this, he follows a comment of Thucydides but neglects Pericles' central point: "We have a form of government not fetched by imitation from the laws of neighboring states (nay, we are rather a pattern to others than they to us) which because in the administration it hath not respect to a few but to the multitude is called a democracy."[39] For Pericles, as Thucydides knew, helped to reform the laws of a participatory democracy. In Athens, the assembly debated every major issue. Six thousand provided a quorum for a meeting, one-fifth of those eligible to attend.[40] Pericles exemplified, in many ways, democratic leadership, one relying on the strengths of Athenians, not simply catering to popular passions. At the same time, however, his celebration of empire ultimately nurtured Athenian defeat.

Now, "gallantnesse of courage" would prove more widespread in subsequent democracy than Hobbes imagined. As Pericles saw, for Athenians, pride in freedom, justice, creativity, magnanimity, and tolerance disdains mere conquest and brutality.[41] Though motivated by public concerns, however, the realization of character requires self-possession. As Aristotle suggests, those who seek gain from others—friendships of convenience or for money—lack the self-*possession* to be concerned with the good of another, independent person. They are possessed, as it were, by the objects of their pursuits. Thus, Greek history, philosophy, and public life are continuous.[42] In a gradual public corruption characterized by an absence of self-possession, the emergence of Cleon—the most "violent" man of his time—had horrifying consequences for Athenians.

Only the personality of Pericles, however, separates his leadership from that of demagogues. Later liberal institutional arrangements, for instance, the weakened, but constitutional, authority of the U.S. Congress to declare war, attempt to limit the capriciousness of democratic leadership.

In Greek politics as well as political theory, individual character shapes and is shaped by the regime. A great leader, who adheres to *gnome*—reason—and *arete*—virtue—however, such as Pericles, differs from, is more independent of regime structure than, most citizens. Thucydides sometimes speaks of *arete*—attributing this trait, for example, to Nicias in book 7—without approval, as a customary virtue. Thus, the character of a democratic leader, for Thucydides, exceeds, as it were, democracy and parallels to a limited extent the autonomy, in Plato, of a philosopher. Consider, in *Crito*, Socrates' deliberated allegiance to democratic laws,[43] which reveals their impact—he "was raised by them" and, as the *Apology* notes, "stayed at his post" in war—and his independence. At seventy, he noted the short span he had yet to live; his execution for what would come to be called civil disobedience did more to bring Athenian laws into disgrace than the whisperings of its later enemies.

As Plato maintains, each form of public life yields a typical citizen. A timocracy nurtures those concerned with honor, an oligarchy those hungry for money, a democracy citizens focused on freedom.[44] In distortion, a democratic regime may instigate license. Rightly ordered, however, as Pericles emphasized, its citizens may freely concern themselves with a regime's grandeur, as shown, most strikingly in their triumph, against the odds, over Persian imperialism. They may exhibit a stake in public things.

Now good character for Athenians does not reflect, anachronistically, a Kantian concern to do what is right as a categorical imperative. Instead, such character was the creation of a regime-focused education (the Greek word for gentleman, *kaloskagathos*, combines the terms for the beautiful and the good). An individual Athenian would be less than himself, as it were, if he stooped to murder or conquest. Thucydides' conception, later to be theorized by Aristotle, unites pride in intrinsic goods—freedom, openness, and courage in war—with insight into human limits (humans are a mean between beasts and gods) and self-acceptance. The moral goods and virtues flow from and strengthen other goods of character and regime; they are part of a *common good*.[45] These themes contrast with Pericles' emphasis on Athenian grandeur.

Although Thucydides is constantly aware of the war against Persia— the previous "greatest event" in the history of the Greeks—he does not often comment on it. As we will see, however, he draws startling implicit parallels between the attitudes of the Melian magistrates and Athenian resisters.

Yet endorsing a widespread stereotype, Gilpin contrasts Plato, "the idealist," and Aristotle, "the realist," and likens the latter to Thucydides. But Gilpin overemphasizes the "city in speech," which is depicted, in the *Republic*, as an unusual regime, one nearly impossible to realize. He fails to see Socrates' motivation for proposing this idea in the murderous class struggles and dangers of conquest highlighted by Thucydides. As contemporary Athenians would have known, by the time the *Republic* was written, Polynices, a leader of the democrats, Niceratus,[46] and Socrates were slain. Athens had fallen. The setting gives poignancy to Hegel's dictum that philosophy takes flight at social dusk. Gilpin misses Socrates' criticism of hubris. Thus, he fails to see the concordance of Thucydides, Aristotle, and Plato on central political themes.[47]

4. HOBBES AGAINST ATHENS

Even Hobbes admires democratic Athens as a power. He sees the source of that power, however, as distinct from rule by the people. Thus, he ignores the funeral oration's celebration of democracy[48] as well as Thucydides' account of Athenian decline and its defeat by democratic Syracuse. As Hobbes puts it,

For his opinion concerning the government of the state [sic—city], it is manifest that he least of all liked the democracy. And upon divers occasions he noteth the emulation and contention of the demagogues for reputation and glory of wit; with their crossing of each other's counsel, to the damage of the public; the inconsistency of resolutions, caused by the diversity of ends and power of rhetoric in the orators; and the desparate actions undertaken upon the flattering advice of such as desired to attain, or to hold what they had attained, of authority and sway amongst the common people.[49]

Yet Hobbes also mentions Thucydides' criticisms of the oligarchy and suggests that he "praiseth the government of Athens [in book 8] when it mixed *the few and the many*." For Hobbes, however, but not Thucydides, the latter's criticisms of Athens are sufficient commendation of monarchy.[50] One might emphasize the fearsome revolutionary context of Hobbes's sometimes remarkable distortions of the ancients. Thus, he depicts Aristotle—perhaps because the latter had influenced the hated "Schoolmen"—as a radical: "For who can be a good subject of monarchy, whose principles are taken from the enemies of monarchy, such as . . . Aristotle of Athens, who seldom speak(s) of kings but as wolves and other ravenous beasts."[51] Ironically in so great a classics scholar and translator, Hobbes regrets the impact of ancient republics: "there was never any thing so dearly bought, as these western parts have bought the learning of the Greek and Latin tongues."[52] That great work, *Leviathan*, exhibits a novel simplicity of deduction, modeled on ancient geometry and Newtonian mechanics.[53] In contrast, however, Hobbes supposes, Aristotle's complex views caused disagreement in ethics and dissension among the poor. He implausibly reduces, for instance, Aristotle's and ordinary citizens' reasoned distinctions between monarchy and tyranny, aristocracy and oligarchy, "commonwealth by institution" and "commonwealth by acquisition," and the like, to putatively unjustifiable expressions of preference.

Hobbes's sole argument for this reduction contrasts government— equated with monarchy—with no government. But the worst tyranny is not superior to anarchy. As Rousseau notes, following Locke, the companions of Odysseus in the cave of Cyclops, waiting to be devoured, had—temporary—security: "What do they gain if that tranquillity itself is one of their miseries?" [Qu'y gagnent-ils si cette tranquilité même est une de leurs misères?].[54]

By depicting the zeal, cruelty, and fate of imperialism, Thucydides aims to warn democrats. Furthermore, in opposition to Hobbes, modern democracy has made gradual headway, achieved longevity and stability. In today's context, Thucydides' insight into the interplay of individual character—what we would call individuality—and a democratic regime, ordered by a common good, provides a coherent structure of explanation, of which reductionist neorealism is but a caricature. Still, as the introduction notes, the elements are inverted. Pericles stressed an imperial, slaveholding, only *partly* democratic regime that, nonetheless, permits a private life for citizens, a *democratic* individuality. In contrast, we admire the individuality, including public expressions, fostered by a regime, a democratic *individuality*.

Further, Thucydides concurs with, and yet immediately limits, Pericles' embodiment of Athenian pride. For the plague, reducing the city to abject self-serving, follows swiftly upon Pericles' speech. Though the latter survives, his influence is eclipsed. The juxtaposition of these two episodes, of public grandeur and horror, motivates a clichéd realist reading: pride leads to a fall. But this "realism" neglects the distinction between what is honorable in Athens—pride in democratic character though also dominion—and subsequent, blind pride, involved in slaughter and decline. One might, more aptly, reformulate the realist cliché: even largely justified pride, adhered to steadily, leads to a fall. For Pericles celebrated imperial grandeur. Perhaps the *History* is even more critical of imperial destiny—and consequent Athenian downfall—than many have thought. For in creating the funeral oration, Thucydides had already experienced Athenian decline. Pericles articulated Athenian glory "in remembrance." Others, however, are not willingly dominated. The slaughter at Syracuse is inglorious.

Thucydides likens the impact of the plague to Athenian conduct in others' civil wars, the Melian massacre, and finally, the misery of Athenians, dying in the quarries of Syracuse. The Athenians were originally high—noble, in memory, and, then, as predators[55]—and finally low. Official realism overlooks the political shadings of Thucydides' theme, which is not a message to all "powers" in the abstract, but a warning to Athens that imperialism will lead to democratic collapse.[56]

5. OFFICIAL "REALISM" AS CORRUPTION: THUCYDIDES VERSUS HOBBES II

Great leaders are unusual.[57] Pericles ruled the Athenians from 461 or 459 to 429, better than a third of Athens' history as a free regime, and presided, as Thucydides does not mention, over imperial expansion.[58] He survives only briefly, until book 3, of the *History*. Thus, his role as military leader condenses that long rule into two years, emphasizes, in the destructive optic of war, pride and frailty. After Pericles' death, demagogues, who pandered to popular conceptions of the "use" of policies and eschewed ideas of character or justice, shaped Athens' policy. Cleon, in particular, advocated genocide in response to the Mytilinean revolt (he sought to kill all the men).[59] Yet Diodotus, whose views prevailed and limited the slaughter, also appealed to the "usefulness" rather than the

justice of his policy. Athenians still, "moderately," put a thousand Mytilinean men to death.[60]

At the end of book 3, Corcyran class war compounds brutality and,
thematically, shapes the remaining, *post-Periclean* books.[61] As Corcyra
reveals, devastating class rivalry between rich and poor may divide any
regime. In such a conflict, attempts to reach a common good—nearly a
balance of competing claims, as Aristotle interprets it—cease; words
change meaning. For democrats, who trap and kill their—oligarchic—
enemies, need an ideological rationale:

> [M]any and heinous things happened in the cities through this sedition. . . .
> war, taking away the affluence of daily necessaries, is a most violent master
> and conformeth most men's passions to the present occasion. . . . The re-
> ceived value of names imposed for signification of things was changed into
> arbitrary. For inconsiderate boldness was counted true-hearted manliness;
> provident deliberation, a handsome fear; modesty, the cloak of cowardice;
> to be wise in everything, to be lazy in everything. A furious suddenness was
> reputed a point of valour. To re-advise for the better security was held for a
> fair pretext of tergiversation. He that was fierce was always trusty, and he
> that contraried such a one was suspected. He that did insidiate, if it took,
> was a wise man; but he that could smell out a trap laid, a more dangerous
> man than he. But he that had been so provident as not to need to do the one
> or the other was said to be a dissolver of society and one that stood in fear
> of his adversary. In brief, he that could outstrip another in the doing of
> an evil act or that could persuade another thereto that never meant it was
> commended.[62]

Hobbes sees in Thucydides' description of the debasement of all sides
at Corcyra a cause for the latter's abstention from Athenian politics. He
misinterprets Corcyran politics as the inevitable trend of *all* politics and
omits Thucydides' praise of Periclean democracy:

> But it seemeth he [Thucydides] had no desire at all to meddle in the govern-
> ment, because in those days it was impossible for any man to give good and
> profitable counsel for the commonwealth, and not incur the displeasure of
> the people. For their opinion was such of their own power, and of the facility
> of achieving whatsoever action they undertook, that such men only swayed
> the assemblies, and were esteemed wise and good commonwealth's men, as
> did put them upon the most dangerous and desperate enterprises. Whereas
> he that gave them temperate and discreet advice, was thought a coward, or
> not to understand, or else to malign their power. And no marvel: for much
> prosperity (to which they had now for many years been accustomed) maketh
> men *in love with themselves*, and it is hard for any man to love that counsel
> which makes him love himself the less.[63]

Although, as Hobbes recognizes, Pericles confronted popular disapproval after the plague, he ignores Pericles' celebrated leadership of the Athenian polis, to whose grandeur his funeral oration attests, for thirty years before it.

In this citation, however, we can see the identification of Hobbes's notion of love of self with Greek and biblical pride (hubris). In contrast, Aristotle rightly distinguishes justified love of self—being a self—from selfishness.[64] In Thucydides, Pericles' pride in offering the funeral oration—his self-confidence in the nobility of a democratic way of life—illustrates the distinction lost in Hobbes. Yet in the tragedy of Athenian defeat, we may also see Pericles' blind pride in empire.

Many Christians, however, erase the Greek contrast. They see life as selfishness—original sin—and envision self-abnegating altruism as an alternative. Thus, the Christian term *humility* mistranslates the Greek *sophrosune* (moderation). The triumph of Christianity—even its subtle influence on so great an opponent as Hobbes—helps to explain much of the later misreading of Thucydides. Nonetheless, Niebuhr's sense of Lincoln's mercy, stemming from "a broken spirit and a contrite heart," can cohere with a more subtle, psychological view of "love of self."

Following Thucydides, the political criticism of pride—identified with blind arrogance—and greed or overreaching of human limits (*pleonexia*)[65] become central themes of Greek realism, Christianity, and modern political theory. These themes illustrate a (near) commonality between Thucydides and Hobbes. In this context, however, today's neo*realists*, who imagine that they are value-neutral, shockingly misunderstand the long-standing moral impulse of realism.

From this common point, however, Hobbes proceeds sharply in his own, non-Thucydidean direction. As the sole alleged alternative to murderous anarchy or civil war, the estate of what he memorably calls "masterless men," Hobbes defends monarchy: many do not "consider that the state of man can never be without some incommodity or other, and that the greatest, that in any form of government can possibly happen to the people in general, is scarce sensible in respect of the miseries, and horrible calamities, that accompany a civil war, or that dissolute condition of masterless men, without subjection to laws, and a coercive power to tie their hands from rapine and revenge."[66]

In illustrating this theme, Hobbes relies on and yet distorts Thucydides. For the international and civil wars, depicted in the *History*, illumine Hobbes's fear of the Puritan Revolution. In fact, such paradigms are far more striking than his own, a much more debatable account of human rapaciousness in a putative state of nature. Hobbes sees Leviathan as ruler over the *children of pride*. Unlike Athenians and modern liberals, for whom toleration is a central public good,[67] Hobbes interprets every slight, every ostensible slight, as an inevitable cause of inter-Greek and civil war, and English rebellion: "considering what value men are naturally apt to set upon themselves; what respect they look for from others; and how little they value other men; from whence continually arise amongst them, emulation, quarrels, factions, and at last war, to the destroying of one another, and diminution of their strength against a common enemy."[68]

In contrast, as Thucydides favorably notes in book 8, Alcibiades persuaded the democrats at Samos not to attack the oligarchy at Athens because intensified civil war would expose all Athenians to conquest by nearby enemies. Seeing Pericles or Alcibiades as nondemocratic leaders, however, Hobbes identifies a one-sided, non-Thucydidean psychology of pride and indignity as the cause of strife: "[A]ll men are by nature provided of notable multiplying glasses, that is, their passions and self-love, through which every little payment appeareth a great grievance; but are destitute of those prospective glasses, namely moral and civil science, to see afar off the miseries that hang over them, and cannot without such payments be avoided."[69]

Hobbes has, notably, dropped away Thucydides' themes of the possibility of a rightly ordered democratic politics as well as individual restraint or self-possession. In fact, as we have seen, to explain Thucydides' abstention from Athenian politics, Hobbes wrongly identifies the best with the worst, Periclean Athens with Corcyra. He even avers in *Leviathan* that tyranny is merely "monarchy misliked."[70] For to legitimize his reductionist psychology—that all pride is subjective and unjustified—Hobbes erases central moral, psychological, and political distinctions emphasized by Thucydides and Greek political theory.

Now Hobbes condemns Corcyran shifts of word and practice. The deterioration in the "value" of terms does not diminish the "evil" of acts.[71] The license of a prevailing power—also a "Leviathan," not merely the parliamentary "Behemoth" that Hobbes decries—does not mean that a deterioration in common verbal currency conveys what Hobbes rightly considers moral substance. Contrary to Hobbes's reductionism, to see the deterioration or corruption, as he does, one must cleave to that substance.[72] Thucydides, however, goes farther than Hobbes. He contrasts a common good-ordered democracy with rapacious, ultimately doomed, imperial politics.

Under the progressive influence of war, Thucydides depicts Corcyran democrats and oligarchs as abandoning virtue and operating on a murderous renaming of standards. An image, exaggerated at the expense of the rest of Thucydides' account, of a mainly shifty, ruthless human nature—exhibiting a "perpetual and restless desire for power after power, that ceaseth only in death"[73]—shapes both Hobbes's translation of the

History (1628) and his subsequent interpretations of politics in *De Cive*, *Leviathan*, and *Behemoth*. In *Leviathan*, for example, Hobbes insists, moral terms may "arbitrarily" change significance not only as a factual matter—or matter of sociology—as in Corcyra, but, by decree of the sovereign, as an ethical one (*a transience of moral standards claim*): "For these words of good, evil, and contemptible, are ever used with relation to the person that useth them: there being nothing simply or absolutely so; nor any common rule of good and evil, to be taken from the nature of the objects themselves; but from the person of the man, where there is no commonwealth; or, in a commonwealth, from the person that representeth it."[74] Thus, Hobbes substitutes legal or ethical positivism for ethics.

In contrast, Locke's *Second Treatise* rightly responds that injustices are committed—rights, as conditions of respect for human capacities and well-being, are violated—even in a putative state of nature. In such cases, "every man hath a *right* to punish the offender and be executioner of the law of nature."[75] *Leviathan*'s initial claim that each has but to look into her (or his) own perceptions and feelings to experience the truth of Hobbes's core doctrine, however, also contradicts his relativism.[76]

Hobbes's legal positivism partly prefigures the ethical positivism of today's neorealists (that the moral stands of statespersons are but "expressions of power"). Hobbes's reductionism, however, plays a different political role in his argument from that of contemporary scholars: an able sovereign must disguise the human provenance of laws from citizens.[77] But such positivism is inconsistent with the core of his argument. For Hobbes emphasizes fear of violent death—and hence, the good of life—which licenses, but also limits, Leviathan's power.[78]

Thus, a prisoner, sentenced to death, may "rattle his chains" and resist: "they but defend their lives, which the guilty man may as well do, as the innocent."[79] Further, as Hobbes puts it, "no man can transfer, or lay down, his right to save himself from death, wounds, and imprisonment, the avoiding whereof is the only end of laying down any right."[80] In these cases, the rule of Leviathan threatens to overturn its underlying, *natural* justification. Hobbes's theory that all seek to avoid violent death can not consistently underpin the instability of *moral* meanings that his sociological reductionist misreading of Corcyra requires. Further, starting from the good of preserving life, Thucydides, in contrast to Hobbes, defends a good life, at least a justly ordered democracy.

Hobbes's inference, however, licenses not only his famed but inconsistent moral relativism, but also his specific version of *conservativism*. On a Hobbesian view, all non-Hobbesian political arguments—ones not immediately based in the preservation of life—become secondary, arbitrary matters of opinion (as we saw in chapter 2, Morgenthau's distinction between public "duty" and "personal morality" to deprecate the profound issue of slavery exemplifies this weakness). For where Hobbes's underlying moral insistence on fear of death should lead to a direct response to such views, deciphering whether they would better succeed in preserving life than his own, he offers, instead, unreasoned rejection—a rejection without consideration—simply because they fail to coincide with the positive will of the sovereign. Though Hobbes starts from Thucydides' account, the secondary apparatus of *Leviathan* is inconsistent both with Thucydides and in its own terms.

Theoretically, Leviathan is, then, not so powerful a figure as Hobbes infers. The monarch's justification stems from preserving the life—though not, as with Aristotle, mainly a good life—of each citizen. Contrary to Hobbes, if Leviathan fails, he becomes—as an Aristotelian might note—a tyrant, an illegitimate Behemoth. Further, in addition to life, Hobbes wants a decent regime to facilitate a "commodious life" for each[81] rather than the eudaemonist goods of activity, relationship, and virtue. As Hobbes's view of justice reveals, however, he sometimes affirms the latter as well. Moreover, he speaks "without affectation to either side, and not as a lover of country, but of truth."[82] Like Thucydides and Morgenthau, and in contrast to today's official realism, Hobbes makes no attempt to be "value-free."[83]

Cleaving to Hobbes's mistaken, secondary notion that moral terms have no intrinsic meaning and that "men" are solely motivated by hunger for power, modern realists and neorealists adopt an amoral and apsychological concept of power to explain political action. Hobbes's morally inspired, psychologically sophisticated, antidemocratic realism is, thus, a far more accurate account both of Thucydides and of public life than reductionist neorealism.

Yet in contrast to Hobbes, Thucydides means to depict the grandeur of Athenian democracy—as in Pericles' funeral oration—as well as its moral collapse, adumbrated by the Athenian role in class war at Corcyra, and, later, fully realized in Athens. Thus, Thucydides' image of justice highlights public *corruption*—a Greek, but not a Hobbesian concept—in the Corcyran civil war. For the Greeks, corruption was the opposite of a common good, a frightening, narrowly self-seeking response to extreme circumstances.[84] In Plato, Thrasymachus, in the *Republic*, who maintains that "justice is the advantage of the stronger," Callicles in the *Gorgias*, Anytus in the *Meno*, and Meletus in the *Apology* speak in the voice of decadent Corcyra. Contrary to Hobbes and official realism, however, neither Plato nor Thucydides—who aptly render that misshapen voice—do.[85]

In plotting about Mytilene, a precursor to the genocide at Melos, the language of mere advantage (*to sumpheron*) of the moderate Diodotus as well as the violent Cleon, supplants the Periclean idiom of grandeur, justice (*to dikaion*), freedom, and openness.[86] Where, in his final speech, Pericles considered the empire as "like a tyranny" (*hos tyrannida*), for Cleon and later, Euphemus, it became, simply, a "tyranny."[87] Such distinctions are available neither to Hobbes nor to official realism. In Corcyra, civil war, intensified by international conflict—antidemocratic feedback—reduces oligarchs and democrats to murderous shadows of citizens. In acts even more than words, Athens has declined from Pericles and entered upon a cycle of aggression, conquest, and, ultimately, defeat.

6. THE OFFICIAL REALIST MISINTERPRETATION OF MELOS

For beginning students, John Vazquez's *Classics of International Politics* reproduces four pages of Thucydides' *History*—the indelibly fierce exchange between the Athenian delegation and the Melian magistrates as a prelude to conquest and genocide at Melos.[88] The Athenians speak privately to magistrates rather than publicly to citizens. They ask to deliver, and the Melians respond with, unparalleled short speeches (here, Thucydides prefigures Platonic dialogue). This technique accentuates the seeming frankness, the lack of need for public "legitimation," of the Athenian ambassadors. They invoke the law of conquest—"the law of the stronger"—that realists treat as the central lesson of the *History*: "they that have the odds of power exact as much as they can, and the weak yield to such conditions as they can get."[89] Against this compelling theme, the Melians can summon only "hope" (*elpis*) in a future in which the cautious Spartans somehow adventure to save them—they lack strength to defend themselves—and pride in their seven-hundred-year independence. On a realist view, one might say, small wonder, then, that the Athenians slaughter them.

In the setting of book 5, however, this dialogue exhibits a remarkably different, nonrealist context. For the Melians echo the words of Herodotus's daring, but seemingly outnumbered Athenians against the Persian Empire at Salamis.[90] Hope and justice—resisting Persian aggression and conquest—are political causes of Greek victory, not just mechanical comparisons of numbers of soldiers and sailors (what neorealists think of, apolitically, as power).[91] Further, in contrast to Melos, which had existed for seven hundred years as a free and independent city, Athens had been a democracy, and then an empire, for less than a hundred years. One recalls the injured, daring citizens of Melos in admiring the daring of the people of another island, Syracuse, and being daunted by the massacre in Syracusan quarries of the Athenians.

In addition, Hermocrates had already invoked to Syracusans the power of those who resist and not just those who aggress: "for it is the nature of man everywhere to command such as give way and to be shy of such as assail." Resistance to injustice is as much a law as conquest by the powerful: "We are to blame that know this and do not provide accordingly and make it our first care of all to take good order against the common fear. Of which we should soon be delivered, if we would agree amongst ourselves."[92] At Melos, the Athenians speak in a kind of soulless desperation; their fate already hovers in the words.

Put differently, the law of history is of struggle by the seemingly weak—class struggle from below by those who are victimized—not only the crass triumph of the powerful. Thucydides' account of Syracusan resistance, linking citizens to sustain a common good, strikingly illustrates *democratic internationalism*. The Athenians maintain a law of the stronger as a putative apology: "Neither did we make this law nor are we the first that use it made; but as we found it, and shall leave it to posterity for ever, so also we use it, knowing that you likewise, and others that should have the same power which we have, would do the same."[93] But Pericles represents a different possibility. If Thucydides had meant to praise, as a theme, the supposed "law of the stronger," he would not have concluded with the Athenian defeat at Syracuse and internal collapse. He would have stopped, instead, ahistorically, with the account of Melos.[94]

Thus, Hermocrates articulated a central theme of the *History* and prefigured democratic internationalism: those who stick together, who fight for a common good, can overcome the odds of power and withstand fearsome external attack. In Thucydides, those who remain divided by class war end up like the bloody oligarchs and democrats at Corcyra.[95] Class strife, culminating in the oligarchy of the Four Hundred, the Tyranny of the Thirty, and Spartan conquest—rather than the defeat at Syracuse taken by itself—leads to the destruction of Athens. In contrast to neorealism, Athenian history and political science thus emphasize the interplay of global and domestic politics. The study of public corruption, of the decline of a common good and the emergence of international, and then domestic, murderousness is central to Greek thought. It captures the *antidemocratic feedback* involved in the Tyranny of the Thirty—the violent triumph of oligarchy—as well as in expansionary, decadent, ultimately defeated democracy.[96]

The official realist failure to see the role of resistant democratic Syracuse mirrors the blindness of American politicians, officers, and academics in Vietnam. Swollen with arrogance, the "ignorant" Athenians end up, dying, demoralized and cowardly, in Syracusan quarries.

In the Melian dialogue, the Athenian speakers, as compared even to their predecessor, the "violent" Cleon, have become nameless[97]—a contrast not to be discovered from the standard neorealist excerpt. For Pericles, citizenship in the Athenian assembly gave names and voices to different strategies and allowed deliberation and judgment:[98] "For also in this we excel others, daring to undertake as much as any and yet examining what we undertake; whereas with other men ignorance makes them dare and consideration dastards. And they are most rightly reputed valiant who, though they perfectly apprehend both what is dangerous and what is easy, are never the more thereby diverted from adventuring."[99] This contrast concurs with Walzer's between hypothetical debate in the Athenian assembly and "law-like realism."[100]

Thus, contrary to democratic grandeur, the ambassadors at Melos are mere "realist" voices of a conquest that prefigure the subsequent Athenian defeat at Syracuse. To emphasize the interconnection of the two events, Thucydides does not conclude the fifth book (where he usually says: "thus ended the battle at . . . ," no such sentence occurs here). The slaughter by Athenians at Melos thus blends with the slaughter of Athenians at Syracuse: hunger for power transforms citizens into the shadow of self-aware democrats. In the opening sentence of book 6, Thucydides foreshadows the cause: "The same winter the Athenians, with greater forces than they had before set out with Laches and Eurymedon, resolved to go again into Sicily, and, if they could, wholly to subdue it, being for the most part ignorant both of the greatness of the island, and of the multitude of people, as well Greeks as barbarians, that inhabited the same, and that they undertook a war not much less than the war against the Peleponnesians."[101] Parallel to Athens in Syracuse, no one in the American State Department, at the time of the Kennedy and Johnson escalations of the war, knew Vietnamese.

Eschewing the sea that Pericles had hailed as the decisive Athenian military advantage, Nicias, leading forty thousand disheartened troops, echoed the "empty" words of the Melian magistrates about hope:

> Nicias, perceiving the army to be dejected, and the great change that was in it . . . exalted his voice more than ever before. . . .[102]
>
> "Athenians and confederates, we must hope (*elpida*) still, even in the present state. Men have been saved ere now [note the passive voice] from greater dangers than these are. . . . And yet I have worshipped the gods frequently according to the law (*es theous nomima dedietemai*) and lived justly (*dikaia*) and unblameably toward men. For which cause my hope (*elpis*) is still confident of the future, though these calamaties, as being not according to the measure of our desert, do indeed make me fear."[103]

He thus expressed hope in the gods, as did the Melian magistrates, as well as fear of divine retribution.[104]

But while he noted, in passing, that he still commanded forty thousand Athenians, Nicias failed to grasp the real relations of power, which now favored Syracuse. He also omitted the causes: Athenian arrogance—

ironically, he had, originally, opposed the invasion, and his extreme caution, uncharacteristic for an Athenian, had brought his troops to their current, desperate pass—and Syracusan unity in self-defense.[105] As Connor stresses, Nicias's own timidity highlights the fatedness, public and individual, of Athenian aggression in Sicily. Personal worth within Athenian mores and faith in a measure of divine justice for individuals carry no weight in this historic struggle. The *public* greed and wantonness of Athens lead to its decline. For Thucydides, the battle at Syracuse parallels the Greek defeat of the Persians at Salamis. Recalling his initial passage on the "greatness of the war" that motivates the work, Thucydides summarizes Athenian defeat as, shockingly, the "greatest" event in Greek history: "And this was the greatest action that happened in all this war, or at all, that we have heard of amongst the Grecians, being to the victors most glorious and most calamitous to the vanquished. For being wholly overcome in every kind and receiving small loss in nothing, the army and fleet and all perished . . . with an universal destruction. Few of many (*oligoi apo pollon*) returned home. And thus passed the business concerning Sicily."[106]

Thus, contrary to neorealism, the core of Greek democratic realism is moral insight into pride and self-restraint. Those enthralled with and driven by power are destroyed by it.[107] In tragedy, for instance Sophocles', we see this corruption in the fate of Creon, who refuses to allow Antigone's brother burial and sentences her to death, sealed in a cave, for covering him. As vultures cast Polynices' unclean flesh over the city, Creon's son, who loves Antigone, and then his wife, commit suicide. Only too late does Creon see.[108]

For Socrates, democratic public life invites hubris and leads to destruction. Plato and Aristotle stress the dangers of Athenian imperialism.[109] Unjust conquest abroad, as Aristotle suggests, might persuade a powerful figure at home, driven by ambition and possessing sufficient skill and resources, to become tyrant.[110] Plato's *Republic* is the leading argument in political theory that suffering injustice is better than any temporary "gain" derived from committing it. For even a rare tyrant with a reputation for utter justice reveals a lack of self-possession that accompanies and ends in horror.[111]

7. WAR BETWEEN DEMOCRACIES: THE SYRACUSAN DEFEAT OF ATHENS

Syracuse's war with, and defeat of, Athens also undercuts the newly prevalent, mainly post–Cold War thesis that democracies—merely as a result of the form—do not war against other democracies. In convening assemblies of citizens, Athens was, of course, more democratic than today's

America, which is an oligarchy with parliamentary forms. Yet Athenian democracy was highly restricted. Aristocrats like Pericles dominated its politics. Ordinary citizens, Thucydides notes, "judge but do not originate." As Connor puts it, the *phauloi* or *poneroi* lacked organization, in contrast to the friendships that leagued the influential, the *chrestoi*. Further, Aristophanes' *Peace* mocks demagogues like Cleon, around whom "a snake-like mass of flatterers writhed." Some offices were not open to all citizens.[112]

As I have noted, though the assembly was comparatively participatory, imperial tribute paid for attendance. Moreover, the Athenian and Syracusan regimes held slaves. Even though Aristotle does not understand that institution's horror, he rightly emphasizes the class structure that underlies such regimes, an insight lost to contemporary proponents of neorealism and the democratic-peace hypothesis.[113] Denying the humanity of those whom they enslaved, Athenians could not see humanity in other democrats. Similarly, denying the humanity of Asians through racism, the American "democratic" empire would come to stunning defeat in Vietnam.

American leaders ignored the long struggle of the Vietnamese against colonialism.[114] A little country, smaller than Syracuse, far off, they might have said . . .

Since the defeat of Athens by Syracuse, central in ancient history, conflicts with the newly prevailing thesis, one might expect that international-relations experts, who pay obeisance to Thucydides as the first "realist," would have considered it. Until recently, they have not.[115] To save the contemporary thesis, however, one could emphasize the novelty of ancient democracy, as well as its class character: interdemocratic wars occur only in regimes where the demos is highly restricted. One might note that modern democracies—at least formally—recognize each citizen and rule out slavery.[116] Perhaps this extension of freedom and an increased impact for citizen resistance might explain a lesser likelihood of contemporary interdemocratic war. For instance, as we have seen, Kant stresses "citizen" opposition to imperialism compared to a monarch's wanton sacrifice of "subjects."

Recognizing intra-Greek democratic conflict, however, requires a more fundamental revision of the thesis that *democracies do not go to war against one another*. For if, given initial class analysis, we insist on the importance of slaveholding in Athenian arrogance, we may also notice the role of imperial oligarchy in U.S. arrogance.[117] Thus, as the first two chapters emphasize, the American regime has intervened against elected regimes in Iran, Guatemala, Brazil, Indonesia, Chile, Nicaragua, Guyana, the Congo, Haiti, and, through barring fulfillment of the Geneva Accords that provided for internationally supervised elections in 1956, Vietnam.[118] The omission by contemporary political "science" of American antidemocratic belligerence—on behalf of a thesis that purports to defend democratic "peacefulness"—has, as I have stressed, a misguided, operationalist justification: an insistence that only the loss of a thousand soldiers on each side characterizes an intervention as a war. Thus, the existence of an American empire and aggressive acts comparable, though not even motivated by memories of democratic grandeur, to Athens at its worst, has, ironically, escaped the attention of many political scientists concerned with democracy. Advocates of democratic peace also fail to respond to Chomsky, Klare, and other critical observers.[119]

Still, a class-oriented account of democracy might save the thesis. For the more genuine the democracy, as chapter 5 argues, the greater the degree of popular control of, or influence over, foreign policy, coupled with easier access to the truth about specific policies, the more likely that citizens will defend their basic interests in life, well-being, and liberty, and limit war and intervention.[120] In contrast, only an oligarchy with parliamentary forms, a democratic internationalist might suggest, is imperialist.

Further, we might reformulate this thesis: advanced capitalist, comparatively stable European and American parliamentary regimes have not gone to war with one another.[121] As a realist might note, most of these regimes are, comparatively, great powers—the cost of the United States, England, France, or Germany warring with each other would be enormous. In addition, rulers would have difficulty stigmatizing others among these regimes, through racism, as "enemies." Nonetheless, "peace" among parliamentary oligarchies is distantly—though still importantly—related to citizen pressure against war.

Now some post–Cold War American interventions, for instance in Somalia, are, also, more humanitarian than imperialist. But given American oligarchy, such humanitarian efforts are, if there is significant risk, unlikely to be forceful even to save the most needy, as the long European and American failure to act in Bosnia revealed. To articulate a reasonable critique of American foreign policy is, thus, to reveal how far removed much of prevailing journalism and academic work is from democratic values or responsibility. What Morgenthau named the "academic-political complex" remains in place.

8. THUCYDIDES THROUGH THE LENS OF VIETNAM

Influenced by the early Cold War, American classicists like Pouncey read Thucydides through a lens of pessimism, in which the USSR and the United States assumed the roles of Sparta and Athens.[122] More exactly, allegiance to democracy provided an ideological rationale for American Cold War policy, but, as realists recognized, its policies need not—in the less developed countries, did not—further democracy. In contrast, W. Robert Connor reveals, the experience of Vietnam transformed his understanding of the *History* and accentuated moral themes: the link of America to Athens and Vietnam to Syracuse.

> I had long been struggling with the tensions between detachment and involvement, optimism and pessimism, morality and power in Thucydides. But I can be quite precise about the moment when I began to think about Thucydides in a new way. In the middle of the Vietnamese War, when it seemed impossible to think of almost anything else, I remember reading an essay in the *New Yorker* on the destruction of Vietnam. The issue was dated March 9, 1968—the very height of the conflict. Five hundred and forty-two American soldiers had been killed the previous week; the following day the papers reported General Westmoreland's request for 206,000 troops to be added to the existing American force of 510,000. The essay, by Jonathan Schell began "The following article is about what is happening to Vietnam— to the people and the land—as a result of the American military presence. I shall not discuss the moral ramifications of that presence. I shall simply try to set down what I saw and heard first hand during several weeks I spent with our armed forces in South Vietnam last summer. . . . I have no wish to pass judgment on the individual Americans fighting in Vietnam. I merely wish to record what I witnessed." As I read on in the article, I was repeatedly reminded of Thucydides and his descriptions that avoided moral rhetoric and made the audience visualize what was happening.[123]

Is such an experience, even so vivid a one as that of American aggression in Vietnam, merely the founder of a new ideology? Ironically, Cold War scholars—and earlier scholars—had offered an arcane interpretation of Thucydides in which pieces of the work, though separately coherent, were thought to be dissimilar, explained somehow by patterns in a—largely unknown—life.[124] Further, older classicists disregarded the theme of democracy and decay. Now, an identification of ideology, let alone a *series* of ideologies, especially in so careful a writer as Thucydides, requires striking demonstration of anomalies. Otherwise, the interpretation appears as a mere attempt, nurtured in a reactionary political climate—the Truman-McCarthyism of the Cold War—to force an uncongenial interpretation on the *History*:

> [T]he prevalent assumptions about the text made it easy for political philosophers and political scientists to extract from the work a series of propositions about his [Thucydides'] political views on the empire, democracy, Realpolitik, and the like. If this sounded suspiciously like the construction of the prose-paraphrases that the New Critics so deplored, it was at least a convenient approach, one that made it possible to treat Thucydides as a

thinker and to extract some useful messages from his work: that peace and freedom required power and preparedness; that great powers had to be tough and constantly alert; that sea-power ought, if properly directed, to have a great strategic advantage over continental powers. These and other inferences could be debated, of course, and none was explicitly stated by Thucydides, but it seemed fully appropriate to view his text as containing propositions that could be explicated and brought into a coherent system and identified as "Thucydides' Political Philosophy," or even as a series of laws about the science of politics.[125]

Ironically for an interpreter of so famous an historian, Connor learned from the New Criticism in literature, which stressed close readings of text, largely ignoring context.[126] Informed by the Vietnam War, Connor's subtle reading emphasizes the critique of imperial democracy that forms the central thread of Thucydides' work.

Connor also acknowledges his debt to the pathbreaking studies of Jacqueline de Romilly,[127] who read Thucydides in the context of the defeat of French colonial wars in Indochina and Algeria. De Romilly's original breakthrough, however, concentrated on imperialism, but downplayed the theme of democracy. Having changed his view, Connor provides an exceptionally self-aware account of the differences between Cold War–based and Vietnam-based interpretations of Thucydides.

In international politics, however, American neorealism—and, later, the democratic-peace hypothesis—developed independently of new classical insights into Thucydides. Nonetheless, few American realists fail to criticize the Vietnam War—as an overexpansion of power—after the fact. But they condemn the war without explicit interest in democracy. American "power," they say, lost the support of the citizenry (this criticism could, however, note a fact about *any* regime). It waged a brutal, hopeless war against the Vietnamese; it made a "mistake." Curiously blasé, many adherents to the democratic-peace hypothesis tend not to discuss this—or other disturbing—cases.[128]

In Thucydidean perspective, however, as Connor suggests and Morgenthau's analysis affirms, the American oligarchy waged a genocidal war against a people *able* to defend itself. Analogous to Hermocrates, Ho Chi Minh led a forty-year resistance first against French colonialism, then (allied with the U.S. government!) against Japanese aggression, then, again, against French colonialism (treacherously aided by the U.S. government), and, finally, against the United States itself.[129] Given the pro-colonial and genocidal character of those invasions, that long war of self-defense was just. Analogous to the violent Cleon, President Johnson had to lie about the Vietnam War, persecute internal critics, and violate a common good. Following Aristotle's conception of antidemocratic feedback, an internationalist might link (oligarchic) violation of democracy at home to unjust expansion—violation of democracy—abroad. As the introduction stresses, party competition, based on defaming opponents as "weak" on Communism and hounding opposition, laid the basis for these violations. But comparable to Athens in Syracuse, LBJ's blindness— his escalation of an imperial war and persecution of critics—led to unforeseen American defeat. In addition, advice by those committed to "power"-rivalry and opposed to democracy—Bundy, Kissinger, and other components of an "academic-political complex"—contributed to that downfall. For an individual and a people, Thucydides knew what the honor of a citizen or a regime meant. Two thousand years later, Morgenthau followed him. But worshiping power at the expense of democracy, unable to listen to this oldest of international-relations texts, an oligarchic establishment launched the brutal, self-defeating war against which Thucydides warned.

TABLE 6
Why Democracy and Public Corruption Are Central for Thucydides and Anomalies
for Hobbes and Neorealism

	Original Democratic Realism (Thucydides, de Romilly, Connor)		
	Democratic Realist Thesis	*Socratic Critique*	*Democratic Internationalist Critique*
Thesis 1	Innovative democracy could withstand the odds and resist aggression (the Athenian-led defeat of Persian imperialism). It thus defended the lives—and equal liberties—of its citizens	Same as democratic realist thesis	Same as democratic realist thesis
Thesis 2	This democracy took pride in its accomplishments, the equal freedom of each, deliberation, magnanimity, and openness	The downfall of Athenian democracy stems from the nature of politics. Pericles' commitment to imperial grandeur unleashed policies that culminated in decline	Same as democratic realist thesis
Thesis 3	Athens held a limited empire originally through acceptance, among its subject peoples, of its vigor and virtue. Pericles celebrates imperial "grandeur." As memories of the defeat of Persian imperialism faded, however, that empire became oppressive.[b] Athenians would expand at their own risk (Pericles)	A nonexpansionary democracy could not maintain peace;[a] only a justly ordered hierarchical regime, led by a philosopher-king, could do so	As with internal slaveholding, external subordination inevitably leads to corruption. In opposition to Thucydides, even limited empire is not for "the good of the governed"—a broader, antidemocratic-feedback thesis
Thesis 4	Appeals to narrow "interests," money, or use degraded the public concerns of citizens and led, over time, to corruption		Same

TABLE 6 (*cont.*)

Original Democratic Realism (Thucydides, de Romilly, Connor)

	Democratic Realist Thesis	Socratic Critique	Democratic Internationalist Critique
Thesis 5	Decadence exacerbated restless Athenian character, led to the ignoring of Pericles' advice, and resulted in warring on others, particularly democrats, of whom Athenians were ignorant (Syracuse)		In a modern—Kantian—reformulation of Thucydides' argument, democrats have common interests, in opposition to their state(s), against wars on other democracies and wars of aggression
Thesis 6	Defeat in war encouraged violent class strife and regime-change at home—antidemocratic feedback—and, after the *History* concludes,[c] collapse		Same

Classical, Hobbesian, Antidemocratic Realism

	Classical Realist Thesis	Democratic Realist—or Internationalist—Thesis
Thesis 1	The aim of a regime is to prevent the violent death of any (and, hence, to ward off aggression)	Same
Thesis 2	A state of nature is thus a state of war, a condition without justice. The "children of pride" conduct such a war	No state of nature exists; murder is wrong (alternately, as Locke suggests, even in a state of nature, murder is wrong)
Thesis 3	Even in a civil state (*civitas*), prideful citizens war with each other over—interpreted—slights. Any slight tends to lead to war	Justice is based on—minimally—the preservation of the life of each citizen. Thus, Hobbesian realist theses 1 and 7—in ethics, a *moral* realism[d]—contradict theses 3–6

continues on next page

TABLE 6 (*cont.*)

Classical, Hobbesian, Antidemocratic Realism

	Classical Realist Thesis	Democratic Realist—or Internationalist—Thesis
Thesis 4	Moral terms mean simply what the interested—ideologues, or the children of pride—want them to mean (moral relativism)	No necessary psychological and social slippage exists between slights in (an extensive) democracy—a regime that ignores and often even fails to elicit "censorious looks"—and war
Thesis 5	Rule by an absolute monarch is the only alternative to war	The reasonable alternatives are between a just regime—one that seeks a common good and is characterized by toleration—and tyrannies. Hobbes's opposition of monarchy to no government is false
Thesis 6	Justice is what the Leviathan, by law, declares it to be (legal positivism)	The aim of each to avoid violent death is Hobbes's central ethical claim and rules out his moral relativism. That the meanings of ethical terms shift, *sociologically,* does not alter their intrinsic moral reference: the *horror* of a state of war
Thesis 7	Nonetheless, justice is (also) a "gallant-nesse of courage" by which a person disdains advantage from fraud or breach of promise (moral realism)	Same, except that the sovereign disdains to prey on the lives and well-being of citizens. These goods are more fundamental than—do not arise from—what Hobbes calls "promise"
Thesis 8	Prisoners, sentenced to death, may violently resist Leviathan	Murderers do not *rightly* rebel against punishment[e]
Thesis 9		Capital punishment may, nonetheless, reflect an inadequate respect for the nature and dignity of a democratic regime[f]

Thin, Neorealist Reductionism

	Neorealist Thesis	Democratic Realist—or Internationalist—Rejoinder
Thesis 1	No common good exists	Hobbes's theses 1 and 7 are right against neorealism. By officially denying the good of life as well as of its common protection, the latter removes any justification for state interests.
Thesis 2	In the international arena, regimes are based upon and seek power. There is no moral or analytic distinction to be	

TABLE 6 (*cont.*)

Thin, Neorealist Reductionism

	Neorealist Thesis	Democratic Realist—or Internationalist—Rejoinder
	drawn between a democracy, however it honors the lives and consciences of citizens, and a tyranny, however severe	Neorealist thesis 4 contradicts neorealist theses 1–3
Thesis 3	No consideration of justice, no Hobbesian magnanimity, enters into the theory of international politics (legal positivism)	
Thesis 4	The interests of a state are justified by the goal of protecting citizens against aggression	

The Democratic-Peace Argument

	Democratic-Peace Thesis	Democratic Realist—and Internationalist—Rejoinder
Thesis 1	Democracies do not go to war with one another	The defeat of Athens by Syracuse shows otherwise. In addition, the American regime has a pattern of anti-democratic belligerence in the less developed countries
Thesis 2		Advanced capitalist, comparatively stable European and American democracies—oligarchies with parliamentary forms—do not war on one another. To some extent, that "peacefulness" reflects the will and interests of the citizens of those regimes

[a] Nonetheless, according to Plutarch's "Nicias," Socrates warned against invading Sicily.

[b] As a just war that led to empire, the Athenian-led defeat of Persia parallels the Soviet Union's defeat of Nazism. That mobilization inspired Soviet legitimacy—long after World War II—although its influence among subject peoples, as with the legitimacy of Athenian empire, swiftly declined.

[c] Book 8 breaks off after the twenty-first year of the war.

[d] Gilbert, *Democratic Individuality*, chaps. 1–3. Moral realism insists that ethical terms—often—refer to real properties of human freedom, cooperation, and well-being. In less determinate cases, however, the sovereign—notably a democracy—may, so long as it does not unnecessarily harm any person, decide what is just.

[e] Rightly criticizing Hobbes, Hegel, *Philosophy of Right,* pars. 258, 275–79, sees punishment as restoring the prisoner's rationality as a free individual, which is realized in honoring the *substance*—the impersonal laws—of a free regime.

[f] Hobbes's core thesis 1 contradicts theses 2, 4, and 6. If Hobbes's characterization of a state of nature were right, thesis 8 would follow from thesis 1. But equal citizens rightly protect themselves from murder. Though a murderer may appeal, he or she does not have a *right* to resist punishment violently.

Part Three

DELIBERATIVE DEMOCRACY AND

"GAMBLING FOR RESURRECTION"

Deliberation as a Medium for Internationalism

> [The tyrant's] next step, however, so that the people
> will always be in need of a leader is to undertake an
> ongoing search for pretexts to make war.
>
> I dare say.
>
> Moreover, the imposition of war taxes is likely to
> impoverish the citizenry sufficiently so that they must
> tend more diligently to earning their livelihood with
> correspondingly less time to plot against the leader.
>
> A telling observation.
>
> Then, too, I suppose he would suspect the continu-
> ing presence of free men in the city who resist his
> domination. What better way to get rid of them than
> to send them off to the wars to take their chances
> with the enemy? All these provide the tyrant with
> compelling reasons for constantly provoking wars.
>
> (Plato, *Republic*, 566e–567a)

> The laws will never make men [and women] free. It is
> men who have got to make the laws free. They are the
> lovers of law and order, who observe the law when
> the government breaks it.
> (Henry David Thoreau, "Slavery in Massachusetts")

> When asked what he thought about "Western civili-
> zation," Gandhi replied: "It would be nice."

1. INTERNATIONALISM VERSUS PLURALISM

This chapter deepens internationalism's conception of a common good
by exploring a theory of deliberative democracy. It then considers the
promise of novel, nonviolent movements, a panoply of possible reforms
to make contemporary oligarchy more democratic, and new international
regimes, prefigured in the Ottawa Convention Banning Land Mines, restrictions on greenhouse gases, and other initiatives of the post–Cold War
era.

The first section contrasts internationalism with pluralism. The second examines the contemporary American intensification of oligarchy. The third shows how a conception of deliberative democracy permits principled resolutions of otherwise intractable ethical disputes. Focusing on hard cases, the fourth highlights limits of public deliberations where they attempt to override individual conscience. It suggests that deliberative democracy is primarily a *conscience-sustaining regime*. The fifth assesses nonviolent movements for social change. The sixth proposes reforms—greater toleration for civil disobedience, referenda on major issues, and abolition of secret police—to further domestic deliberation. Upholding the *fair value* of equal public liberties (Rawls), the seventh defends public financing of campaigns as well as, to contest referenda, issue-oriented committees. It also suggests treatment of news media as, on important political concerns, a public trust, mandating advocacy of diverse opinion.

The eighth section criticizes abstract visions of cosmopolitan governance, but suggests, instead, the importance of global regimes on particular issues such as outlawing land mines, curtailing the emission of greenhouse gases, barring the use of children as soldiers, and founding an international criminal court. Though not previously applied to the international arena, pluralism explains American diplomatic isolation on each of these issues as a consequence of unchecked particular interests. In contrast, internationalism maintains that only movements from below—perhaps multilateral in setting—can realize these and other common good-sustaining regimes. The ninth section traces the threat of renewed conflict between the United States and Iraq. The tenth explores the possibility, given strong movements from below, of barring major wars. The eleventh examines, in the absence of international devastation, the prospects for revolution against domestic injustice. The twelfth focuses on Downs and Rocke's principal/agent account of presidential escalation of a losing war or intervention abroad to resurrect a candidacy. That view suggests the likely corruption—to some extent—of any democratic regime. But internationalism stresses the energy of citizens rather than—solely—political forms. The thirteenth section considers a sophisticated realist objection to this argument as a whole. That criticism might contend that antidemocratic feedback harms most citizens rather than instigates political cooperation, supporting realism, not internationalism. The last section notes the impermanence of reform and the distance, as well as promise, of deliberative democracy.

Internationalism is a theory and policy appropriate to any nonaggressive democratic regime or movement.[1] Since Aristotle, Plato, and Thucydides, political theorists and historians have considered it. Yet the absence of internationalism in contemporary political science, until now, reveals an oligarchic skew.

In the post–Cold War era, however, broad interest has also emerged in the thesis that democracies do not go to war with one another. As neorealism and internationalism stress, some versions of this view conceal a pattern of American aggression against democracies in the less developed countries. Nonetheless, the very existence of the interdemocratic-peace argument underlines a novel, post–Cold War hope that section 8 examines: that the realization of democratic regimes in many countries may limit belligerence.

Internationalism reinforces this trend. For it raises a question *internal* to neorealism about what effect great-power rivalry has on a domestic common good—antidemocratic feedback—and demonstrates that any well-formulated realist view, supposedly concerned only with power, *must* include harms to citizens at home. It thus shows that the dominant paradigm in the American Cold War "science" of international relations cannot sustain its argument against democracy.

Through striking historical examples, internationalism warns citizens against the likelihood that presidents will intervene against democracy abroad to circumscribe political alternatives and "resurrect" themselves.[2] It identifies a hierarchically controlled press, academia, and mainstream politics—Morgenthau's "academic-political[-media] complex"—as obstacles to nonaggressive democratic practices. It emphasizes the fierce ideologies of antiradicalism, racism, and sexism that stigmatize others as "enemies" (in refusing to commute a sentence of death on Ethel and Julius Rosenberg for "stealing nuclear secrets," President Eisenhower, for instance, focused hostility on her).[3] Thus, internationalism sanctions insurgencies from below like the anti–Vietnam War movement to make an oligarchy with parliamentary forms more democratic. In addition, it suggests that further steps toward democracy could reduce the possibility, and domestic harms, of aggression.

Now on a pluralist view of American democracy, organization by the disadvantaged, that is, the union movement, the civil rights movements among blacks, Chicanos, and Native Americans, feminism, the gay and lesbian movements, and the like can balance the power of the rich and secure a common good. A disconcerting international consequence of that view, however, has long gone unnoticed.[4] For what group in America, one might ask, defends the autoworkers for U.S. companies in Santiago or Johannesburg and offsets the political power of GM and Ford?[5] On a pluralist theory, no one does. Section 8 of this chapter probes this unacknowledged consequence of pluralism that accounts for the isolation of the U.S. government, in thrall to particular interests, on treaties concerning land mines, exploitation of children as soldiers, and the like.

Contrary to pluralism, internationalism underlines the damage done by global rivalry to democracy at home, and the interest of most citizens in opposing (neocolonial) aggression. It creates some hope that domestic protest can accompany international resistance to U.S.-sponsored domineering and restores the moral attractiveness of pluralism (we might thus see democratic internationalism as a *sophisticated* pluralism). Further, only activity from below would realize innovative regimes, possibly including, as we will see, the outlawing of major war.

2. THE NARROWING OF AMERICAN OLIGARCHY

Pluralism also fails as a domestic account of American politics. For as the startling augmentation in inequalities of income and wealth over the past two decades indicates, domestic groups do not have equal power. Through lobbying and clubs, elite education and acquaintance, the rich influence government vastly more than unions, let alone weaker popular organizations, short of mass, extraparliamentary revolt.[6]

At a 1996 thousand-dollar-a-plate Democratic fund-raising dinner honoring Rosa Parks, even President Clinton reminded attendees of those "too many Americans who could no more come to this dinner than the man in the moon, because they're still looking for a job."[7] Corporations held lavish parties at the conventions, spending an estimated $9 million at the Republican and $7 million at the Democratic. One in every five Republican delegates was—usually *him*self—a millionaire. One in fifty had a family income under twenty-five thousand dollars. For the Democrats, the latter ratio was one in fourteen.[8]

In addition, in the past two decades, the elite has acquired the bulk of its earnings through special government programs. Between 1979 and 1995, for example, Robert Goizueta, CEO of Coca-Cola, deferred $2,946,132 and received in restricted stock incentives and related tax-offsets $933,501,756. His taxed income was $75,659,626. His untaxed—and, thus, *unmeasured in inequality statistics*—earnings were 12 times greater: $936,447,888, for a total of more than $1 billion.[9] Yet corporations cut back pensions for most managers and workers. They even "downsize" executives who had once, comparatively, had job security.[10]

Voting among the poor has temporarily declined from its already low level.

Shifting welfare to the states, congressional leaders listened to no witnesses actually on welfare.[11]

3. DEMOCRATIC DELIBERATION AND MORAL CONTROVERSY

In a democratic regime, citizens sometimes engage in fierce moral disputes, which, if untempered by mutual regard across conscientious differences, can lead to violence. Influenced by metaethical relativism, however, many scholars believe that such clashes derive from incommensurable, *underlying* ethical premises. Holders of different positions live, as it were, in disparate moral worlds.

That account, however, *denies* the possibility of the central, democratic virtue of civility or what Thompson and Gutmann call *civic magnanimity*. Such magnanimity recognizes "the moral point of view of others even though we disagree with it"[12] and derives from liberalism's core moral standard: mutual regard among persons of differing comprehensive views.[13] In addition, as chapters 1 and 2 illustrate, we can often discern a common ethical basis in complex moral disputes that pivot mainly on social theoretical and factual clashes. Such empirical conflicts frequently make political as well as theoretical disagreements intractable.

For instance, at a high level of abstraction, plausible social and political theories start from the core *moral* insight that securing a common interest among citizens is a decisive political good (level 1). They then add factual and social theoretical claims (level 2) that, if challenged— as democratic internationalism questions the silence of pluralism on global affairs—lead to clashing, complex ethical and political judgments (level 3).[14] Thus, the deliberative democratic critique of realism in chapters 1 and 2 applies to pluralism, Marxism, and other well-stated social theories.

That critique also clarifies the structure of the public controversies that are the subject matter of Thompson and Gutmann's *Democracy and Disagreement*.[15] Starting from Morgenthau and Niebuhr, my argument shares Thompson and Gutmann's aim of defining a reasonable deliberative process that can mitigate *often intractable* clashes (clashes to which there is, at least currently, no objective resolution).[16] Such deliberations, however, as I have emphasized, arise from core *recognition of persons*: a mutual insight into equal basic liberties and sufficiently cooperative economic arrangements—the difference principle—to uphold democracy (Rawls) or into the substantive, fundamental rights of each person—liberty, basic opportunity, and fair opportunity—and relevant, derivative conditions—reciprocity, publicity, accountability.[17] Although Thompson and Gutmann see *reciprocity* as a "condition" for deliberation, my way of putting it—that reciprocity derives from a core insight into the dignity of each person—underlines its *substantive*, political content.

Their other conditions—accountability that involves a growing recognition of members of other cultures and those not yet born; publicity to each individual of the laws and policies that affect her—have similar, substantive content.

Thompson and Gutmann rightly suggest that a history of deliberations often shifts and strengthens—by a bootstrapping process—its conditions: "This capacity of deliberative democracy to encourage changes in its own meaning over time illustrates one of its most important qualities. Deliberative democracy expresses a bootstrap conception of the political process: the conditions of reciprocity, publicity, and accountability that define the process pull themselves up by means of the process itself."[18] Over time, they hope that such a democracy can "meliorate" core injustices: "[T]he level of opportunity [for example] does not represent some immutable standard, objectively determined outside the political process. . . . Just as citizens and public officials in the 1930s came to see social security for financial protection in old age as part of a social minimum, so in the 1990s the vast majority are coming to regard guaranteed health care as a basic opportunity."[19]

Thompson and Gutmann contrast their vision with a "proceduralism" that encourages citizens to adhere to certain common rules and, as it were, keep their differences out of the public sphere. But such an approach hardly erases those disputes, especially concerning basic questions of justice, such as the oppression of workers, women, and minority groups, that eventually surface in extraparliamentary conflict. Thompson and Gutmann also reject a "constitutionalism" that downplays elections and looks for public reasons solely to a Supreme Court. For such a regime removes the people—and political deliberation—from democracy.

On behalf of that view, however, one might note that protection of the core liberties of each citizen underlies any decent process of deliberation. Ideally, a Court can defend or expand these liberties against transient, popular pressures. Some such judicial institution must play a central role in an equal-rights-based theory of democracy. Thus, Dworkin's vision of a Constitution of abstract principle, registered especially in the Bill of Rights, models a Rawlsian or Rousseauian conception. That view contrasts with a notion of judicial decisions as an ad hoc historical process so that, for example, the Court might grant "due process" to blacks but not to gays.[20] But even the best Court cannot, by and large, substitute its reasons for democratic deliberations, and, as we will see, protest movements among citizens.[21]

Through public reasoning—reasoning that appeals, however inadequately, to the interests of all—deliberative democracy provides some chance to mitigate basic injustices:

We do not presume that these background circumstances [for deliberative democracy] are easily created or maintained. But citizens and officials should not use the injustice of inequalities in liberty and opportunity as an excuse for neglecting to deliberate or failing to develop a more deliberative form of democracy. On the contrary, because deliberative democracy relies on reciprocity, publicity and accountability, it stands a better chance of identifying and meliorating social and economic injustices than a politics that relies only on power, which is more likely to reproduce or exacerbate existing inequalities.[22]

Despite its virtues, however, Thompson and Gutmann's argument has two fundamental flaws. First, they fail to discuss relevant questions in social theory, in particular, why deliberation has worked so slowly to overcome glaring injustices or how deliberation can remake growing oligarchic influence over government policy.[23] By contrast, this argument stresses the existence of oligarchy and *antidemocratic feedback* that undermine such deliberations.

Further, a social theoretical emphasis would strengthen Thompson and Gutmann's restrictively moral account of internationalism. For instance, they praise the shift to a wider *accountability* to American citizens and others involved in the Clinton administration's endorsement of the International Biodiversity Treaty. If such diversity is protected, "the human world will be better off," have "more intrinsic value."[24] The antidemocratic-feedback argument, however, underlines the nonmoral as well as moral interests of citizens in a panoply of such proposals.

Second, Thompson and Gutmann fail to see struggle from below as a *driving force* in democratic deliberations. For instance, social security became an issue in American politics through the radical-led formation of unemployment councils and union drives; sit-down strikes created industrial unions. As in the case of the Vietnam War, deliberation often occurs *only* as a result of such conflict. In this context, the Montgomery bus boycott and sit-ins at southern lunch counters suggest a democratic promise in civil disobedience to which I will return.

4. CONSCIENCE AND THE LIMITS OF PUBLIC DELIBERATION

Now, questions of fact and social/biological theory may frequently—at least for a long time—prove as hard to resolve in complex ethical disagreements as rarer, underlying moral clashes.[25] In addition, political interests exacerbate such disputes. We can therefore explain the intensity of (complex) ethical conflicts without supposing disagreement on underlying moral standards. In fact, such common standards—conjoined with empirical clashes—generate what everyone recognizes as distinctively *ethical* disputes. Thus, deliberative democracy has a principled justification as the best method of wrestling with comparatively intractable moral controversies.

In rare cases, however, public decision may compromise underlying rights, notably freedom of conscience. Investigation of such cases yields a second justification for deliberative democracy as, centrally, a conscience-sustaining regime.

To take a paradigm case—when does a fetus become a child?—both pro- and antiabortion advocates recognize the good of life: no side commends postpartum infanticide. Yet Thompson and Gutmann note, "Both pro-life and pro-choice advocates argue from fundamentally different but plausible *premises* to conflicting public policies. . . . Pro-life advocates believe the fetus to be a human being. . . . Pro-choice advocates believe the fetus to be only a potential constitutional person. . . . The principle they invoke for defending legalized abortion is that women should have the liberty to decide to bear a child."[26]

Thompson and Gutmann do not, however, distinguish underlying moral disagreements from the empirical/social theoretical conflicts that ordinarily fuel complex disputes. Part of the reason for this failure is an unusual, different weighing of real moral claims—the good of life, the good of a woman's individuality[27]—by the two sides in this case. Yet *reasonable* advocates of each position—ones who understand their own commitment, as Dworkin creatively emphasizes, to the sacredness of life—could concur that serious moral claims are being advanced by the other, and, as Thompson and Gutmann suggest, achieve livable resolutions of—or at least truces about—the conflict.

Further, Dworkin's insight into the underlying, ethical thinking on seemingly "incommensurable" sides of this issue provides a model for decent, deliberative settlement. For each side could recognize the importance of—though not the weight given to—the ethical standards invoked by the other. Not just any reaction to abortion would be moral. This hard case is thus not a counterexample to, but rather confirms, an analysis of limited moral objectivity.[28]

More precisely, antiabortionists view the fetus as not only a potential life, but an actual one. They treat abortion as infanticide and rule out consideration of the woman's—and possibly the child's—well-being. Yet as Dworkin suggests, they can have a nuanced attitude: consider the special hostility to late-term abortions. Ironically, for putative defenders of antistatism, their view seeks *state* protection of the fetus by overriding the mother's freedom.

In contrast, though recognizing the evil of infanticide, defenders of a woman's individuality insist that the fetus is not yet a person and, thus, that decisions about abortion should be made privately (by the person most affected). Following Dworkin,[29] Thompson and Gutmann articulate this claim in a somewhat unattractive, technical way: a fetus, they say, is not yet a "constitutional person" or "lacks interests," until he or she becomes, in some sense, conscious.

Dworkin identifies a range of cases in which the controversy is severe, and asks how, in a democratic regime—one that rests on individual rights—they may be decided:

> The sanctity of life is a highly controversial, *contestable* value. It is controversial, for example, whether abortion or childbirth best serves the intrinsic value of life when a fetus is deformed, or when having a child would seriously depress a woman's chance of making something valuable of her own life. Does a state protect a contestable value best by encouraging people to accept it as contestable, understanding that they are responsible for deciding themselves what it means? Or does the state protect a contestable value best by deciding, through the political process, which interpretation is the right one, and then forcing everyone to conform?[30]

This unusual case suggests rights-based *limits* to democratic deliberation. For a public decision that demands too great a sacrifice of individual *responsibility*, as Dworkin puts it, undercuts a basic right—equal freedom of conscience—that is a precondition for such deliberation. The boundary of reasonable public deliberation in this case shows how sharply a modern democracy is a conscience-sustaining or conscience-dependent regime.

Put differently, there is a two-tier structure to democratic deliberations. The first tier concerns individual rights that are objective—those that derive from the general human capacity for moral personality—and are a precondition for such deliberation.[31] If, in fundamental matters, public deliberation coerces conscience, it is illegitimate. The second tier includes the enormous variety of complex cases in which democratic deliberation must, provisionally, decide, for example, the public preference for abortion during the first three months of pregnancy.[32]

Emphasizing public debate, however, Barber—and others—mistakenly treat all decisions as second tier. He speaks of "an absence of an independent ground" in democratic politics. But Barber confuses an important, *pragmatic* point—no right can be enforced without political struggle; a functioning democracy is vital to the upholding of rights—with a self-refuting, epistemological one.[33] In Rousseau's idiom, he treats every decision as a "will of all." But the upholding of the equal basic rights of each—a precondition for democracy—is the aim of a general will. Such a will—and the equality to which it tends—have a different epistemological status from that of most decisions stemming from (rights-based) democratic deliberations. In a modern idiom, this distinction captures Aristotle's contrast between natural[34] and conventional justice.

Dworkin's responsibility names a central *condition*—in Thompson and Gutmann's terms—as well as justification, for public deliberation. In matters of conscience, individual responsibility is precisely what mutual regard aims to protect. Transient democratic decisions may no more overrule a woman's right to procreative autonomy than they can decide, for individuals, whether to participate in a(n unjust) war. The American regime currently recognizes conscientious objection to all wars. A genuine democracy would, however, also affirm *selective* conscientious objection—the right to refuse conscription in particular wars for articulated reasons of injustice, and seek some form of alternate service.[35] Other than in wars countering aggression, such a right would, by improving the quality of public deliberations, render belligerence more difficult.[36] Honoring conscience, these cases reveal the clearest constraints on such deliberations.

5. EXPERIMENTS IN NONVIOLENCE

Internationalism encourages us to imagine favorable conditions for democratic deliberation, ones arising either from the reform, due to mass rebellion, of existing regimes, or from nonviolent or violent revolution. A refined pluralism or deliberative view, however, can see civil disobedience, or more radical protest, as an instrument to offset the elite's power and promote public reflection.[37] In addition, although, in a nuclear era, violent revolution has been possible as in China, Vietnam, Cuba, Algeria, Guinea-Bissau, Mozambique, Nicaragua, and elsewhere, radicals have lacked the vision to sustain novel, more democratic regimes. In this context, we might envision, as an alternative, militant, nonviolent movements, respectful of the humanity and dignity of others, which, nonetheless, relentlessly challenge unjust authority.[38] For in protesting the waste of human life by current governments, nonviolence emphasizes the value of life. Through self-sacrifice, it offers hope for a transformative regime, one less responsive to aggression with additional bloodshed and more tolerant of political differences. From Henry David Thoreau[39] to Martin Luther King Jr. and Barbara Deming,[40] Americans have contributed to the theory and practice of civil disobedience. They have celebrated the capacity of each individual to say no to great injustice.[41] They have thus participated in a still embryonic, international movement, that of Tolstoy, Gandhi, Dom Helder Camara,[42] Denise Levertov,[43] and many others, which has led so far to a few, striking, twentieth-century examples—the struggles for independence in India and Ghana, the American civil rights movement, and the South African Truth Commission.

Some critics of nonviolence mistakenly argue, however, that proponents, like older utopians, seek merely to petition an elite. They take the fact that a ruling class will not peacefully abjure even horrifying injustices to rule out, by itself, successful nonviolent campaigns. But as Deming notes, nothing about a mass, militant, nonviolent movement requires "begging." For instance, noncooperation overturned the Kapp putsch in Germany (1920) and the French generals' revolt in Algeria (1961). The collapse of Soviet-style dictatorships in Eastern Europe occurred without violence.[44] A self-conscious nonviolent movement would only have deepened these changes.

Put differently, some suppose that a Gandhian movement could work against the "nice" British but not against the Nazis. But this objection disregards the brutality of English colonialism. It also ignores the need for a revolutionary situation, as in Eastern Europe in the late 1980s, that will allow a movement—whether nonviolent or violent—to succeed.

Deming concurs with Stokely Carmichael's critique of utopianism: "Look, you guys are supposed to be nice guys and we are only going to do what we are supposed to do. . . . We demonstrated from a position of weakness. We can not be expected any longer to march and have our heads broken in order to say to whites: come on, you're nice guys. For you are not nice guys. We have found you out."[45] Conjuring Lorenz's biology of aggression[46]—she might better have invoked Niebuhr's realism—Deming insists that almost no one is politically "nice" in the required sense, and emphasizes the power of revolt.

Further, in the experience of nonviolent movements, the leaders' visions came to encompass "a beloved community." Thus, Gandhi renamed the "untouchables" *harijans* (the children of God) and fought for Hindu-Muslim unity. Martin Luther King Jr. opposed the Vietnam War, supported the Memphis sanitation workers' strike, and initiated the poor people's movement.[47] Each foresaw a revolution in social as well as political equality. In a last speech to the Southern Christian Leadership Conference, King mused:

> There are forty million poor people here, and one day we must ask the question, why are there forty million poor people in America? When you begin to ask that question, you are raising questions about the economic system, about a broader distribution of wealth. When you ask that question, you begin to question the capitalistic economy. I am simply saying that more and

more we've got to begin to ask questions about the whole society. We are called upon to help the discouraged beggars in life's market place, but one day we must come to see that an edifice which produces beggars needs restructuring. It means that questions must be raised. You see, my friends, when you deal with this you begin to ask the question: who owns the oil? You begin to ask the question: who owns the iron ore? You begin to ask the question, why is it that people have to pay water bills in a world that is two-thirds water? These are the questions that must be asked.[48]

King had "been to the mountain top" in a vision; he did not expect to join others there:

Like anybody I would like to live a long life. Longevity has its place. But I'm not concerned about that now. . . . I may not get there with you but I want you to know tonight that we as a people will get to the promised land.[49]

If the means can work, nonviolent movements can undertake radical democratic projects. Thus, despite historic differences, a nonviolent revolution might simply *be* a communist or radical democratic movement. Further, not just novelty or elite attack, but psychological insecurity and status differences within the movement have long inhibited fair conversation between advocates of violence and nonviolence—communists look down on "Quaker-vegetarian prattle" (Trotsky); "(*I* am a good person; I would never consider violence." In contrast, Gandhi saw violent resistance as better than acquiescence to oppression.[50] Millions of people have participated in twentieth-century battles, nonviolent as well as violent, against injustice. We need respectful, mutual conversation not only in the current disarray, but as a characteristic of democratic resurgence.

6. CIVIL DISOBEDIENCE, REFERENDA, AND ABOLITION OF SECRET POLICE

Though an internationalist perspective primarily reassesses the internal qualities of radical movements as the driving force of a *deliberative* regime, it also suggests major institutional reforms of contemporary and/ or radical democracies. Consideration of such measures would also strengthen theories of deliberative democracy. For today's elections in oligarchies with parliamentary forms display a "deliberative deficit."[51] They are mainly personality contests, characterized by negative campaigning and the irrelevance of—or dishonesty about—issues. Further, given inequalities of wealth and elite influence on government, voting alone has not altered large-scale injustices—slavery, denial by group or sex of the right to vote, aggressive wars such as Vietnam, homelessness, the oppression of poor children and the feminization of poverty, and the like. As another way of putting it, the democratic deliberations on which the American regime prides itself—those leading to abolition, women's suffrage, unions, unemployment insurance and social security, civil rights, and the like—stemmed mainly from nonparliamentary protest from below, not from electoral activity.[52]

Thus, first, a democratic regime, here and now, would look to *augmented civil disobedience* as a vehicle to raise comparable issues. It would consider obstruction—temporary violations of property rights such as the Berrigans' pouring of blood on draft files—or tax resistance far less weighty than the patterned violations of civil rights, impositions of suffering, and the threat of (nuclear) war, characteristic of mainstream American politics.[53] Lengthy sentences for damage to property during Vietnam,[54] a democrat might say, highlight a regime where "property" has rights, people do not. In this context, disobedience becomes an instigator of deliberative democracy.

In Rawls's dialectical idiom, for a "nearly just" regime, civil disobedience resists a particular unjust law within the context of overall "fidelity to law"[55] (since no existing democracy is "nearly just," civil disobedience must often have broader goals). Such disobedience also illustrates Thompson and Gutmann's criterion of *civic magnanimity*. For although militantly opposing unjust policies, disobedience respects not only the capacity for moral personality but the souls of the powerful. It seeks to generate a comparable reflectiveness in the rich,[56] to *civilize* American politics.

In a frequent, fierce response to civil disobedience, however, hubris, as Thucydides and Niebuhr suggest, preys on the seemingly weak, and highlights the *incivility* of injustice: consider Bull Connor's police dogs in Birmingham. Disobedients must expect a price. Further, while such disobedience can focus on *wide* issues of injustice (once again, revolutionary ones, where necessary), it does not seek to broaden others. It thus also affirms Thompson and Gutmann's criterion of "an economy of moral disagreement."[57] Finally, this conception of civil disobedience extends the First Amendment. To instigate *public* debate, it underlines a deliberative justification—beyond respect for the consciences of individuals—for refusal to participate in (unjust) war.[58] Such a conception reveals the central role of Dworkin's criterion of individual responsibility in a theory of democratic deliberation.

Mainstream public opinion, however, influenced, to a considerable extent, by an elite-controlled media, shuns the core liberal value of equal freedom of conscience. For instance, in 1995, Mahmoud Abdul-Rauf, a Muslim who played basketball for the Denver Nuggets, refused to stand for the national anthem. He rightly thought that the American flag has historically served as a symbol of racism and aggression, not just—or even mainly—as a symbol of liberty (it has unambiguously symbolized liberty only after 1863—though one must abstract from genocide against Native Americans—and, despite internal racism, during World War II).

But even if Abdul-Rauf had been wrong, he could still have striven, in conscience, to express his conviction. Nothing gave the employer of his basketball skills, the National Basketball Association, an additional right to demand his conscience. Moreover, he sought courteously only to register his considered view, not commenting, except by difference, on teammates or the audience. For most of the season, he waited, during the Anthem, in the locker room. In contrast, a crowd that drinks, retreats to the bathroom, or, in the case of journalists, gawks at or scrambles to get pictures of Abdul-Rauf, does not, as Nuggets coach, Bernie Bickerstaff, noted, "honor the flag."[59]

In *The New York Times'* words,

> By [finally] agreeing to stand in silent prayer during the national anthem, Mahmoud Abdul-Rauf . . . has acted to end a confrontation with the National Basketball Association that threatened his team's playoff chances and his $11.2 million contract. . . . in the process of coercing Mr. Abdul-Rauf to rethink his position, the clever patriots who run the N.B.A. have lost sight of what the pre-game ritual celebrates.
>
> Just as a reminder, the ceremony is meant to honor a nation that respects freedom of expression, and the right of individuals to hold personal and religious beliefs that may depart from the mainstream. In other words, it means allowing a devout Muslim like Mr. Abdul-Rauf to decide, based on his personal and religious beliefs, not to take part in the national anthem ceremony. . . . [The real issue in the dispute all along] was the N.B.A.'s blindness to the fact that trying to force participation in a patriotic exercise undermines democratic values.[60]

Furthermore, Abdul-Rauf has overcome Tourette's syndrome and is an unusually humble, honorable person. Yet the arrogant fell upon him, highlighting the psychological mechanism—that of bullying where one can "get away with it"—which makes nonviolence, in general, a dangerous strategy. Deming, however, rightly invites us to consider, comparatively, the cost in lives of violent and nonviolent resistance. The initial price of nonviolence in lives—entirely of protestors—may, she suggests, be high. In the long term, however, where the strategy is workable, fewer lives will be lost.

Similarly, President Bush's 1988 campaign attempted to require of citizens the "Pledge of Allegiance" *against* conscience.[61] As section 3 maintains, as a result of *Roe v. Wade*, public opinion allows individual responsibility for abortion. Yet it does not appreciate the role of such responsibility in selective conscientious objection. In addition, it fails to consider such deliberative consequences of a commitment to freedom of conscience as broader toleration for civil disobedience. For democracy is, first and foremost, a *conscience-sustaining regime*. Contrary to a common American misconception that majority rule and basic rights conflict, this argument shows how sharply a decent, democratic regime grows out of and sustains such rights.

As a second measure to facilitate deliberation, a democratic regime might also institute two or three referenda a year, on such central issues as war (where time allows), welfare, or universal health coverage. In striking contrast to modern America, even in the slaveholding Roman republic, citizen-soldiers pledged to engage this "enemy," in this particular war. Along with selective conscientious objection, referenda would limit the executive's capacity to coerce individuals to forfeit their lives in unjust causes.

We might, for example, have two readings of referenda, at say, three-month intervals, with dual passage required for the measure to take effect.[62] Such a practice would encourage deliberative discussion rather than transient, popular decision, a striving to realize Rousseau's "general will" as opposed to the edicts of a sometimes tyrannical, "will of all." Referenda would bar military efforts that do not receive a high degree of popular authorization, for instance, the Gulf War. For the latter resulted in massive slaughter of Iraqis—civilians as well as soldiers—and a devastation of the environment, coupled with the domestic strengthening of racism: in the words of a "patriotic" T-shirt, "I'd go ten thousand miles to smoke a camel."[63] In addition, though restoring the royal family in Kuwait, the war failed to topple the recent American client and "asset" of President Bush, now demonized, Saddam Hussein. A reasonably stated referendum might have sanctioned continued boycott or other measures of condemnation, short of war.[64]

As another example, a referendum might have permitted earlier American intervention to sustain democracy in Haiti, where the CIA, long a supporter of dictatorship, apparently worked even against President Clinton to defeat President Jean-Bertrand Aristide. In backing the military coup against Aristide's election in 1991—a post–Cold War instance in which the American government warred against democracy—the CIA paid "several leading members of the military junta" as well as of the paramilitary group FRAPH.[65] An accomplice has since accused Emmanuel Constant, the leader of FRAPH, while on the CIA payroll, of murdering the minister of justice, Guy Malary. In any case, FRAPH engaged in wanton killing—"as many as 3,000."

In June 1996, "under a secret deal struck with the US government and over the protests of the Haitian Government," a county jail in Maryland freed Constant. He went to Brooklyn to live with his mother. In March 1995, Secretary of State Warren Christopher had written to Attorney

General Janet Reno: "Nothing short of Mr. Constant's removal from the United States can protect our foreign policy interests in Haiti. . . . [The Justice Department should] take all steps possible to effect his deportation to Haiti."

A year later, however, "the State Department, National Security Council, Justice Department and Immigration and Naturalization Service struck a deal."[66] Even in the *Times'* story, however, the CIA, which probably alone has the influence to engineer such high-level coordination for a jailed immigrant against opposition from the secretary of state, drops out of the picture (imagine an ordinary, impoverished Haitian, waiting in American immigration detention).[67] With some publicity and debate, however, a referendum might have cut off American military and police—as well as CIA—"aid" to the Haitian elite.

Thus, even after the Cold War, the CIA secretly overturns democratic regimes.[68] In addition, in its fifty-year history, it has carried out few pro-"democratic" covert actions. For as Walzer suggests, a democratic power would find it hard to intervene in another country for democratic or radical purposes (ones that serve a common good). Thus, the CIA has repeatedly succeeded only in betraying Kurdish resistance movements to Saddam. Such causes are best left to a people organizing from within.[69]

By contrast, intervening to support military oligarchies and license random murder is comparatively easy. Robert White, former U.S. ambassador to Salvador, reports a forty-year-old Latin and Central American sarcasm about covert activity:

"Why do you think it is the United States that is the most stable government in the hemisphere." I groaned inwardly for I knew what was coming. "The United States is the most stable country in the hemisphere," he said, "because there is no American embassy in Washington."[70]

As a third reform, no reasonable justification has existed, during or after the Cold War, for secret belligerence by a democracy against other regimes, particularly parliamentary ones.[71] A democracy would restrict intelligence activities to knowledge gathering.[72] Put differently, the CIA should no longer be the government agency charged with disproving the "democracies do not go to war with one another" thesis. Yet post–Cold War Congresses have failed even to mention this honorable alternative.

Further, the government has suborned academics, clergy and journalists for subversive purpose.[73] In 1996 congressional testimony, echoing the long disregarded words of Morgenthau and with some bitterness, Ted Koppel avowed:

I am unalterably and categorically opposed to the notion of the CIA having the legal option of using journalism as a cover for its officers or agents. . . . [Legalization] will certainly make life much more difficult for my colleagues and me. It will also place an even greater strain on the one thread of credibility that exists between American journalists and our readers and viewers if they are left to wonder which of us are still trying to maintain some ethical and professional standards and who among us is actually working for U.S. intelligence. Those of my colleagues who devoted a lifetime striving for fairness and objectivity in their work, who have genuinely reported without fear or favor, will now have to settle for the assumption that they were just maintaining their cover.[74]

An array of fundamental democratic criteria, focused on domestic issues, support the abolition of "covert activities." For, as chapter 2 stresses, the pluralist argument for a decent, democratic regime *requires* the independence of diverse institutions from the government. But CIA policy routinely violates this criterion. Further, the practices of the "secret government" conflict with Thompson and Gutmann's condition of *democratic publicity*. Invoking CIA director Richard Helms's deliberately misleading Congressional testimony about Chile and Oliver North's lying during the Iran-Contra affair, they suggest, such officials use "secrecy insidiously to protect questionable policies which they believe are right." In a realist idiom, these antidemocrats act as zealous, "high-minded secret-keepers." Where temporary secrecy can benefit a public good, Thompson and Gutmann's criterion allows it.[75] But CIA "operations" are neither temporary nor friendly to democracy.

As another example of antidemocratic feedback, the CIA apparently *protected* the trafficking of "crack" in ghettos to raise money for the Contras (the "cocaine-Contra scandal"). The *San Jose Mercury News* provided detailed documentation. Yet the CIA, backed by Attorney General Reno, issued bare denials unaccompanied by evidence or comment and let friendly newspapers apologize. For instance, the *Los Angeles Times* maintained that Nicaraguan groups *only* "distributed $50,000" to the Contras. Incompetence here is taken for innocence.[76]

The *Mercury-News* has withdrawn its initial assertion that the CIA was *centrally* responsible for crack distribution. But that retraction does not weaken the claim that the CIA protected this traffic and its beneficiaries. Further, as White emphasizes, Contra "drug-running into Florida" is far more widely acknowledged than in California."[77]

In a democratic break with previous policy, at the invitation of congressional representative Juanita Millander-McDonald, CIA director Deutsch spoke before a hostile town hall gathering in Watts, urging the audience to "withhold judgment" about crack pushing until a full investigation could be conducted.[78]

The outlook for significant disclosure, however, is not promising. Given habits of secrecy, a record of similar drug dealing in Vietnam,[79] sustained criminal activity,[80] and a policy of creating "deniability," a reasonable social scientist might conclude that the evidence suggesting CIA instigation of crack traffic is powerful.

In addition, crack offenders receive *ten* times the sentence for sale or possession as "ordinary" cocaine users. This policy alone has resulted in the disproportionate jailing of young blacks (the government has sentenced approximately a third of young men between nineteen and thirty-four to some jail time or is currently prosecuting them).[81] At Senate hearings, Lawton Chiles, Democrat of Florida, distorted the testimony of Dr. Robert Byck, a Yale specialist on drugs, to fantasize that crack is "50 times more addictive than cocaine" and justify disparate sentencing.[82] One might recall, however, Montesquieu's injunction that a sentence should bear some proportion to the crime.[83] Fearful of being thought "soft" on drugs in an election year, Congress rejected a recommendation by a special board to annul this unusual sentencing—the first such recommendation it had refused in twelve years.[84]

The three reforms, I have suggested, might have a dramatic effect on foreign and domestic policy, for example, making universal health coverage a possibility. European capitalist democracies introduced such coverage fifty years ago. The American regime, however, has a comparatively vast territory and institutional "balance of powers"—a "republican remedy for the diseases of republicanism" (Madison)—as well as special traditions of racism and intervention abroad; it is unusually resistant to common-good-sustaining reforms.[85] Despite what Thompson and Gutmann rightly see as increasing recognition in the United States of this "basic opportunity," Congress still does not guarantee health care for all citizens. Yet according to a Harvard School of Public Health study, 31 percent of Americans, especially the most ill, cannot obtain adequate care.[86]

As another example, if true knowledge of their activities became widespread *and* politically effective, cigarette companies might lose out.[87] In 1994, these corporations misguidedly abandoned "bipartisanship" and funded Republicans at a roughly three-to-one ratio.[88] Belatedly and unevenly, the Democrats have since made the danger of cigarettes an electoral—and, perhaps, even a legal—issue. As with asbestos, however, which was shown to cause asbestosis by the early 1950s, corporations can traffic murderous substances for decades with impunity.[89]

7. THE FAIR VALUE OF LIBERTY

Most corporations, however, are extremely adaptable in avoiding campaign reform laws. Even with the three reforms listed above, oligarchic policies would still have a better chance in most political competitions than democratic alternatives.

To counter these inequalities, a democratic regime might provide for (1) multiparty or proportional representation in citizen-financed elections, (2) equal public funding for diverse, issue-oriented committees to contest referenda, and (3) alteration of communications media to become, with regard to major issues, a public trust.

The Supreme Court's *Buckley v. Valeo* decision, however, rejected any egalitarian limits on campaign contributions and warned only against bribery rather than a fundamental corruption of the democratic process through oligarchy. The justices affirmed the oligarchic conception that each individual should be able to influence elections according to his "wealth." As Sunstein puts it,

> According to the Court, such restrictions [a limitation of contributions to one thousand dollars per candidate] are a kind of First Amendment "taking" from rich speakers for the benefit of poor ones. In the key sentence, the Court pronounced that "the concept that the government may restrain the speech of some elements of our society in order to enhance the relative voice of others is wholly foreign to the First Amendment."[90]

By a similar reasoning, perhaps the Court should accord extra votes to wealth.

First, as a counter to prevailing oligarchy, a Rawlsian or deliberative democratic conception emphasizes the *priority* of the equal liberties of each citizen. It requires equal influence on *basic* political and institutional decisions. On Rawls's account, as a member of an ideal sovereign assembly, each must be able to judge such institutions and policies as reasonable. Rawls also makes a secondary argument about "the unequal worth of liberty" to differing citizens:

> Thus liberty and the worth of liberty are distinguished as follows: liberty is represented by the complete system of the liberties of equal citizenship, while the worth of liberty to persons and groups is proportional to their capacity to advance their ends *within the framework the system defines*. Freedom as equal liberty is the same for all; the question of compensating for a lesser than equal liberty does not arise. But the worth of liberty is not the same for everyone. Some have greater authority and wealth, and therefore greater means to achieve their aims. The lesser worth of liberty is, however, compensated for, since the capacity of the less fortunate members of society to achieve their aims would be even less were they not to accept the existing inequalities whenever the difference principle is satisfied.[91]

As a *democratic* arrangement, however, a functioning "unequal worth of liberty" depends on two conditions: *(a)* the absence of oligarchy—the priority of the equal-liberty principle rules out those inequalities that allow the rich to dominate parliamentary forms, even if they are justified under the difference principle—and *(b)* the securing of economic benefits to the least advantaged. Thus, Rawls also insists on the *fair value* of equal liberties to each citizen. For instance, he proposes restrictions on campaign funding—*public* financing of campaigns—and suggests that measures to uphold equal liberty "never seem to have been seriously entertained" in the United States:

> Historically, one of the main defects of constitutional government has been the failure to insure the *fair value* of political liberty. The necessary corrective steps have not been taken, indeed, they never seem to have been seriously entertained. Disparities in the distribution of property and wealth that far exceed what is compatible with political equality have been tolerated by the political system. Public resources have not been devoted to maintaining the institutions required for the fair value of political liberty. . . . Moreover, the effects of injustices in the political system are much more grave and long lasting than market imperfections. Political power rapidly accumulates and becomes unequal; and making use of the coercive apparatus of the state and its law, those who gain the advantage can often assure themselves of a favored position. Thus inequities in the economic and social system may soon undermine whatever political equality might have existed under fortunate historical conditions. Universal suffrage is an insufficient counterpoise; for when parties in an election are financed not by public funds but by private contributions, the political forum is so constrained by the wishes of the dominant interests that the basic measures needed to establish just constitutional rule are seldom property presented.[92]

In 1996, the mainstream candidates, Clinton and Dole, debated on television before 70 million people but did not mention the augmented level of American inequality and its political consequences. In a separate, little-watched—"minor party"—debate on cable, Ralph Nader, the Green Party candidate, stressed this issue. Public financing of campaigns, coupled with democratic criteria for qualification, could, however, undermine such oligarchic practices.

Now Thompson and Gutmann rightly reject as a "bottomless pit" a public redistribution of resources to guarantee the special needs of individuality: "Basic liberty should not be expanded to include positive claims on society for all those resources that one may need to pursue one's own way of life. We distinguish, as also do a wide range of theorists, between liberty and the worth of liberty or the opportunity to live a good life. If a deliberative democracy were to broaden the scope of liberty to include the goods necessary to its exercise, it would set virtually no limit on justifiable intervention by government."[93] Their argument, however, overlooks the priority and fair value of basic liberties. It does not distinguish between a sufficient *political* and *social* equality to ensure basic liberty—a *democratic or public goal* of providing effective[94] resources so that each may influence the political agenda equally—and the potentially exaggerated resources "that one may need to pursue one's own way of life." Put differently, Thompson and Gutmann confuse an egalitarian "broaden[ing of] the scope" of *public* liberty to include "those goods necessary to its exercise" and an inegalitarian "broaden(ing)" of mainly private, individual liberty to pursue a good life.

Now any liberal political theory accepts some degree of government intervention, for example, to uphold the physical and moral security of citizens. Such intervention secures democratic conditions for debate— thus, Thompson and Gutmann insist on individual liberty and opportunity as *substantive* constraints on public deliberation. Further, the priority of the equal basic liberties, as Rawls suggests, underlies majority rule on specific issues and cannot be abridged without transforming a general will into an oligarchic will of all. Thus, concern for *equal liberty* or *democratic deliberation* drives the foregoing justification of campaign contribution egalitarianism.[95]

We might, for example, adopt Ralph Nader's proposal that each citizen contribute up to one hundred dollars out of taxes for political campaigns, that such funds be distributed equally among candidates seeking comparable offices, and that no candidate accept private contributions. This criterion would rule out illegitimate advertising, for instance the legion Republican and Democratic National Committee "spots" in 1996 that urged citizens to "write" to the opposing candidate. Such a criterion could also employ some test of electability through effort,[96] though nothing like the current requirement of 5 percent of the vote in the last national election. For what can one say about the barring from presidential debates by a "bipartisan,"[97] judicially sanctioned commission of even a multibillionaire, Ross Perot, who had received 20 percent of the vote in the previous election? Along with the correlative reforms suggested here—all of which would have to be enacted to make any of them effective—a minimal number, say two hundred thousand votes in the last national election seems reasonable as a criterion for equal funding. Such a standard empowers ordinary citizens—not as, at present, a corporate elite—and encourages diversity. Contrary to *Buckley v. Valeo*, this change would require a democratic interpretation of the Constitution; it might also lead to proportional representation.[98]

As a second reform to counter oligarchic influence, we might adopt equal funding of diverse committees to campaign on specific issues— those subject to referendum, for instance. That practice would make a parliamentary regime far more deliberative.

Third, a democracy might require less centralized control of the major communications media and treat them, on important, political issues, as a *public trust*. Currently, almost no radicals can write columns in mainstream American newspapers—the spectrum is "just left of center to middle right"[99]—or host a TV or radio talk show.[100] But a democratic regime could require that all news and cultural enterprises reflect a diversity of opinion, including *currently unpopular* opinion and allow all candidates roughly equal air time.[101]

The Supreme Court, however, currently restricts equal public access to the parks and streets, used for this purpose in the nineteenth century. As Sunstein rightly notes, "Other arenas—perhaps mailboxes, probably railroad stations and airports, certainly broadcasting stations—are the modern equivalents of streets and parks. In Justice Kennedy's words, 'public forum doctrine ought not to . . . convert what was once an analysis protective of expression into one which grants the government authority to restrict speech by fiat.' "[102] Given the debilities of power and the limitations of even radical democratic forms, however, no movement should expect "equal funding" or courteous treatment by authorities. As chapters 2 and 4 emphasize, hubris plays a continuing role in politics. Civil disobedience and mass protest about central issues alone create circumstances in which democratic institutions might live up to the form.

Yet while excluding radical opinions, today's elite-controlled media "officially" considers only pseudoscientific, racist opinions "unpopular," largely as an excuse to propagate them. For instance, it widely publicized Herrnstein's and Murray's *The Bell Curve*,[103] which alleges the genetic inferiority in intelligence of blacks. Now, as Rawls, Sunstein, Cohen, Thompson and Gutmann, Meiklejohn, and many others emphasize, in a deliberative democracy, equal freedom of speech is a central public good.[104] But even a wide-ranging notion of such freedom, attentive to eccentricity, does not protect racist doctrines. For arguments that discredit persons by color, sex or class, deny the mutual regard among those of diverse comprehensive views central to a modern liberal political theory; they aim to intimidate, silence or even kill specific groups of people, and thus directly, and unusually, undermine the justification of equal freedom of speech.[105]

Sunstein invokes Justice Frankfurter's majority opinion in *Beauharnais v. Illinois*, which upheld

> an Illinois law making it unlawful to publish or exhibit any publication which "portrays depravity, criminality, unchastity or lack of virtue of a class of citizens, which [publication] exposes the citizens of any race, color, creed or religion to contempt, derision, or obloquy or which is productive of breach of the peace or riots." The law was applied to ban circulation of a petition urging "the need to prevent the white race from becoming mongrelized by the negro," and complaining of the "aggressions, rapes, robberies, knives, guns and marijuana of the negro."

... Frankfurter referred to the historical exclusion of libel from free speech protection; to the risks to social cohesion created by racial hate speech; and to the need for judicial deference to legislative judgments on these complex matters. Justice Frankfurter placed less emphasis on the interest in equality—in the elimination of caste-like features of current society—but this interest, with its roots in the Civil War Amendments to the United States Constitution, would certainly have fortified his conclusion. Many countries in Europe accept the same analysis and do not afford protection to racial or ethnic hate speech.[106]

One might also underline crimes against individuals incited by racist speech, for instance, lynching.

The ideology of eugenics spawned the Ku Klux Klan and the Nazis. In addition, American federal and state governments passed immigration, sterilization, and miscegenation laws, legitimized by these ideas. Further, authorities used IQ testing to justify turning away boatloads of Jews fleeing Hitler, State Department silence, during World War II, about genocide, medical experimentation on blacks, sterilization of "feeble-minded" immigrants, restrictive quotas for Jews in universities, and the like.[107]

Today's revived eugenics underpins the 1997 "welfare reform" that will force an estimated one million additional children into poverty.[108] As Senator Moynihan notes, not the locus of funding, but a reduction in funds and experimentalism with children's lives make the legislation so dangerous. That an author of the "matriarchal family structure" thesis in the Johnson administration and a follower of Arthur Jensen in the Nixon administration should defend children—he speaks of his Catholic background as ensuring a grasp of "simple morality"—is a startling comment on the current congressional and presidential spectrum of opinion.

Nonetheless, fair publicizing of opponents' views would be sufficient to discredit eugenics.[109] Today, however, the mainstream press ignores the literature that highlights the flaws—they range from fraudulent (Sir Cyril Burt) to funny—in this pseudoscience.[110] This spurious example of "unpopularity"—hawked by the elite, dogged by protest from below—underlines the need to require equal funding of candidates and issues to further genuine debate.

8. GLOBALIZATION AND COSMOPOLIS

Internationalism favors the realization of a common good within each country and strengthens democratic arrangements domestically; it also stresses, across borders, mutual support from below. Nonetheless, a critic might suggest, it does not adequately address the threat to such goods represented by globalization. As chapter 1 emphasizes, contemporary regimes—for instance, the IMF that makes loans contingent on "anti-inflationary" cutbacks in social programs—already enforce economic antidemocratic feedback.[111] The globalization of capital, this critic might maintain, further undercuts the possibility of local democratic transformations.

Moreover, the augmenting inequality in the United States, which this chapter stresses, mirrors, though less shockingly, a worldwide pattern. Recalling Honderich, Thomas Schelling notes:

> If we were to think about a "new world order" that might embark on the gradual development of some constitutional framework within which the peoples of the globe would eventually share collective responsibility and reciprocal obligations, . . . what actual nation, existing now or in the past, might such an incipient world state resemble? . . .
>
> I find my own answer stunning and embarrassing: [apartheid] South Africa.
>
> . . . We live in a world that is one-fifth rich and four-fifths poor; the rich are segregated into the rich countries and the poor into the poor countries; the rich are predominantly lighter skinner and the poor darker skinned; most of the poor live in homelands that are physically remote, often separated by oceans and great distances from the rich.[112]

The term *apartheid*, which Falk also stresses, underlines the *excessive*, racist evil of contemporary international distribution and indicts "geo-governance." Yet this name conceals the harms done to many whites, and the way racism is used, as a form of divide and rule, to legitimize such practices.

In amplifying existing inequalities, global and domestic capitalism follow a course long ago theorized by Marx.[113] Oppression highlights the optimism, utopian temper, and, ironically, vagueness—despite an underlying critical impulse—of David Held's cosmopolitan countervision:

> The achievement of taking steps towards the realization of democratic autonomy within a nation-state or region—important as it unquestionably is—would be but a milestone on the road to the establishment of a cosmopolitan democracy with global reach. While, initially, those communities which enable policy and law to be shaped by their citizenry are likely to pursue such a future, the possibility is held out [the passive grammar betrays the questions: by whom? through what measures?] that the conflict between a person's obligation *qua* citizen to obey the regulations of a particular community, and his or her obligation to obey internationally recognized rules, might eventually be overcome, as more and more states and agencies affiliated to the new democratic order. The principles of individual democratic

states and societies could come to coincide with those of cosmopolitan democratic law. . . . democratic citizenship could take on, in principle, a truly universal status.[114]

Held contends that some form of federated democracy—one might imagine Marx's communism or radical democracy—is desirable, but suggests few measures to achieve it.[115] Further, despite securing arms for humanitarian interventions, that regime would have to be mainly federal, noncoercive, and restricted. As Held acknowledges, following Kant, any *armed* global *state*—for instance, one generated by repeated humanitarian interventions—would pose a significant danger of despotism.[116] As we will see, the starvation occasioned by the U.N. boycott of Iraq adumbrates this possibility. Puzzlingly, however, Held also advocates substituting an "efficient, accountable, international military force" for those of particular states.

His coeditor, Daniele Archibugi, envisions reforming the United Nations. She recommends creation of a "people's assembly" alongside the state representatives in the General Assembly to give voice to citizens and minorities, abolition of the great-power veto in the Security Council, and the like. Though improvements, such reforms would only make a federation of diverse powers a little less unequal. To trumpet modest reforms as "democratic" world governance is misleading.[117]

Similarly, on Kaldor's account, the European Community, for instance through launching multilateral, humanitarian intervention in the former Yugoslavia, has eroded state sovereignty. Projecting the Helsinki Citizens' Assembly's attempt to inject serious debate into the wasteland of contemporary politics—Kaldor invokes Havel's concept of "Living in Truth"—she envisions a more participatory regime.[118] Though morally compelling, however, like Falk's image of humane governance, her account is frail.

In addition, as chapter 1 shows, capitalism has long been international, and, in Marx's phrase, "battered down all Chinese walls."[119] Visions of globalization as an instigator of oppression—or a generator of democratic cosmopolis—are both, probably, overstated.[120]

Nonetheless, an objection to democratic internationalism based on globalization has an important grain of truth. No arrangements in a particular country or group of countries—even those resembling the radical democracy I have sketched—will halt the fluidity of international capital; unchecked from below, capitalism exacerbates inequalities. Yet in particular cases, furthering deliberations and a common good, such political arrangements would be a striking improvement. Moreover, radical example might inspire democratic feedback. Thus, three international movements of workers and other oppressed people as well as peace—notably in Eastern Europe—and green movements that go beyond national borders, illustrate such possibilities.

Further, for particular international goods, such as outlawing land mines, diminishing greenhouse gases, forbidding the use of children as soldiers, establishing an international criminal court, and barring major wars, nongovernmental—including non–United Nations—groups can play a decisive role. These examples illustrate Keohane's notion of cooperative regimes.[121] Yet in the post–Cold War era, they also highlight surprisingly backward features of American diplomacy, underlining the difference between pluralism, which abandons foreign policy to uncountered oligarchic interests, and internationalism, which remedies this foreign-policy defect of pluralism through democratic resistance.

First, the unusual award of a 1997 Nobel Prize to Jody Williams and the Committee to Ban Land Mines—composed of one thousand organizations from sixty nations that led an impromptu, successful campaign—provoked Russia's President Yeltsin to reverse his stand and support an antimines treaty. Only the United States holds out. Though the Clinton administration insists that South Korea needs mines, the South produces twenty times the wealth of the North, and, with a massive American presence,[122] is able to defend itself. What is the "security" value of continuing to seed mines between these regimes for the next ten years compared to that of an international agreement that would outlaw use of mines, gradually cutting back on the annual killing of twenty-six thousand civilians and the maiming of others? In the poor countries, wars have already "planted" 100 million such weapons, claiming dozens of new victims daily. Yet led by Secretary Cohen, the Pentagon plans to use mines widely in any future war and strives to undo even a separate, yearlong ban on this weapon.[123]

Ironically, Americans initiated this campaign. Bobby Muller, a paraplegic veteran, formed Vietnam Veterans of America, which galvanized the international Committee to Ban Land Mines. [124] As he underlines: "$3 antipersonnel land mines have killed more people than all the Cold War weapons of mass destruction combined."[125] In 1992, Senator Patrick Leahy of Vermont fought for a U.S. ban on exporting land mines as well as for a rehabilitation fund for victims. The Canadian regime broke with the Cold War model of "consensus" and supported the treaty. Yet President Clinton told Muller flatly that he could not risk a breach with the Pentagon.[126] Once again, in Morgenthau's words, the American government squanders the *substance* of democratic power to chase its illusory shadow. In November 1997, diplomats from 120 countries approved the antimines treaty. As Muller reflects, "It is . . . sad that this country, which played so important a part in getting this campaign off the ground, is, at the end of the day, a no-show."[127]

Second, to stem greenhouse gas emissions, Europe has cut back on coal. Britain and the Netherlands, for instance, base electricity on natural gas. In the late 1980s, East Germany burned 300 million tons of lignite; in 1995, reunified Germany consumed only 130 million tons. In contrast, coal burning generated 56 percent of American electricity in 1996 compared to 50 percent in 1980.[128] As German foreign minister Klaus Kinkel remarked: "How can the Americans, with around 5 per cent of the world's population, go on accounting for a quarter of its greenhouse gases?"[129]

Though still an issue of controversy,[130] most scientists recognize the role of human activity in causing dire, long-run shifts in the earth's climate. Transparent to sunlight, carbon dioxide, methane, and nitrogen oxide, generated by fuel combustion, trap heat emitted by the Earth. Further, according to a 1995 U.N. report, carbon dioxide stands at a 30 percent higher level in the atmosphere than in preindustrial times. Scientists predict that emissions could push up the Earth's temperature two to six degrees by the year 2100—current temperatures exceed by only five to nine degrees those of the last ice age—and elevate sea levels six to thirty-seven inches. Heat would expand ocean volume and melt glaciers, inundating islands and shorelines. Contributing to Western arrogance, these changes would especially affect such less developed countries as poor, populous, and low-lying Bangladesh.[131] These alterations would shift climate zones, worsen floods and droughts, make heat waves more lethal, and extinguish some ecosystems.[132]

At the December 1997 Earth Summit in Kyoto, the European Community proposed cutting three gases that contribute to the greenhouse effect 7.5 percent below 1990 levels by the year 2005 and 15 percent by 2010. The Clinton administration, initially, held out for a 1990 standard, but finally agreed to a level 7 percent below that of 1990, to be achieved by 2012.[133] Withdrawing its original offer, Europe then agreed to cut back only 8 percent from 1990 by 2012, Japan 6 percent. In addition, against European resistance, the conference adopted a U.S. suggestion to curtail three other gases—hydroflourocarbons, perflourocarbons, and sulfur hexachloride.[134]

America had previously resisted such measures. At the 1992 Earth Summit in Rio, because of U.S. opposition, other nations made reduction to a 1990 standard by the year 2000 a "voluntary" goal.[135] Through gas burning, automobiles contribute centrally to global warming.[136] Yet American manufactures have shifted production from cars to light trucks, which emit 20 percent to 100 percent more carbon dioxide.[137] In 1990, after Iraq invaded Kuwait, Senator Richard Bryan of Nevada introduced legislation to increase the fuel economy of all vehicles 40 percent by 2001. To lobby against this bill, the auto companies hired FMR Group and

John R. Bonner. Despite support from fifty-seven senators, a filibuster defeated it.

In 1992, backed by environmentalists, Clinton won the Democratic nomination. Speaking in Detroit on August 21, however, the candidate alleged that fuel efficiency might not be technically feasible, a justification for subsidizing industry "research" instead of enacting higher efficiency. When the Sierra Club editorialized against the wastefulness of sport utility vehicles, the Big Three pulled their ads from *Sierra*.[138] But the Sierra Club is not president.

Thus, with the exception of the Biodiversity Treaty, the U.S. government has not only refused to lead for an international common good, but rather, catering to *particular* interests, lagged behind. As I have emphasized, pluralism explains, though it does not counter, this ignoble pattern. Yet according to a *New York Times* poll, 65 percent of Americans support swift, even unilateral, action to restrict greenhouse emissions.[139] As internationalism stresses, however, without mass protest, democratic opinion cannot check oligarchy. In a global context, internationalism, once again, appears to be a sophisticated pluralism. Yet for the present, Americans are, comparatively, unorganized. In Europe, green movements—and, consequently, more effective public awareness of ecology—stimulate better policies.

Still, having just rejected the land mines treaty and cognizant of the dangers of global warming, the Clinton administration agreed to a decent accord. By the year 2000, scientists project that, unchecked, the United States would emit 13 percent more greenhouse gases than in 1990, 30 percent by 2010. Thus, if upheld by the Senate,[140] the treaty would significantly curtail U.S. emissions.

In addition, the Clinton administration will offer five billion dollars of research incentives for companies to adopt fuel-efficient technologies. For instance, boards of education might commission new schools with geothermal heat pumps, mirroring the Choptank Elementary School in Cambridge, Maryland, which will cut greenhouse gases 40 percent compared to conventional technology, and save, over the next twenty years, four hundred thousand dollars in energy and maintenance costs; according to Terry Peterson, manager of green-power marketing at the Electric Power Research Institute, financed by the energy industry, in many parts of the United States, wind power will soon underprice fossil fuel; for an Energy Department study, Ford predicted that it could manufacture an electric van, using fuel cell technology, that would get 32 to 34 miles per gallon, more than double today's Econoline; with research subsidies, the Solar Energy Association estimates that its growth might accelerate from 27 percent to 40 percent per year, and reduce the cost of clean—sun-based—

electricity by 25 percent.[141] After the Kyoto conference, the auto companies announced the possibility of cutting out 99 percent of carbon dioxide emissions. Underlining the comparative ease of transition, this startling alternative highlights the corruption of presidential policy since Reagan as well as that of the auto manufacturers.[142]

At Kyoto, the United States proposed setting overall goals to curtail greenhouse gases in each country and issuing allowable emissions certificates to specific corporations. These firms could then try to undercut their targets and sell the remaining certificates, at a profit, to less fortunate companies domestically or internationally: "emissions trading." The treaty would also establish a multilateral organization to encourage firms in the rich nations to invest in cleaner emissions in the poor ones.

Stressing that industrialized nations have caused the problem yet seek to fob off the cost of curtailing global warming on poor countries, the latter, led by China, have demanded serious cuts. Neither the U.S. Senate nor the Clinton administration, however, will sign the treaty unless the industrializing countries join. In addition, even though the treaty creates a novel international framework to deal with global warming, scientists warn of its inadequacy, distinguishing between serious climatic disruptions—now regarded as probable—and catastrophic ones, for instance flooding Bangladesh or New York, which further action may avert.[143]

Third, 191 governments have now ratified the international Convention on the Rights of the Child, which bans the use of soldiers younger than eighteen. Yet the United States is one of only two countries that have not signed. Catering to conservative ideologues who fear "government intervention" in the family—as if war were not a government activity affecting families—the United States resists a ban on a malevolent practice of which it is not even a part.

Selective American commitment based on economic convenience or strategic interest, the *Human Rights World Report for 1998* contends, poses a growing threat to efforts to defend the rights of, for instance, Chinese or Central Africans. Invoking a realist insight, it concludes: "U.S. arrogance suggests that in Washington's view, human rights standards should be embraced only if they codify what the U.S. government already does, not what the United States ought to achieve."[144] In Keohane's idiom, in an increasingly established human-rights regime, such conduct exacts costs in contempt—as well as lack of cooperation—from others.

But lone U.S. opposition to global treaties on behalf of particular interests did not emerge in the Clinton administration. For thirty years, from Truman until Ford, the United States refused to ratify the United Nations' Convention on Genocide, for fear it would be applied to American persecution of blacks.[145] This tyrannical interest is more that of a ruling class than of the specific companies, suggested by pluralism. But what in the Cold War appeared narrow—vicious—self-interest now appears as arrogant, isolated, inexplicable.[146]

Fourth, to deal with genocide and other war crimes by individuals, many governments support a permanent international criminal court. The Security Council has, so far, mandated ad hoc tribunals for the former Yugoslavia and Rwanda. But beyond the 22 million civilians already forcibly uprooted, the U.N. high commissioner on refugees estimates that 35 civil wars may force another 25 million to abandon their homes. Provoked by rape and other forms of sexual abuse in the Balkans and Central Africa, women's organizations and human-rights groups have successfully campaigned for the naming of crimes against women—a major moral advance—in crimes of war.[147]

Across diverse state systems of common law, military justice and civil law, the ad hoc tribunals have worked out common standards. Testifying to a United Nations committee of legal experts, American Justice Gabriel Kirk McDonald noted: "We at the Yugoslavia tribunal brought together 11 judges, all from different systems in different countries, and we were able to draft rules of procedure and evidence that we believe met the needs of all systems."[148] Further, as chief prosecutor in Bosnia, Louise Arbour of Canada, warned: "[T]here is more to fear from an impotent than from an overreaching prosecutor."

Yet the United States holds out for a Security Council veto over cases to be brought before this tribunal. The Pentagon fears that American soldiers might be charged with war crimes. As Arbour responds: "an organization should not be constructed on the assumption that it will be run by incompetent people, acting in bad faith, for improper purposes."[149] But the worry probably reflects a deeper sense about American policy. To protect particular interests, for instance past criminality in Vietnam, continuing CIA involvement in torture and murder as in Haiti, and possible future misconduct, the United States seeks to place itself above an international law that applies to others (except those nations that also have a veto on the Security Council).[150]

As Connie Ngondo, executive director of the Kenyan branch of the International Commission of Jurists, suggests: "the . . . criminal court could be used to harass the nations of the south." Thus, parochial American policy encourages defection from an impartial, common-good-oriented court, undermining the rule of law. The British Labour government, however, has broken with the United States. Instead of allowing a veto by any permanent member over each case by refusing to send it to the court, England proposes joint state action—if the Security Council is already discussing a conflict—to postpone proceedings for a *limited* period.

9. IRAQ, "MONICAGATE," AND SECRETARY ANNAN

An even more striking possibility for international agreement is the abolition of major war. As with the ending of slavery, this idea, as Forsberg stresses, cuts against conventional strategic thinking.[151] In Kennan's words, however, major wars are exceedingly costly in lives, "genetic and environmental damage," and wealth. Still, politically influential corporations find weapons profitable; so do strategic consultants—who traffic an arcane jargon to hide their judgments from public view—and a military elite. As publicity about renewed war with Iraq juxtaposed with sexual scandals at the White House indicates, bombing or swift strikes are a plausible, though temporary, presidential alternative to "Monicagate."[152] Further, the principle that nonviolent resolution of conflict is desirable—a matter in which the United States might provide an example—has not yet occurred to the leaders of the lone remaining superpower. The forces who envision war as a useful alternative currently outweigh those who oppose it.

Renewed threats of U.S.-prompted war against Iraq underscore this danger. Resolving the publicized aim of the conflict, the initial Gulf War reversed Saddam's invasion of Kuwait. Yet according to two representatives of the United Nations' Food and Agricultural Organization in Iraq, since the U.N. imposed sanctions, a million civilians—567,000 of them children—have died.[153] Contrasted to the period before the boycott, infant mortality has doubled; the number of children who die before the age of five has multiplied by six. Philippe Heffinck, a UNICEF representative, estimates that from hunger or disease, 4,500 children perish each month: "it is the singular characteristic of warfare in our time that children suffer most."[154] The Department of Humanitarian Affairs records the breakdown of Iraq's public health services and the lack of clean water (50 percent of rural Iraqis have none).[155]

United Nations' Resolution 986 permits Iraq to use oil revenue to secure food. America and its allies, however, resist steps—either by approving enough Iraqi sales to head off starvation or by providing food to civilians directly—to prevent massive harm to innocents. Pointing out that Saddam is vicious and deceptive—that renewed war would be his "fault," as Clinton and Secretary of State Madeline Albright reiterate—is not sufficient to hide the depravity of the boycott.[156] The failure to discuss, for instance, "bombing" Iraq with food, suggests that harm to noncombatants is the aim of current policy.[157]

By the end of May 1997, Iraq had exported 120 million barrels of oil and received 692,000 metric tons of "food," 29 percent of what had been expected. Of 574 contracts involving "humanitarian supplies," the Sanctions Committee approved 311, placed 191 on hold, denied 14, and sought clarification on 38. Of $2 billion in Iraqi oil revenues authorized for a six-month period, 30 percent went to war reparations, 5–10 percent to U.N. operations, and 5–10 percent to maintenance of the oil pipeline. Only 15 percent of this revenue purchased humanitarian supplies for the Kurds in the North. In addition, the government spent eight hundred thousand dollars on civilians in central and southern Iraq. In a country of imposed *general* suffering, this amount breaks down to twenty-five cents per person per day.[158] Displaying a bad conscience in the crisis, the Security Council doubled the revenue from permissible sales.

The day after negotiated settlement, the *New York Times* interviewed a Baghdad pharmacist, Kazem Hani, who had only two kinds of medicine—a painkiller and a prescription antidepressant—on depleted shelves, and turned away ten of thirteen customers: "Sorry, brother, I don't have it." Asked if he intended to purchase a gas mask, Hani responded: "You are talking to someone who has not eaten a banana in seven years. I last had meat a month ago. When I come to work every morning here, I say good morning to six engineers who are peddling cigarettes on this street to supplement their incomes. Do you believe anyone here is worried about gas?"[159] The engineers sell single cigarettes out of open packs.

Thus, the U.N. boycott mutes Saddam's considerable crimes. Symbolic of internal war against the Kurds, Hussein murdered with chemical weapons the inhabitants of the village of Halabja. He stations innocents—women and children—around military targets.[160] He wasted tens of thousands of Iraqi lives—aided by the United States—in a seven-year war against Iran. Four days *after* the settlement, the *New York Times* detailed the difficult U.N. investigation of secret Iraqi biological weapons production and cover-ups.[161] Nevertheless, as Youssef Rashid, chairperson of the Theatre Department at the School of Fine Arts in Baghdad, asks: "Is it Saddam who has imposed the embargo? . . . This is a country with thousands of years of culture that is now watching its babies dying of malnutrition."[162]

At the behest of the United States, McDowell suggests, "The United Nations, chartered to protect civilian populations from the ravages of war, is, instead, engaged in a . . . war of mass destruction against the people of Iraq."[163] As Secretary Annan's visit to Baghdad indicated, however, the U.N. unified neither behind renewed war nor continued boycott. French and Russian interests—as Yeltsin's brief threat of world war underlined—conflict with those of the United States.

President Clinton's ratings after his State of the Union message were high enough to render bombing Baghdad less likely. Yet the leadership of both parties and the media—against growing resistance from below—agitated for war. Clinton[164] and Secretary Albright claim that, in contrast to other leaders, Saddam actually used biological weapons against Iran. They omit, however, that Presidents Reagan and Bush armed Iraq in that war and were silent about that deployment of those weapons. Put differently, Saddam is at least as evil as the American media depicts him—and it "demonizes" him—but so are many rulers whom the United States, without blinking, supports. For other Middle Eastern powers have biological, chemical, or nuclear weapons, as does America, which apparently, without contemporary domestic publicity, used "depleted uranium" in the first Gulf War.[165] The hubris of American policymakers stands out.

Mistakenly from its own perspective, the White House scheduled, on February 19, a quasi-democratic "town meeting" at Ohio State. More democratic than normal events,[166] this forum, as a questioner pointed out, was nonetheless dominated by Secretary of State Albright, Secretary of Defense Cohen, and National Security Advisor Berger. Still, pointed queries as well as protest from a substantial part of the audience revealed belligerent official ducking of issues. One protestor noted the hypocrisy of American policy in singling out Iraq while ignoring other brutal U.S. clients, such as Suharto in Indonesia. Albright replied: "I am really surprised that people feel it is necessary to defend the rights of Saddam Hussein." The questioner responded: "You're not answering my question, Madame Albright." Another asked the secretary to comment on former president Carter's worry that one hundred thousand Iraqis might be killed. Again shifting the subject, Albright boasted: "I am willing to make a bet to anyone here that we care more about the Iraqi people than Saddam Hussein does."[167]

Though noting the Columbus protest, the American press swiftly closed ranks. It downplayed demonstrations in other cities and failed to publicize a CNN[168] poll showing that despite the White House's campaign of justification, on February 15, 54 percent of Americans opposed bombing in contrast to February 1, when only 39 percent did. In a half-hour program featuring a consensus on the broad outlines of U.S. policy, the National Public Radio moderator abruptly cut off the lone critic, Sarah Flounders of the International Action Center. NPR also removed her comments from the transcript. Similarly, to repair damage, Ted Koppel's *Nightline* interviewed the Clinton officials, but no protestors, and followed up, the next evening, with an admiring piece on Secretary Albright's "day." Still, the persistence and sharpness of protest from below—an example of democratic internationalism,[169] the fact that officials could only avoid, not answer, questions, and the murkiness of U.S. objectives contributed to a (temporary) solution negotiated by U.N. secretary-general Annan.

If Iraq complies with weapons inspections, Russia, France, and other members of the Security Council will seek to end the boycott. Clinging to its pattern of arrogant isolation throughout the crisis, only the United States held out for sanctions to continue until Iraq obey all provisions of the initial Gulf War treaty. As part of the settlement, however, President Clinton apparently acceded to the others.[170]

10. THE ABOLITION OF WAR

As protest at Ohio State demonstrates, internationalism constrains elite options. Further, given strong movements from below, much of the professorial wing of Morgenthau's academic-political complex, as well as politicians, could, on the issue of major war, provide some counterweight to an array of bellicose interests.[171] As a side effect, a movement against large-scale war might check executive "gambling for resurrection."

On Forsberg's account, a series of agreements by the leading democracies to scale down conventional forces and adopt a primarily defense-oriented military strategy—one to stave off aggression and combat genocide through multilateral, humanitarian intervention—could create an international *regime* to handle conflict *without war*. Given "the security dilemma" and the potential "idealism" of merely paper agreements, attention to defensive preparations in each power would have to be considerable. Thus, movements from below would need to fight for such a regime, including inspections concerning defensive weapons, and force leaders to renounce both invasion and unilateral intervention. Nonetheless, efforts by the major powers—and the use of incentives by global institutions to curb aggression—might phase out war.[172]

Similar considerations apply to nuclear weapons. A movement of major powers toward a defense-oriented nuclear strategy and successive arms-reduction agreements might, as Goldfischer argues, encourage outsiders to adopt the same policies.[173] In the long run, efforts to enforce nonproliferation will probably fail; relying on mechanical, neo-Waltzian hopes about giving "deterrents" to each significant power, the opposite policy would also be unlikely to eliminate war.[174] In contrast, creating a regime that fosters defense and reduces nuclear arms—one that, along with those initially unimaginable regimes barring the killing of ambassadors, slavery, chemical weapons, and mines, outlaws nuclear and other major wars—is a conceivable goal.

11. REVOLUTION IN A WORLD WITHOUT WAR

An end of war, however, a critic might note, would still not remedy the distributive injustices named by Schelling and Honderich.[175] But first, none of the strictures barring major belligerence need apply to revolutionary violence from below against patterned denials of rights. Second, nonviolent strategies of resistance are, as this chapter suggests, promising. Finally, movements of the oppressed are more likely to adopt mass, nonmurderous means of protest than elites, thus pressing state leaders toward the abolition of war.[176]

As Falk and Zolo stress, though "multilateral" in form, the initial Gulf War[177] advanced American and European control over Middle Eastern oil and manipulated the United Nations. The boycott maintains war against civilians. Otherwise, however, in the post–Cold War era, novel possibilities for international humanitarian intervention have emerged. For those settings especially damaging to human rights—Bosnia, Somalia, and the like—the United Nations has an unprecedentedly large military budget.[178] Such interventions are today more frequent, and, by and large, an improvement, compared to rare instances of humanitarian action by individual states. Walzer, for instance, highlights only the example of India in Bangladesh in 1971.[179]

Yet as Zolo stresses, multilateral efforts to restore peace often have limited support within the targeted country—consider Somalia—and stave off immediate murderousness only by reinforcing long-run conflict.[180] For not only democracy and communism but even minimal decency are difficult to impose. Except for the case of genocide, Walzer's invocation of Mill's conception of self-help for democratic movements deepens this realist theme.[181] Yet Mill's criticism does not bar all such interventions. Instead it underlines the sharp limits in which interventions may, successfully, be pursued. In addition, this perspective deflates current enthusiasm for cosmopolitan governance, which, if a global regime became too strong militarily, would probably become despotic, and even in a stripped-down form, needs carefully specified objectives. Nonetheless, concrete proposals, such as Archibugi's, seem remarkably modest.

In place of "cosmopolitan governance," Zolo suggests four quite cautious international activities: (1) mapping and monitoring ethnic and class conflict (these clashes often reflect violations of basic rights and distributive injustices that need to be resolved through mass resistance—preferably nonviolent), (2) encouraging direct interaction between representatives of groups advancing and those hostile to nationalist claims (he thinks of Jimmy Carter's efforts),[182] (3) instead of establishing headquarters in New York, decentralizing global institutions, and (4) halting the arms trade (and one might add, restricting arms production). In 1996, for instance, promoting belligerence in regional conflicts, the U.S. government marketed jets to Chile and a warship—for $350 million—to Venezuela. As Edward Luttwak notes sarcastically: "[T]he money was borrowed on the New York market, augmenting the 'investment in Latin America' statistics, and forcing Venezuelans to pay interest on a non-income earning, cost-generating, non-asset."[183]

In contrast, as Falk stresses, in 1993 and 1994, the International Association of Lawyers against Nuclear Arms held meetings to forge a Draft Convention on the Monitoring, Reduction, and Abolition of the International Arms Trade.[184] Further, U.S. congressional representative Ron Dellums estimates that the American government could save between 150 and 200 billion dollars per year in military cutbacks—the vanished "peace dividend"—and use these funds to begin to restore cities and curb income inequality.[185] Although the United States is, in Marx's terms, the leading "parasite state,"[186] other countries could institute modest "savings" and comparatively humane policies.

At a minimum, Zolo's and related measures might limit murder and "ethnic cleansing." Further, short of committing troops, the global "community" might also curb belligerence by, for example, economic boycott, though, in contrast to the one against Iraq, with a proviso that harms to civilians be circumscribed. Such practices might lay the groundwork for an international regime against war, and a widening and deepening of the other treaties noted above.[187]

In addition, as I have emphasized, although the Gulf War shows how a great power can mobilize the United Nations to serve its seeming interests, the results—protecting Kuwaiti princes and grotesque sexist practices among allies,[188] leaving Hussein in power, killing 250,000 Iraqis immediately, poisoning the environment, gassing American troops (probably through mistargeted bombing) and having the Pentagon and CIA, for years, in the face of growing evidence and outcry, lie about it, continuing a boycott that has killed another 750,000 Iraqis, mainly children, and opening the United States to continual provocation by Saddam[189]—do not serve such interests well. Once again, they trade the substance of democracy for its imperial shadow.[190] Given governmental clumsiness and the scale of modern war, the gain from current policies—except in "welfare" to some officers, executives, political and "intelligence" leaders, and academics—is unclear.

Falk pits an abstract, humane image of international rule against contemporary "geogovernance" with its apartheid-like inequalities, destruction of the environment, sanctimony about the poor joined to rapacity, and U.S.-stunted "multilateralism." Without movements from below, however, such proposals are utopian. Insisting on statism or the limited independence from imperial control of a federated organization of un-equal states,[191] advocates of official realism, the democratic-peace hypothesis and cosmopolis miss this domestic, rebellious lynchpin of the future of human rights and democracy.

12. WON'T LEADERSHIP IN A DEMOCRATIC MOVEMENT EVENTUALLY BECOME PROBLEMATIC?

Using a principal/agent model, Downs and Rocke contend that compared to prime ministers, presidents have electoral incentives to prolong losing wars or intervene against other representative regimes. The agent has knowledge that the principal—the voters—lack, and can use this information selectively to lend illusory promise to such ventures.[192] If a war's costs are too high, the principal has only belated electoral rejection as a way to punish the agent (as Downs and Rocke note, this mechanism could dismiss a president who made reasonable decisions that turned out badly).[193]

Any belligerence, however, may transcend a public threshold for loss of life, after which de-escalation or withdrawal cannot prevent electoral defeat. Through escalation and calls for patriotism, however, a leader may still hope to survive an election.[194] Comparatively, parliamentary systems more easily translate citizen discontent into shortening the prime minister's term and diminish "gambling for resurrection."[195] Though fought against a dictatorship, Thatcher's war with Argentina over the Malvinas is, however, a counterexample. To a lesser extent, even parliamentary leaders engage in temporarily popularity-instigating foreign adventures.

Downs and Rocke's theory contrasts with George Ball's assumption that, with escalation, chauvinism sweeps the whole citizenry: "Once we suffer large casualties, we will have started a well-nigh irreversible process. Our involvement will be so great that we cannot—without national humiliation—stop short of achieving our complete objective."[196] But such arguments deny the possibility—in the case of Vietnam, the reality—of movements from below. They disregard institutional alternatives.

Given the privileges and psychology of leadership[197]—a tendency to domineer—and the principal/agent separation, distortion is likely in any system (even a radical democratic one). Though more concerned with the common-good-sustaining potentials of protest movements than most realisms, Downs and Rocke's view also suggests the likely deficiencies of any democratic politics.

But internationalism accepts these cautions. A radical democratic regime need not be Clintonesque—or Reaganesque—in its corruption. Yet short of vibrant movements from below, it would, very likely, become somewhat corrupt.

Downs and Rocke's argument underlines the distance between reasonable practices and presidential "gambling." Critical of U.S. interventions against parliamentary regimes, it allows for a vigorous—nonapologetic—version of the democratic-peace hypothesis: except where the elite can drape "the enemy" in racist, antiradical garb, the principal's knowledge about the good of other free regimes curbs the agent's belligerence. This theory also reinforces a democratic internationalism *from below*, one cognizant of the importance of institutional reforms, but focused on citizen action rather than the beneficence of (ordinary) leaders.

13. A DEMOCRATIC REALIST CRITICISM AND AN INTERNATIONALIST REJOINDER

Considering this internationalist critique as a whole, a sophisticated realist might respond: doesn't the emphasis on antidemocratic feedback underscore the harms to most citizens arising from great-power rivalry? Realists, however, expect such abridgments of the common good; democratic internationalists do not. Thus, your argument shows that some version of realism must be right.[198]

But this criticism makes three errors. First, it overlooks causally important variations in domestic institutions. Though antidemocratic feedback affects every regime, if Downs and Rocke are right, when compared to presidencies, parliaments mitigate "gambling for resurrection." Thus, the fundamental realist move—an abstraction of powers competing in international affairs from generalized regime types as well as particular configurations of institutions—fails. Further, even a democratic realism, such as Morgenthau's concerning Vietnam, cannot account for such institutional variations without abandoning this core realist starting point. In contrast, democratic internationalism highlights the interplay of global conflict *and* particular domestic settings.

Second, international politics results in *democratic*, not just antidemocratic, feedback. Such feedback can involve solidarity from below, for instance, in other countries, for the Spanish republic or between the Jacobins and the Haitian Revolution,[199] as well as from above, for example, to compete effectively with rivals, today's adoption of parliamentary forms—and perhaps some civil liberties for citizens[200]—by formerly dictatorial regimes.

Robert Putnam stresses two-level games in which international settings stimulate particular domestic policies, and, contra the unitary state model employed by neorealism, otherwise minority domestic groups invoke global pressures to push for preferred measures[201] ("from above" here refers to groups within the elite in contrast to a "unitary state"). Putnam uses the example of negotiations over energy prices at the Berlin Summit of 1978 and domestic conflicts. But interactive pressures for adopting parliamentary institutions, preventing major wars, or barring the use of nuclear weapons might also be considerable.[202]

A sophisticated realism might, however, take such democratic effects into account. Since democratic feedback contributes to a common good, however, it undercuts *this* objection. Further, as ordinarily formulated, realism is a statist view. In contrast, internationalism stresses robust citizen democracy and transnational solidarity.

Third, democratic internationalism does not say that citizens *must* achieve a common good domestically, but rather, that they *can*. It suggests reforms from below to make a realization of such goods more likely. Contrary to the self-misinterpretation of official realism, sophisticated realism also envisions a common good and, through internal critique, merges with an internationalist view. But the first response—that, in explanations, domestic institutions matter, and that interplay of spheres, not one-sided emphasis on powers in the global realm, is vital—differentiates democratic internationalism from even a sophisticated realism.

14. THE EROSION OF REFORM AND DEMOCRATIC MOVEMENTS

Even in a radical democratic conception, pluralism depends on the truth of the claim that disadvantaged people can organize themselves to offset prevailing interests and policies. In an oligarchy with parliamentary forms, however, such organization yields, at best, temporary results. Though reform movements have sometimes won particular demands, they then tend to decline. Mainstream political and media hostility speeds their erosion. For instance, in contrast to the vibrant civil rights movement of the 1950s[203] and 1960s, most black teenagers today face unemployment, gangs, or the army. Despite the emergence of an integrated elite, American cities are divided into two worlds. Further, income inequality, harming most whites as well as minorities, is growing.

Antidemocratic feedback exacerbates these trends. In the Reagan-Bush era, for example, warnings of "Evil Empire," a rapidly increasing military budget, a soaring deficit ("supply-side economics"), and borrowing from Japan fused with the Iran-Contra and Cocaine-Contra affairs and cutbacks in domestic social programs.

In contrast, the power of democratic example is unusual—consider the impact of Gandhi on King[204]—and often occurs through internationally influential or internationally influenced, slow-to-emerge movements. Where elite power is covert, concentrated, near to office, and costless to individuals,[205] democratic power falls outside prevailing circles of influence, is surveilled[206] and thus dangerous to participants, and often stems from mass revolt from below.

Now democratic theory mandates for each citizen not just a right to vote or even to participate in deliberations but an equal voice in setting the public agenda. If we imagine ourselves in a Rawlsian ideal sovereign assembly, we would need to be able to say that the basic institutional structure and policies of our society uphold equal freedom. But mainstream arrangements stem or reverse democratic movements and undercut such freedom. As this book has emphasized, *antidemocratic feedback* has been a decisive, though long unrecognized, obstacle to a deliberative regime.[207] Further, shadowing a narrowing oligarchy, even once-dominant pluralism is a declining theory in American universities.[208] The policies, institutional reforms, and international agreements noted above would go a long way toward allowing citizens a genuine say on important issues. Some of these measures could, even now, be realized. Within American and other parliamentary regimes, however, the emergence of even this degree of democracy would probably require nonviolent social revolution.

Must global politics constrain democracy? No. Does such politics constrain democracy in the United States and elsewhere? Markedly. In the gulf between these two responses lies the need for renewed debate and democratic movements.

Notes

Epigraphs

1. The Thaelmann column from Germany, the first brigade to arrive in Spain, contributed to holding off Franco in a battle for Madrid, November 7, 1936. Only a few of the initial five hundred survived the Spanish Civil War.

Defying racism and Roosevelt's blockade, thirty-three hundred black, brown, and white men and women served in the Abraham Lincoln Brigade. Nearly half—sixteen hundred—died in Spain. The survivors were later blacklisted or hauled before the House Un-American Activities Committee as "premature anti-fascists."

Rather than a democrat or communist, Robert Jordan in Hemingway's *For Whom the Bell Tolls* speaks of what it meant to be an "anti-fascist." In a 1938 farewell to the Americans at Barcelona, Dolores Ibarruri ("Passionara") named the significance of their action:

> For the first time in the history of people's struggles, there has been the spectacle, breathtaking in its grandeur, of the formation of the International Brigades to help save a threatened country's freedom and independence. . . .
>
> Communists, Socialists, Anarchists, Republicans . . . they asked us for nothing at all. That is, they did want a post in the struggle, they did aspire to the honor of dying for us.

Quoted in Joe Brandt, ed., *Black Americans in the Spanish People's War against Fascism, 1936–1939* (New York: International Publishers, n.d.), 43.

Introduction

1. The larger speech (4.5.204–14) uses a Crusade to illustrate the maxim and augurs *Henry V:*

> And all my friends . . .
> Have but their stings and teeth newly ta'en out,
> . . . by whose power I well might lodge a fear
> To be again displaced. Which to avoid,
> I cut them off, and had a purpose now
> To lead out many to the Holy Land,
> Lest rest and lying still might make them look
> Too near unto my state. Therefore, my Harry,
> Be it thy course to busy giddy minds
> With foreign quarrels . . .

2. Stephen Krasner, "Realism, Imperialism, and Democracy: A Reply to Alan Gilbert," *Political Theory* 20, no. 1 (1982): 38–52.

3. Michael W. Doyle, "Kant, Liberal Legacies, and Foreign Affairs." *Philosophy and Public Affairs* 12, no. 3 (1983): 205–35, and 12, no. 4 (1983): 323–53. A shortened version—"Liberation and World Politics—subsequently appeared in the *American Political Science Review* 80 (1986): 1151–69.

4. In a Waltzian idiom, the former is a second-image view, the latter a third-image view.

5. Chapter 1, however, also explores Doyle's *internal* critique of realism.

6. My arguments *novelly* challenge prevailing realisms. Yet as Krasner's response

("Realism, Imperialism, and Democracy") to the original version of chapter 1—a reiteration of neorealism—reveals, the spell of prevailing paradigms is strong. Thus, at the conclusion of this introduction and in subsequent chapters, I offer tables of the central theses in each debate.

7. At Kenneth Waltz's lecture at the Graduate School of International Studies in May 1995, I granted the core premise of neorealism and asked about antidemocratic feedback. His cursory reply—"international-relations theory is very limited"—underlines how methodological crochets hamstring neorealism. See J. David Singer, "The Levels-of-Analysis Problem in International Relations," in *The International System: Theoretical Essays*, ed. Klaus Knorr and Sidney Verba (Princeton: Princeton University Press, 1961); K. J. Holsti, *International Politics: A Framework for Analysis*, 5th ed. (Englewood Cliffs, N.J.: Prentice-Hall, 1988), 13–14; Martin Hollis and Steve Smith, *Explaining and Understanding International Relations* (Oxford: Clarendon Press, 1991), 7–9, 32, 89–91, 99–101, 117–18, 143–44, 168, 194–200, 203–16.

8. Sam Keen, *Faces of the Enemy* (New York: Harper and Row, 1991), traces the caricaturing of "enemies," often, in a racist vein, as vilified animals. The practice has psychological resonance—treating one's problems as solely "external"—for many individuals. Even in the rare case where an opponent is evil, such as the Nazis, however, the American war effort employed ordinary caricature, and kept silent about genocide (Leonard Dinnerstein, *America and the Survivors of the Holocaust* [New York: Columbia University Press, 1982], prologue).

9. Morgenthau's courageous anti–Vietnam War essays initiated the critique of anticommunism. Pre-Vietnam American realists denounced "democratic" ideology, which, emblematically, on their view, motivated President Wilson's "crusade."

10. Niebuhr's contrast of *group* "immorality" to individual "morality" underlines this point. Similarly, Morgenthau's *Politics among Nations*, 5th ed. (New York: Knopf, 1973), 9, sees politics as the "domination of man over man" and seeks to identify "interest" defined as "power," regardless of setting. As a response to the Vietnam War, however, and in contradiction to his general theory, he stressed a *common* good and democracy.

11. George Kennan, *American Diplomacy* (Chicago: University of Chicago Press, 1984), 166–67.

12. Others are near competitors, however. World War I was marked by the jailing of Eugene Debs as well as other protestors, and followed by the Palmer Raids; World War II occasioned the imprisonment of Japanese-Americans in concentration camps, the persecution of Trotskyists, the outlawing of strikes, and so forth.

13. As public critics of the war, Michael Walzer and Sheldon Wolin in political theory, Stanley Hoffmann in international relations, were exceptions.

14. He implausibly avers, however, that one can affirm structural Marxism—the existence of an *exploitative* ruling class, a view that he characterizes as nearly indistinguishable from statism—without moral baggage.

15. Branch Davidian leader David Koresh was apparently an abuser of children. Nonetheless, criticism of the Waco slaughter as murder initiated by the central government (FBI) has merit; President Clinton's rejoinder none.

16. Madison spoke of vast territory as well as the governmental division of power as providing "a republican remedy for the diseases of republicanism."

17. Josh Cohen and Joel Rogers, *Inequity and Intervention* (Boston: South End Press, 1986); Michael Reich, *Racial Inequality: A Political-Economic Analysis* (Princeton: Princeton University Press, 1981).

18. Michael K. Brown, "The Segmented Welfare System," in *Remaking the Welfare State*, ed. Brown (Philadelphia: Temple University Press, 1988); Gwendolyn Mink, *Old Labor and New Immigrants* (Ithaca: Cornell University Press, 1986); Richard Cloward and Frances Fox Piven, *Poor People's Movements* (New York: Pantheon, 1977). Indeed, these

claims explain the current spectacle of Republican "revolution," elevating the military and the rich but targeting the poor, and Democratic concessionary "resistance."

19. Bruce Russett, *Controlling the Sword: The Democratic Governance of National Security* (Cambridge: Harvard University Press, 1991), chap. 1.

20. George Downs and David M. Rocke, "Conflict, Agency, and Gambling for Resurrection: The Principal-Agent Problem Goes to War," in *Optimal Imperfection? Domestic Uncertainty and Institutions in International Relations* (Princeton: Princeton University Press, 1995), chap. 3. Before the English-Argentine war over the Falkland Islands, Thatcher's social policies, tolerating widespread unemployment, had fallen into disrepute. In that case, also, a temporarily unpopular, *parliamentary* regime may use foreign adventure to stir up patriotic, antireform support at home.

21. J. Peter Euben, "Corruption," in *Political Innovation and Conceptual Change*, ed. Terence Ball and James Farr (New York: Cambridge University Press, 1989), and *The Tragedy of Political Theory: The Road Not Taken* (Princeton: Princeton University Press, 1990), chap. 6.

22. Krasner, "Realism, Imperialism, and Democracy," 42–43, 45; J. William Fulbright, *The Price of Empire* (New York: Pantheon, 1989).

23. Actual regimes sometimes have a more complex effect. For instance, the European Union's trade policies, arguably, benefit the poor in Spain and Portugal, but harm the least advantaged in nearby countries from which trade is diverted.

24. Mainstream politics objects only to "safety nets" and "welfare" for the poor, not for various elites.

25. Alan Gilbert, *Democratic Individuality* (Cambridge: Cambridge University Press, 1990), chap. 3; Gilbert Harman, "The Inference to the Best Explanation," *Philosophical Review* 74 (1965): 88–95.

26. This contradiction highlights the implausibility of a *reductionist* theoretical project to establish a uniform, amoral currency of "power."

27. *Zeal* is another favored realist term of condemnation.

28. Ironically for this view, however, after World War II, American military rule established parliamentary regimes in Germany and Japan.

29. Given special incentives of power, prestige, and money to leaders, this claim, however, holds for any regime.

30. Thus, Morgenthau averred as a "fundamental rule" that "diplomacy must be divested of the crusading spirit," and cited William Graham Sumner: "If you want war, nourish a doctrine. Doctrines are the most frightful tyrants to which men are ever subject because doctrines get inside of a man's own reason and betray him against himself" (Hans J. Morgenthau, *Politics among Nations*, 2d ed., revised [New York: Knopf, 1964], 540–41).

31. Realists would also have to demonstrate that their skepticism of leadership applies to genuine democratic influence on power. First, none of the existing, mainly elitist, democracies—and not even revolutionary socialist regimes—has facilitated, by and large, that kind of mirroring of popular sentiment by leadership. Second, more strikingly than realism, internationalism captures the need for civil disobedience and other manifestations of democratic power from below.

32. Under democratic pressure, revolutionary state legislatures, reluctantly, abolished the debts of impoverished farmers. The *Federalist Papers* repeatedly warn against this "danger," symbolized by Shays's Rebellion, to "justify" a more centralized regime. See Alan Gilbert, *Emancipation and Independence: The American Revolution, Haiti, and Latin American Liberation*, forthcoming, chap. 4.

33. More accurately, participants *rebelled* against patterned racism, usually motivated, as in Harlem, by murders of young, "suspect" innocents like James Powell by the police.

34. Gilbert, *Emancipation and Independence*, chap. 4; John Rawls, *Political Liberalism* (New York: Columbia University Press, 1993).

35. According to economist Paul Krugman, over the past twenty years, the top 1 percent has gained in real income and wealth, while the income and wealth of the bottom 80 percent has held steady or declined; further, income inequality has increased even *within* the highest 1 percent.

[Being rich] means being part of the 10% of families who own 70 per cent of the nation's wealth.

But the truth is the upper class is indeed pulling away from the middle class. In fact, income is becoming more concentrated all the way up the scale.

It's not just that the top 20 per cent have gotten richer compared with the rest. The top 5 per cent have gotten richer compared with the next 15 per cent; the top 1 per cent have gotten richer compared to the next 4 per cent, and there is pretty good evidence that the top 0.25 per cent have gotten richer compared with the next 0.75 per cent.

The idea that wealth is spreading rather than becoming ever more narrowly concentrated is comforting, but utterly untrue.

Krugman, "The Wealth Gap Is Real and It's Growing," *New York Times*, August 21, 1995. See Kevin P. Phillips, *The Politics of Rich and Poor: Wealth and the American Electorate in the Reagan Aftermath* (New York: Random House, 1990).

36. In Waltzian language, Peter Gourevitch, "The Second Image Reversed: The International Sources of Domestic Politics," *International Organization* 32, no. 4 (1978), names this argument "second image reversed."

37. Krasner, "Realism, Imperialism, and Democracy," 44; Hans J. Morgenthau, *In Defense of the National Interest* (New York: Knopf, 1952).

38. As the *New York Times* reports (April 8, 1995, 1A), even forty years after, the record of CIA—and U.S. government—criminality against democracy in the 1950s, for instance against the elected Arbenz government in Guatemala and that of Mossadegh in Iran, is only hesitantly being made public. In 1993, President Clinton ordered thousands of documents declassified. Probably *none* of these documents now affect "national security," even on a no longer relevant, Cold War calculus. Nonetheless, as a stalling tactic—to prevent insight into covert, antidemocratic belligerence—the CIA has brought forward "experts" to argue about them, one by one.

In 1993, Leo Valladares, the new Human Rights Ombudsman of Honduras, requested information on CIA support of Battalion 316, a secret, government hit squad, which launched a reign of terror in the early 1980s. The Clinton administration promised a prompt response (in 1995, Director Deutsch ordered a review of the CIA's activities in Honduras, saying it would provide lessons on "how not to do things"). A four-part series in the *Baltimore Sun* (June 13, 14, 15, and 18, 1995) by Gary Cohn and Ginger Thompson told the story of Ines Murillo, a guerilla, who was brutalized for seventy-eight days in Battalion 316's secret jails, but—unusually—not murdered because of the threat by her father, a military officer known to the torturers, to reveal the name and address of the CIA man involved (see also their article with Mark Matthews, "Torture Taught by the CIA," *Baltimore Sun*, January 27, 1997). Though the Honduran government has recently indicted some officers who commanded death squads, witnesses fear to come forward. The CIA and Defense Intelligence Agency are "still reviewing their files." On October 10, 1996, A22, a *New York Times* editorial warned of the antidemocratic impact on Honduras of continuing U.S. cover-up.

39. I mean democratic compared to the American presidential election of the same year, which required millions of votes for a third party—5 percent—in a previous election to qualify for the public funding that might enable it to elicit those votes. But even then, such funding would hardly be equal. Thus, Perot, who got 20 percent of the vote in the 1992 presidential election, received only half the federal funds available to the Democratic and

Republican candidates in 1996 (further, that comparison leaves aside the vast, separate spending of the Democratic and Republican national committees). The *New York Times*, September 8, 1996, 1A, estimated that $600 million would be spent in the race, including an allocation of $30 million in federal funds to Perot for the previous campaign, and, if his campaign were to raise it, an additional $30 million (a ratio of 1 to 10; the two other parties have *roughly* nine-twentieths of the funds—$270 million—each). The final figure for expenditures appears nearer to $800 million.

Thus, in recent times, only a multibillionaire has managed to cross these barriers even in one election. Moreover, although Perot was funded, a "bipartisan commission" denied him participation in presidential debates. The dominant Democratic-Republican consensus erects dramatic obstacles to fair electoral competition. Michael Parenti, "Is Nicaragua More Democratic Than the United States?" *Covert Action Information Bulletin* 26 (1986): 48–52. Chapter 5 explores democratic alternatives to current practices.

40. William L. Robinson, "Globalization, the World System, and 'Democracy Promotion' in U.S. Foreign Policy," *Theory and Society* 25, no. 5 (1996): 48–62, and *Promoting Polyarchy* (Cambridge: Cambridge University Press, 1996).

41. Since the Vietnamese postrevolutionary government was not a "democracy," even the American violation of the Geneva Accords vanishes.

42. He does not acknowledge earlier objections by John Mearsheimer, "Back to the Future: Instability in Europe after the Cold War," *International Security* (summer 1990); Krasner, "Realism, Imperialism, and Democracy"; Alan Gilbert, "Power Rivalry–Motivated Democracy: A Response to Stephen Krasner," *Political Theory* 20, no. 3 (1992): 681–89; and others, but only an article by David P. Forsythe, in *Human Rights and Peace: International and National Dimensions* (Lincoln: University of Nebraska Press, 1993.

43. His claim would, for example, make England, following World War II, "unstably democratic." Yet Bruce Russett, *Grasping the Democratic Peace: Principles for a Post–Cold War World* (Princeton: Princeton University Press, 1993), 14–15, rightly rules out preservation of a "free market"—more precisely, of private property in the means of production or other vital resources—as a criterion for democracy (John Rawls, *A Theory of Justice* [Cambridge: Harvard University Press, 1971], 61). Despite Russett's later assertion about "instability," this criterion allows the expropriation of foreign ownership. In addition, as chapter 5 shows, he misguidedly excises civil liberties from his conception of democracy.

44. Russett, *Grasping the Democratic Peace*, 123; emphasis added. Russett (137, 141 n. 15, 142 n. 3) also invokes David Lake, "Powerful Pacifists: Democratic States and War," *American Political Science Review* 86, no. 1 (1992): 24–37, which suggests that in war, democracies, supposedly displaying "low imperialist drive," often defeat authoritarian regimes. Lake's final table, however, conflates the U.S. seizing of Texas from Mexico and other colonial acts of conquest by "parliamentary" governments, with the war against Nazism. *Aggression* is not the same as democratic "strength."

45. He borrows this notion from Huntington (Russett, *Grasping the Democratic Peace*, 16); the regime should have been in power for (nearly) three years. Allegedly "unstable" because Russett imagines Allende was a "Marxist" (121), Chile had been a democracy since the turn of the twentieth century.

46. Russett's chapter 5 adds the previously unmentioned stricture for making Guatemala, Chile, et al. "unstably democratic." His explicit criteria for democracy emphasize competitive elections (*Grasping the Democratic Peace*, 14) but omit any notion of *representation*. Like much behaviorist literature, Russett stresses only *internal* processes; yet he has written a book about *foreign* policy.

47. Russett, *Grasping the Democratic Peace*, 123–24.

48. Noam Chomsky and Edward Hermann, *The Political Economy of Human Rights: The Washington Connection and Third World Fascism*, vol. 1 (Boston: South End Press, 1977), "The Sun and Its Planets," inside cover. Following the example of I. F. Stone, I

emphasize mainstream, journalistic revelations about CIA activities, particularly in chapter 5, to indicate how problematic this avoidance is.

49. In fact, internationalism sharpens awareness of the pattern. Cf. Mearsheimer "Back to the Future"; Krasner, "Realism, Imperialism, and Democracy."

50. From the standpoint of assessing a common good, nonbehaviorist defenders of interdemocratic peace, for instance Doyle, invoke statism more plausibly than neorealists.

51. Samuel P. Huntington, *Political Order in Changing Societies* (New Haven: Yale University Press, 1967), chap. 1, and "The Democratic Distemper," in *The Crisis of Democracy*, ed. Huntington, Michel Crozier, and Joji Watanuki (New York: New York University Press, 1975).

52. John Rawls, "The Law of Peoples," in *On Human Rights: The Oxford Amnesty Lectures*, ed. Stephen Shute and Susan Hurley (New York: Basic Books, 1993).

53. See the Liddell-Scott-Jones *Lexicon* of classical Greek; Jacqueline de Romilly, *The Rise and Fall of States, According to Greek Authors* (Ann Arbor: University of Michigan Press, 1977), chap. 4.

54. *Apology*, lines 23a–b.

55. The term *humility* is distinctively Christian; Kennan, *American Diplomacy*, 178, and Niebuhr, *A Theologian of Public Life: Selected Writings of Reinhold Niebuhr*, ed. Larry Rasmussen (Minneapolis: Fortress Press, 1991), 97–98, 105, 155, strikingly invoke it.

56. As chapter 4 maintains, Thucydides was more a democrat than a realist, a founder of what I call democratic realism or, more accurately, democratic internationalism.

57. This Greek term, which means taking more than one's share, also has a sense of *over*reaching what is needed for a relationship or activity—what is human—a sense that is later lost.

58. Thucydides, *History of the Peloponnesian War*, trans. Thomas Hobbes (Chicago: University of Chicago Press, 1989), 40–41, 108–15.

59. Spoken in the voice of Pericles' mistress, Aspasia, Plato's *Menexenus* mocks the funeral oration: "[I]t is easy to praise Athenians to Athenians." In *Gorgias*, Socrates, misguidedly, ignores Pericles' anti-imperialist advice, and treats him as a mere politician, one who made the Athenians worse over time. Yet as chapter 4 emphasizes, we might see Socrates' insights as linking Thucydides' particular critique of Athenian pride, emerging from restless innovation and culminating in blind hunger for dominion, to narrow political leadership and dogmatism in general.

60. Ancient political philosophy, as in Aristotle, aimed to sustain not just mere life but a good life for each citizen.

61. Will Kymlicka, *Liberalism, Community, and Culture* (Oxford: Oxford University Press, 1989); Rawls, *Political Liberalism*, lecture 5; Gilbert, *Democratic Individuality*, chap. 1.

62. Gilbert, *Democratic Individuality*, chap. 1.

63. Ancient democracy created what Hegel called "beautiful individuality," though at the expense of slavery and a reductionist, functional conception of individuals (*Die Vernunft in der Geschichte* [Hamburg: Meiner Verlag, 1955], 62). Despite lower social and political expectations characteristic of at least its capitalist form—Marx's reference to "influential shoe black dealers" in contrast to Athenian citizens—a liberal regime promises a public equality of those who pursue the life that each sees fit so long as she doesn't harm others. Marx, *Capital*, trans. Samuel Moore and Edward Aveling, 3 vols. (New York: International Publishers, 1967), 1:431, 408.

64. Morgenthau, *Politics among Nations*, 5th ed., 9.

65. As chapter 1 shows, taken logically, Krasner's arguments license belligerent state interests. In practice, however, Krasner often criticizes such interests, for instance, those of the U.S. government in Vietnam (Krasner, "Realism, Imperialism, and Democracy").

66. A large number, Aristotle, *Politics*, bk. 3, notes, may sometimes have more insight

than a single leader. He saw more good in democracy than did Plato, though not than did the "historical" Socrates (contrast the speech of the democratic "Laws" in the *Crito* with the more clearly Platonic *Republic*, bk. 9).

67. Although Thucydides criticizes the weaknesses of this regime, he also, as chapter 4 shows, cautiously befriends democracy (Cynthia Farrar, *The Origins of Democratic Thinking: The Invention of Politics in Classical Athens* [Cambridge: Cambridge University Press, 1988]; Jennifer Tolbert Roberts, *Athens on Trial* [Princeton: Princeton University Press, 1994]). Nonetheless, his admiration for Athenian greatness—the *instrumental* role of democracy in securing imperial dominion over others—limits his insights into that regime as an intrinsic good.

68. Aristotle only warily defended "natural" slavery. He rejected popular justifications for this practice, such as the putative distinction, in the words of Helen of Troy, between Greeks and barbarians; further, he admired a barbarian regime, Carthage, as one of the three best actual regimes. Modern readers often take his apology for natural slavery out of context, the dawning of the first, still limited, *free* regimes (Gilbert, *Democratic Individuality*, chap. 1). In addition, this view is also directed against Socrates, whose illustration of the recollection of geometry by a slave in the *Meno* challenges any such doctrine.

69. In relying on empiricism, as chapter 1 shows, the social "sciences" substitute allegiance to a controversial philosophical picture of science, a supposed *method*, for a particular, mature theory within each domain of knowledge. Thus, investigators attempt to test "hypotheses," without theoretical critique, against "the evidence," which is mistakenly thought not to be "theory-loaded." In this context, however, the vagueness, ambiguity, and implausibility of putative theoretical terms is hardly unique to neorealism; consider, for example, the notion of war in the democratic-peace hypothesis.

70. *New York Times*, September 17, 1973. A9.

71. The U.S. government violated the 1954 Geneva Accords, as President Eisenhower admitted, because Ho Chi Minh would have won the elections mandated for 1956.

72. John Locke, *Two Treatises of Government* (New York: Hafner, 1947), 235.

73. Gilbert, *Democratic Individuality*, chap. 12.

74. Concurring with Marxism, Niebuhr emphasized the injustice of domestic, not just global, "powers." Yet he, ironically, saw the Vietnam War less as an expression of elite interests than did Morgenthau or even Kennan.

75. Marx, letter to Meyer and Vogt, *Selected Correspondence*, trans. I. Lasker, ed. S. Ryazanskaya (Moscow: Foreign Languages Publishing House, 1965), 235–37.

76. Obstacles to unions—ranging from firings and blacklistings to the use of police and injunctions against strikers to preying on ethnic and gender divisions to the stigmatization of antiradical ideology—are considerable. In the United States, for example, at the turn of the twentieth century, the AFL organized only craft workers—about 10 percent of the workforce. Some fifty years after the initial working-class movements, the CIO, occupying factories by sit-down strikes, organized industrial unions and stimulated competitive AFL efforts—and roughly 25 percent of workers joined organizations. Antiunion laws, including the banning of such strikes and Taft-Hartley injunctions—giving workers, for whom going on strike takes organization and enormous energy, and employers "equally" ninety days "to cool off"—have eroded, and continue to erode, that power.

77. Reich, *Racial Inequality*; Gilbert, *Democratic Individuality*, chap. 11.

78. Following Marx, one might suggest that racism toward immigrants (including disfavored groups of "whites"), blacks, Chicanos, and Native Americans, coupled with U.S. support for oligarchies abroad, notably in Mexico and Latin America, has been "the secret of the impotence" of the modern American working class.

79. Ted Honderich, *Political Violence* (Ithaca: Cornell University Press, 1976), 5.

80. Alan Gilbert, "Equality and Social Theory in Rawls' *A Theory of Justice*," *Occasional Review* 819 (autumn 1978): 95–117. Current circumstances are far from just. As

chapter 5 suggests, any serious proposal to implement seemingly quite uncontroversial moral programs—for instance, the priority of Rawls's principle of the equal basic liberties of each, which makes you and I, and the owners of *Time*, equal in resources from the standpoint of shaping the public agenda—turns out to be intensely controversial.

81. This dilemma for ethical theory in today's politics resembles, as chapter 1 shows, that of Keohane's morally well stated liberal institutionalism.

82. Given widening inequalities in the last twenty years, one might add: for the United States as well.

83. Benjamin R. Barber, *Jihad versus McWorld* (New York: Times Books, 1995), 305 n. 22, 14.

84. Roberts, *Athens on Trial*. Many realists, however, rightly fear what they take to be Thucydides' conclusion. For instance, Niebuhr warns that "the moral cynicism and defeatism which easily result from a clear-eyed view of the realities of international politics are even more harmful than the too simple ideals of pure moralists" (Reinhold Niebuhr, *Moral Man and Immoral Society: A Study in Ethics and Politics* [New York: Charles Scribner's Sons, 1944], 126). See also *Reflections on the End of an Era* (New York: Charles Scribner's Sons, 1934), 123.

85. Realist interpretations have often neglected this theme. But a sophisticated realist could still criticize Athenian "overexpansion," à la Krasner and Gilpin, and yet miss Thucydides' focus on *democracy*.

86. Hobbes also emphasizes a "commodious life." As chapter 4 suggests, his views are closer to Aristotle's on a good life than his insistence on preserving life, by itself, seems to imply.

87. Empiricists aim to find measurements for abstract concepts: to *operationalize* them. However justified this goal, one must still offer plausible accounts of these concepts, not, as in social scientific definitions of "I.Q.," "democracy," "' and the like, antidemocratic, tautological, or implausible ones. See Ned Block and Gerald Dworkin, "I.Q., Heritability, and Inequality," *Philosophy and Public Affairs* 3 (1974): 331–409, 4 (1974): 40–99; Alan Gilbert, 'What Then?' The Irrepressible Radicalism of Democracy," in *History and the Idea of Progress*, ed. M. Richard Zinman, Jerry Weinberger, and Arthur Meltzer (Ithaca: Cornell University Press, 1995), sec. 3.

Chapter One

1. Official realism, as chapter 4 argues, misinterprets Thucydides, seeing him not as a critic of democratic imperialism, but as a brutal spokesperson, through the Athenian ambassadors at Melos, for a putative "law of the stronger."

2. Rawls, "The Law of Peoples," emphasizes the centrality of such rights in a decent international perspective. See Friedrich Kratochwil, *Rules, Norms, and Decisions: On the Conditions of Practical and Legal Reasoning in International Relations and Domestic Societies* (Cambridge: Cambridge University Press, 1989).

3. Section 5 of this chapter restates this conception, based on Michael Doyle's version, as an internal critique of realism.

4. Aristotle, *Politics*, 1333b29–33.

5. Kant, *Zum Ewigen Frieden* (Bern: Scherz, n.d.), 18–19.

6. This formulation restates the thesis that citizens often have common—democratic—interests across national boundaries against the predatory policies of their own state(s).

7. All statements of theses refer to the debate charted in table 2 at the conclusion of this chapter.

8. Kenneth N. Waltz, *Theory of International Politics* (New York: McGraw-Hill, 1979), 99, 80. Invoking an eccentric, philosophical image of the natural sciences, Singer, "Levels-of-Analysis Problem, " 77, asserts, "Whether in the physical or the social sciences, the ob-

server . . . may, for example, choose between the flower or the garden, the rock or the quarry, the trees or the forest . . . the micro- or the macro- level of analysis." But, first, the natural sciences rely on particular theories in each domain, and, sometimes, of the relations between them. The Michelson-Morley experiment or quarks are paradigms of a *theoretically* interesting "macro/micro" distinction. In contrast, international relations—and other social "sciences"—pursue a controversial, external portrait of "scientific method" at the expense of theory. Second, both the international and comparative "levels" are "macro." Singer's and neorealism's attempt to force Waltz's "three images"—or his abstraction of the international from the domestic realm—into a macro/micro dichotomy is misguided.

9. Waltz, *Theory of International Politics*, 71; Krasner, "Realism, Imperialism, and Democracy." The first sentence should read "are likely to be subject to" rather than "are subject to." To understand if, and how, great powers "pressure" other states also depends, on a neorealist account, on their domestic politics.

10. Once again, a one-sided picture of Woodrow Wilson's policies symbolizes the error to be avoided.

11. With restricted suffrage for parliament and kingly authority over foreign policy, the Prussian monarchy was, in decisive respects, tyrannical. But it is a borderline case. For in regard to the pattern of antidemocratic U.S. belligerence, "bipartisan" foreign policy often plays a comparable role.

Citing Hegel, Rawls, "The Law of Peoples," 60–68, sketches an ideal "hierarchical" regime, which sustains a common good among its members. In the abstract, his claim makes sense, but one would be hard pressed, as he recognizes, to think of practical examples. Though sexist and oppressive, one might suggest, satirically, that perhaps the Saudi regime preserves the lives of most of its members and realizes, in that respect, a common good. Rawls's claim, however, underlines the critical nature of moral philosophy. Contemporary "democracies" are, as Rawls also recognizes, for quite uncontroversial reasons—for instance, they promise an equal package of basic liberties to citizens that capitalism subverts— far removed from justice rather than "nearly just" regimes. Chapter 6 explores the implications of Rawls's argument for reforming democratic institutions. Rawls, *A Theory of Justice*, 226.

12. Plato, *Republic*, bk. 9.

13. Rawls, "The Law of Peoples," for example, stresses the nonaggressive character of decent regimes. He affirms a modified version of the democratic-peace hypothesis among large, comparatively stable, capitalist democracies, one qualified by condemnation of the pattern of U.S. antidemocratic intervention in the less developed countries.

14. The radical conception of a *united front* advances democratic demands along with liberals: resistance to aggression, checking racism and sexism, striking for higher wages, and the like; yet it also encourages each side to advocate its overall point of view. In fighting for a common good, a radical thinks, state hostility will reveal to participants the need for revolution. Alan Gilbert, *Marx's Politics: Communists and Citizens* (New Brunswick, N.J.: Rutgers University Press and Oxford: Martin Robertson, 1981), chaps. 1, 11, and *Democratic Individuality*, chap. 8.

15. Gilbert, *Marx's Politics*, chaps. 1, 9. Even such sophisticated theorists as G. A. Cohen, *Marx's Theory of History: A Defense* (Princeton: Princeton University Press, 1977), and Shlomo Avineri, *The Social and Political Thought of Karl Marx* (Cambridge: Cambridge University Press, 1970), do not mention internationalism.

16. Doyle, "Kant, Liberal Legacies"; Francis Moore Lappe and Joseph Collins, *World Hunger: Twelve Myths* (New York: Institute for Food and Development Policy, 1986), 115–28; Cohen and Rogers, *Inequity and Intervention*. Radical democratic internationalism often defends (betrayed) liberal values (Micheline Ishay, *Internationalism and Its Betrayal* [Minneapolis: University of Minnesota Press, 1995]).

17. For instance, as chapter 3 stresses, English workers upheld abolitionism in the American Civil War at the expense of their own jobs (Gilbert, *Democratic Individuality*, chap. 7).

18. "Is there anything evil in the regions of actuality or possibility that the *Aurora* has not suggested of me," Adams fumed. "The matchless effrontery of this Duane merits the execution of the alien law" (James Roger Sharp, *American Politics in the Early Republic: The Nation in Crisis* [New Haven: Yale University Press, 1993], 218–19). Though born in America, William Duane, editor of the *Philadelphia Aurora*, moved as a child with his mother to Ireland; he returned after the Revolution.

19. James Morton Smith, *Freedom's Fetters* (Ithaca: Cornell University Press, 1956), 23–24, 152–55.

20. Prefiguring the sinking of the *Maine* and the Tonkin Gulf "incident," Adams charged that unnamed French diplomats, "X," "Y," and "Z," had tried to suborn American representatives.

21. Madison, *Writings*, vol. 6 (New York: Putnam, 1906), 333; Gilbert, *Emancipation and Independence*, chap. 4.

22. Jefferson, *Writings*, ed. Merrill D. Peterson (New York: Library of America, 1984), 453–55. Given Proposition 187 and the current Republican campaign against immigrants, many Californians—and other American workers—might wisely heed Jefferson's counsel.

23. Smith, *Freedom's Fetters*; Michael Hunt, *Ideology and U.S. Foreign Policy* (New Haven: Yale University Press, 1987); Adrienne Rich, "For Ethel Rosenberg," in *A Wild Patience Has Taken Me This Far* (New York: Norton, 1981); Loch Johnson, *America's Secret Power* (Oxford: Oxford University Press, 1989); William W. Keller, *The Liberals and J. Edgar Hoover: The Rise and Fall of a Domestic Intelligence State* (Princeton: Princeton University Press, 1989).

24. Herbert Lüthy, *France against Herself* (New York: Meridian, 1957).

25. Bill D. Moyers, *The Secret Government: The Constitution in Crisis* (Washington, D.C.: Seven Locks Press, 1988).

26. Gilbert, *Democratic Individuality*, chap. 1.

27. In responding to this essay's original version (Alan Gilbert, "Must Global Politics Constrain Democracy? Realism, Regimes, and Democratic Internationalism" *Political Theory* 20, no. 1 [1992]: 8–37), Krasner overreacted to this sentence. I maintain only that the logic of the *official realist* argument, which forgets a morality realists otherwise affirm, is imperialist: to dominate where one can. Given the historic moral impetus of realism in shunning pride and "democratic" expansion, however, sophisticated realists usually concur with Morgenthau's critique of Vietnam, which chapter 2 explores, though they, perhaps, rarely state it so bluntly.

28. This conception affirms Rawls's account ("The Law of Peoples") of *international* human rights.

29. See Gilbert, *Democratic Individuality*, chaps. 1, 2, 13. Morgenthau, *Politics among Nations*, 5th ed., chap. 1, rightly stresses an objective moral view that exists in interplay with the empirical possibilities of prudent international politics. Except for *Truth and Power*, however, Morgenthau does not see—as Niebuhr does—how moral considerations, encompassed in a conception of a common good, are central to a realist view of international conflict.

30. I use *statism* synonymously with *realism*.

31. Arghiri Emmanuel's *Unequal Exchange* (New York: Monthly Review Press, 1972) is the *locus classicus* of this view. As Robert Gilpin, *The Political Economy of International Relations* (Princeton: Princeton University Press, 1987), notes, "From the theorists of economic nationalism, [dependency theorists] take their political program of state building. . . . there are no calls for the workers of the world to unite and throw off their chains" (282). I

will, however, mainly show the unexpected interest of democratic internationalism rather than probe the deficiencies of dependency theory.

32. Gilbert, *Democratic Individuality*, chaps. 1–2; Rawls, *A Theory of Justice*, "The Priority of Right and Ideas of the Good," *Philosophy and Public Affairs* 17 (1988): 251–76, "The Law of Peoples," and *Political Liberalism*.

33. In contrast, as I have emphasized, today's neorealists inconsistently affirm a strict separation between international order, which they suppose is utterly anarchic and domineering, and domestic, ostensibly constitution-bound, democratic politics.

34. Gilbert, *Democratic Individuality*, chap. 5, and Alan Gilbert, "An Ambiguity in Marx's and Engels's Account of Justice and Equality," *American Political Science Review* 76, no. 2 (1982): 328–46; Robert W. Tucker, *The Inequality of Nations* (New York: Basic Books, 1977).

35. For instance, many participants initially saw Vietnam as a "mistake" within the basically benevolent policy of a democratic power, not as an extreme outcome of a consistent imperial policy to sustain reactionary dictatorships and overturn democracies in the less developed countries.

36. Weber's commendation of parliamentary competition, for example, arose from instrumental concerns: "The German philistine . . . believes that he can smugly look down on them [parliamentary institutions] from the heights of his own political impotence and . . . fails to consider that the British parliament became, after all, the proving ground for those political leaders who managed to bring a quarter of mankind under the rule of a minute but politically prudent minority." Max Weber, *Economy and Society*, trans. Gunther Roth and Claus Wittich, 3 vols. (New York: Bedminister, 1968), 3:1420; Gilbert *Democratic Individuality*, chap. 10.

37. *Epistemological realism* centers on the claim that our theory-governed inquiry into the world achieves successively greater approximations to truth and that the nonvisible posits of mature scientific theories, e.g., electrons, by and large, exist. It contrasts with *power state realism* in international relations. See Boyd's and MacMullin's essays in *Scientific Realism*, ed. Jarrett Leplin (Berkeley and Los Angeles: University of California Press, 1984); Dudley Shapere, *Reason and the Search for Knowledge* (Amsterdam: D. Reidel, 1984); Harman, "Inference to Best Explanation"; Gilbert, *Democratic Individuality*, chap. 3.

38. Stephen Krasner, *Defending the National Interest: Raw Materials Investment and U.S. Foreign Policy* (Princeton: Princeton University Press, 1978), 21–26, 32–33, 152–53, 323–25 n. 98.

39. So, I contend in *Democratic Individuality*, chaps. 9–12, does Weberian-inspired social "science."

40. As chapter 5 emphasizes, in Rousseau and Rawls, *democratic autonomy* is the central thesis of modern political theory: to assess the justice of current practices, we may think of ourselves as free and equal citizens, deliberating in favorable circumstances, as part of an ideal sovereign assembly, on the best institutions and policies for our regime. It thus conflicts with realist and Marxian, social theoretical notions of state autonomy (Gilbert, *Democratic Individuality*, chaps. 1, 8).

41. Krasner, *Defending the National Interest*, 344, ignores Wilson's antidemocratic activism. But however decent her initial intentions, a president alone cannot change underlying, patterned policies. See Chomsky and Hermann, *Political Economy of Rights*; Michael T. Klare, *War without End* (New York: Knopf, 1972).

42. Huntington, *Political Order*, chap. 1.

43. Krasner, *Defending the National Interest*, 42–45.

44. Like Krasner, Waltz offers a legal positivist account: "States in anarchy cannot afford to be moral. The possibility of moral behavior rests upon the existence of an effective

government that can deter and punish illegal actions." Robert J. Art and Kenneth N. Waltz, "Technology, Strategy, and the Uses of Force," in *The Uses of Force*, ed. Art and Waltz (Lanham, Md.: University Press of America, 1983), 6. First, however, this putatively categorical dismissal of ethics in global affairs underlines the implausibility of the central, neorealist separation between international and domestic politics: protection of the lives of citizens against aggression—a central goal of "effective" government—is moral. Second, just as individuals may act ethically in the absence of government enforcement, so may regimes (Jack Donnelly, "Realism and the Academic Study of International Relations," in *Political Science in History: Research Programmes and Political Traditions*, ed. James Farr, John S. Dryzek, and Stephen T. Leonard [Cambridge: Cambridge University Press, 1995]). Further, at the conclusion of *Theory of International Politics*, Waltz stresses that joint state action may curb the four *p*s—poverty, population, pollution, and (nuclear) proliferation— and achieve an international "*collective* good" (209–10, 196–98) (this chapter is, unfortunately, the only place where Waltz uses a term equivalent to "common good"). These claims contradict his misguided categorical dismissal of any international morality.

45. Krasner, *Defending the National Interest*, 41.

46. Michael L. Walzer, *Just and Unjust Wars* (New York: Basic Books, 1977); Gilbert, *Democratic Individuality*, chaps. 1, 2.

47. "The statements and preferences of central decision-makers can nevertheless be used to define the national interest if two conditions are met: these preferences do not consistently benefit a particular class or group, and they last over an extended period of time. A public act of the state is one that affects the whole community" (Krasner, *Defending the National Interest*, 43). Overly cautious about morality, however, this misguided formulation includes, as "in the national interest," *tyrannical* policies that consistently harm all groups and negatively "affect the whole community."

48. Nonetheless, Vietnam, Cuba, and Nicaragua indicate the limits of such "ignorance."

49. Rawls, *A Theory of Justice*, and *Political Liberalism*; Ronald Dworkin, *Taking Rights Seriously* (Cambridge: Harvard University Press, 1977), chaps. 6–8.

50. Faced with an unusual threat, however, the role of the Western democracies, aligned with the Soviet Union and resistance movements, in defeating fascism, is a striking, internationalist counterexample.

51. Smaller-scale efforts by former antiwar and church activists, however, including the Sanctuary Movement as well as public protest, also countered U.S. interventions in Nicaragua and Salvador.

52. Gilbert, *Democratic Individuality*, chaps. 8, 10, 12.

53. Krasner, *Defending the National Interest*, 323–25.

54. In other words, trimmed to realist preconceptions, he can imagine only a Marxian theory about *domination*, not one focused, primarily, on "the *emancipation* of the working class" and other oppressed people.

55. In addition, wealthy people find it hard to tell when others offer friendship or applause for the sake of a relationship or activity rather than external gain. Such an elite might be, often irrationally, suspicious. In a society driven by money and "fetishism," the difficulty the rich experience only amplifies a common concern.

56. Gilbert, *Democratic Individuality*, chap. 12.

57. Krasner, *Defending the National Interest*, 339. Only Michael Paul Rogin, *Ronald Reagan the Movie and Other Studies in American Political Demonology* (Berkeley and Los Angeles: University of California Press, 1987); and Gilbert, *Democratic Individuality*, chap. 12, spell out the nature and *mainstream role* of anticommunist or antiradical ideology in American public life.

58. David Goldfischer, *The Best Defense* (Ithaca, N.Y.: Cornell University Press, 1993). As chapter 2 shows, Forrestal also helped engineer the "war scare" of 1948 (Frank Kofsky, *Harry S. Truman and the War Scare of 1948* [New York: St. Martin's, 1993], 86–88).

59. E. P. Thompson, *Beyond the Cold War* (New York: Pantheon, 1982). In the post–Cold War era, Goldfischer's alternative (*The Best Defense*) of a de-escalated nuclear regime focused on military targets—a proposal still isolated among Cold War "security" specialists—deserves consideration.

60. On behalf of his mistaken thesis, Krasner, *Defending the National Interest*, 340–41, invokes Maslow and even the crude *social* Darwinism of E. O. Wilson.

61. At this point, one might combine his argument with Robert Jervis's theory of misperception (*Perception and Misperception in International Politics* [Princeton: Princeton University Press, 1976])to produce a sophisticated realism.

62. Krasner, "Realism, Imperialism, and Democracy," 48.

63. Krasner fails to see that I offer an internal—and hence, often friendly—critique of realism ("Realism, Imperialism, and Democracy," 38). For instance, as I insist, though an emphasis on power at the expense of democracy can camouflage reactionary policies, realists, including Krasner, often—and if they understand the moral underpinnings of well-stated realism, should always—"oppose [imperial] crusades" (Gilbert "Must Politics Constrain Democracy?" 12).

64. As I note below, however, it may sanction multilateral, humanitarian interventions, say, in Somalia or Bosnia.

65. Gilbert, *Democratic Individuality*, chap. 13.

66. Mearsheimer, "Back to the Future"; and Stephen Van Evera, "Primed for Peace: Europe after the Cold War" *International Security* (winter 1990–91) counsel the U.S. government to counteract the ideology of "hypernationalism" in German education. They fail to call for, first, telling the truth about U.S. domineering in American schools.

67. He might have added, Goulart in Brazil, Jagan in Guyana, the Sandinistas in Nicaragua, and Aristide in Haiti. More exactly, the U.S. government—notably, the CIA—organized Contra depredations against civilians, disseminated lies in the American media about alleged Sandinista antidemocratic practices, and, through economic war, reduced Nicaragua to the poorest nation in the hemisphere. Subsequently, the Sandinistas abandoned power through elections. Barbara Kingsolver's novel *Animal Dreams* recalls the case of Ben Linder—an American agricultural volunteer murdered by the Contras.

68. Van Evera, "Primed for Peace."

69. In response to these novel problems, John Herz, who named the "security dilemma," gave up realism as an adequate theory of international rivalry.

70. Oddly, he refers to this claim as an "empirically unsupported assumption" (Krasner, *Defending the National Interest*, 46). Empirically, though aggression is not always repelled, it is always resisted and, short of rare cases that require humanitarian intervention, always despised by a subject population. Neorealists should abandon "geometry-envy."

71. The Nazis motivated people by appeals to a spurious "Aryan" good. The notion of legitimacy, however, fails to differentiate just motivations from ideological—tyrannical—facsimiles.

72. Scholarship follows its own course. Consider Barrington Moore Jr., isolated in the Russian Research Center at Harvard from teaching undergraduates and most graduate students in Social Relations and Government, who spent fifteen years writing *Social Origins of Dictatorship and Democracy* (Boston: Beacon Press, 1965).

73. More than most political scientists, Krasner, Gilpin, and Keohane attend to alternate conceptions. They do not, however, see fair statement of leading theoretical alternatives—going further, where possible, than current proponents—as central to scientific work.

74. Gilpin, *Political Economy*, 1987, 335–36; Krasner, "Realism, Imperialism, and Democracy." See also Fulbright, *The Price of Empire*, 136–37, 142.

75. Gilpin, *Political Economy*, 336.

76. Gilpin, *Political Economy*, 42.

77. Gilbert, *Democratic Individuality*, chap. 10; Gilpin, *Political Economy*, 40.

78. Gilbert, *Democratic Individuality*, chaps. 10–11.

79. Marine invasions as well as U.S. military aid installed and protected Nicaraguan dictatorships for most of this century.

80. The Bush administration's intervention in the Middle East—unusually—opposed aggression (Michael L. Walzer, *Just and Unjust Wars*, 2d ed. [New York: Basic Books, 1992], introduction). In the context of overall U.S. interventionary policy, and its nurturing, until the eve of war, of Iraqi dictatorship, however, as chapter 5 shows, a democratic internationalist might still oppose it.

81. Such well-formulated conservative arguments are broadly liberal or decent, in the sense used in this book. Emerging in the eighteenth century, liberalism highlighted such freedoms against religious persecution and was never a primarily economic doctrine. Extending these historic liberal insights into democratic theory, chapter 5 interprets deliberative democracy as, primarily, a conscience-sustaining regime (Gilbert, *Democratic Individuality*, chap. 1; Rawls, *Political Liberalism*, chap. 1).

82. Robert Gilpin, *Political Economy*, 26–31, and "The Richness of the Tradition of Political Realism," in *Neorealism and Its Critics*, ed. by Robert O. Keohane (New York: Columbia University Press, 1984), 321.

83. Gilpin, *Political Economy*, 55, 41–42, 59 n. 54, 38.

84. Hilary Putnam, "On the Corroboration of Theories," in *Collected Philosophical Papers* (Cambridge: Cambridge University Press, 1975); Imre Lakatos, "Falsification and the Methodology of Scientific Research Programmes," in *Criticism and the Growth of Knowledge*, ed. Lakatos and Alan Musgrave (Cambridge: Cambridge University Press, 1970); Gilbert, *Marx's Politics*, chaps. 1, 9–10.

85. Gilpin, *Political Economy*, 38–40.

86. Keohane also stresses the Coase theorem. Invoking an example of a factory's "reap(ing)" a profit from its capacity to pollute," the latter, however, shows how a victimizer getting a payoff to do slightly less victimizing fulfills Pareto optimality, a claim more favorable to a realist picture of international politics than to Keohane's image of mutual benefit. Robert O. Keohane, *After Hegemony: Cooperation and Discord in World Political Economy* (Princeton: Princeton University Press, 1984), 86, 75–77, 82–83.

87. Keohane, *After Hegemony*, 57.

88. Keohane, *After Hegemony*, 123–25.

89. Keohane, *After Hegemony*, 252–56; emphasis added.

90. Rousseau, *Oeuvres complètes*, 3 vols. (Paris: Gallimard, 1964), 1:355–56. The example is, originally, Locke's (*Two Treatises of Government*, 237).

91. Patrick Ireland, "Facing the True 'Fortress Europe': Immigrant and Politics in the European Community," *Journal of Common Market Studies* 24, no. 5 (1991), and *The Policy Challenge of Ethnic Diversity: Immigration Politics in France and Switzerland* (Cambridge: Harvard University Press, 1994). The emergence of violent neofascist groups throughout Europe is a malevolent, nationalist response to these decent, liberal measures—a *feedback of antidemocratic example.*

92. Keohane, *After Hegemony*, 42.

93. The term *openness* seemingly has liberal moral connotations. Yet it refers here to "free" capital movement, which often harms the least advantaged.

94. Keohane, *After Hegemony*, 119–20. Keohane uses the term *liberal* to refer to the unobstructed "rule" of capitalist markets, not, as this book does, to a regime whose institutions further individuality.

95. Ramonet, "Hope," *Le Monde Diplomatique*, January 1996, 1, also remarks: "This arsenal of social guarantees, hard won by workers' movements, constitutes the heart of modern civilization. The logic of globalization and of planetary free trade leads to the downgrading of salaries and social protection towards the much lower levels prevalent in

Asia and the Pacific." In Marxian terms, such cutbacks seek to lower the social element in subsistence.

96. "German Economy Shows Weakness: Output Down, Unemployment Up," *Denver Post*, December 18, 1996, 32A.

97. The rapid growth of inequality over the last twenty years has restored the U.S. economy to "number one," according to Switzerland's International Institute for Management Development. Germany has slipped back to tenth (*Denver Post*, December 16, 1996, 32A).

98. As chapter 4 shows, Keohane's argument parallels Hobbes's opposition of monarchy to no government: to protect physical security, the latter allows liberals only negativity without imagination.

99. Keohane, *After Hegemony*, 257 n. 2.

100. Gene Sharp, *Making Europe Unconquerable: The Potential of Civilian-Based Deterrence and Defense* (Cambridge, Mass.: Ballinger, 1986), 139. If similar movements could be mobilized to support them, so do Goldfischer's (*The Best Defense*) conception of a deescalated, military target and noncity, non-civilian-oriented nuclear strategy, and George DeMartino and Stephen Cullenberg's proposal ("Beyond the Competitiveness Debate: An Internationalist Agenda," *Social Text* 41[winter 1994]: 11–39) for an international tariff structure offering incentives for antisexist and environmental reforms.

101. Even the British liberation of one hundred thousand blacks in exchange for enlistment, during the American Revolution, drew its momentum from below (Gilbert, *Emancipation and Independence*, chap. 1).

102. At the margins, however, outlaw slavery—for instance, importation into the United States of impressed labor from Mexico or Asia—still exists.

103. In the war of 1812, early U.S. and English parliamentary regimes—with very limited suffrage—clashed. In 1798, the United States nearly went to war with France (Gilbert, *Emancipation and Independence*, chap. 4; Fulbright, *The Price of Empire*). One might speak of a modified *Keohane-Doyle-Fulbright thesis*.

104. John Jay, Alexander Hamilton, and James Madison, *The Federalist Papers* (New York: Mentor, 1961), 46; Gilbert, *Democratic Individuality*.

105. See chapters 3 and 5 of this book; Reich, *Racial Inequality*; Gilbert, "An Ambiguity" and *Democratic Individuality*, chaps. 7, 10–11; Krugman, " Wealth Gap Is Real"; Phillips, *Rich and Poor*.

106. Keohane, *After Hegemony*, 167–69; emphasis added. A radical academic work could probably not have included so blunt a formulation. See also Doyle, "Kant, Liberal Legacies," 331–38; Russett, *Grasping the Democratic Peace*, 121–24.

107. John McCamant, "Intervention in Guatemala," *Comparative Political Studies* 17 (1984): 373–407; Robinson, *Promoting Polyarchy*.

108. Huntington, *Political Order*; Sheldon Wolin, "Political Theory as a Vocation," in *Machiavelli and the Nature of Political Thought*, ed. Martin Fleisher (New York: Atheneum, 1972), 21; Gilbert, *Democratic Individuality*, chap. 9.

109. One may, however, interpret Machiavelli as defending a (slaveholding) republic, not an empire. Weber is the prototypical *predatory* "democrat."

110. Wendy Brown, *Manhood and Politics* (Lanham, Md.: Rowman and Littlefield, 1988); J. Ann Tickner, "Hans Morgenthau's Principles of Political Realism," in *Gender and International Relations*, ed. Rebecca Grant and Kathleen Newland (Bloomington: Indiana University Press, 1991).

111. Julia Kristeva, *Strangers to Ourselves* (New York: Columbia University Press, 1991); Tzvetan Todorov, *The Conquest of America* (New York: Harper and Row, 1985); William Connolly, "Identity and Difference in Global Politics," in *International/Intertextual Relations*, ed. James Der Derian and Michael Shapiro (Lexington, Mass.: Lexington Books, 1989).

112. The conflicts of fledgling "democracies" at the turn of the nineteenth century seem far less horrible than their contemporary counterparts. *At most*, the democratic-peace hypothesis holds for large, comparatively stable, capitalist, mainly white oligarchies with parliamentary forms.

113. Rawls, "The Law of Peoples"; Gilbert, *Democratic Individuality*, chap. 1.

114. Alternately, in a Waltzian vein, neorealism may be regarded as, at most, articulating *constraints* posed by the existing structure of power for policies, events, and changes in the international setting, rather than explaining or predicting such phenomena. I am grateful to Jack Donnelly for this point.

115. Gilbert, *Emancipation and Independence*, chap. 3. The success of the revolution in Saint Domingue—named Haiti upon independence in 1804—led to the fusion of emancipation and independence in Venezuela and throughout Latin America. English emancipation and the defeat of abolition in the American Revolution foreshadowed the uniqueness and tragedy of a Civil War in which slavery became the central issue.

116. G. A. Cohen, "Reconsidering Historical Materialism," in *Nomos: Marxism*, ed. J. Roland Pennock (New York: New York University Press, 1984), 239.

117. Gilbert, *Democratic Individuality*, chap. 10.

118. Gilbert, *Emancipation and Independence*, chap. 4.

119. Through factories in Nazi Germany, General Motors and Ford produced tanks and jet engines to support Franco's revolt; the Roosevelt administration harassed ordinary Americans who defended the Spanish Republic. As a 1974 congressional hearing revealed, the U.S. government subsequently paid GM thirty-two million dollars and Ford three million dollars for damages to their German plants from Allied bombing during World War II (Bradford Snell, *Ramparts*, June 1974, 14–16). See also Michael Dobbs, "Ford and GM Scrutinized for Alleged Nazi Cooperation: Firms Deny Researcher's Claims on Aiding German War Effort," *Washington Post*, November 30, 1998, A1, who reports: " 'General Motors was far more important to the Nazi war machine than Switzerland,' said Bradford Snell, who has spent two decades researching a history of the world's largest automaker. 'Switzerland was just a repository of looted funds. GM was an integral part of the German war effort. The Nazis could have invaded Poland and Russian without Switzerland. They could not have done so without GM.' "

In 1938, Hitler awarded Henry Ford and James Mooney of GM the Grand Cross of the German Eagle for "distinguished service to the Reich." These men engaged in betrayal. According to documents in German and American archives: "[I]n certain instances, *American managers of both GM and Ford went along with the conversion of their German plants to military production at a time when U.S. government documents show they were resisting calls by the Roosevelt administration to step up military production in the plants at home*" (emphasis added).

GM and Ford also battened off slave labor. On Dobbs's account, "The story of Elsa Iwanowa, who brought a class-action suit against Ford last month, is typical. At the age of 16, she was abducted from her home in the Southern Russian city of Rostov by German soldiers in October 1942 with hundreds of other young women to work at the Ford plant in Cologne. 'The conditions were terrible. They put us in barracks on three-tier bunks,' she recalled in a telephone interview from Belgium, where she now lives. 'It was very cold; they did not pay us at all and scarcely fed us. The only reason we survived was that we were young and fit.' "

A U.S. army report by investigator Henry Schneider, September 5, 1945, accused the German branch of Ford of serving as an "arsenal of Nazism, at least for military vehicles," with the "consent" of the parent company in Dearborn. He was ignored. Congress, in league with the CIA, resettled war criminals from Eastern Europe in the United States while barring "displaced persons" from the same region, notably Jews. As I noted above, Congress also voted compensation to GM and Ford for "damage" to their German operations.

In "What's Good for General Motors . . . May Have Been Good for Hitler," *New York Times*, December 2, 1998, A31, Frank Rich notes: "When I read GM's latest statement of denial [of complicity to Rich and Dobbs] to Bradford Snell, a historian who is completing a book on the auto giant to be published by Knopf, he laughed and dismissed it as 'baloney.' . . . In his book, he will devote 'several hundred pages' to G.M.'s wartime history—a story he has assembled over 20 years through interviews with former G.M. employees and Albert Speer as well as from documents in Nazi, British, Polish and U.S. archives. G.M., though, has given him 'zero' information to help set the half-century-old record straight."

120. Hannah Arendt, *On Violence* (New York: Harcourt Brace Jovanovich, 1977); George Kateb, "Nuclear Weapons and Individual Rights," *Dissent* 33, no. 2 (1986): 161–72; Thompson, *Beyond the Cold War*.

Chapter Two

1. Hans J. Morgenthau, "The Shadow and Substance of Power," in *Vietnam and the United States* (Washington, D.C.: Public Affairs Press, 1965).

2. Morgenthau, "Shadow and Substance," 15.

3. Contrary to this stereotype, however, leading realists—Morgenthau, Niebuhr, Kennan, and Herz—all criticized American Cold War policies. To be concerned with the intelligent use of power does not mean merely to serve existing power.

4. Morgenthau, "Prologue," in *Truth and Power: Essays of a Decade* (New York: Frederick Praeger, 1970), 5.

5. Stanley Hoffmann at Harvard and George Kennan, a diplomat who had become a professor of history at the Institute for Advanced Study—both sophisticated realists—were the only international-relations specialists, besides Morgenthau, to speak out against Vietnam. Niebuhr—a theologian—also criticized the war. Though few in number, realists were, nonetheless, a high percentage of outspoken tenured opponents of the war. Among political theorists, Sheldon Wolin and Michael Walzer stood out as public critics.

6. Morgenthau, *Truth and Power*, 24–25.

7. More precisely, sophisticated realism begins from Thrasymachus's formula that so-called "justice is the advantage of the the stronger," but modifies it with Socrates' insight that justice is—more rarely—the realization of a *common* good (Plato, *Republic*, bk. 1).

8. Richard Barnet, *Intervention and Revolution: America's Confrontation with Insurgent Movements around the World* (New York: World, 1968), 164–75. In a triumph of American "intelligence," many of those on the list were absent from the Dominican Republic in 1965.

9. The desire to achieve security and, perhaps ultimately, leadership by offering obsequious advice is different from—not as central to Morgenthau's abbreviated view of human nature as—the desire to dominate.

10. Morgenthau, *Politics among Nations*, 5th ed., 34. Contrary to Morgenthau, Hobbes insists *only* on the fear of violent death and would have rejected a putative innate, not situational, desire to dominate.

11. Thomas Hobbes, *Leviathan or the Matter, Forme and Power of a Commonwealth Ecclesiasticall and Civil*, ed. Michael Oakeshott (New York: Collier, n.d.), 184; John Herz, "Idealist Internationalism and the Security Dilemma," in *The Nation-State and the Crisis of World Politics* (New York: D. McKay, 1976), 72–73.

12. Tickner, "Hans Morgenthau's Principles"; Jean Baker Miller, *Toward a New Psychology of Women* (Boston: Beacon Press, 1976), chap. 1. As the study and practice of war, international politics has displayed prototypical sexism (Gilbert, *Democratic Individuality*, 380). Increasing awareness of feminism and the participation of women, however, has sometimes accompanied articulation of the moral core of international relations, for instance, Secretary of Energy Hazel O'Leary's break with secrecy about the murderous

activities of the U.S. government—the raining down of nuclear poisons on unsuspecting patriots in Utah, and the like. The Advisory Committee on Human Radiation Experiments' investigation revealed that "scientists" had injected plutonium into eighteen, now terminally ill patients, without consent. Tom Bailie, a Washington farmer, who lived in "Death Mile" downwind from the Hanford atomic plant, commented: "They were atomic Gods. They played God with our lives" ("In Cold War's Shadow, All of U.S. a Laboratory," *Denver Post*, June 13, 1995, A7; Susan Griffin, *A Chorus of Stones* [New York: Vintage, 1992]).

13. Morgenthau, *Truth and Power*, 9.

14. Morgenthau, *Truth and Power*, 47.

15. Interview with Lawrence Colburn, *60 Minutes*, March 29, 1998.

16. Nixon commuted Calley's sentence.

17. Leslie Zganjar, "GI Who Halted My Lai Massacre to Be Honored," *Denver Post*, March 2, 1998, A2, 7. Responding to the British film, David Egan, a Clemson professor, led a campaign to recognize humane conduct. Kevin Clement, a lieutenant colonel, has repeatedly urged his Pentagon superiors to praise Thompson's actions to recruits as a model of allegiance to the laws of war, against criminality. Thompson and Colburn—Andreotta died in Vietnam—were finally awarded Soldier's medals, given to those who risk their lives in situations which involve no enemy troops.

> Shortly after My Lai, [Thompson] and his crew received Bronze stars. . . :
> "It was only to keep me quiet," he says.

Colburn notes that the My Lai memorial prompted the U.S. government to issue new medals: " 'Just to save face,' he says" (A7).

18. Morgenthau's insight recalls Marx's invocation of Dante in the preface to *Capital*: "Segui il tuo corso e lascia dir le gente" [follow your own course and let people talk].

19. A paradigm of official realism, Huntington's claim (*Political Order*, chap. 1; 'The Democratic Distemper") that the "national interest" is "the interest of state institutions" rewords Thrasymachus's assertion that "justice is the advantage of the stronger" (Plato, *Republic*, bk. 1).

20. Cited in Theodore Draper's review of *Kissinger*, by Walter Isaacson, *New York Times Book Review*, Sept. 16, 1992.

21. Stanley Hoffmann, *Janus and Minerva: Essays in the Theory and Practice of International Politics* (Boulder, Colo.: Westview Press, 1987), 72–73, notes the tension between Morgenthau's abstract formulations and his subtle analysis of specific situations.

22. Morgenthau, preface to *Politics among Nations*, 2d ed., xiii. Montesquieu, however, defended a novel regime, a modern commercial republic (England) (Gilbert, "Individuality and Political Association in Montequieu," *Political Theory* 22, no. 1 [1994]: 45–70, and *Friendless Aliens, Friendless Citizens*, forthcoming, chap. 1). For fear of censorship, his writing is subtler.

As Morgenthau's invocation of Montesquieu indicates, however, he saw no wall between international relations and political theory. Leo Strauss commented on the second edition (foreword to *Politics among Nations*, 2d ed., xiii). Morgenthau was a dear friend of Arendt's and authored a eulogy, in a form mirroring the essays in Arendt's *Men in Dark Times*, "An Appreciation of Hannah Arendt (1906–1975)," *Political Theory* 4, no. 1 (1976): 5–8. He opened with the elegant, sad wish that he might have died first, for he had always hoped that she—friend and master of the form—might have written an epitaph for him. As his friendship and admiration for Niebuhr shows, he also saw no hard separation between international relations and theology.

23. Morgenthau, *Politics among Nations*, 5th ed., 9. Robert W. Tucker's insightful critique ("Professor Morgenthau's Theory of Political Realism," *American Political Science*

Review 46, no. 1 [1952]: 214–24) of Morgenthau's *In Defense of the National Interest* emphasizes the opposed—alternately: incoherent—moral consequences one could draw from the latter's attempt to reduce ethics to power. Mistakenly persuaded by the empiricist doctrine of "value-freedom," however, Tucker misses Morgenthau's endorsement of uncontroversial moral standards. Morgenthau's self-indulgent rejoinder ("Another 'Great Debate': The National Interest of the United States," *American Political Science Review* 46, no. 4 [1952a]) devotes exactly one sentence, in a footnote, to Tucker. I am grateful to Timothy Fuller for alerting me to this important exchange.

24. "Power covers the domination of man by man, both when it is disciplined by moral ends and controlled by constitutional safeguards, as in Western democracies, and when it is that untamed and barbaric force which finds in laws nothing but its own strength and its sole justification in aggrandizement" (Morgenthau, *Politics among Nations*, 5th ed., 9). The later editions feature a comparatively terse formulation about power. For instance, contrast the second edition's (13–14) repeated, ungainly definition of power as "man's control over the minds and actions of other men."

25. Gilbert, *Democratic Individuality*, chaps. 1, 13.

26. Morgenthau, *Politics among Nations*, 2d ed., xii, emphasis added. Hoffmann, *Janus and Minerva*, chap. 4, underlines the absence of this insight in many of Morgenthau's general formulations.

27. Gilbert, *Democratic Individuality*, chap. 12, 423–26.

28. Donnelly, "Realism and Academic Study."

29. He spoke of "eternal laws by which man moves in the social world. There are, aside from the laws of mathematics, no other eternal laws besides these." *Scientific Man versus Power Politics* (Chicago: University of Chicago Press, 1946), 220.

30. In its devotion to a philosophical picture of "method" and an ironic, for empiricists, dismissal of theoretical alternatives without investigation, neorealism is also often arrogantly argued.

31. Morgenthau, *In Defense of the National Interest* (New York: Knopf, 1952), 987.

32. Today's empiricists study "power" apolitically, as if the *truth* about important public institutions and movements could be neutral. Yet as Charles Taylor, "Neutrality in Political Science," in *Philosophy, Politics, and Society*, ed. Peter Laslett, 3d series (New York: Barnes and Noble, 1964), has shown, such institutions inevitably affect "human wants, needs and purposes," or what I call underlying ethical standards. In addition, an implausible *reduction* of ethics to "values" haunts this empiricist formulation. For if every value, for instance, Nazi genocide, is moral, then the notion of the moral becomes self-refuting (a self-refuting argument reveals its falseness by its assertion, for example, if I say to you, "I do not exist") (Gilbert, *Democratic Individuality*, 4).

33. Morgenthau, *Politics among Nations*, 5th ed., 14.

34. Morgenthau, *Politics among Nations*, 5th ed., 12.

35. Morgenthau, *Politics among Nations*, 5th ed., 11, 14.

36. Morgenthau, *Scientific Man*, 177.

37. Hans J. Morgenthau, *The Decline of American Politics*, vol. 1 of *Politics in the Twentieth Century* (Chicago: University of Chicago Press, 1962), 47.

38. Morgenthau, *Decline of American Politics*, 10. "There is one moral code . . . [that] is something objective that is to be discovered." Morgenthau, "Human Rights and Foreign Policy," in *Moral Dimensions of American Foreign Policy*, ed. Kenneth Thompson (New Brunswick, N.J.: Transaction Books, 1984), 10; *The Purpose of American Politics* (New York: Knopf, 1960), 222–23, 252; *The Restoration of American Politics*, vol. 3 of *Politics in the Twentieth Century* (Chicago: University of Chicago Press, 1962), 237.

39. Morgenthau, *Politics among Nations*, 1st ed. (New York: Knopf, 1948), 177. I am grateful for the latter examples to Jack Donnelly.

40. Morgenthau, *Politics among Nations*, 1st ed. 177; *Scientific Man*, 176; *Decline of American Politics*, 130, 126, 373; *Truth and Power*, 65.

41. Gilbert, *Democratic Individuality*, chap. 13, stresses the diverse levels of ethical argument and possible confusions about what drives comparatively intractable, complex moral disagreements. It sees core ethical standards as level 1, social theoretical and empirical differences as level 2, and complex moral judgments as level 3. Chapter 5 suggests that this analysis justifies a theory of deliberative democracy, and examines those unusual cases that involve a conflict of public deliberations with core standards—notably, freedom of conscience—and limit the role of the former.

42. Morgenthau, *Scientific Man*, 193. His reductionist insistence on "man's will to power" is Nietzschean.

43. Morgenthau's contemporary, John Herz, named such a view a "realist liberalism" ("Idealist Internationalism," chap. 1). Such terms illustrate, once again, the conjunction of controversial empirical theses about international power-rivalry with ordinary, underlying ethical standards about a regime's decency.

44. Morgenthau, *Politics among Nations*, 5th ed., 9.

45. Morgenthau, *Politics among Nations*, 5th ed., 7.

46. Morgenthau, *Politics among Nations*, 5th ed., 7–8; "Shadow and Substance," 18–19. More than twenty-five years later, with hesitation, secretary of defense and architect of war Robert McNamara (Robert McNamara with Brian VanDeMark, *In Retrospect: The Tragedy and Lessons of Vietnam* [New York: Times Books, 1995]) finally admitted that such criticisms were right. See *New York Times*, "McNamara's War," April 12, A12, letters; April 14, 1995, A10; April 15, 1995, A1.

47. Tickner, "Hans Morgenthau's Principles," rightly criticizes Morgenthau's statement of political realism in *Politics among Nations* for ignoring a common good. Overly reliant on today's literature on realism, however, she disregards Morgenthau's writings on Vietnam, particularly *Truth and Power*, which provide both an abstract formulation and examples of possible democratic empowerment. She also, unfortunately, reads *Politics among Nations* uncritically, failing to see the internal tensions in Morgenthau's misguided theoretical attempt to reduce the ethical complexities of power to amoral domineering.

48. Morgenthau, *Truth and Power*, 31. The previous sentence notes: "The great decisions democratic governments are called upon to make are always justified in terms of the common good—that is, of the benefits which, at least in the long run, will accrue to the great mass of citizens." As Morgenthau notes, such claims can sometimes be right.

49. Gilbert, *Democratic Individuality*, chaps. 5–6; "Historical Theory and the Structure of Moral Argument in Marx," *Political Theory* 9, no. 3 (1981): 173–206; and "An Ambiguity."

50. Rawls's prioritization of the equal-liberty principle over the difference—the common, though unequal, economic benefit—principle in a decent—"well-ordered"—regime highlights this point (Rawls, *A Theory of Justice*).

51. Morgenthau, "Freedom and Freedom House," in *Truth and Power*, 50. He rightly juxtaposes the likely fate of the Freedom House "statement" to that of the fatuous 1914 manifesto, denying Prussian aggression against Belgium, signed by many German intellectuals.

52. In the *Crito*, line 48c, Socrates suggests that most people might "frivolously" condemn a man to death but later, if only they could, wish that person back to life.

53. For instance, Kennan conjured this virtue to reject "our military-industrial addiction" (*American Diplomacy*, 178).

54. Morgenthau, *Politics among Nations*, 5th ed., 11. Though a political liberal, Morgenthau shared Michael Oakeshott's hostility to social tinkering. This concurrence of attitude stems from a sense of how easily "benevolent" attempts to change social conditions can

go awry. Hence, Morgenthau chose the title *Scientific Man versus Power Politics*; Oake-shott's striking review (Michael L. Oakeshott, "Scientific Politics," in *Religion, Politics, and the Moral Life*, ed. Timothy Fuller [New Haven: Yale University Press, 1993]), however, questions Morgenthau's misguided identification of scientism with science.

55. Even Kissinger is a more complex figure, a student and friend of Morgenthau, than stereotypical dismissals of realism allow. His *New Republic* obituary for his teacher, "A Gentle Analyst of Power: Hans J. Morgenthau," *New Republic*, August 2–9, 1980, 12–14, makes it clear that they shared—or, at least, he yearned for—the latter's kindness. Kissinger has, however, committed himself to abusive uses of power.

56. Niebuhr emphasized the coming into being of "things that are not." To its detriment, however, as chapter 1 shows, "structural realism" does not recognize transformation.

57. Morgenthau, "Quisling Show," *New Republic*, December 21, 1959. The movie *Quiz Show* also underlines this point.

58. The United Nations' Convention identifies this crime as the deliberate "destruction of a people, in whole or in part" (United States Civil Rights Congress, *We Charge Genocide*, ed. William L. Patterson [New York: International Publishing, 1949]). Hugu Adam Bedau, "Genocide in Vietnam?" in *Philosophy, Morality, and International Affairs*, ed. Virginia Held, Sidney Morgenbesser, and Thomas Nagel (Oxford: Oxford University Press, 1974), carefully weighs whether the U.S. government committed genocide in Vietnam and con-cludes with an ironic, Scottish verdict—"Not proven, not quite."

59. Morgenthau, "What Ails America?" in *Truth and Power*, 33, "Freedom and Free-dom House," 47, "Shadow and Substance," 19–20.

60. Morgenthau, "Freedom and Freedom House," 47.

61. Morgenthau, "Shadow and Substance," 9–13, 22–23, and "Johnson's Dilemma," in *Truth and Power*, 404–5. As chapter 4 illustrates, Morgenthau's distinction between sub-stance and shadow recalls Thucydides' contrast between Pericles' funeral oration and the crazed "realism" of Athens's representatives at Melos, whose hunger for power ultimately led to the slaughter of the Athenians in Syracusan quarries. I am grateful to Lucy Ware for bringing Morgenthau's distinction to my attention.

62. Morgenthau, *Politics among Nations*, 5th ed., 38; *From Max Weber: Essays in Soci-ology*, ed. and trans. H. H. Gerth and C. Wright Mills (New York: Oxford University Press, 1958), 384–85; Gilbert, *Democratic Individuality*, 376. As chapter 4 contends, Thucydides' *History* unforgettably illustrates this point—for those who read it, which did not, unfortu-nately, include American policymakers during the Cold War.

63. Krasner, "Realism, Imperialism, and Democracy."

64. Morgenthau, "What Ails America?" 31.

65. Morgenthau, *Truth and Power*, 28.

66. Morgenthau, "Human Rights and Foreign Policy," in *Moral Dimensions of Ameri-can Foreign Policy*, ed. Kenneth Thompson (New Brunswick, N.J.: Transaction Books, 1984), 344; Gilbert, *Democratic Individuality*, chap. 2. Morgenthau described the empiri-cal—sociological—variability of moral standards. From this fact, his essay mistakenly infers an *epistemological* relativism—the absence of any reasonable claims about a decent life for humans.

67. Gilbert, *Democratic Individuality*, 337–38.

68. Herz, "Idealist Internationalism," 74; Morgenthau, "Human Rights," 344.

69. That complex ethical disputes are hard to resolve (level 3) does not mean that they are motivated by differences about underlying moral standards (level 1) as opposed to social theoretical and empirical disagreements (level 2). Furthermore, given that clashes of social and class interest exacerbate such empirical disagreements, complex ethical disputes might prove remarkably intractable (Gilbert, *Democratic Individuality*, chaps. 1, 13).

70. As a 1993 episode of *Nightline* underlined, White House publicity generates the lead stories—the right-hand column on the first page—in the *New York Times* and the

Washington Post, as well as leading columns, spread throughout urban newspapers by the Associated Press and the United Press.

71. "Truth and Power," in *Truth and Power*, 22–23.

72. McNamara, *In Retrospect*, 322.

73. *New York Times*, April 15, 1995, 8.

74. McNamara, *In Retrospect*, 258.

75. Corruption—a political and social atmosphere characterized by abject self-serving and the inverted meaning of all moral concepts—is central to the ancient Greek critique of tyranny. Chapter 4 explores Thucydides' emblematic account of Corcyra (Euben, *Tragedy of Political Theory*, chap. 6).

76. Morgenthau, "How Totalitarianism Starts," in *Truth and Power*, 52.

77. *Denver Post*, March 23, 1995, A18.

78. *Denver Post*, April 2, 1995, A5.

79. *Denver Post*, April 8, 1995, A2; Noam Chomsky, *What Uncle Sam Really Wants* (Berkeley: Odonian Press, 1989), 46–49.

80. *Denver Post*, June 29, 1996, A2.

81. *New York Times*, March 3, 1997, A1.

82. Morgenthau, *Truth and Power*, 54, and "Epilogue," 434.

83. Morgenthau, *Truth and Power*, 434.

84. Cohen, *Marx's Theory of History*, 237–38.

85. Unsuccessful critiques of imperial wars mark American history, for instance, Lincoln's and Thoreau's of President Tyler's aggression against Mexico in 1846, William James's of the Spanish-American War. Morgenthau, again, misguidedly idealized the American past.

86. I speak as one of the leaders of the Harvard strike. Ironically, Morgenthau appeared at teach-ins in the Midwest; I and many others at Harvard did not realize how forceful his critique of the war sometimes was. Morgenthau's stereotypical fear of SDS, however, which he stigmatized—representing "youth"—for "aimlessness," was misguided (*Truth and Power*, 53, 36–37).

87. If Niebuhr had not been ill, he might have played a similar role.

88. Morgenthau wrongly derogated Senator Fulbright, whose criticisms were as courageous as Morgenthau's, and, given the latter's role as an adviser, just as near to power (*Truth and Power*, 21–22). President Johnson also instructed the FBI to investigate Fulbright's potential "Communism" (Randall Bennett Woods, *J. William Fulbright, Vietnam, and the Search for a Cold War Foreign Policy* [Cambridge: Cambridge University Press, 1998], 408–12).

89. Morgenthau, *Politics among Nations*, 5th ed., 9–10. To defend "neorealism" in the contemporary debate, Christopher Layne, "Kant or Cant?" *International Security* 17, no. 2 (1994): 11, misguidedly invokes Morgenthau as a "realist"—a supposed opponent of contingent pacifism—against democracy.

90. Morgenthau, *Politics among Nations*, 2d ed., 542–43.

91. Morgenthau, *Politics among Nations*, 1st ed., 439.

92. Morgenthau, "Prologue," in *Truth and Power*, 5. This view accords with the Marxian critique of "utopian" socialism.

93. Morgenthau stressed the prevalence of racism and the threat of nuclear war, as well as "a failed 'war' on poverty, the decay of cities, the destruction of a livable natural environment and [the denial of] public responsibility for individual health," among other causes, meriting revolution (*Truth and Power*, 4).

94. Morgenthau, *Truth and Power*, 25.

95. For instance, as a radical, the famous philosopher of science Hilary Putnam was denied raises at Harvard and subjected to a vicious whispering campaign by envious, mainly prowar figures in the American Philosophical Association.

96. Morgenthau, *Politics among Nations*, 5th ed., 10–11, *Defense of National Interest*, 987, and "Human Rights," 348. As chapter 4 shows, Morgenthau's distinction between "duty" and "personal morality" is a Hobbesian claim, one that mistakenly implies, but does not argue, that the official stance is also comparatively a common good.

97. Walzer, *Just and Unjust Wars* (1977), 101–8, and "The Politics of Rescue," *Dissent* 42, no. 1 (1995): 35–41. John Brown's statement upon being captured at Harper's Ferry illustrates this point (Thoreau, "The Last Days of John Brown," in *The Portable Thoreau*, ed. Carl Bode [New York: Penguin, 1982], 676–82). In contrast, exploring potential English intervention on the side of the South, Layne, "Kant or Cant?" 16–22, ignores a pro-abolitionist, near civil war waged by workers in England that, as chapter 3 shows, halted an elite crusade (Royden John Harrison, *Before the Socialists: Studies in Labour and Politics, 1861–1881* [London: Routledge and Kegan Paul, 1965], 64, 66, 76–77). Layne treats pre–Civil War America as, unambiguously, a democracy and omits the central moral/political issue of slavery.

98. Moore, *Social Origins*, chap. 3. Sadly, in the original "Revolution," only the British freed those slaves who would fight on their side: perhaps as many as one hundred thousand (one-quarter of all slaves). The fourth-generation slaveholder George Washington would not recruit free blacks until large numbers of ex-slaves were fighting for the British (*New York Times*, August 4, 1996, A10). Thus, despite British opportunism, their cause became, among slaves, that of emancipation—a quasi-*humanitarian intervention*, in Walzer's terms—and rendered the Revolution a much more ambiguous vehicle of human freedom than it has usually been presented. Further, in a different kind of antidemocratic feedback, imperial emancipation and the antislavery leadership of Quakers who were at most neutral in the Revolution chilled growing American abolitionism (Gary B. Nash, *Race and Revolution* [Madison: Madison House, 1990], chap. 3; Gilbert, *Emancipation and Independence*).

99. We admire Lincoln, however, for other reasons. "With malice toward none, with charity for all"—Lincoln's sense of mercy stands out against today's stigmatizing of slight differences as "demonological" signs of "the enemy" (Morgenthau, *Truth and Power*, 6).

100. Gilbert, *Democratic Individuality*, chaps. 10, 12.

101. Krasner, *Defending the National Interest*. As chapter 1 notes, however, unlike Morgenthau, Krasner misguidedly separates the international sphere—in which he deems regime structure, notably democracy, irrelevant—from domestic politics.

102. Morgenthau, *Defense of National Interest*, 5.

103. Morgenthau, "Another 'Great Debate,' " 972.

104. Niebuhr, *Theologian of Public Life*, 104, notes the coincidence between his insights and Hegel's and Marx's dialectics.

105. Marx, *The Poverty of Philosophy* (New York: International Publishers, 1963), 121, 112.

106. *Equal justice* is not a precise term. As chapter 5 emphasizes, liberal theory envisions mutual regard among persons of differing conscientious views as the central egalitarian feature of a good society. Marx's emphasis on social individuality or mine on democratic individuality are thus forms of liberalism. To check corruption of the equal basic liberties of each individual by unequal wealth, theorists now offer a variety of egalitarian economic proposals: equal resources over a lifetime (Dworkin), equal incomes (Levine, Gilbert), support for the basic capabilities of each (Sen), and the like.

107. In 1929, the Detroit Bethel Evangelical Church refused applications for membership from blacks. Niebuhr, who had previously been minister there, was appalled by this decision and doubted, self-critically, that he had been willing to engage in the controversy about racism that, on his view, being a Christian requires. Richard Fox, *Reinhold Niebuhr: A Biography* (New York: Panthcon, 1985), 118–21.

108. Niebuhr, *Moral Man*, 234–35. In contrast to Niebuhr, to distinguish his realism from Lenin's view, Morgenthau implausibly characterized any attempt to overturn an

existing balance of power as an "act of imperialism." He thus, ironically, made what for any liberal are *anticolonial* struggles "acts of imperialism." As with tyranny, Morgenthau wrongly insisted that "the term 'imperialism' has lost all concrete meaning" and strove to find an "ethically neutral, objective and definable meaning" (*Politics among Nations*, 5th ed., 45–46).

109. In a recent lecture, Waltz misguidedly extenuated neorealism's incapacity to account for the disappearance of the USSR by arguing that alternatives in the international-relations literature—often caricatured—fare even more poorly (Graduate School of International Studies, University of Denver, May 1996).

110. In contrast to Amos and Niebuhr, one might note that art, especially that of experiment and individuality, emerges out of suffering and reaches no complacent destiny.

111. Amos 5:21, 23–24, quoted in Niebuhr, *Theologian of Public Life*, 1991, 272. Niebuhr's "The Wise Men and the Mighty Men" notes: "Since the dawn of history, there have been men of wisdom and virtue who stood before the king to speak the truth. The court preachers and prophets of righteousness of every age have had something of that confidence [that they will be heard]. . . . [Their speaking] is symbolic of the contest between the conscience of society and its imperial impulses, a contest in which conscience does not frequently gain the victory" (*Reflections*, 39–40). Niebuhr's "man of power" prefigures LBJ, who beguiles "court preachers" and excoriates "prophets of righteousness" (*Reflections*, 42–43).

112. Amos 7:10–13, quoted in Niebuhr, *Theologian of Public Life*, 270.

113. While neorealists rightly distinguish international anarchy from domestic constitutional regimes, their point is a relative one, not, as they mistakenly suggest, one of "levels of analysis." Again, they substitute a methodological assertion for what would have to be, if plausible, a specific political argument.

114. *Reflections*, 11.

115. Niebuhr, *Theologian of Public Life*, 105.

116. Niebuhr, *Moral Man*, xii.

117. Niebuhr, *Reflections*, 3.

118. Morgenthau, "The Intellectual and Moral Dilemma of History," *Christianity and Crisis*, February 8, 1960, 7. The work of these leading realists was closely affiliated. On October 14, 1963, *Christianity and Crisis*, which Niebuhr edited, also published Samuel H. McGill's "The Thought of Hans J. Morgenthau."

119. Niebuhr, *Moral Man*, xv; Fox, *Reinhold Niebuhr*, 136–37. The other great Protestant theologian of mid-twentieth-century America, Paul Tillich, an exile from Nazism, had defended the dictatorship of the proletariat. As a pastor in the Ruhr, he had seen coal miners organize "Red Hundreds" to fight Weimar capitalism and armed Nazi gangs. For Tillich, religious principles always congeal to serve oppressive power—Niebuhr's Amaziah. The Protestant principle, he suggests, is the critical—in Niebuhr's terms, the prophetic—principle (Tillich, "The Protestant Era and the Proletarian Situation," in *The Protestant Era* [Chicago: University of Chicago Press, 1948]); Fox, *Reinhold Niebuhr*, 160–61, 257–59.

120. Niebuhr, *Reflections*, 32.

121. Niebuhr, *Theologian of Public Life*, 97–98.

122. Niebuhr, *Theologian of Public Life*, 105, commends a "decision between religious *humility* and sinful pride."

123. Niebuhr, *Theologian of Public Life*, 155. In "The Life and Death of Civilizations," he also suggested: "The self-deception of the academics is derived from a special kind of detachment from the inertia and brutality of impulsive life peculiar to the learned man" (*Reflections*, 11–12).

124. Niebuhr, *Theologian of Public Life*, 156.

125. Niebuhr, *Theologian of Public Life*, 106–7. Niebuhr had a subtle interest in con-

temporary socialist and Communist politics, but a weak grasp of Marx's theory. Larry Rasmussen, "Introduction: A Biographical Sketch," in Niebuhr, *Theologian of Public Life*, 35–37; Beverly Wildung Harrison, *Making the Connections: Essays in Feminist Social Ethics*, ed. Carol Robb (Boston: Beacon Press, 1985), 58–63.

126. Niebuhr, *Reflections*, 51; Gilbert, *Democratic Individuality*, chap. 5.

127. Niebuhr, *Reflections*, ix.

128. Niebuhr, *Moral Man*, xi–xii.

129. Rasmussen, "Introduction," 34.

130. Niebuhr, *Moral Man*, 176.

131. Gilbert, *Democratic Individuality*, chap. 1; Fox, *Reinhold Niebuhr*, 1985, 138. Once again, a *liberal* theory sanctions those social, economic, and political institutions that facilitate the individuality of each person, *so long as she does not harm others.*

132. Niebuhr, *Moral Man*, xxiv.

133. Fox, *Reinhold Niebuhr*, 115–16.

134. A Yale radical, editor of *The New Masses*, and—unlike Niebuhr—a mystic, Waldo Frank became a friend of Niebuhr's (Fox, *Reinhold Niebuhr*, 171–72).

135. *Moral Man*, 197–98. Niebuhr, again, invoked the term "inevitable" as a substitute for argument, rhetorically, even pridefully (Gilbert, *Democratic Individuality*, chaps. 7–8).

136. Fox, *Reinhold Niebuhr*, 157.

137. Niebuhr, *Reflections*, 118.

138. Niebuhr, *Theologian of Public Life*, 270.

139. In 1934, the board fired Joseph Matthews as executive secretary for his advocacy of proletarian violence in resisting capitalism; Niebuhr resigned (Fox, *Reinhold Niebuhr*, 118–21; Niebuhr, "Why the Christian Church Is Not Pacifist," in *Christianity and Power Politics* [New York: Charles Scribner's Sons, 1940]).

140. Gilbert, *Democratic Individuality*, chap. 1.

141. Rawls, *Political Liberalism*, lecture 4. For example, is the divine female, male, or neither; impersonal, as in Buddhism or Hinduism, or personal?—and the like.

142. Niebuhr, *Theologian of Public Life*, 279. As Marx noted, this criterion is not limited to slaveowning. Despite Niebuhr's ethical justification of rebellion, however, he, like Morgenthau, is silent about John Brown.

143. Niebuhr, *Theologian of Public Life*, 278. Niebuhr aptly entitled one essay in *Reflections on the End of an Era* "The Peril of Barbarism in the Spirit of Vengeance."

144. *Christianity and Crisis*, February 8, 1960, 2–3.

145. Niebuhr, *Theologian of Public Life*, 279; emphasis added. Though Morgenthau did not use the word *mercy*, his sense that the lives and basic interests of others are of equal value to one's own also invokes forgiveness. Further, *Politics among Nations* conjures Edmund S. Morgan's depiction of John Winthrop, the first governor of Massachusetts, who "had many . . . occasions to notice how self-righteousness extinguished charity" (4th ed. [New York: Knopf, 1967], 541).

146. Rasmussen, "Introduction," 13; Victor S. Navasky, *Naming Names* (Middlesex: Penguin, 1981), 52, 56; Fox, *Reinhold Niebuhr*, 332.

147. Griffen Fariello, *Red Scare* (New York: Norton, 1995), 233. In 1950, recalling the World War II detention of Japanese-Americans, Hubert Humphrey demanded that radicals be put in concentration camps during "national emergency" (Title 2 of the National Security Act). Arthur Schlesinger Jr. advocated informing on others to the McCarthy committee and outlawing membership in the Communist Party (Navasky, *Naming Names*, 260, 53, 52–56). Such "liberalism" is hard to distinguish from fascism.

148. John Bennett, "From Supporter of War in 1941 to Critic in 1966," *Christianity and Crisis*, February 21, 1966, 13–14. The editors also published a lengthy defense of the war by Ramsey, written "to keep them sane," as the author, with some lack of humility and, perhaps, projection, put it.

149. *Christianity and Crisis*, February 25, 1966.

150. By the height of the war, Niebuhr was an invalid; he cut back his activity in the journal and did not participate in public protest. Yet as a leading theologian and inspiration for many, his influence, in an unusual, ungrudging way, pervades *Christianity and Crisis*.

151. Morse reported Cordell Hull's memory of Roosevelt. Morse and Ernest Gruning of Alaska were initially alone among senators in opposing the War. *Christianity and Crisis*, November 2, 1964, 209.

152. *Christianity and Crisis*, November 2, 1964, 210.

153. Wayne Morse, "The US Must Withdraw," Frank N. Trager, "To Guarantee the Independence of Vietnam," and Alan Geyer, "Vietnam's Greatest Need: Political Aid," in *Christianity and Crisis*, November 2, 1964.

154. *Christianity and Crisis*, March 7, 1966; emphasis added. This theme echoes Morgenthau's insights into Christian prophecy. Oddly, Niebuhr did not sign this piece.

155. *Christianity and Crisis*, March 7, 1966, 33; emphasis added.

156. This issue, Berger rightly suggested, overrode tactical considerations: "*The crime consists of waging a war that, by its very method and routine manner, involves the killing of large numbers of helpless people*" [his emphasis] ("A Conservative Reflection on Vietnam," *Christianity and Crisis*, March 7, 1966, 33). In a 1968 article on Niebuhr's *The Irony of American History*, Henry F. May noted, "[W]e must immediately stop slaughtering civilians in Vietnam; here the young prophets have been more right than the middle-aged skeptics" (*Christianity and Crisis*, May 27, 1968, 122).

157. Denise Levertov, "Goodbye to Tolerance," in *The Freeing of the Dust* (New York: New Directions, 1975); John Bennett, "It Is Difficult to Be an American," *Christianity and Crisis*, July 25, 1966, 165–66.

158. *Christianity and Crisis*, March 7, 1966, 33.

159. I am indebted to Dan Wessner for this point.

160. Niebuhr, "The CIA: Tool or Policy-Maker," *Christianity and Crisis*, May 30, 1966, 105, speaks of it as an "invisible government." See also Leon Howell, "The CIA Debacle: Growing Up in America," *Christianity and Crisis*, March 20, 1967, 49–52.

161. Arthur J. Moore, "The Mysterious Case of the AFL-CIA," *Christianity and Crisis*, May 29, 1967, 117.

162. Niebuhr, "Politics, Patriotism, and Integrity," *Christianity and Crisis*, March 20, 1967, 45–46. Largely an elite organization, the NSA had little support on American campuses and was extraneous to the antiwar movement; its leaders took part in international "student" gatherings.

163. "Mr. Safer Reports," *Christianity and Crisis*, June 27, 1966, 140; Richard T. Baker, "The Harrison Salisbury Reports," *Christianity and Crisis*, February 6, 1967, 2–3. David Schonbrun's "Vietnam: The Case for Extrication," *Christianity and Crisis*, February 6, 1967, 4–9, also explores the problems that honest reporters faced in covering the war.

164. "Mr. Safer Reports," 141.

165. Michael Novak, "Hypocrisies Unmasked," *Christianity and Crisis*, May 12, 1969.

166. Paul Bernstein, "When a University Confronts a Crisis," reprinted from the *Stanford Observer*, *Christianity and Crisis*, August 4, 1969, 220.

167. *Christianity and Crisis* published distinguished but cautious opponents of the war and, except for Father Phillip Berrigan, ignored militant protest. Thus, it took the Harvard strike for *Christianity and Crisis* to echo the sudden press discovery of the previously unrecognized, now defamed "progressive labor militants"—actually, this group called itself the "worker-student alliance caucus"—as opposed to "gentler SDS factions who recall the humanism of the Port Huron statement." "Gentler": much of the SDS leadership became Weathermen. Perhaps gentleness, compassion, and insight, as well as harsh opposition to the war's horrors, were not so defined by "faction" as Novak surmised ("Hypocrisies Unmasked," 125).

168. The dean whose name Novak does not mention was Franklin Ford, a fine European historian; as an administrator, one might say, he forgot himself.

169. Novak, "Hypocrisies Unmasked," 126.

170. The ferocity and irrationality of administration attacks, I can attest as an activist, inspired an unyielding response.

171. Novak, "Hypocrisies Unmasked," 126.

172. Novak, "Hypocrisies Unmasked," 126–27. A sit-in against the Stanford Research Institute also triggered Paul Bernstein's article—"the truth is, we wouldn't even have been talking about the goals or the concerns until this slight removal from normal procedure [the sit-in] made us aware of the lies we were living"; similarly, the police attack on People's Park generated discussions at Berkeley and in *Christianity and Crisis* (Bernstein, "University Confronts a Crisis," 221).

173. The Soviet invasion to squelch the Dubček reforms had occurred in spring 1968. *Christianity and Crisis*, June 9, 1969, 169.

174. Mark Juergensmeyer, "The Battle of People's Park," *Christianity and Crisis*, June 9, 1969, 170–71.

175. Except for official murderousness, however, the contrast is relative; democratic movements also have eccentricities. In addition, while at Harvard the Student-Faculty Advisory Committee was ignored, Princeton administrators regularly met with students. Yale officials supported William Sloane Coffin against attack. In the latter cases, there was, comparatively, less militancy.

176. Robert McAfee Brown, "Dissent in the Great Society," *Christianity and Crisis*, May 15, 1967; emphasis in original. See also Brown, "Treating Dissent Seriously," *Christianity and Crisis*, April 18, 1966.

177. Richard F. Hamilton, *Restraining Myths: Critical Studies of U.S. Social Structure and Politics* (Beverly Hills, Calif.: Sage Publications, distributed by Halsted Press, New York, 1975).

178. Norman Morrison, a Quaker, burned himself in 1965.

179. Berrigan, *Christianity and Crisis*, May 17, 1968, 169. Citing King's "Letter from a Birmingham Jail," Berrigan would not choose such a name; the editors, however, thought that the letter merited it. Authorities sentenced Father Berrigan to six years in prison for pouring his own blood on draft records. "My brother and I have had experience with legitimate dissent for 10 years, the Melvilles nearly as long in Guatemala [thirty years before the Harbury protest described above], Tom Lewis and David Eberhardt nearly as long. We have seen legitimate dissent first ridiculed, then resisted, then absorbed." He rightly identified blind "love of property" as cause for the harsh sentences (*Christianity and Crisis*, May 17, 1968, 169–70).

In 1995, at age seventy-two, Berrigan was sentenced to ten months in federal prison for "raining hammer blows and pouring blood" on a F-15 fighter-bomber at a North Carolina base. Perhaps the judge—and the *New York Times* reviewer of Berrigan's autobiography (J. Anthony Lukas, February 9, 1997, *Book Review*, 16)—thought the jet was frail.

180. As a member of the Boston Draft Resistance Group, I discussed my own situation with others and counseled those faced with conscription.

181. Shinn, *Christianity and Crisis*, June 27, 1966. As a graduate student at Harvard, I gave up 2-S; so did many other members of the worker-student alliance caucus of SDS.

182. John C. Bennett, "The Boston Four," *Christianity and Crisis*, July 8, 1968, 149.

183. Compare Plato's *Crito*, lines 50a–54d. Arendt, "Civil Disobedience," in *Crises of the Republic* (Harmondsworth, Middlesex: Penguin, 1973), pt. 3, discusses the Supreme Court's refusal to take up the "political question" of war-motivated actions by the executive or legislative branches.

184. *Christianity and Crisis*, July 8, 1968, 149–50.

185. Driver, *Christianity and Crisis*, April 18, 1966, 78.

186. *Christianity and Crisis*, June 14, 1966, 116.

187. *Christianity and Crisis*, January 23, 1967, 314.

188. The Johnson administration responded to the sit-in movement and rebellions in American cities with the Civil Rights Act of 1964. Yet even Johnson continued to make racist and sexist attacks on black people. At Howard University in 1965, for instance, he invoked Daniel Patrick Moynihan's matriarchal family structure thesis: the idea that racism had largely vanished in American society since 1865, and, consequently, that black "lack of success" must stem from the inadequacies of single mothers in bringing up boys. The speech provoked widespread protest (William Ryan, *Blaming the Victim* [New York: Vintage, 1976]).

189. Niebuhr, *Moral Man*, 206. Once again, Niebuhr asserted too easily the "inevitable" victory of patriotism.

190. Carl E. Schorske, *German Social Democracy: 1905–1917* (New York: Harper and Row, 1972); Arno J. Mayer, "Domestic Causes of the First World War," in *The Responsibility of Power*, ed. Leonard Krieger and Fritz Stern (Garden City, N.Y.: Doubleday, 1967), "Internal Causes and Purposes of War in Europe, 1870–1956: A Research Assignment," *Journal of Modern History* 41, no. 3 (1969): 291–303, and "Internal Crises and War since 1870," in *Revolutionary Situations in Europe, 1917–22: Germany, Italy, Austria-Hungary*, ed. Charles L. Bertrand (Montreal: Centre interuniversitaire d'études européennes, 1977).

191. Compare Father Berrigan's account of the inequality of wealth (*Christianity and Crisis*, May 17, 1968, 169).

192. Niebuhr, *Christianity and Crisis*, June 3, 1966, 125–26.

193. *Christianity and Crisis*, June 3, 1966, 126. Arguably, the hierarchical structure of academia harms participants. Following Socrates, one might shun the heights: though some become aware of and transcend it, that life seems full of petty tyranny, insincerity, and grief; more obviously, for most, the desire to seek truth must offset the lonely long-distance run of monastic preparation for a steadily disappearing set of (tenured) jobs.

194. *Christianity and Crisis*, September 15, 1969, 225. Similarly, Bennett's editorial "End the War Now!" refers to "the emptiness of the cause for which we and they [the Thieu government] have been fighting"; he sees the war as a "tragedy," but no longer a "mistake" (*Christianity and Crisis*, 262–63).

195. *Christianity and Crisis*, March 17, 1969, 49. The National Liberation Front engaged in mass revolutionary violence; in contrast, the CIA's ostensibly nonterrorist Operation Phoenix assassinated roughly twenty thousand village leaders.

196. Harding was a friend of as well as political adviser to Martin Luther King; he spent the summer of 1965 studying the history of Vietnam and drafted King's Riverside speech against the war. For a striking tribute to the forgotten radical King who called for a "poor people's movement" to unite the oppressed of all races and fought against the Vietnam War, see Vincent Harding, *Martin Luther King: The Inconvenient Hero* (Maryknoll, Mass.: Orbis, 1996).

197. Vincent Harding, "Vietnam: History, Judgment, and Redemption; Repentance Is Called For," *Christianity and Crisis*, October 18, 1965, 216–17.

198. As Morgenthau put it, "Political realism refuses to identify the moral aspirations of a particular nation with the moral laws that govern the universe. . . . All nations are tempted—and few have been able to resist the temptation for long—to clothe their own particular aspirations and actions in the moral purposes of the universe" (*Politics among Nations*, 5th ed., 11).

199. John David McGuire, "Martin Luther King and Vietnam," *Christianity and Crisis*, May 1, 1967, 89–90; Nicholas D. Picque, "The President and the Congress," *Christianity and Crisis*, March 21, 1966.

200. Vincent Harding, "The Irony of Vietnam," *Christianity and Crisis*, July 25, 1966, 178–79.

201. Harding, *The Inconvenient Hero*, 135

202. *Christianity and Crisis*, March 17, 1969, 50.

203. *Christianity and Crisis*, March 17, 1969, 51.

204. At a 1941 celebration of his teacher, Samuel Press, at Union Theological Seminary, Niebuhr had remarked that "all theology begins with Amos" (Rasmussen, "Introduction," 269).

205. Rasmussen, "Introduction," 269.

206. Stanley Hoffmann, *Gulliver's Troubles* (New York: McGraw-Hill, 1968), 136, 139–40, and *Janus and Minerva*, 70–71.

207. David Mayers, *George Kennan and the Dilemmas of US Foreign Policy* (Oxford: Oxford University Press, 1988), 277; Woods, *J. William Fulbright*.

208. At an American Political Science Association panel, "Realism: For and Against," September 1992, with Krasner, Doyle, and myself, John Mearsheimer stressed that realists initially affirm the integrity of states *to avoid genocide*. Thus, he insisted, Jews in the 1930s, Moslems in Bosnia today, require a state for their defense. His argument reveals that (neo)realism is not only a scientific view but an *intensely* moral one.

209. Kennan, *American Diplomacy*, 61–62.

210. Kennan, *American Diplomacy*, 173.

211. Kennan, *American Diplomacy*, 175, echoes the theme of Walzer's *Just and Unjust Wars*. But Walzer made explicit the justice of defeating aggression and protecting civilians. In moral terms, his view elucidates and *justifies* realist statism. Thus, the remarkable, otherwise sophisticated realist John Herz made a false, official realist inference from the need of a state to preserve its citizens from aggression to a vague, potentially infinite aggrandizement of power: "Groups or individuals living in such a constellation [of international powers] must be, and usually are, concerned about their security from being attacked, subjected, dominated or annihilated by other groups and individuals. Striving to attain security from such attack, they are driven to acquire more and more power in order to escape the impact of their power of others. This, in turn, renders the others more insecure and compels them to prepare for the worst" (Herz, "Idealist Internationalism," 73). But the realist argument only works when such power is restricted, given *plausible* international competition, to defense against aggression. Ignored by today's pseudoscientific neorealists, Walzer's account, ironically, provides the *best version* of contemporary realism (Paul Kan, "Realism and Its Discontents," *Journal of Public and International Affairs* 5 [spring 1994]: 7–16). For a critique of even this realism, see Gilbert, *Democratic Individuality*, 63–68.

212. Kennan, *American Diplomacy*, 171–72; Walzer, *Just and Unjust Wars* (1977), 21–22; Stanley Hoffmann, *Duties beyond Borders* (New York: Syracuse University Press, 1981), 73–74.

213. Following World War II, the aircraft industry nearly went bankrupt; its leadership helped to foment the "scare" (Kofsky, *Truman and War Scare*, chap. 2).

214. Clifford cited in Charles L. Mee Jr., *The Marshall Plan: The Launching of the Pax Americana* (New York: Simon and Schuster, 1984), 244.

215. George Kennan, *Memoirs, 1925–1950* (Boston: Little, Brown, 1967), 400–404, emphasis added; Horrigan, "Resisting the Drawdown," 46–50.

216. Kennan, foreword to Sharp, *Making Europe Unconquerable*, xiii; emphasis added.

217. Gilbert, *Democratic Individuality*, 423–26.

218. Sharp, *Making Europe Unconquerable*, 44, 123–25. In 1939, Kennan, then second secretary in the embassy in Berlin, resisted congressional pressure to protest German persecution of Jews (Robert Schulzinger, *The Making of the Diplomatic Mind* [Middletown, Conn.: Wesleyan University Press, 1975], 134). As Sharp points out (105–7), conquered regimes like Denmark, which, nonetheless, resisted genocide through civil disobedience— the king wore a yellow star—saved lives; in contrast, under the influence of eugenic ideology in the foreign service, the U.S. as well as Britain, chose to firebomb a quarter of a million

German civilians in Dresden rather than target the tracks that took victims to the camps. Walzer, *Just and Unjust Wars* (1977), 253, rightly suggests that one has merely to point to Nazism to illustrate evil. Defining novel *crimes against humanity*, anti-Nazism was a paradigm case, if one exists, of a just cause.

219. Kennan, foreword to Sharp, *Making Europe Unconquerable*, xvi.

220. Kennan, foreword to Sharp, *Making Europe Unconquerable*, xvii.

221. Morgenthau, "Shadow and Substance," 1965, 19; Krasner, *Defending the National Interest*, 321–25. Senator Fulbright rightly stigmatized American Cold War policies as driven by "paranoid" or "obsessive anti-communism" and the—often murderous—repudiation of any nonviolent reform as "communist." It is ironic how lively and pointed Fulbright's arguments are compared to most academic ones—another sign of Morgenthau's *academic*-political complex (Fulbright, *The Price of Empire*, 159–61; Gilbert, "What Then?" pt. 2). Emphasis on the causal role of antiradical ideology in Vietnam and elsewhere, as chapter 1 underlines, characterizes both sophisticated realism and democratic internationalism.

222. Gilbert, "What Then?" pt. 2; and Kennan, *American Diplomacy*, 164, stress the ideological tendency to see diverse opponents as creations of a single "evil" center.

223. As vice president, Humphrey fiercely supported the Vietnam War; after Iran, Carter launched a "rapid deployment" strategy in the Middle East and initiated murderous, "counterinsurgency" policies in Salvador (later extended by Reagan). Both could maintain that their opponents had wrongly accused them of lacking "anticommunist fervor." As Carter's subsequent conduct reveals, however, he is a more complicated and decent man than most American politicians.

224. I should emphasize Kennan's probity: he comes to the moral point without "realist" antimoralism. Under the influence of an official realist view, however, he sometimes mistakenly considered the state's interest a "natural" one and neglected the crime of aggression ("Morality and Foreign Policy," *Foreign Affairs* 63, no. 2 [1985]: 206).

225. Kennan, *American Diplomacy*, 165–66.

226. He clashed with his son, Christopher, over the latter's involvement (Mayers, *George Kennan*, 285, 62, chap. 12).

227. These stands undercut his previous, fiercely antidemocratic convictions (Mayers, *George Kennan*, chap. 4).

228. Gilbert, *Democratic Individuality*, chaps. 9–11, and "What Then?" advance additional arguments that the American regime is oligarchic, not democratic.

229. Gilbert, *Democratic Individuality*, chap. 13.

230. Taylor, "Neutrality in Political Science"; Gilbert, *Democratic Individuality*, chaps. 1–2.

231. Though the idea of value-freedom can provide an ideological screen for crimes, empiricist social science need not justify such policies; hunger for power requires many intellectual errors.

232. Scientific realism holds that many entities unobservable by the naked eye but discovered by modern science, such as electrons, exist (Gilbert, *Democratic Individuality*, chap. 3).

233. Kant's neglected but pointed realism about prevailing international politics and diplomacy—under monarchies—also deserves emphasis. Immanuel Kant, *Political Writings*, trans. H. B. Nisbet (Cambridge: Cambridge University Press, 1992), 93, 94, 119–21.

Chapter Three

1. Gilbert, *Marx's Politics*, chaps. 1–2, 10.

2. Gilbert, *Democratic Individuality*, chap. 11.

3. Marx's historical and political writings feature insights into internationalism; economic determinist interpretations of his theory, implausibly, ignore them.

4. Richard N. Hunt, *The Political Ideas of Marx and Engels: Marxism and Totalitarian Democracy, 1848–50* (Pittsburgh: University of Pittsburgh Press, 1974); Avineri, *Social and Political Thought*; Cohen, *Marx's Theory of History*.

5. Alan Gilbert, "Salvaging Marx from Avineri," *Political Theory* 4, no. 1 (1976): 9–34, and *Marx's Politics*, chaps. 1–2, 9.

6. Karl Marx and Friedrich Engels, *Selected Works* (Moscow: Foreign Languages Publishing House, 1962), 1:64–65, 22, 46.

7. Oscar J. Hammen, *The Red '48ers: Karl Marx and Friedrich Engels* (New York: Scribner's, 1969), 250; Karl Marx, *Letters to Dr. Kugelmann* (New York: International Publishers, 1934), 126.

8. Gilbert, *Democratic Individuality*, chaps. 5–8. Marx's theory seeks to implement a political liberalism which he interprets as a promise for each person of fair conditions to pursue individuality, largely made idle by capitalism. As Marx and Engels aver in the *Manifesto*, for example, a communist society is one in which "the free development of each is the condition for the free development of all." Karl Marx and Friedrich Engels, *Selected Works in One Volume* (New York: International Publishers, 1974), 52.

9. Amartya Sen, *Inequality Reexamined* (Cambridge: Harvard University Press, 1992).

10. Joan Edelman Spero, *The Politics of International Economic Relations* (New York: St. Martin's, 1977), 142; Hollis Chenery et al., *Redistribution with Growth* (Oxford: Oxford University Press, 1974), xiv–xv. With the rapid spread of AIDS in less developed countries and the high cost of even palliative treatment, the differential in life expectancy may worsen.

11. For discussions of possible Rawlsian views on justice in international distribution, see Gilbert, "Equality and Social Theory"; Peter Singer, "Famine, Affluence, and Morality," *Philosophy and Public Affairs* 1, no. 3 (1972); Charles R. Beitz, "Justice and International Relations," *Philosophy and Public Affairs* 4, no. 4 (1975).

12. Marx and Engels, *Selected Works*, 1:46.

13. Marx and Engels, *Selected Works*, 1:37–38.

14. Marx and Engels, *Selected Works*, 2:11.

15. Marx and Engels, *Selected Works*, 1:386, 384.

16. Marx and Engels, *Selected Works*, 1:64; emphasis added.

17. On the role of auxiliary statements in Marx's theory, see Gilbert, *Marx's Politics*, chaps. 1, 9–10.

18. Even radicals had just begun to recognize the oppression of women (Gilbert, *Marx's Politics*, chap. 1).

19. Marx and Engels, *Works in One Volume*, 204–5; Marx, *Politische Schriften*, ed. Hans-Joachin Lieber, 2 vols. (Stuttgart: Cotta Verlag, 1960), 1:398.

20. Karl Marx and Friedrich Engels, *Werke*, 39 vols. (Berlin: Dietz Verlag. 1959–), 5:154.

21. The Russian Revolution of 1917 and the German Democratic Revolution of 1918 also resulted from world war, but after defeat.

22. See also Mayer, "Domestic Causes," "Internal Causes," and "Internal Crises and War."

23. Hegel, *Elements of a Philosophy of Right*, par. 248, addition, and 269. Yet Hegel also commended the antidemocratic feedback of belligerence: "[N]ations troubled by civil dissension gain internal peace as a result of wars with external enemies" (par. 324, addition, and 362). Hegel's favorable attitude toward monarchies that sustain themselves through aggression, however, contradicts his core notion that a modern state is a complex "architectonic" for the realization of the *freedom of individuals*; it differs decisively from democratic internationalism.

24. Marx and Engels, *Werke*, 5:202.

25. Gilbert, *Democratic Individuality*, chap. 1.

26. Frederick Douglass, "Did John Brown Fail?" address delivered in Harpers Ferry,

West Virginia, May 30, 1881, reprinted in *The Frederick Douglass Papers*, ed. John W. Blassingame and John R. McKivigan, vol. 5 (New Haven: Yale University Press, 1979); Thoreau, "Last Days." America, however, celebrates Lincoln, who issued the Emancipation Proclamation only in 1863. That view, curiously, concurs with Marx, who came to praise Lincoln's statesmanship, though he, also, initially admired "Old John Brown." Niebuhr's account of Lincoln's mercy, however, does the latter justice. Crystallizing U.S. racism, Hollywood imaged "Brown" as a Christian madman in *The Santa Fe Trail* (gaunt Raymond Massey portrayed John Brown as well as a fanatic Jacobin in the contemporaneous *Scarlet Pimpernel*)

27. Marx, *On America and the Civil War*, ed. Saul K. Padover (New York: McGraw-Hill, 1972), 153, 247, 271, 272.

28. Marx, *America and Civil War*, 92–93, 237.

29. Marx, *Capital*, 1:301.

30. Allen W. Trelease, *White Terror: The Ku Klux Klan Conspiracy and Southern Reconstruction* (New York: Harper and Row, 1971).

31. Marx, *America and Civil War*, 112–13, 157–60, 266, 152–56, 161–63.

32. Harrison, *Making the Connections*, 66, 64, 76–77.

33. Marx, *On the First International*, ed. Saul K. Padover (New York: McGraw-Hill, 1973), 35–36; Marx and Engels, *Selected Works*, 1:384.

34. Thus, in June 1996 in Colorado, Teamster truckers supported thirteen thousand Safeway and King Sooper's strikers.

35. Marx and Engels, *Selected Works*. 1:426.

36. At that time, workers fought to organize unions *at all*, not to be ruthlessly exploited through child labor, and the like. *If* there are serious defenses of capitalism as furthering individuality—or, more likely, harming it less than alternative economic and social arrangements—they do not apply to that system's initial epochs. Gilbert, *Friendless Aliens, Friendless Citizens*, chap. 5.

37. Marx, *On the First International*, 41.

38. The information is courtesy of Patrick Ryle, chief shop steward, International Longshoreman's and Warehouseman's Union, and Dwight Threepersons, member, International Boilermakers' Union.

39. Once again, Hegel prefigures such a view.

40. Marx, *On Colonialism and Modernization*, ed. Shlomo Avineri (Garden City, N.Y.: Doubleday, 1968), 132–34. Avineri's introduction omits Marx's internationalism. The collection concentrates on the so-called Third World and also, unfortunately, leaves out Marx's theoretically charged writings on Ireland. Finally, Avineri ignores Hegel's view that in the battle over colonialism, liberation has moved to the side of the colonized.

41. Marx, *On Colonialism and Modernization*, 137.

42. Marx's theory of racism would stress this insight (Gilbert, *Democratic Individuality*, chap. 11; Reich, *Racial Inequality*).

43. Marx, *On Colonialism and Modernization*, 206, 443–44, 49–50. Relying entirely on the opinion of the English consul, Marx, however, produced an uncharacteristically negative evaluation of the Taiping rebellion for *Die Presse*.

44. The United States once rebelled against English colonialism; yet Hollywood omits English brutality and depicts crazed worshippers of Kali, say in *Gunga Din* or *Indiana Jones and the Temple of Doom*. This erasure of American revolutionary history began with the 1798 Irish revolt in which President Adams supported England; American political scientists' hostility to revolution—including forgetfulness about the Revolution of 1776—in the 1950s and early 1960s, unfortunately, echoes it. Marx opposed English colonialism in India more thoroughly than even Gandhi did until after 1921 (Mahatma Gandhi, *Essential Writings of Mahatma Gandhi*, ed. Raghavan Iyer [Oxford: Oxford University Press, 1994]).

45. Marx, *On Colonialism and Modernization*, 224–234. Though properly noting

Marx's original skepticism about the revolt's military chances, Avineri's introduction ignores all of Marx's arguments in defense of the rebellion (see 25–26, 29). Chomsky and Hermann, *Political Economy of Rights*, study the contemporary American elite's similar response to "terror."

46. Marx, *On Colonialism and Modernization*, 238, 19, rightly emphasizes this point.

47. Marx, *On Colonialism and Modernization*, 463.

48. Ironically, for the *Manifesto*, twentieth-century radicalism, for instance in China, Vietnam, and Algeria, would move mainly from the outlying, weaker countries toward "the center"; in resistance to fascism, however, European Communist movements also grew strong.

49. Marx and Engels, *Selected Correspondence*, trans. I. Lasker, ed. S. Ryazanskaya [Moscow: Foreign Languages Publishing House, 1965] 230, 232, 235, 236–237; Marx and Engels, *Works in One Volume*, 290, 161–62.

50. Marx and Engels, *Selected Correspondence*, 236–37.

51. Gilbert, *Democratic Individuality*, chap. 11, contrasts Marx's theory with Weber's on the possibility of multiracial movements, such as the Farmers' Alliance, early Populism, and the Tenants' Union in the South.

52. Outside of revolutionary situations, as the introduction and Lenin's *State and Revolution* stress, capitalism hinders workers even from forming grass-roots organizations for self-defense.

53. *Selected Correspondence*, 236–237; see also Marx and Engels, *Works in One Volume*, 162. From the inception of the IWA, Marx advocated Irish independence and supported arrested Fenian leaders on many occasions. An advocate of *mass* revolutionary violence, however, he opposed conspiratorial and terrorist tendencies within the Fenian movement (Marx and Engels, *Selected Correspondence*, 513, 514; Marx, *America and Civil War*, 128, 143, 440–41, 145, 149, 281, 285).

54. Gilbert, *Democratic Individuality*, chap. 5, and "An Ambiguity"; Engels, *Anti-Dühring* (New York: International Publishers, 1939).

55. Gilbert, *Marx's Politics*, chaps. 1, 9–10.

56. While one might frame an economic determinist argument against capitalism internationally, activists and scholars who hold such views rarely do.

57. Marx and Engels, *Selected Works*, 1:377–381, and *Works in One Volume*, 163.

58. Gilbert, *Democratic Individuality*, 344. As section 1 shows, radicalism or democratic internationalism is a *sophisticated realism*, with an explicit democratic and moral foundation. In a debate on my critique of neorealism, however, David Goldfischer emphasized this central, realist objection: wouldn't you, he said, if a revolution, radical as you like, came to power and you could advise it, be tempted to expand? As the introduction underlines, democratic internationalism shares—and even sharpens—realist misgivings: a restriction to example.

59. Marx, *On Colonialism and Modernization*, 471, 473; V. I. Lenin, *Collected Works*, 45 vols. (Moscow: Foreign Languages Publishing House, 1974–), 22:143–56, 320–60. The same tension, however, exists, on Lenin's argument, between support for an independence movement, led by a national bourgeoisie, and socialism, as the tension between democratic and proletarian revolution that had troubled Marx in 1848 (Gilbert, *Marx's Politics*, chap. 13, and "Changing the World: The Revolutionary Strategies of Marx and Lenin," in *American Political Science Association Proceedings* [Ann Arbor: University of Michigan Press, 1976], 20).

60. Lüthy, *France against Herself*, 205.

61. For differing criteria on the injustice of wars of this kind, see Rawls, *A Theory of Justice*, sec. 58; Beitz, "Justice and International Relations," 386–87.

62. Three million people emigrated. Antonio de Figueiredo, *Portugal: Fifty Years of Dictatorship* (New York: Holmes and Meier, 1976), 180; Rona M. Fields, *The Portuguese*

Revolution and the Armed Forces Movement (New York: Praeger, 1976), 73; Hamilton, *Restraining Myths*, 184 and chap. 5.

63. Figueiredo, *Portugal*, 251.

64. Gilbert, *Marx's Politics*, chaps. 1, 9.

65. Fields, *Portuguese Revolution*, chap. 3.

66. For instance, the Algerian revolution produced relatively little redistribution. Arnold Fraleigh, "The Algerian Revolution as a Case Study in International Law," in *The International Law of Civil War*, ed. Richard Falk (Baltimore: Johns Hopkins University Press, 1971), 243; Arslan Humbaraci, *Algeria: A Revolution That Failed* (London: Pall Mall Press, 1966), 271.

67. John Westergaard and Henrietta Resler, *Class in a Capitalist Society: A Study of Contemporary Britain* (New York: Basic Books, 1975), 356–57; Stephen Castles and Godula Kosack, *Immigrant Workers and Class Structure in Western Europe* (Oxford: Oxford University Press, 1973), 418; Richard R. Fagen, "The Realities of U.S.-Mexican Relations," *Foreign Affairs* 55, no. 4 (1977): 689.

68. Suzanne Paine, *Exporting Workers* (Cambridge: Cambridge University Press, 1974) is an important exception.

69. J. L. Brierly, *The Law of Nations* (Oxford: Oxford University Press, 1963), 279; Rawls, *A Theory of Justice*, sec. 58.

70. Rawls, "The Law of Peoples."

71. Spero, *Politics of Economic Relations*, chap. 6; Castles and Kosack, *Immigrant Workers*, 427–29.

72. Edmund Faltermeyer, "Who Will Do the Dirty Work Tomorrow?" *Fortune*, January 1974; Manuel Castells, "Immigrant Workers and Class Struggles in Advanced Capitalism: The West European Experience," *Politics and Society* 5, no. 1 (1975): 56–57, 64; Castles and Kosack, *Immigrant Workers*, 341.

73. Alexander Saxton, *The Indispensable Enemy* (Berkeley and Los Angeles: University of California Press, 1971), 271–82.

74. Ireland, "Facing the True Fortress Europe," and *Policy Challenge*; Rawls, "The Law of Peoples."

75. Psychologically, fascism hurts not only the middle classes but, arguably, the elite. Socrates' arguments against doing injustice in the *Republic* underline this point.

76. Castells, "Immigrant Workers," 61–65; Castles and Kosack, *Immigrant Workers*, 152–75, chap. 11.

77. Michael Reich, "The Economics of Racism," in *The Capitalist System*, ed. Richard C. Edwards, Michael Reich, and Thomas Weisskopf (Englewood Cliffs, N.J.: Prentice-Hall, 1972), 313–25, and *Racial Inequality*; Gilbert, *Democratic Individuality*, chaps. 10–11.

78. Gilbert, *Democratic Individuality*, chaps. 10–11. Rawls's first principle highlights the priority of the equal basic liberties of each person. In sociology and psychology from the late 1960s until today, the spectrum of theories on the condition of blacks, ranging from a putative genetic explanation of IQ tests (Jensen, Herrnstein, Murray) to "lower-class culture" (Banfield, Mischel) is superficial, subject to contemporary pointed but, in a parody of "science," unanswered challenge, and blames the victim (Richard Miller, *Fact and Method* [Princeton: Princeton University Press, 1987], 173–75; Reich, *Racial Inequality*; Block and Dworkin, "I.Q., Heritability, and Inequality"; Alan Garfinkel, *Forms of Explanation* [New Haven: Yale University Press, 1981]). Mainstream antiracist views focus largely on "prejudice" among ordinary whites and are also, as sociological theories, superficial (Allport, the Kerner Commission Report). Sadly, the greater the importance of the issue for democracy, the more rudimentary the analysis provided by empiricist-inspired scholarship (aside from Reich) and the more unwilling to engage radical theories.

79. Marx, *Capital*, 1:171, 236; Emmanuel, *Unequal Exchange*, chap. 3, especially 116–20.

80. Gandhi's campaign for Indian cloth—spun on the *chakra*—emphasizes this point (*Essential Writings*, 369–71, 108).

81. Hari P. Sharma, "The Green Revolution in India: Prelude to a Red One?" In *Imperialism and Revolution in South Asia*, ed. Sharma and Kathleen Gough (New York: Monthly Review Press, 1973); James Scott, *The Moral Economy of the Peasant: Rebellion and Subsistence in Southeast Asia* (New Haven: Yale University Press, 1976), chap. 6.

82. For the latter's role in Battalion 316's reign of terror in Honduras, see the *Baltimore Sun*, June 12, 14, 15, and 18, 1996; Chomsky and Hermann, *Political Economy of Rights*.

83. Michael T. Klare, "Pointing Fingers," *New York Times*, August 10, 1977, and *War without End*, chaps. 9–10.

84. So does the current struggle in Peru between these elites and the Tupac Amaru and Sendero Luminoso movements. David Cusack, *Revolution and Counterrevolution in Chile* (Denver: Graduate School of International Studies Monograph Series, 1977), 114. Cusack, an American citizen and Ph.D. from the Graduate School of International Studies of the University of Denver, was an expert on covert activity against Allende. He was murdered in Bolivia, probably at the instigation of the CIA, shortly after he completed this monograph.

85. As chapters 1 and 2 emphasize, for example, the nurturing of a large, surveillance apparatus, the restriction of political alternatives, and the draft all harm ordinary citizens.

86. In contrast, reactionaries could mix a primary appeal to restoration of a nation's previous power with others, for instance, the necessity to curtail rival economic and, perhaps, political imperialisms, like that of Japan. Justifications for such policies to some sectors of the population could even include formulations much like an international-difference principle: we must intervene in country X because its elite refused to use foreign aid to help the least advantaged. Robert Amdur, "Rawls' Theory of Justice: Domestic and International Perspectives," *World Politics* 29, no. 3 (1977), argues that one might even, from the standpoint of Rawls's original position, attempt to justify such intervention ideally. Given the actual network of relationships between rich nations and poor ones, however, those interventions would not achieve the desired result.

Chapter Four

1. Krasner, "Realism, Imperialism, and Democracy."

2. Robert Gilpin, "The Theory of Hegemonic War," in *The Origin and Prevention of Major Wars*, ed. Robert I. Rotberg and Theodore Rabb (Cambridge: Cambridge University Press, 1989), 18, 23.

3. Russett, *Grasping the Democratic Peace*, chap. 3, is, however, an exception.

4. Among political theorists, Farrar, *Origins of Democratic Thinking*, rightly sees Thucydides as an unusual, though critical, defender of Athenian democracy.

5. De Romilly, *Rise and Fall*, 58.

6. As a concomitant of imperialism, Athenian democracy grew corrupt. So too, one might think, has the American regime. One reason for the adoption of "value-free," merely "operational" definitions of democracy—"democracy exists when the two parties compete"; "no common good among citizens exists internationally or domestically"—is that they apologize for an imperial state—"the military-industrial" and "academic-political complexes"—as well as antidemocratic interventions.

7. A. H. M. Jones, *Athenian Democracy* (Baltimore: Johns Hopkins University Press, 1986), 41–42, 47. Perhaps the Truman-McCarthy period in the United States also deserves emphasis, for these persecutions drove Moses Finley from Rutgers, later to become

professor at Cambridge and be knighted in England, opponent of slavery and a great classi-cal scholar (Ellen Schrecker, *No Ivory Tower* [New York: Oxford University Press, 1986], 165, 167, 171–79, 182, 185, 196, 267, 272–76, 282, 293, 338; David Caute, *The Great Fear: The Anti-Communist Purge under Truman and Eisenhower* [New York: Simon and Schuster, 1978]).

8. Krasner, "Realism, Imperialism, and Democracy."

9. Russett, *Grasping the Democratic Peace*, 121, however, characterizes Arbenz and Allende as Marxists, Ortega as a Leninist, and accepts the State Department's rationaliza-tions for overturning democracies as preventing totalitarianism. He seems a victim of this ideology.

10. Chomsky and Hermann, *Political Economy of Rights*.

11. From Buddhists to peasant radicals, the Vietnamese anti-imperialist movement at-tended to a common good against forty years of French, Japanese, French, and American aggression and had democratic allegiances that Hermocrates' speeches foreshadow. After gaining power, however, the Vietnamese leadership has not tolerated even parliamentary opposition.

12. De Romilly, *Rise and Fall*, 58; Gilbert, *Democratic Individuality*, chap. 1.

13. Hobbes, *Behemoth; or, The Long Parliament* (Chicago: University of Chicago Press, 1990), 28, 30. Roberts, *Athens on Trial*, traces the unrelieved hostility to Athenian democ-racy of most subsequent interpretation.

14. W. Robert Connor, *Thucydides* (Princeton: Princeton University Press, 1984), intro-duction. Even so sophisticated a commentator as David Grene envisions Thucydides as a perhaps sorrowful realist.

15. Thucydides, *Peloponnesian War*, trans. Hobbes, 126; Peter Pouncey, *The Necessi-ties of War: A Study of Thucydides' Pessimism* (New York: Columbia University Press, 1980), appendix, "Human Nature in Hobbes."

16. Farrar, *Origins of Democratic Thinking*, 166. Donald Kagan suggests that Pericles warned only, in this speech, against a single decision. He fails to realize that that decision—to wage war on a second front, against a powerful, unknown enemy—was fateful for Athens. He exaggeratedly compares Pericles and Cleon (*The Archidamian War* [Ithaca, N.Y.: Cornell University Press, 1974], 350–62). See W. Robert Connor *Greek Political Leadership* (Princeton: Princeton University Press, 1969), 120–21, 134. Following Thu-cydides, Jacqueline de Romilly, *Thucydides and Athenian Imperialism*, trans. Philip Thody (Oxford: Basil Blackwell, 1963), 332, pits Cleon, as spirited, but pandering *thumos*, against Pericles, as *nous*.

17. Thucydides, *Peloponnesian War*, trans. Hobbes, 126.

18. Thucydides, *Peloponnesian War*, trans. Hobbes, 238–41.

19. Thucydides, *Peloponnesian War*, trans. Hobbes, 240; emphasis added.

20. Thucydides, *Peloponnesian War*, trans. Hobbes, 83–84.

21. Thucydides, *Peloponnesian War*, trans. Hobbes, 397–98. In the democratic revolu-tion of 1848, Engels would hail Danton's insight that the "defensive is the death of every armed rising," his call for "de l'audace, de l'audace et encore de l'audace" (Friedrich Engels, *Revolution and Counterrevolution in Germany*, trans. Eleanor Marx Aveling [New York: Capricorn Books, 1971], 90); Gilbert, *Marx's Politics*, 194–95). Marx and Engels looked to a political boldness whose importance they learned, with vividness, from Thucydides.

22. Thucydides, *Peloponnesian War*, trans. Hobbes, 40–41, 126.

23. In book 7 of the *Politics*, Aristotle defends a limited empire—perhaps one more restricted than Pericles envisioned—for "the good of the governed." Hobbes's view, which shockingly identifies "commonwealth by acquisition" (conquest) with "commonwealth by institution" (consent)—tracing both, allegedly, to fear—fails to make even this distinction (*Leviathan*, 132–33, 151–55). Standard later justifications for colonialism—such as Mill's—make appeals like Aristotle's, with the modified aim that the colonized will, ulti-

mately, be free. As chapter 3 shows, Marx's "justification" of colonialism in India looks to the revolt of the oppressed.

We have now learned that self-determination is a great good. Aside from very unusual circumstances, claims about external rule for the "good of the governed" are false (But, as a limited counterexample, one might invoke some aspects of postfascist, U.S. domination in Germany and Japan [Gilbert, *Democratic Individuality*, chap. 2]).

24. Thucydides, *Peloponnesian War*, trans. Hobbes, 110.

25. Thucydides, *Peloponnesian War*, trans. Hobbes, 110. A. Geoffrey Woodhead, *Thucydides on the Nature of Power* (Cambridge: Harvard University Press, 1970. 31–32, ignores Pericles' oration and Thucydides' admiration for the transient nobility of Athenian democracy.

26. As no church, and hence no church doctrine, existed in Greece, Hobbes's translation is a seventeenth-century anachronism.

Contrasting otherworldly Christianity to natural "Greek and Roman" civil religion, Hobbes, *Behemoth*, 63–64, condemns sedition: "[C]onsider what harm may proceed from a liberty that men have, upon every Sunday and oftener, to harangue all the people of a nation at one time, whilst the state is ignorant of what they say; . . . there is no such thing permitted in all the world out of Christendom nor therefore any civil wars about religion." To a modern reader, Hobbes's promonarchical antipathy to Christianity sounds strange. In the context of the Puritan Revolution, it makes sense. As first causes of Puritan revolt, Hobbes, *Behemoth*, 2–3, emphasizes three kinds of negative Christian influence, notably Presbyterian and even—doubtfully—"Papist." Holmes's introduction to *Behemoth* (xxviii–xxxiv), a scathing but one-sided Hobbesian indictment of Christianity, fails to note the liberating, and, ultimately, liberal, force of the Reformation, its defense of the consciences, the souls of individuals.

27. Thucydides, *Peloponnesian War*, trans. Hobbes, 110–11. In Plato's *Laws*, bk. 1, 642c–d, Megillus, the Spartan legislator, also celebrates Athenian character: "They alone are good by their own nature without compulsion, by a divine dispensation; they are truly, and not artificially, good."

28. Thucydides, *Peloponnesian War*, trans. Hobbes, 124–25.

29. Thucydides, *Peloponnesian War*, trans. Hobbes, 111. Criticizing the embroidery of Hobbes's translation, Grene aptly suggests: " 'We are lovers of beauty but with cheapness; we are lovers of culture [or wisdom], but without softness [philokaloumen te gar met' euteleias kai philosophoumen aneu malakias].' "

30. Thucydides, *Peloponnesian War*, trans. Hobbes, 111; Aristotle, *Nicomachean Ethics*, bk. 4.

31. Russell Meiggs, *The Athenian Empire* (Cambridge: Harvard University Press, 1972).

32. *Gorgias*, lines 515e–516c.

33. In Plutarch's life of "Nicias," by contrast, Socrates, that "divine guide," warns against invading Syracuse. Perhaps because Plato writes, as an Athenian, after the defeat of Athens, this fact, as it were, no longer warrants recall.

34. Socrates' appraisal of philosophical pride is far more woven into the tapestry of his dialogues than Niebuhr's essayistic critique.

35. *Apology*, lines 24b–28a.

36. In this case, the Athenians had the zeal of Khomeini, pronouncing a death sentence on Salman Rushdie.

37. His poverty suggests a kinship with contemporary ascetic Buddhist and later Christian traditions.

38. Hobbes, *Leviathan*, 116–17; Michael L. Oakeshott, *Rationalism in Politics and Other Essays*, ed. Timothy Fuller (Indianapolis: Liberty Press, 1995), 289–93.

39. Thucydides, *Peloponnesian War*, trans. Hobbes, 109. Christian Meier, *The Greek Discovery of Politics*, trans. David McLintock (Oxford: Clarendon Press, 1990), 140,

comments: "Both statements are true, and the difference between them is not that one relates to theory, the other to reality. Rather, the leadership of Pericles accorded with the will of the people, who enjoyed substantial participation in public affairs. It rested partly on the fact that it was he who had created, improved and facilitated this participation. His leadership was deliberately limited to the broad lines of policy." On Meier's view, Pericles resembles Rousseau's legislator more than a proficient statesman.

40. Meier, *Greek Discovery of Politics*, 150.

41. De Romilly, *Thucydides and Athenian Imperialism*, 153–55.

42. Aristotle, *Nicomachean Ethics*, 1156b10–1157a28; Gilbert, *Democratic Individuality*, chap. 7.

43. The argument about accepting death has a mystical as well as rational character. Socrates follows his daimon, hearing the "droning murmur of the pipes of the Corybants" that drowns out Crito's narrower considerations (*Crito*, line 54d). In contrast to the reputation for injustice that would be brought on Athens by a particular death sentence enacted "by men," the idea of democratic laws inspires Socrates

44. Plato, *Republic*, bk. 9.

45. Laurie Bagby, "The Uses and Abuses of Thucydides in International Relations," *International Organization* 48, no. 1 (1994), rightly criticizes neorealism for misinterpreting Thucydides. But she treats character in isolation from regime and, surprisingly, overlooks the central issue of democracy.

46. Niceratus attended the dialogue; the Thirty later murdered him. His father, Nicias, whom Plato also mentions, as we will see, commanded the fateful invasion of Syracuse.

47. Gilpin, "Theory of Hegemonic War," 18. Gilpin has read more Thucydides than many contemporaries. As chapter 1 reveals, he is also a leading, sophisticated scholar of international politics. A democratic study of Thucydides will, however, I suggest, help transform the theory of international politics.

48. Despising *political* equality, Hobbes traces only a supposed natural equality, one of pride, power-seeking, indignity, and brutality, which forces even the "diffident" to violence. He puts that equality at the center of the *natural* order to sanction a *social* escape: an absolute monarch.

49. Thucydides, *Peloponnesian War*, trans. Hobbes, 572; Woodhead, *Thucydides on Power*, 31; Jones, *Athenian Democracy*, 41.

50. G. E. M. de Sainte-Croix, *The Origins of the Peloponnesian War* (Ithaca: Cornell University Press, 1972), 27–28, criticizes Hobbes's misreading. For instance, Hobbes ignores a distinctive feature of ancient democracy—the absence of factions—that differentiated it, positively, from oligarchy (Meier, *Greek Discovery of Politics*, 151).

51. Hobbes, *Behemoth*, 158, 23, 17.

52. Hobbes, *Leviathan*, 163.

53. Combined with Hobbes's eloquence, the simplicity of the core argument—and its unique, materialist emphases—make *Leviathan* one of the great, innovative works of political philosophy in English.

54. Rousseau, *Oeuvres complètes*, 1:355–56; Locke, *Two Treatises of Government*, 237.

55. Like Thucydides, Gandhi distinguishes the abject law of force as characteristic of "brutes" from what he, quite differently, views as fully human. Gandhi, "Non-Violence—The Greatest Force," *Hindu*, November 8, 1926, in *Essential Writings*, 240–41.

56. Aristotle, *Politics*, bk. 7; Gilbert, *Democratic Individuality*, chap. 2.

57. De Romilly, *Rise and Fall*, chap. 4, underlines the fragility of Greek regimes and the later Roman solution: the elevation of citizens of conquered territories to the status of Roman. Hobbes, *Behemoth*, 33–34, also praises Rome's policy. Farrar, *Origins of Democratic Thinking*, 165–67; Montesquieu, *Oeuvres complètes*, ed. Andre Masson (Paris: Edi-

tions Gallimard, 1950–55), 2:150, however, reveals the aptness of Thucydides' concerns for the destiny of the Roman republic.

58. De Romilly, *Thucydides and Athenian Imperialism*, 110; David Grene, *Man in His Pride* (Chicago: University of Chicago Press, 1950), 139–40.

59. In, sadly, attempting a "Thucydidean" apology for Vietnam, Woodhead, *Thucydides on Power*, 26, invokes Cleon. He reveals the failure of older scholars to *read* the *History* as a literary work.

60. Sainte-Croix, *Origins of Peloponnesian War*, 13 fails to place Diodotus's views in the context of those of Pericles and mistakenly concludes that the former expresses Thucydides' "realism."

61. Ignoring the grandeur of Periclean democracy, Grene, *Man in His Pride*, 8–14, highlights only three "realist" events—the Athenian ambassador's brazen speech in book 1, Corcyra, and the chilling Athenian formulations at Melos.

62. Thucydides, *Peloponnesian War*, trans. Hobbes, 204–5.

63. Thucydides, *Peloponnesian War*, trans. Hobbes, 571–72.

64. Rousseau's *Second Discourse* also differentiates each individual's natural "amour de soi" from destructive "amour-prôpre."

65. De Romilly, *Thucydides and Athenian Imperialism*, 332–33.

66. Hobbes, *Leviathan*, 141; see also 162: "[A]s amongst masterless men, there is perpetual war of every man against his neighbor."

67. For instance, affirming reasonable pluralism in modern societies based on insight into the bloody history of religious wars, Rawls makes toleration of differing comprehensive—conscientious—views a central value (*Political Liberalism*, chap. 1).

68. Hobbes, *Leviathan*, 139. Hobbes defines the "value or worth of a man as his price, that is, so much as would be given for the use of his power" (73). C. B. MacPherson, *The Political Theory of Possessive Individualism: Hobbes to Locke* (Oxford: Oxford University Press, 1962), misinterprets this point as a practical, *bourgeois* foreshadowing of the Marxian theoretical definition of abstract, socially necessary labor-time and labor-*power*. But in contrast to *Capital*, Hobbes insists on differing *subjective* valuings by each individual—rooted in envy—and their role in hierarchical English status structure: "[V]alue . . . is not absolute, but a thing dependent on the need and judgement of another." He strikingly elaborates: "[M]en have no pleasure, but on the contrary a great deal of grief, in keeping company, where there is no power able to over-awe them all. For every man looketh that his companion should value him, at the same rate he sets upon himself; and upon all signs of contempt, or undervaluing, naturally endeavors, as far as he dares (which amongst them that have no common power to keep them in quiet, is far enough to make them destroy each other) to extort a greater value from his contemners, by dommage; and from others, by example" (99). In emphasizing competitive valuations leading to war, Hobbes's account prefigures Montesquieu's of monarchical honor and Rousseau's of "amour-prôpre" as distinctive evils of civil society.

69. Hobbes, *Leviathan*, 141.

70. Hobbes, *Leviathan*, 142.

71. Holmes, introduction to Hobbes, *Behemoth*, xvii–xx, vividly portrays Hobbes's judgments. He reads them, however, in the light of Hobbes's famous, though, as Holmes notes in passing, secondary and contradictory "value-subjectivism" (xix n. 24).

72. John Wilson, "The Customary Meanings of Words Were Changed—or Were They? A Note on Thucydides 3.82.4," *Classical Quarterly* 32, no. 1 (1982): 20, criticizes translations of this passage, suggesting that not the meanings of terms but their "evaluative significance" has shifted: "[P]oliticians and other wicked men are greatly assisted not by enforced and arbitrary changes in the meanings of words (something no one would be persuaded by), but by more or less plausible redescriptions of phenomena within the existing vocabulary."

But this interpretation draws, misguidedly, on an ostensible fact/value distinction. Instead, one might suggest that in today's philosophical terms, due to public corruption, the terms come to have (moral) referents *opposed* to the original meanings.

73. Hobbes, *Leviathan*, 80.

74. Hobbes, *Leviathan*, 48–49. In *Behemoth* Hobbes also remarks: "For several men praise several customs, and that which is virtue with one, is blamed by others; and contrarily, what one calls vice, another calls virtue, as their present affections lead them" (45).

75. Locke, *Two Treatises of Government*, 125; emphasis added.

76. Hobbes, *Leviathan*, 20.

77. Holmes, introduction to *Behemoth*, xlvii.

78. In a Harvard lecture in 1967, Michael Walzer stressed this point.

79. Hobbes, *Leviathan*, 165, 164.

80. Hobbes, *Leviathan*, 110.

81. Hobbes, *Leviathan*, chap. 13.

82. Hobbes, *Leviathan*, 580. As *Behemoth* also indicates, Hobbes's insights into the psychologies of interconnected participants in civil society are diverse and, as Holmes emphasizes, funny (Hobbes, *Behemoth*, 155, 22, 176, 32, 89, 159; Holmes, introduction, xxxviii–xxxix).

83. For a political history of this positivist doctrine, see Robert N. Proctor, *Value-Free Science? Purity and Power in Modern Knowledge* (Cambridge: Harvard University Press, 1991).

84. Euben, *Tragedy of Political Theory*, chap. 6.

85. Thrasymachus and Callicles echo the depraved Athenian delegates at Melos.

Though de Romilly briefly gestures at the similarity of Plato and Thucydides (*Thucydides and Athenian Imperialism*, 365–68), her first exploration of this comparison (299 and n. 1) misses Thucydides' critique of "realism."

86. Following Thucydides, Hobbes refers to Cleon as "the most violent sycophant in those times" (Thucydides, *Peloponnesian War*, trans. Hobbes, 574). Clifford Orwin, *The Humanity of Thucydides* (Princeton: Princeton University Press, 1994), chap. 7, esp. 151–56, 200–206, suggests that an appeal to justice underlies Diodotus's account of what is advantageous. Like Hermocrates, he contends, Diodotus insists that the Mytilenians, as a matter of humanity, resist Athenian domination. Orwin even celebrates Diodotus rather than Pericles. Nonetheless, the need for Diodotus to shift words represents a decline.

87. Thucydides, *Peloponnesian War*, trans. Hobbes, 124, 175. See also the Corinthians' indictment in book 1 (39), and Euphemus's affirmation of tyranny at Camarina in book 6 (426) (Connor, *Thucydides*, 234). The change in how Athens conducted—and saw—the empire, from the Delian League to combat Persia, to imperial oppression, is a central theme of the *History*.

88. John A. Vazquez, ed., *Classics of International Relations*, 2d ed. (Englewood Cliffs, N.J.: Prentice-Hall, 1990), 16–20, and *The Power of Power Politics: A Critique* (New Brunswick, N.J.: Rutgers University Press, 1983) is a critic of realism. That he, too, accepts the "realist" misreading of Thucydides testifies to its paradigm-like quality.

89. Thucydides, *Peloponnesian War*, trans. Hobbes, 365; Woodhead, *Thucydides on Power*, 9, 11; Pouncey, *The Necessities of War*, 143. Omitting Syracuse, Pouncey stresses only the divisiveness and self-seeking of later Athenian and Spartan leaders. Thucydides, however, praises the Athenian democrats at Samos (Connor, *Thucydides*, 220–21).

90. Herodotus, *History of the Greek and Persian War*, bk. 8, traces omens, as well as strategies, for the surprising victory of Athenian—and Greek—freedom (Connor, *Thucydides*, 154–56).

91. Numbers, evidently, are important. The history of twentieth-century guerilla war, however, once again, reveals the fallacy of claims about mere numbers or superior technol-

ogy. For, contrary to abstract, neorealist characterizations of "power," Vietnamese people's war defeated the U.S. government. Vo Nguyen Giap, *People's Army, People's War*, foreword by Roger Hilsman (New York: Praeger, 1967).

92. Thucydides, *Peloponnesian War*, trans. Hobbes, 263.

93. Thucydides, *Peloponnesian War*, trans. Hobbes, 368.

94. Hunter R. Rawlings, *The Structure of Thucydides' History* (Princeton: Princeton University Press, 1981), suggests that Thucydides intended to make this decisive dialogue the exact center, the turning point, of the *History*.

95. Historical circumstances, however, vary; modern class structures are larger and more diverse. Thus, internal strife led to French upper-class support for Vichy treachery. Yet democratic resistance united a broad variety of groups—echoing Thucydides—and allied with external forces, notably the Soviet Union, but also England and the United States. Broad opposition to French colonialism and Vietnamese landlords in Indochina played a similar, creative role.

96. Hence, Aristotle contrasted "politeia"—a regime organized around a common good—to democracy—the decadent rule of the freeborn as a *particular* interest.

97. So are the Athenians at Lacedaemon who, invoking the justice and courage of their role against Persia, first defend the empire (Thucydides, *Peloponnesian War*, trans. Hobbes, 42–46).

98. In the concluding book 8, no individuals give public speeches; except for the complex case of Alcibiades, actions by named leaders are self-interested.

99. Thucydides, *Peloponnesian War*, trans. Hobbes, 111.

100. Walzer, *Just and Unjust Wars* (1977), chap. 1.

101. Thucydides, *Peloponnesian War*, trans. Hobbes, 375; 126–27.

102. Inverting the Corinthian's praise of Athenians in book 1, Thucydides startlingly depicts a false public appearance that belies incomprehension and fear (*Peloponnesian War*, trans. Hobbes, 40).

103. Thucydides, *Peloponnesian War*, trans. Hobbes, 491, 367–68; Connor, *Thucydides*, 201–9.

104. De Romilly, *Thucydides and Athenian Imperialism*, 328 n. 1. Farrar, *Origins of Democratic Thinking*, 174, misguidedly stresses Nicias's distant echo of Pericles, which, however, highlights the former's desperation, his inadequacy as a leader.

105. Nicias failed to win the debate in the assembly (Thucydides, *Peloponnesian War*, trans. Hobbes, 380–84). Ironically, factional strife, which led to the flight of Alcibiades, left Nicias to command an invasion against which he had warned.

106. Thucydides, *Peloponnesian War*, trans. Hobbes, 498–99, 1–2. Connor, *Thucydides*, 249; 207–9, emphasizes Thucydides' alliterative interweaving of language. The text indelibly registers the theme of decline. That many classicists should, nonetheless, have disregarded it highlights the effect of a misguided paradigm—official realism—on research (Roberts, *Athens on Trial*).

107. De Romilly, *Thucydides and Athenian Imperialism*, 327–29.

108. Hegel, *Phenomenology of Spirit*, trans. A. V. Miller (Oxford: Oxford University Press, 1977), 267–89. Euben, *Tragedy of Political Theory*, highlights the kinship of tragedy and theory. Meier, *Greek Discovery of Politics*, explores Aeschylus's *Eumenides* and "the rise of the political."

109. Farrar, *Origins of Democratic Thinking*, 266–74, too easily depicts these theorists as antidemocratic. As Athenian slaveholding and imperialism reveal, democracies are capable of criminal practices. Chapter 5 stresses the upholding of each citizen's basic rights—a precondition—and the nonaggressive character that are central to a decent, democratic regime.

110. Aristotle, *Politics*, 1333b29–33. See Plato, *Republic*, book 9, on the nurturing and psychology of tyrants.

111. In the Myth of Er, the first chooser of a fate is a man entranced by a previous happy life—one enacted through habit, not virtue—and a subsequent, thousand-year, heavenly journey. He hastily picks the life of a tyrant and only later observes that he must consume his children. He then wails and blames the Fates rather than himself. As the text indicates, however, these three weavers of destiny reflect rather than determine human psycholog(ies). Gandhi adopted Plato's stand on the importance of suffering injustice and refusal to become one who could commit it.

112. Connor, *Greek Political Leadership*, 89, 93.

113. Layne, "Kant or Cant?"; Russett, *Grasping the Democratic Peace*, chap. 3 (with William Antholis).

114. Even after American defeat, Kissinger, *Diplomacy* (New York: Simon and Schuster, 1994), 625–27 bafflingly fails to credit the Vietnamese with resisting Japanese aggression as well as French colonialism. To acknowledge this fact, however, would bring out the alliance of Vietnamese nationalism, led by Communists, with American democracy against Japanese fascism; it would reveal the subsequent affiliation of the Vietnamese movement with the *substantive* tradition of American anticolonialism against the U.S. government-supported French effort to reconquer them. It would thus undercut the propagandistic force—projecting himself onto others—of Kissinger's characterizations of Vietnamese Communist motives as "cold-blooded" (645). As Morgenthau comments in "What Ails America?" "This [the U.S. war in Vietnam] is a counterrevolutionary war waged by a revolutionary nation. It is Metternich's war waged by the nation of Jefferson and Lincoln" (33). By omission, Kissinger strives to sanction Nixon's—and his own—genocidal policies. See also William Bundy, *A Tangled Web: The Making of Foreign Policy in the Nixon Presidency* (New York: Hill and Wang, 1998), cited in Tony Judt, "Counsels on Foreign Relations," review of William Bundy, *A Tangled Web: The Making of Foreign Policy*," *New York Review of Books*, May 24, 1998, 8, on centralization and deception of the State Department and Congress during the Nixon-Kissinger period: "[W]hen one of his staffers objected to the plan to invade Cambodia in April 1970, Kissinger responded revealingly: "Your views represent the cowardice of the Eastern Establishment."

115. Russett, *Grasping the Democratic Peace*, chap. 3 (with William Antholis), however, explores Athenian aggression against Syracuse and other interdemocratic wars. Yet he worries that the Athenians did not "perceive" Syracuse as a democracy (59). Further, he omits the decisive issue of slavery as a limit on Athenian democracy. Finally, though he praises Thucydides in his own idiom—"Thucydides' great book actually is a penetrating analysis of the role and weaknesses of democratic politics in formulating security policy" (62)—he neglects most of what is interesting both about Thucydides' argument and the conflict.

116. Gilbert, *Democratic Individuality*, chap. 1.

117. Illustrating the decadence of neorealism, Layne, "Kant or Cant?" omits the evil of slavery and treats even the pre–Civil War United States as simply a democracy. Similarly, except for noting that a democratic public may tolerate covert interventions short of "overt" war, Russett ignores the impact of oligarchy.

118. More exactly, in Vietnam, the U.S. government intervened to prevent the *election* of regimes.

119. Ignored during the Cold War, however, Michael Doyle, "Kant, Liberal Legacies, and Foreign Affairs," *Philosophy and Public Affairs* 12, nos. 3–4 (1983): 205–35, 323–53, courageously defended the theme of interdemocratic peacefulness and was aware of American cruelty in the less developed countries. See also Russett, *Grasping the Democratic Peace*, 121–24.

120. Josh Cohen, "Do Values Explain Facts? The Case of Slavery," in *American Political Science Association Proceedings* (Ann Arbor: University of Michigan Press, 1986).

121. Rawls, "The Law of Peoples." One might also include post–World War II Japan.

122. Connor, *Thucydides*, 3–4.

123. Connor, *Thucydides*, 7. For a shallow, "Thucydidean" apology for American policy in Vietnam, see Woodhead, *Thucydides on Power*, 22–26.

124. Hobbes's biographical essay begins by questioning, of which Thucydides ancient fragments may speak. De Romilly, *Thucydides and Athenian Imperialism*, general introduction, reversed an earlier trend of studying the *History* itself as fragments.

125. Connor, *Thucydides*, 5, 231–32; de Romilly, *Thucydides and Athenian Imperialism*, 374.

126. Connor, *Thucydides*, 4–5, 231–32. "Now, in a different intellectual climate, with a less naive conception of history, the work appears in a different light, and a new participant enters into the discussion of how the text works and what it means. As the reader comes into view, a new set of relationships and new interpretive possibilities demand consideration. . . . 'Not the book needs to be a complete thing, but the reader of the book does,' as Whitman says. At the same time, the 'objectivity' of the text can be understood in a new way, not as a goal or standard, but as a means by which the reader is drawn into the work, and made 'to do something for himself'" (232).

127. Connor, *Thucydides*, 4.

128. Other scholars do, however. For instance, Downs and Rocke's modeling of presidential incentives to intervene—"gambling for resurrection"—in "Conflict, Agency, and Gambling for Resurrection," shares central concerns with this study.

129. In World War II, American democracy intervened justly to combat Japanese fascism.

Chapter Five

1. Rawls, "The Law of Peoples."

2. Downs and Rocke, "Conflict, Agency, and Gambling for Resurrection"; Russett, *Controlling the Sword*, chap. 1. As Clinton's 1996 bombing of Iraq illustrates, a president may also—though insecurely—be leading in the polls. Nonetheless, the circumscription of this effort—"not one American life was lost"—betrays democratic influence. Jack S. Levy, "Domestic Politics and War," *Journal of Interdisciplinary History* 18, no. 4 (1988), contrasts the frequent examples provided by historians of the uses of foreign intervention to check domestic reform or regenerate the leader's popularity with broad, quantitative, international politics studies so badly "operationalized" that they sometimes fail to capture it.

3. Rich, "For Ethel Rosenberg."

4. Gilbert, *Democratic Individuality*, 318 n. 20.

5. As obvious illustrations, Charles Wilson and Robert McNamara, CEOs respectively of GM and Ford, became secretaries of defense under Presidents Eisenhower and Kennedy.

6. Richard Cloward and Frances Fox Piven, *Poor People's Movements* (New York: Pantheon, 1977).

7. *Denver Post*, August 15, 1996, A26.

8. *Denver Post*, August, 13, 1996, A1; Adam Clymer, "Class Warfare: The Rich Win by Default," *New York Times*, August 11, 1996, E1.

9. "Special Tax Breaks Enrich Savings of Many in the Ranks of Management," *New York Times*, October 13, 1996, A1, A14. In 1995, K-Mart froze the benefits that 280,000 workers could receive from its government-guaranteed pension plan. In hiring a chief executive in the same year, however, it "handed out millions of dollars in deferred stock grants and left its supplemental pension benefits for executives intact." Lewis Hubble, an Illinois warehouseman, noted: "There are a lot of hard feelings" ("Special Tax Breaks," A15).

10. In a new era, one wonders about the political fate of so unstable a capitalism.

11. Clymer, "Class Warfare," E1.

12. Dennis Thompson and Amy Gutmann, *Democracy and Disagreement* (Cambridge: Harvard University Press, 1996), 84–91.

13. Rawls, *A Theory of Justice*, 1993b, chap. 1; Thompson and Gutmann, *Democracy and Disagreement*, 79–91, invoke "mutual respect."

14. Gilbert, *Democratic Individuality*, chaps. 5, 13.

15. Thompson and Gutmann's *Democracy and Disagreement* identifies features of deliberative democracy that encourage provisional resolutions to specific moral disputes. It thus represents a step forward compared to Habermas's and Benhabib's conception, which stresses a noncoercive, "ideal speech situation," and Cass R. Sunstein's exploration of freedom of speech in *Democracy and the Problem of Free Speech* (New York: Free Press, 1993). Such deliberative conceptions make Dewey's notion of a "democratic public" more specific.

16. As I have suggested for the case of slavery, once apparently intractable controversies—sometimes only after historical epochs—become clear (Gilbert, *Democratic Individuality*, chap. 1).

17. Rawls's conception applies Rousseau's notion of a *general will* as a will to equality—a will to uphold the basic freedom and independence of each citizen—to a modern, plural regime. Thus, respect for the rights of each is a *precondition* for democratic deliberation. For the rule of mere democratic procedure could result, through successive majorities—"wills of all"—in favor of disenfranchising different groups, in a steadily shrinking electorate.

18. Thompson and Gutmann, *Democracy and Disagreement*, 352.

19. Thompson and Gutmann, *Democracy and Disagreement*, 218.

20. Ronald Dworkin, *Life's Dominion* (New York: Knopf, 1993), chap. 5, especially 119–20. The latter conception is Justice Antonin Scalia's.

21. See Gilbert, *Democratic Individuality*, chap. 1, and *Emancipation and Independence*, chap. 5.

22. Thompson and Gutmann, *Democracy and Disagreement*, 349, 347.

23. Many current deliberative conceptions share this flaw. For example, Sunstein, *Democracy and Free Speech*, overemphasizes Madison's commitment to deliberation at the expense of his primary fealty to commerce (Gilbert, *Emancipation and Independence*, chap. 5).

24. Thompson and Gutmann, *Democracy and Disagreement*, 161–62.

25. At a 1996 APSA panel on Thompson and Gutmann's book, Alan Wertheimer suggested that isolating social theoretical and empirical elements in moral disputes would decrease their intensity. But such controversies (level 2) rest on underlying moral standards (level 1) and feed in, unavoidably, to complex ethical clashes (level 3). Pointing out the empirical character of many disputes—as opposed to offering significant evidence and argument about them—will not diminish their force. In contrast, isolating the moral standard(s) underlying the position of each participant, might, to some extent—as we will see in Dworkin's approach to abortion—increase mutual regard and civility.

26. Thompson and Gutmann, *Democracy and Disagreement*, 74; emphasis added.

27. Among those who respect the sacredness of life, Dworkin distinguishes the good of life, biologically speaking, from the human contribution to a (good) life. Differences involving that distinction create space for a woman's "right to procreative autonomy" (Dworkin, *Life's Dominion*, chap. 3).

28. Gilbert, *Democratic Individuality*, chaps. 1, 13.

29. Thompson and Gutmann, *Democracy and Disagreement*, 75–76.

30. Dworkin, *Life's Dominion*, 151. Postmodernists stress what are allegedly "essentially contestable values." The adverb "essentially," however, obscures what are often complex conflicts based on common, underlying moral standards. Nonetheless, with its weighing of different, underlying ethical elements, this special case is a paradigm of *core* moral contestability.

31. Gilbert, *Democratic Individuality*, chap. 1.

32. Such conventional decisions often, however, stem far more from deliberation than what economists term "preferences." But they still contrast with an adherence to individual rights which underlies all decent conventions.

33. Benjamin R. Barber, *Strong Democracy* (Berkeley and Los Angeles: University of California Press, 1984), 23; Gilbert, *Democratic Individuality*, 76–78.

34. Abortion causes great psychological harm to the mother. Patriarchs are not more reflective on this issue than those most affected. The decision is best left with the latter.

35. Barber, *Strong Democracy*, rightly stresses the importance of public service to democratic citizenship.

36. I would extend the right of conscientious refusal to soldiers who sign up for military service before a particular war is contemplated. In case of attack against the territory of one's country, however, the laws might make the exercise of that right, comparatively, difficult.

37. For example, after World War II, Togliatti—the Italian Communist leader—proposed such a view.

38. Barbara Deming, "On Revolution and Equilibrium," in *Revolution and Equilibrium* (New York: Grossman, 1971).

39. Thoreau rightly admired John Brown and had no paradigm of mass, nonviolent resistance.

40. Adrienne Rich's "The Hermit's Scream," in *What Is Found There: Notebooks on Poetry and Politics* (New York: Norton, 1993), 57–61, explores Deming's thoughtful, passionate activism, her eventual linking of the struggle for peace to combating violence against women.

41. Kateb, "Nuclear Weapons."

42. As Bishop Helder Camara put it, "When I gave charity to the poor, people called me a saint. But when I asked *why* men and women are poor, people called me a communist" (Harding, *Martin Luther King*, 126).

43. Levertov, "With the Seabrook Natural Guard in Washington," in *Light Up the Cave* (New York: New Directions, 1981); Gilbert, "Must Politics Constrain Democracy?"

44. Sharp, *Making Europe Unconquerable*, chap. 2.

45. Deming, "On Revolution and Equilibrium," 10–13.

46. Before he emigrated to the United States, Lorenz was a Nazi. His (socio)biology has reactionary undertones.

47. Yet Gandhi warned against strikes and tended to control too tightly the movement he led. Under pressure from LBJ, King tried to talk the Mississippi Freedom Democratic Party out of demanding full recognition—replacing the racist Mississippi delegation—at the Democratic Convention of 1964; he also, reluctantly, supported use of the national guard against the Watts rebellion. Both traveled a complex, ambiguous course toward important clarities.

48. Cited in Harding, *Martin Luther King*, 125.

49. Cited in Harding, *Martin Luther King*, 127.

50. Gandhi, *Essential Writings*, 253.

51. Thompson and Gutmann, *Democracy and Disagreement*, 12.

52. Cloward and Piven, *Poor People's Movements*; Miller, *Analyzing Marx*.

53. Rawls, *A Theory of Justice*, secs. 53–59; Gilbert, *Democratic Individuality*, chap. 1; Arendt, "Civil Disobedience." In an oligarchy with parliamentary forms, Thoreau's stand against slavery is a paradigm of such resistance.

54. Similarly, in 1996, as a result of civil disobedience against the training of Central and Latin American officers at Fort Benning, Georgia, the courts sentenced Father Roy Bourgeois and others to six months in prison.

55. Rawls, *A Theory of Justice*, secs. 53–59. Since no existing democracy is "nearly just," civil disobedience must often have broader goals.

56. Gandhi, *Essential Writings*, 310.

57. Thompson and Gutmann, *Democracy and Disagreement*, 84–91. In response to a question at the 1996 APSA panel on their book, Thompson concurred with the importance of civil disobedience in instigating deliberation. Written at an ebb of democratic protest (with the exception of "pro-life" activity), however, *Democracy and Difference* does not discuss such disobedience.

58. Rawls, *A Theory of Justice*, secs. 53–59; Dworkin, *Taking Rights Seriously*, 200–201, chap. 8.

59. Editorials about Abdul-Rauf in the Denver newspapers were unusually vicious. Bob Kravitz's columns in the *Rocky Mountain News*, however, stood out for decency and intelligence.

60. "Star-Spangled Coercion," *New York Times*, March 15, 1996, A14.

61. Though a mob burned down a Jehovah's Witness's Hall near Kennebunkport, Maine, where George Bush lived as a teenager, he did not come to value this central principle of liberalism. His rival, Dukakis, belatedly responded to Bush's flagwaving with "pride in being a Democrat." Alone among mainstream American politicians, Jesse Jackson pointedly affirmed freedom of conscience.

62. Barber, *Strong Democracy*, 281–89.

63. One night outside Penrose Library at the University at Denver, an Afghani-American woman was assaulted by a thug with a baseball bat. Her crime: wearing a sweater with an inscription in Arabic. Democratic patriotism differs from chauvinism.

64. In contrast, we will see, the continued boycott against Iraq—despite U.N./U.S. victory and secret from the American people until the recent crisis—has killed more civilians, especially children, than even the Gulf War. In justifying referenda, Barber, *Strong Democracy*, suggests careful phrasing of policy alternatives.

65. William Blum, *Killing Hope: U.S. Military and CIA Interventions since World War II* (Monroe, Maine: Common Courage Press, 1995). "Most of the coup leaders and members of the junta that directly conducted the systematic repression, and the political figures such as Honorat and Bazin that tried to legitimize a post-Aristide order, had long since established extensive relations with Washington through the CIA and the DIA, the NED [National Endowment for Democracy], and other programs. And Haitian army officers, in fact, continued to receive training *after the coup* in U.S. military facilities. 'Virtually all observers agree that all it would take is one phone call from Washington to send the army leadership packing,' noted the *New York Times* a year after the coup" (William L. Robinson, *Promoting Polyarchy* [Cambridge: Cambridge University Press, 1996], 302–3).

66. FRAPH leaders "were not only on the CIA payroll but were also integrated into post-coup and later post-invasion, U.S. political and economic aid programs" (Robinson, *Promoting Polyarchy*, 304).

67. The document accusing Constant surfaced during a lawsuit by Alerte Balance, a Haitian human-rights activist who "was severely wounded by four hatchet wielding FRAPH thugs three years ago." "CIA Report Said Haitian Agent May Have Helped Plan Killing," *New York Times*, October 13, 1996, A7.

68. Surprisingly, Russett, *Grasping the Democratic Peace*, 121, misses this point. Despite rightly supporting only rare and multilateral interventions in the post–Cold War era (136) and acknowledging "deep (American) culpability" for overturning parliamentary regimes (124), he does not call for an end to covert action.

69. Walzer, *Just and Unjust Wars* (1977), chap. 6. Nothing, however, prevents the U.S. government from issuing statements of support for democratic or radical causes.

70. Robert White, "An Address to the National Women's Democratic Club," October 29, 1996, ⟨http://www.us.net/cip/speech.htm⟩. The Guatemalan legislator who told this story, "a man with an outstanding democratic and centrist record," doubted the admirable aims of Ambassador Marilyn McAfee, hinting that "there were officials in the embassy who contravened and subverted her policy." Subsequent revelations about the murders of Mi-

chael Devine and Efrain Bamaca Velazquez, for instance, have, as White notes, underlined the truth of the legislator's suspicions.

71. The usual "rationale" stresses short-term, state expediency at the sacrifice of democracy.

72. To clarify, this argument calls for abolition of *current* secret apparatuses. It does not rule out subsequent, congressionally controlled activity aimed only at securing knowledge about potential aggression. Further, an ideal democratic regime might engage in *rare* covert actions in cases requiring—hopefully, multilateral—humanitarian intervention.

73. In 1966, at the Universite del Valle in Cali, Columbia, attempting to combat U.S. covert action, students locked John McCamant, recently appointed at the Graduate School of International Studies, out of his classroom for one day, along with other Americans. McCamant has since become an important critic of the CIA and American intervention ("Intervention in Guatemala"). Since 1986, GSIS has maintained a policy of active non-cooperation with the CIA, barring funding, "reporting" on others, and recruitment.

74. "Hearings of the Senate Select Intelligence Committee on the Use of Journalists and Members of the Clergy in Intelligence Gathering," July 17, 1996, ⟨http://www.us.net/cip/senintl.htm⟩. In 1995–96, fifty-five American journalists were killed in the less developed countries (Mortimer Zuckerman, editor of *US News and World Report*). Other witnesses included Don Argue, president of the National Association of Evangelicals and Claudette Laverdiere, president of the Maryknoll Sisters. Resisting the 1992 Boren bill, which saw the Department of Defense as an appropriate funder of language study, the South Asia Council of the Association for Asian Studies and the Joint Committee on South Asia of the Social Science Research Council and the American Council of Learned Societies insisted: "Past experience, in South Asia as elsewhere, amply demonstrates the perils of connections, however tenuous, between scholars and U.S. national security agencies. Possible consequences range from mistrust and lack of cooperation to physical violence against U.S. scholars and their colleagues abroad." This statement is representative of those of Latin American, Middle Eastern, and African studies associations.

75. Their criterion of publicity also permits exemptions to defend the privacy of individuals.

76. Oscar Danilo Blandon, the Nicaraguan ring's "Los Angeles point man" was not, the *Times* insisted, "the Johnny Appleseed of crack in California [as the *Mercury-News* had suggested]. . . . There is no evidence that *any significant drug profits* from the Nicaraguan rights were pumped back to the contras—less than $50,000 went to the rebel cause, according to a contra supporter and a business partner who sold drugs with Blandon" ("Paper Disputes CIA-Crack Report," *Denver Post*, October 20, 1996, A2; see also *New York Times*, October 25, 1996).

77. White, "Address," October 29, 1996. In addition, on November 21, 1996, a Miami grand jury indicted General Robert Guillen, head of a Venezuelan "antidrug" unit, for shipping 22 million tons of cocaine into the United States from 1987 to 1991:

> The officials say the shipments approved by the CIA were allowed to be sent under the premise that letting the drugs reach their destination in the U.S. without hindrance would enable the CIA to gather intelligence about drug-smuggling networks and strengthen the position of a key confidential informant within Columbia's drug cartels. The Drug Enforcement Administration opposed the plan. . . "We always told US authorities. . . . Nothing could be done without their authorization," says General Guillen. "I defend the CIA. I believe they did an excellent job."
>
> No CIA officials were indicted. The grand jury reported: "We have found no intent to profit, no nothing, just stupidity."

"Former CIA Ally Faces Charges of Smuggling Drugs into U.S.," *Wall Street Journal*, November 22, 1996. The CIA-sponsored drug smuggling of Panamanian general Manuel Noriega is another noteworthy example.

78. As Deutsch rightly noted, "[N]o one previously has come forward and told you there was going to be an investigation." But to make the investigation credible, he cited only the inspector-general's apprehension of credit card fraud, as if he did not understand what the uproar was about. "CIA Chief Takes Heat: Cocaine Link Focus of L.A. Town-Hall Meeting," *Denver Post*, December 16, 1996, 2A.

79. McCamant, "Intervention in Guatemala"; Alfred W. McCoy, *The Politics of Heroin: CIA Complicity in the Global Drug Trade* (New York: Lawrence Hill, 1991).Those whom American newspapers routinely referred to as the "CIA-supported Meo tribesmen" in Laos grew and supplied heroin, at the cost of addiction of roughly half the adult Meo population. The CIA then flew it on Air America to Vietnam to be pushed among U.S. soldiers. Frontline troops were disproportionately black. Many soldiers returned to become homeless.

The UN Convention defines genocide as the deliberate destruction of a people, "in whole or in part." Thus, for foreign-policy purposes, the CIA already has a long record of promoting genocide against blacks as well as harming other Americans. Although Reagan and Bush initiated support for crack traffic, the Clinton administration now covers it up. As an example of "bipartisanship," Bob Dole, William Safire, Rush Limbaugh, Alphonse D'Amato, Ken Hamblin et al. raised improprieties with FBI files, Indonesian contributions and so on, but utter no whisper of a government policy that has ravaged blacks.

80. For instance, the CIA employed the Mafia in eight congressionally documented attempts to assassinate the president of Cuba.

81. Jerome Miller, *Search and Destroy: African-American Males in the Criminal Justice System* (Cambridge: Cambridge University Press, 1996), analyzes the public policy war on blacks.

82. Two medical researchers, Dorothy Hatsukama (Minnesota) and Marian Fischman (Columbia), found that "cocaine is cocaine. Regardless of whether you shoot it up or smoke it, it has the same stimulant effect." "Crack Sentences Unfair, Doctors Say," *Denver Post*, November 20, 1996, 16A.

83. Montesquieu, *De l'esprit des lois*, ed. R. Derathé, 2 vols. (Paris: Editions Gallimard, 1973), bk. 11.

84. "Cocaine Sentencing Hammers Blacks," *Denver Post*, September 13, 1996, A35. A democratic argument might also strip the FBI of police powers, at least in regard to "political" crimes. For the FBI has persecuted dissidence, often as under "foreign influence." Now acts of terrorism by individuals, like the Oklahoma City bombing, represent a danger. But the cessation of massive state *terrorism* exercised through the CIA and other covert agencies might limit many grievances that give rise to anti-American terror. Further, officials and scholars have used the term *terrorism* to stigmatize disempowered groups and shield the U.S. government. This ideological campaign against dissidents and violation of civil rights threatens American democracy. Only a carefully circumscribed capacity to check terrorism would be appropriate.

85. Cohen and Rogers, *Inequity and Intervention*.

86. *Denver Post*, October 23, 1996, A6. Those with inadequate coverage include 17 million insured adults and 13 million uninsured. As corporations lay off full-time employees and hire part-timers without benefits, the report suggests, the proportion of the uninsured will increase.

87. Addicted to tobacco contributions, Republican presidential candidate Bob Dole, mused that this substance "is only addictive for some people."

88. The largest reporting campaign contributor, Phillip Morris, gave $2,131,955 to Republicans out of a total of $2,741,659 (a ratio of 3.5 to 1). These figures include soft money to the national parties, PAC money to candidates, PAC and individual contributions to the Clinton and Dole campaigns, and individual campaign contributions to all federal candi-

dates. "Business Is Biggest Spender in Presidential Race, Study Says," *New York Times*, October 18, 1996, C20.

89. White-collar workers across the street from production plants have contracted cancer from breathing asbestos fibers. Thus, Johns Mansville moved its corporate headquarters to Denver, *away* from production sites.

90. Sunstein, *Democracy and Free Speech*, 94–95; Josh Cohen, "Freedom of Expression," *Philosophy and Public Affairs* 22, no. 3 (1993): 247–48. Many well-known law professors, including John Rawls, who has a Harvard Law School appointment as well as an appointment in Philosophy, recently issued a statement criticizing *Buckley v. Valeo* (*New York Times*, November 10, 1996, A18).

91. Rawls, *A Theory of Justice*, 204. As we will see, however, the "fair value" of liberty bars those of "greater authority and wealth" from a systemic—oligarchic—influence on the public agenda.

92. Rawls, *A Theory of Justice*, 226, and *Political Liberalism*, lecture 8, secs. 7, 12; emphasis added. In *Political Liberalism* (357–58), Rawls adds:

> [T]he instituted arrangements must not impose any undue burdens on the various political groups in society and must affect them all in an equitable manner. Plainly, what counts as an undue burden is itself a question, and in any particular case is to be answered by reference to the purpose of achieving the fair value of the political liberties. For example, the prohibition of large contributions from private persons or corporations to political candidates is not an undue burden (in the requisite sense) on wealthy persons and groups. Such a prohibition may be necessary so that citizens similarly gifted and motivated have roughly an equal chance of influencing the government's policy and of attaining positions of authority irrespective of their economic and social class. It is precisely this equality which defines the fair value of the political liberties.

See also Gilbert, "Equality and Social Theory"; Norman Daniels, "Equal Liberty and Unequal Worth of Liberty," in *Reading Rawls*, ed. Daniels (New York: Basic Books, 1975); and Garfinkel, *Forms of Explanation*.

93. Thompson and Gutmann, *Democracy and Disagreement*, 204–5.

94. By "effective" here, I mean, for example, a restriction of campaign financing to a public fund contributed to equally by citizens and allocated equally among candidates for comparable offices, coupled with a barring of additional private contributions.

95. See Gilbert, *Democratic Individuality*, chaps. 7–8 for related arguments on equal incomes as a vehicle to promote individuality.

96. This criterion, perhaps pallidly, recalls Mill's and Walzer's test of self-help: "It is during an arduous struggle to become free by one's one efforts that these virtues [of liberty] have the best chance of springing up" (Walzer, *Just and Unjust Wars* (1977), 87, chap. 6).

97. A commission divided between six Democrats and six Republicans.

98. Sunstein, *Democracy and Free Speech*, 98. In the state of New York, minor parties can nominate a candidate jointly with others. This practice allows a voice to citizens who support such parties' programs, yet worry that particular votes will not be effective. Under rigid, "bipartisan" control, however, many states bar this democratic practice. With impressive legal and academic support, the New Party has recently challenged such policies in Wisconsin before the Supreme Court, to no avail.

99. In conversation, the editor of the *Rocky Mountain News*, Vincent Carroll, critically characterized "reasonable" opinion in this way. A conservative journal, the *News*—alone among mainstream U.S. papers—initially opposed the Gulf War as a betrayal of the national interest. With the invasion, however, it sprouted flags on the front page.

100. Along with Freud and Keynes, Noam Chomsky has offered one of perhaps the five most significant theories in the social sciences of the twentieth century. Since the Vietnam

War, he has written prolifically on American-sponsored violations of human rights. Yet even Chomsky appears only rarely on National Public Radio.

101. Consider Sunstein, *Democracy and Free Speech*, 119, on a "New Deal for speech."

102. Sunstein, *Democracy and Free Speech*, 102–3.

103. Despite an academic facade, *The Bell Curve* offers no new arguments or research on behalf of its conclusions, fails to answer central arguments and evidence critical of its thesis, and sneakily relies, as if objective, on neo-Nazi sources supported by the Pioneer Fund or published in the *Mankind Quarterly* (Charles Lane, "The Tainted Sources of *The Bell Curve*," *New York Review of Books*, December 1, 1994). Its "success" in the media in 1994—fifty years after the defeat of Nazism—raises the question of why researchers of racist sympathies gravitate to IQ testing, what camouflage the methodological doctrines surrounding this enterprise may provide. See Gilbert, "What Then?" sec. 3.

104. Rawls, *Political Liberalism*, lecture 8, secs. 10–12; Cohen, "Freedom of Expression."

105. Sunstein, *Democracy and Free Speech*, chap. 6; Cohen, "Freedom of Expression." This criterion rules out not only derogations of workers and other poor people in capitalist society, but also stigmatization of disagreed-with views as class-based, procapitalist, "petit bourgeois," or "revisionist"—by radicals. Put differently, as in the tradition of nonviolence, the aim is to treat persons as opponents of (potential) integrity and "souls," not as "enemies." Once again, Thompson and Gutmann's criterion of civic magnanimity is central to democratic debate.

106. Sunstein, *Democracy and Free Speech*, 185–86, 193, also discusses the apparent reversal of this decision in *New York Times v. Sullivan*.

107. The Nazis modeled sterilization and miscegenation laws on those of Indiana and Virginia; they then went further.

108. Charles A. Murray, *Losing Ground* (New York: Basic Books, 1984). Eugenics also legitimizes differential sentencing (Miller, *Search and Destroy*, chaps. 1–5).

109. Cohen, "Freedom of Expression."

110. Canadian J. Phillippe Rushton proffered a supermarket questionnaire to males of different ethnic groups about "length of ejaculation" and published his "findings" (Adam Miller, "Professors of Hate," *Rolling Stone*, October 20, 1994, 110). Richard Herrnstein and Charles Murray, *The Bell Curve* (New York: Free Press, 1994), cite eight of Rushton's articles.

111. Cheryl Payer, *The Debt Trap* (New York: Monthly Review Press, 1974). The IMF could require cutbacks of, say, military budgets. The elite in the borrowing state would, however, resist: hence, the Fund's preference for harming the poor and ravaging a common good.

112. T. C. Schelling, "The Global Dimension," in *Rethinking America's Security*, ed. Graham Allison and Gregory F. Treverton (New York: Norton, 1992), 200; Richard Falk, *On Humane Governance: Toward a New Global Politics* (University Park: Pennsylvania State University Press, 1995), 51–52.

113. John Cassidy, "The Return of Karl Marx," in a fashionable magazine—the *New Yorker*, October 20–27, 1997, 248–59—now recalls this, from a capitalist standpoint, disquieting fact.

114. David Held, *Democracy and the Global Order: From the Modern State to Cosmopolitan Governance* (Stanford: Stanford University Press, 1995), 232–33.

115. Held, *Democracy and Global Order*, 278–80. In "Democracy and the New World Order," in *Cosmopolitan Democracy: An Agenda for a New World Order*, ed. David Held and Daniele Archibugi (Cambridge: Polity Press, 1995), 88, 114–15, he notes, in passing, "the deficiencies" of the United Nations—its domination and financing by the great powers, particularly the United States—which he traces to the state system "with its deep structural embeddedness in the capitalist economy." Likewise, Norberto Bobbio, "Democracy and the

International System," in Held and Archibugi, *Cosmopolitan Democracy*, 32, gestures at contemporary obstacles.

116. Held, *Democracy and Global Order*, 229–30.

117. Daniele Archibugi, "From the United Nations to Cosmopolitan Democracy," in Held and Archibugi, *Cosmopolitan Democracy*, 140–42, 152–58. Held also suggests two changes at the U.N.

118. Mary Kaldor, "European Institutions, Nation-States, and Nationalism," in Held and Archibugi, *Cosmopolitan Democracy*, 90–93.

119. Stephen Krasner, "Compromising Westphalia," *International Security* 20, no. 3 (1995–96): 115, emphasizes comparable erosions of sovereignty throughout the epoch of "Westphalia."

120. Stressing positive features of the contemporary global environment, David Held, "Democracy: From City-States to a Cosmopolitan Order?" *Political Studies* 40 (1992): 26, unlike Marx, downplays its harms: "What is new about the modern global system is the spread of globalization in and through new dimensions of activity—technological, organizational, administrative and legal, among others—and the chronic intensification of patterns of interconnectedness mediated by such phenomena as the modern communications industry and new information technology."

121. Overlapping with Waltz's emphasis in *Theory of International Politics* on restricting the four *p*s—poverty, pollution, population, and proliferation—they realize international public goods.

122. The U.S. stations thirty-eight thousand troops in South Korea.

123. *New York Times*, May 3, 1998.

124. After recovering from his wounds, Muller organized both veterans against the war and the first postwar citizen missions of mercy to Vietnam.

125. Francis X. Clines, "Militant Veteran Wages War against Land Mines," *New York Times*, December 3, 1997.

126. Clines, "Militant Veteran Wages War." Even General H. Norman Schwartzkopf signed a letter to the president, supporting the ban.

127. Clines, "Militant Veteran Wages War."

128. James Gerstenzang, "Germany Powering Way to Efficiency," *Denver Post*, November 17, 1996, A12.

129. William Drozdiak, "World Increasingly Disdainful of Powerful U.S.," *Denver Post*, November 13, 1997, A27.

130. Questioning current models of climate change, MIT professor Richard Lindzen dissents from the consensus in the scientific community. William K. Stevens, "Skeptic Asks: Is It Really Warmer?" *New York Times*, June 17, 1996.

131. William K. Stevens, "Kyoto Agreement Only a Beginning in Fight against Global Warming," *New York Times*, December 12, 1997.

132. William K. Stevens, "Talks on Global Warming Open in Kyoto," *New York Times*, December 2, 1997.

133. Future presidential candidate Gore's appearance at the conference presaged this change. Retreating from, though not quite abandoning, his onetime stand on global warming, Gore moved cautiously between environmentalists and the oil companies. James Bennet, "Senate Fight to Be Tough," *New York Times*, December 11, 1997. Within the administration, Tim Wirth, undersecretary of state for environmental affairs, fought for major reductions, lost, and resigned (John H. Cushman Jr. and David F. Sanger, "No Simple Fight: The Forces That Shaped the Clinton Plan," *New York Times*, November 28, 1997).

134. William K. Stevens, "Global Emissions Accord Gets Nod: But U.S. Hedges on Volatile Issue," *New York Times*, December 11, 1997.

135. Charles J. Hanley, "Warming Hot Topic for 150 Nations," *Denver Post*, November 30, 1997, A30.

136. So does the burning of rain forests—in 1997 at a record high—in Indonesia and Brazil. Such burning diminishes absorption of carbon dioxide by trees. Todd Lewan, "Amazon Rain Forest a Spark Away from Disaster," *Denver Post*, December 4, 1997, A12.

137. Keith Bardauer, "License to Pollute: Trucks, Darlings of Drivers, Are Favored by the Law, Too," *New York Times*, November 30, 1997, A24. The figure varies from city to city with the severity of auto inspection.

138. Bardauer, *New York Times*, November 30, 1997, A24. This withdrawal cost the journal 7 percent of its advertising revenue and forced the editors to shorten it.

139. John H. Cushman Jr., "Most Favor U.S. Action on Warming," *New York Times*, November 28, 1997, A14.

140. Bennet, "Senate Fight Tough."

141. John H. Cushman Jr., "How Climate Change Treaty Could Affect U.S.," *New York Times*, December 12, 1997.

142. Warren Brown and Martha M. Hamilton, "New Cars Would Cut Emissions by 99%," *Washington Post*, December 18, 1997.

143. Stevens, "Kyoto Agreement Only Beginning," and "The Coming Battle over Kyoto," editorial, *New York Times*, December 12, 1997.

144. Robin Wright, "Rights Group Argues U.S. Poses a 'Growing Threat,'" *Denver Post*, December 5, 1997, A3.

145. United States Civil Rights Congress, *We Charge Genocide*. After the civil rights movement, President Carter signed the agreement. Yet during his tenure, the larger pattern of U.S. human-rights policy remained abysmal (Chomsky and Hermann, *Political Economy of Rights*). Since leaving office, however, Carter has provided striking leadership for a common good.

146. Like Carter, Clinton and Gore are aware of the relevant moral and intellectual issues. That these two men—who have sought "leadership" relentlessly since they were teenagers—cave in to particular interests is sad.

147. Secretary of State Madeleine Albright has spoken out on this issue. Barbara Crossette, "Legal Experts Agree on an Outline for a World Criminal Court," *New York Times*, December 14, 1997.

148. Barbara Crossette, "World Criminal Court Having Painful Birth," *New York Times*, August 13, 1997.

149. War crimes are uncommon. With the highest stakes, however, for instance concerning an armed world state, an analogous response would not be persuasive.

150. Barbara Crossette, "Prosecutor Proposes Permanent International Criminal Court, *New York Times*, December 9, 1997.

151. Randall Forsberg, "Toward the End of War," *Boston Review*, October–November 1997, 4–9. This issue includes a symposium on the possibility of abolishing war.

152. Worried about bombing by Saddam, citizens of Tel Aviv use this term (*Denver Post*, January 30, 1998, A1). A young Iraqi pharmacist, Kazem Hani, remarked: "I think this may be the first time a lot of people may die because your President has turned the White House into a brothel" (Youssef M. Ibrahim, "Standoff with Iraq: Listen to the People Caught in the Crosshairs," *New York Times*, February 23, 1998, A7). See also *Time*'s cover story, "Double Trouble," March 2, 1998, on the interplay of the two crises. Contrasted to the criminal threat to the Constitution posed by Watergate, however, this analogy is an exaggeration.

153. Drs. Mary Sarton-Fawzi and Peter Pellett probably base their overall figures on Iraqi Ministry of Health reports. Nonetheless, these estimates indicate a magnitude of suffering. United Nations Food and Agricultural Organization, *Evaluation of Food and Nutrition Situation in Iraq* (Rome, December 1995).

154. United Nations International Children's Emergency Fund, "Disastrous Situation of Children in Iraq," press release, October 4, 1996. See also the March 26, 1997 UNICEF

press release; UNICEF, "Nearly One Million Children Malnourished in Iraq," New York, November 1997; World Health Organization, "The Health Conditions of the Population in Iraq since the Gulf Crisis," March 1996.

155. Rick McDowell, "Iraq—as the People Suffer," *Catholic Worker*, January–February 1998. Averring "freedom" from government control, the American press questions Iraqi "claims" that the boycott has killed civilians: "In a government organized march 62 small empty coffins [were] carried through Baghdad in a symbolic funeral for children *Iraq says* have died because of a shortage of medicine under U.N. sanctions" ("Related News," *Denver Post*, February 22, 1998, A9; emphasis added).

156. Albright, remarks at Ohio State, *New York Times*, February 19, 1998, A9.

157. Walzer, *Just and Unjust Wars*.

158. McDowell, "Iraq—as People Suffer."

159. Ibrahim, "Standoff with Iraq," A7.

160. Ved Nanda, "Put Saddam on Trial," *Denver Post*, February 25, 1998, B9.

161. William J. Broad and Judith Miller, "Iraq's Deadliest Arms: Puzzles Breed Fears," *New York Times*, February 26, 1998, A1. Miller requested information from Francis A. Boyle, professor of international law at the University of Illinois and author of Congress's 1989 Biological Weapons Anti-Terrorism Act. Yet these reporters did not include his account of continuing American biological weapons production as well as *U.S. shipment of weapons-specific agents, including anthrax, to Iraq during the Iran War*. They also omitted inspector Richard Zalinskas's contention on National Public Radio that the U.N. had investigated "all reasonable weapons sites" and "destroyed whatever potential existed." Ironically, Miller's initial letter notes: "The American shipments of anthrax strains to Baghdad are now well known." Yet in its sudden account of the Iraqi biological "threat," no mass media source included this fact. Boyle offered an e-mail response to the article as well as the correspondence at fboyle@Law.UIUC.edu.

162. Ibrahim, "Standoff with Iraq."

163. McDowell, "Iraq—as People Suffer."

164. Pentagon speech, *New York Times*, February 16, 1998.

165. The Pentagon authorized the use of three hundred tons of depleted uranium shells against Iraq ("The Depleted Uranium Project," press release, June 24, 1997; *New York Times*, February 26, 1998, A26). In contrast, as Hani notes, "We [Iraq] have no army. Anyone can see that we cannot defend ourselves" (Ibrahim, "Standoff with Iraq").

166. Unfortunately, the president will almost certainly not repeat such an event. The next day, the *New York Times* ran James Bennet's "White House: Bad Vibes from the Heartland Launch Fleet of Finger-Pointers," February 19, 1998, A9. *Time* reporters (March 2, 1998, 38) insisted that "the forum could have been held in a smaller hall, with a crowd carefully prescreened in the usual fashion for the White House roadshow. Instead it was the wrong people in the wrong place in front of the wrong audience; the hecklers put the panel on the defensive, three Budweiser frogs bobbing weakly on gusts of mob [better, no doubt, to have White House campaigns for war undeterred by democracy] emotion."

167. "War of Words: The Administration, Its Critics, and Questions of Moral Right," *New York Times*, February 19, 1998, A9. Her claim may well be true: while the U.S. turned ships bearing refugee Jews from Europe away in the late 1930s, it "cared" more about them than Hitler did.

168. CNN, of course, belongs to the mainstream press. Patriotism sweeps the media more through consensus—the shunning of anyone with a critical view—than coercion. CNN, however, initially tried to depict the protestors as a "couple of dozen," whereas in an audience of six thousand, two hundred activists had many sympathizers (*New York Times*, February 19, 1998, A9). Nonetheless, CNN's owner opposed bombing ("Ted Turner to Shalala: Don't Attack," *Denver Post*, February 21, 1998, A2).

169. In response to Ohio State, Clinton decided to seek a hard-to-get congressional vote before bombing (*Time*, March 2, 1998, 38).

170. Daniel Schor, *All Things Considered*, National Public Radio, February 22, 1998.

171. As in the cases of continuing CIA "covert activity" or the impact of the boycott on Iraqi civilians, no strong movement from below means no policy consistent with democracy.

172. Robert D. Putnam, "Diplomacy and Domestic Politics: The Logic of Two-Level Games," *International Organization* 42, no. 3 (1988): 427–60.

173. David Goldfischer, "Rethinking the Unthinkable after the Cold War: Toward Long-Term Nuclear Policy Planning," paper presented to the Annual Meeting of the American Political Science Association, 1997, 36–37.

174. John Mearsheimer, "Back to the Future: Instability in Europe after the Cold War," *International Security* 15, no. 1 (1990).

175. As in Russia, China, and Vietnam, the carnage of world war has often instigated twentieth-century revolutions. One might, however, envision more favorable—*comparatively* humane—circumstances for future social transformations.

176. For instance, Marx's *Civil War in France* juxtaposes the honor of Communards with Versaillese murderousness. In contemporary Peru, the unwillingness of the Tupac Amaru to kill any of their hostages contrasts—except in the inverted perspective of the mainstream media—with Fujimori's bloodthirstiness.

177. Danilo Zolo, *Cosmopolis: Prospects for World Government*, trans. David McKie (Cambridge: Polity Press, 1997), chap. 1; Held, *Democracy and Global Order*, 95 n. 12, briefly concurs.

178. Thus, Held, *Democracy and Global Order*, 88 n. 10, rightly, if sourly, stresses that the total U.N. budget, about $8 billion, "is approximately what was spent last Christmas [1994] on Western children, or approximately what U.S. citizens spend each year on cut flowers and potted plants." The U.N. spends half that amount—$4 billion annually—on interventions ("peacekeeping") and emergency relief.

179. Walzer, *Just and Unjust Wars* (1977), 105–6.

180. Zolo, *Cosmopolis*, 159. Cases of torture or murder of Somali civilians by Italian and Belgian soldiers under U.N. command highlight the debilities of humanitarian *intervention* (Jennifer Gould, "UN Soldiers Acquitted," *Village Voice*, July 9–15, 1997; "Beasts in Blue Berets," *New American*, September 29, 1997).

181. Walzer, *Just and Unjust Wars* (1977), 87–96.

182. Zolo, *Cosmopolis*, 156–57.

183. Luttwak, "Paradoxes of Conflict," *Boston Review*, October–November, 1997, 12. In an unwitting self-parody of the professional strategist, however, Luttwak mourns the "nondiversified emotional investment" of mothers with one son, which, he "fears," presents a substantial obstacle to war. See also Carol Cohn, "Sex and Death in the Rational World of Defense Intellectuals," *Signs* 12, no. 4 (1987): 687–718.

184. Falk, *On Humane Governance*, 238–39.

185. Ron Dellums, "The High Cost of Failure," *Boston Review*, October–November 1997, 14–15.

186. Marx and Engels, *Selected Works*, 1:284–85, 332; Gilbert, *Marx's Politics*, chap. 11.

187. Widening refers to the range of issues, deepening to the realization of particular measures.

188. The Saudi monarchy, for instance, forbids driver's licenses to women.

189. In this setting, the comparatively army-less Hussein has acquired the initiative.

190. These results mirror those Krasner, *Defending the National Interest*, traces for evidently *unilateral* American interventions.

191. Falk stresses the economic "G7" as an imperial substitute even for the U.N. He

rightly looks to "globalization from below" that may "give political weight to renewed movements to achieve social and economic rights" (*On Humane Governance*, 106–7).

192. This knowledge is often problematic. Two friends of mine, both Vietnam veterans, relate the routine in their companies. They would go as far away from battle as possible, get high, return after five to seven days, and report a "bloated body count."

193. Downs and Rocke, "Conflict, Agency, and Gambling for Resurrection," 67.

194. Downs and Rocke, "Conflict, Agency, and Gambling for Resurrection," 59–67, 72–75, offer a striking mathematical interpretation of their theory.

195. Scholars who admire England sometimes recommend Parliament to Americans overly easily as, comparatively, efficient. As an antidote to aggression, however, Downs and Rocke's argument is compelling.

196. Cited in Downs and Rocke, "Conflict, Agency, and Gambling for Resurrection," 69.

197. Plato's "city in speech" deprives guardians of spouses, children, and personal property. Marx's proposal that worker-officials, modeled on those of the Paris Commune, should receive wages no higher than those of a skilled worker also attempts to counter this danger (Gilbert, *Democratic Individuality*, chap. 8).

198. I owe this objection to George Downs.

199. Robin Blackburn, *The Overthrow of Colonial Slavery, 1776–1848* (London: Verso, 1988), 222–26, 258–59, stresses this high point of Jacobinism.

200. The failure to consider individual rights in the democratic-peace literature is startling.

201. Putnam, "Diplomacy and Domestic Politics," 428–29, 434–35.

202. Glenn H. Snyder and Paul Diesing, *Conflicting Nations: Bargaining, Decision-Making, and System Structure* (Princeton: Princeton University Press, 1977), 510–25. William Clark of Georgia Tech and Kenneth Schultz of Princeton are currently working on the role of such interactions in the expansion of democracy.

203. The Montgomery bus boycott.

204. Sudarshan Kapur, *Raising Up a Prophet: The African-American Encounter with Gandhi* (Boston: Beacon Press, 1992).

205. Perhaps I should say: costless in terms of official persecution or sentencing. The wretchedness and servility, characteristic, just below the surface, of elite politics, is—at least for some—a detriment.

206. Michel Foucault, *Surveiller et punir. Naissance de la prison* (Paris: Editions Gallimard, 1975); Caute, *The Great Fear*; Schrecker, *No Ivory Tower*; Fariello, *Red Scare*.

207. Among democratic theorists, Cohen and Rogers, *Inequity and Intervention*, discuss the domestic impact of U.S. war on Nicaragua. See also Rawls, "The Law of Peoples."

208. The original proponents of pluralism—Dahl and Lindblom—now believe that the "power of large corporations" is inconsistent with democracy. Charles Lindblom, *Politics and Markets* (New York: Basic Books, 1977), 356; Robert A. Dahl, *A Preface to Economic Democracy* (Berkeley and Los Angeles: University of California Press, 1985). Only radicals like Walzer and Joseph M. Schwartz, *The Permanence of the Political* (Princeton: Princeton University Press, 1995), hold to it, as a postrevolutionary conception (Gilbert, *Democratic Individuality*, 350–51).

Bibliography

Amdur, Robert . "Rawls' Theory of Justice: Domestic and International Perspectives." *World Politics* 29, no. 3 (1977).

Archibugi, Daniele. "From the United Nations to Cosmopolitan Democracy." In *Cosmopolitan Democracy: An Agenda for a New World Order*, ed. David Held and Daniele Archibugi. Cambridge: Polity Press, 1995.

Arendt, Hannah. *Crises of the Republic*. Harmondsworth, Middlesex: Penguin, 1973.

——. *On Violence*. New York: Harcourt Brace Jovanovich, 1977.

Aristotle. *Nicomachean Ethics*. Trans. H. Rackham. Loeb Classical Library. 1975.

Art, Robert J., and Kenneth N. Waltz. "Technology, Strategy, and the Uses of Force." In *The Uses of Force*, ed. Art and Waltz. Lanham, Md.: University Press of America, 1983.

Ashley, Richard K. "The Poverty of Neo-Realism." *International Organization* 38 (1984).

Avineri, Shlomo. *The Social and Political Thought of Karl Marx*. Cambridge: Cambridge University Press, 1970.

Bagby, Laurie. "The Uses and Abuses of Thucydides in International Relations." *International Organization* 48, no. 1 (1994).

Barber, Benjamin R. *Jihad versus McWorld*. New York: Times Books, 1995.

——. *Strong Democracy*. Berkeley and Los Angeles: University of California Press, 1984.

Barnet, Richard. *Intervention and Revolution: America's Confrontation with Insurgent Movements around the World*. New York: World, 1968.

Bedau, Hugu Adam. "Genocide in Vietnam?" In *Philosophy, Morality, and International Affairs*, ed. Virginia Held, Sidney Morgenbesser, and Thomas Nagel. Oxford: Oxford University Press, 1974.

Beitz, Charles R. "Justice and International Relations." *Philosophy and Public Affairs* 4, no. 4 (1975).

Berrigan, Philip, and Fred A. Wilcox. *Fighting the Lamb's War: Skirmishes with the American Empire. The Autobiography of Philip Berrigan*. Monroe, Maine: Common Courage Press, 1997.

Blackburn, Robin. *The Overthrow of Colonial Slavery, 1776–1848*. London: Verso, 1988.

Block, Ned, and Gerald Dworkin. "I.Q., Heritability, and Inequality." *Philosophy and Public Affairs* 3 (1974): 331–409, 4 (1974): 40–99.

Blum, William. *Killing Hope: U.S. Military and CIA Interventions since World War II*. Monroe, Maine: Common Courage Press, 1995.

Blunt, Anthony. *Picasso's "Guernica."* New York: Oxford University Press, 1969.

Bobbio, Norberto. "Democracy and the International System." In *Cosmopolitan*

Democracy: An Agenda for a New World Order, ed. David Held and Daniele Archibugi. Cambridge: Polity Press, 1995.

Boeck, Wilhelm, and Jaime Sabartes. *Picasso*. New York: Henry N. Abrams, 1955.

Brandt, Joe, ed. *Black Americans in the Spanish People's War against Fascism, 1936–1939*. New York: International Publishers, n.d.

Brierly, J. L. *The Law of Nations*. Oxford: Oxford University Press, 1963.

Brown, Michael K. "The Segmented Welfare System." In *Remaking the Welfare State*, ed. Michael K. Brown. Philadelphia: Temple University Press, 1988.

Brown, Wendy. *Manhood and Politics*. Lanham, Md.: Rowman and Littlefield, 1988.

Bundy, William. *A Tangled Web: The Making of Foreign Policy in the Nixon Presidency*. New York: Hill and Wang, 1998.

Butterfield, Herbert. *Christianity and History*. New York: Charles Scribner's Sons, 1950.

Cassidy, John. "The Return of Karl Marx." *New Yorker*, October 20–27, 1997, 248–59.

Castells, Manuel. "Immigrant Workers and Class Struggles in Advanced Capitalism: The West European Experience." *Politics and Society* 5, no. 1 (1975).

Castles, Stephen, and Godula Kosack. *Immigrant Workers and Class Structure in Western Europe*. Oxford: Oxford University Press, 1973.

Caute, David. *The Great Fear: The Anti-Communist Purge under Truman and Eisenhower*. New York: Simon and Schuster, 1978.

Chan, Steve. "Mirror, Mirror on the Wall . . . Are Freer Countries More Pacific?" *Journal of Conflict Resolution* 28, no. 4 (1984).

Chenery, Hollis, et al. *Redistribution with Growth*. Oxford: Oxford University Press, 1974.

Chomsky, Noam. *What Uncle Sam Really Wants*. Berkeley: Odonian Press, 1989.

Chomsky, Noam, and Edward Hermann. *The Political Economy of Human Rights: The Washington Connection and Third World Fascism*. Vol. 1. Boston: South End Press, 1977.

Cloward, Richard, and Frances Fox Piven. *Poor People's Movements*. New York: Pantheon, 1977.

Cohen, G. A. *Marx's Theory of History: A Defense*. Princeton: Princeton University Press, 1977.

———. "Reconsidering Historical Materialism." In *Nomos: Marxism*, ed. J. Roland Pennock. New York: New York University Press, 1984.

Cohen, Josh. "Do Values Explain Facts? The Case of Slavery." In *American Political Science Association Proceedings*. Ann Arbor: University of Michigan Press, 1986.

———. "Freedom of Expression." *Philosophy and Public Affairs* 22, no. 3 (1993).

Cohen, Josh, and Joel Rogers. *Inequity and Intervention*. Boston: South End Press, 1986.

Cohn, Carol. "Sex and Death in the Rational World of Defense Intellectuals." *Signs* 12, no. 4 (1987): 687–718.

Connolly, William. "Identity and Difference in Global Politics." In *International/Intertextual Relations*, ed. James Der Derian and Michael Shapiro. Lexington, Mass.: Lexington Books, 1989.

Connor, W. Robert. *Greek Political Leadership*. Princeton: Princeton University Press, 1969.

———. *Thucydides*. Princeton: Princeton University Press, 1984.

Cusack, David. *Revolution and Counterrevolution in Chile*. Denver: Graduate School of International Studies Monograph Series, 1977.

Dahl, Robert A. *A Preface to Economic Democracy*. Berkeley and Los Angeles: University of California Press, 1985.

Daniels, Norman. "Equal Liberty and Unequal Worth of Liberty." In *Reading Rawls*, ed. Norman Daniels. New York: Basic Books, 1975.

Dellums, Ron. "The High Cost of Failure." *Boston Review*, October–November 1997, 14–15.

DeMartino, George, and Stephen Cullenberg. "Beyond the Competitiveness Debate: An Internationalist Agenda." *Social Text* 41 (winter 1994): 11–39.

de Romilly, Jacqueline. *Thucydides and Athenian Imperialism*. Trans. Philip Thody. Oxford: Basil Blackwell, 1963.

———. *The Rise and Fall of States, According to Greek Authors*. Ann Arbor: University of Michigan Press, 1977.

Deming, Barbara. "On Revolution and Equilibrium." In *Revolution and Equilibrium*. New York: Grossman, 1971.

Dewey, John. *The Public and Its Problems*. Chicago: Gateway, 1946.

Dinnerstein, Leonard. *America and the Survivors of the Holocaust*. New York: Columbia University Press, 1982.

Donnelly, Jack. "Realism and the Academic Study of International Relations." In *Political Science in History: Research Programmes and Political Traditions*, ed. James Farr, John S. Dryzek, and Stephen T. Leonard. Cambridge: Cambridge University Press, 1995.

Douglass, Frederick. "Did John Brown Fail?" Address delivered in Harpers Ferry, West Virginia, on May 30, 1881, reprinted in *The Frederick Douglass Papers*, ed. John W. Blassingame and John R. McKivigan, vol. 5. New Haven: Yale University Press, 1979.

Downs, George, and David M. Rocke. "Conflict, Agency, and Gambling for Resurrection: The Principal-Agent Problem Goes to War." In *Optimal Imperfection? Domestic Uncertainty and Institutions in International Relations*. Princeton: Princeton University Press, 1995.

Doyle, Michael W. "Kant, Liberal Legacies, and Foreign Affairs." *Philosophy and Public Affairs* 12, nos. 3–4 (1983): 205–35, 323–53.

———. "Liberalism and World Politics." *American Political Science Review* 80, no. 4 (1986): 1151–69.

Dworkin, Ronald. *Life's Dominion*. New York: Knopf, 1993.

———. *Taking Rights Seriously*. Cambridge: Harvard University Press, 1977.

Emmanuel, Arghiri. *Unequal Exchange*. New York: Monthly Review Press, 1972.

Engels, Friedrich. *Anti-Dühring*. New York: International Publishers, 1939.

———. *Revolution and Counterrevolution in Germany*. Trans. Eleanor Marx Aveling. New York: Capricorn Books, 1971.

Euben, J. Peter. "The Battle of Salamis and the Origins of Political Theory." *Political Theory* 14, no. 3 (1986).

———. "Corruption." In *Political Innovation and Conceptual Change*, ed. Terence Ball and James Farr. New York: Cambridge University Press. 1989.

———. *The Tragedy of Political Theory: The Road Not Taken*. Princeton: Princeton University Press, 1990.

Fagen, Richard R. "The Realities of U.S.-Mexican Relations." *Foreign Affairs 55*, no. 4 (1977).

Falk, Richard. *On Humane Governance: Toward a New Global Politics*. University Park: Pennsylvania State University Press, 1995.

Faltermeyer, Edmund. "Who Will Do the Dirty Work Tomorrow?" *Fortune*, January 1974.

Fariello, Griffen. *Red Scare*. New York: Norton, 1995.

Farrar, Cynthia. *The Origins of Democratic Thinking: The Invention of Politics in Classical Athens*. Cambridge: Cambridge University Press, 1988.

Fields, Rona M. *The Portuguese Revolution and the Armed Forces Movement*. New York: Praeger, 1976.

Figueiredo, Antonio de. *Portugal: Fifty Years of Dictatorship*. New York: Holmes and Meier, 1976.

Finley, M. I. *Politics in the Ancient World*. Cambridge: Cambridge University Press, 1994.

Fischer, Fritz. *War of Illusions*. New York: Norton, 1975.

Fleisher, Martin, ed. *Machiavelli and the Nature of Political Thought*. New York: Atheneum, 1972.

Forsberg, Randall. "Toward the End of War." *Boston Review*, October–November 1997, 4–9.

Forsythe, David P. "Democracy, War, and Covert Action." *Journal of Peace Research* 29, no. 4 (1992).

———. *Human Rights and Peace: International and National Dimensions*. Lincoln: University of Nebraska Press, 1993.

Foucault, Michel. *Surveiller et punir. Naissance de la prison*. Paris: Editions Gallimard, 1975.

Fox, Richard. *Reinhold Niebuhr: A Biography*. New York: Pantheon, 1985.

Fraleigh, Arnold. "The Algerian Revolution as a Case Study in International Law." In *The International Law of Civil War*, ed. Richard Falk. Baltimore: Johns Hopkins University Press, 1971.

Fry, Michael G., and Arthur Gilbert. "A Historian and Linkage Politics." *International Studies Quarterly* 26 (1982).

Fulbright, J. William. *The Price of Empire*. New York: Pantheon, 1989.

Gandhi, Mahatma. *Essential Writings of Mahatma Gandhi*. Ed. Raghavan Iyer. Oxford: Oxford University Press, 1994.

Garfinkel, Alan. *Forms of Explanation*. New Haven: Yale University Press, 1981.

Giap, Vo Nguyen. *People's Army, People's War*. Foreword by Roger Hilsman. New York: Praeger, 1967.

Gilbert, Alan. "An Ambiguity in Marx's and Engels's Account of Justice and Equality." *American Political Science Review* 76, no. 2 (1982): 328–46.

———. "Changing the World: The Revolutionary Strategies of Marx and Lenin."

In *American Political Science Association Proceedings*. Ann Arbor: University of Michigan Press, 1976.

————. *Democratic Individuality*. Cambridge: Cambridge University Press, 1990.

————. *Emancipation and Independence: The American Revolution, Haiti, and Latin American Liberation*. Forthcoming.

————. "Equality and Social Theory in Rawls' *A Theory of Justice*." *Occasional Review* 819 (autumn 1978): 95–117.

————. "Exquisite Balances." *Denver Quarterly* 27, no. 1 (1992): 22–42.

————. *Friendless Aliens, Friendless Citizens*. Forthcoming.

————. "Historical Theory and the Structure of Moral Argument in Marx." *Political Theory* 9, no. 3 (1981): 173–206.

————. "Individuality and Political Association in Montesquieu." *Political Theory* 22, no. 1 (1994): 45–70.

————. "Marx on Internationalism and War." *Philosophy and Public Affairs* 7, no. 4 (1978): 346–69. Reprinted in *Marx, Justice, and History*, ed. Marshall Cohen, Thomas Scanlon, and Thomas Nagel. Princeton: Princeton University Press, 1981.

————. *Marx's Politics: Communists and Citizens*. New Brunswick: Rutgers University Press and Oxford: Martin Robertson, 1981.

————. "Must Global Politics Constrain Democracy? Realism, Regimes, and Democratic Internationalism." *Political Theory* 20, no. 1 (1992): 8–37.

————. "Power Rivalry–Motivated Democracy: A Response to Stephen Krasner." *Political Theory* 20, no. 3 (1992): 681–89.

————. "Salvaging Marx from Avineri." *Political Theory* 4, no. 1 (1976): 9–34.

————. " 'What Then?' The Irrepressible Radicalism of Democracy." In *History and the Idea of Progress*, ed. M. Richard Zinman, Jerry Weinberger, and Arthur Meltzer. Ithaca: Cornell University Press, 1995.

Gilpin, Robert. *The Political Economy of International Relations*. Princeton: Princeton University Press, 1987.

————. "The Richness of the Tradition of Political Realism." In *Neorealism and Its Critics*, ed. by Robert O. Keohane. New York: Columbia University Press, 1984.

————. "The Theory of Hegemonic War." In *The Origin and Prevention of Major Wars*, ed. Robert I. Rotberg and Theodore Rabb. Cambridge: Cambridge University Press, 1989.

Goldfield, Michael. *The Color of Politics: Race and the Mainsprings of American Politics*. New York: New Press, 1997.

Goldfischer, David. *The Best Defense*. Ithaca: Cornell University Press, 1993.

————. "Rethinking the Unthinkable after the Cold War: Toward Long-Term Nuclear Policy Planning." Paper presented to the Annual Meeting of the American Political Science Association, 1997.

Gomme, A. W. *A Historical Commentary on Thucydides*. 3 vols. Oxford: Oxford University Press, 1945.

Gordon, Michael R. "Domestic Conflict and the Origins of the First World War: The British and German Cases." *Journal of Modern History* 46 (1974).

Grene, David. *Man in His Pride*. Chicago: University of Chicago Press, 1950.

Griffin, Susan. *A Chorus of Stones*. New York: Vintage, 1992.

Hamilton, Richard F. *Restraining Myths: Critical Studies of U.S. Social Structure and Politics*. Beverly Hills, Calif.: Sage Publications, distributed by Halsted Press, New York, 1975.

Hammen, Oscar J. *The Red '48ers: Karl Marx and Friedrich Engels*. New York: Scribner's, 1969.

Harding, Vincent. *Martin Luther King: The Inconvenient Hero*. Maryknoll, Mass.: Orbis, 1996.

Harman, Gilbert. "The Inference to the Best Explanation." *Philosophical Review* 74 (1965): 88–95.

Harrison, Beverly Wildung. *Making the Connections: Essays in Feminist Social Ethics*, ed. Carol Robb. Boston: Beacon Press, 1985.

Harrison, Royden John. *Before the Socialists: Studies in Labour and Politics, 1861–1881*. London: Routledge and Kegan Paul, 1965.

Hastings, Max, and Simon Jenkins. *The Battle for the Falklands*. New York: Norton, 1983.

Hegel, G. W. F. *Elements of the Philosophy of Right*. Trans. H. B. Nisbet. Cambridge: Cambridge University Press, 1991.

———. *Phenomenology of Spirit*. Trans. A. V. Miller. Oxford: Oxford University Press, 1977.

———. *Die Vernunft in der Geschichte*. Hamburg: Meiner Verlag, 1955.

Held, David. "Democracy: From City-States to a Cosmopolitan Order?" *Political Studies* 40 (1992): 10–39.

———. *Democracy and the Global Order: From the Modern State to Cosmopolitan Governance*. Stanford: Stanford University Press, 1995.

———. "Democracy and the New World Order." In *Cosmopolitan Democracy: An Agenda for a New World Order*, ed. David Held and Daniele Archibugi. Cambridge: Polity Press, 1995.

Held, David, and Daniele Archibugi, eds. *Cosmopolitan Democracy: An Agenda for a New World Order*. Cambridge: Polity Press, 1995.

Hemingway, Ernest. *For Whom the Bell Tolls*. Philadelphia: Blakiston, 1940.

Herrnstein, Richard, and Charles A. Murray. *The Bell Curve*. New York: Free Press, 1994.

Herz, John. "Idealist Internationalism and the Security Dilemma." In *The Nation-State and the Crisis of World Politics*. New York: D. McKay, 1976.

Hobbes, Thomas. *Behemoth; or, The Long Parliament*. Chicago: University of Chicago Press, 1990.

———. *Leviathan or the Matter, Forme and Power of a Commonwealth Ecclesiasticall and Civil*. Ed. Michael Oakeshott. New York: Collier, n.d.

———. "Of the Life and History of Thucydides." In *History of the Peloponnesian War*, trans. Thomas Hobbes. Chicago: University of Chicago, 1989.

Hoffman, Stanley. *Dead Ends: American Foreign Policy in the New Cold War*. Cambridge, Mass.: Ballinger, 1983.

———. *Duties beyond Borders*. New York: Syracuse University Press, 1981.

———. *Gulliver's Troubles*. New York: McGraw-Hill, 1968.

———. *Janus and Minerva: Essays in the Theory and Practice of International Politics*. Boulder, Colo.: Westview Press, 1987.

Hollis, Martin, and Steve Smith. *Explaining and Understanding International Relations*. Oxford: Clarendon Press, 1991.

Holmes, Stephen. "Aristippus in and out of Athens." *American Political Science Review* 73 (March 1979).

———. "Introduction" to Hobbes, *Behemoth*. Chicago: University of Chicago Press, 1990.

Holsti, K. J. *International Politics: A Framework for Analysis*. 5th ed. Englewood Cliffs, N.J.: Prentice-Hall, 1988.

Honderich, Ted. *Political Violence*. Ithaca: Cornell University Press, 1976.

Horrigan, Brenda L. "Resisting the Drawdown: Interests, Ideology, and the U.S. Defense Community in the Post–Cold War Era." Ph.D. diss., University of Denver. Ann Arbor: University Microfilms, 1996.

Humbaraci, Arslan. *Algeria: A Revolution That Failed*. London: Pall Mall Press, 1966.

Hunt, Michael. *Ideology and U.S. Foreign Policy*. New Haven: Yale University Press, 1987.

Hunt, Richard N. *The Political Ideas of Marx and Engels: Marxism and Totalitarian Democracy, 1848–50*. Pittsburgh: University of Pittsburgh Press, 1974.

Huntington, Samuel P. "The Democratic Distemper." In *The Crisis of Democracy*, ed. Huntington, Michel Crozier, and Joji Watanuki. New York: New York University Press, 1975.

———. *Political Order in Changing Societies*. New Haven: Yale University Press, 1967.

Ireland, Patrick. "Facing the True 'Fortress Europe': Immigrant and Politics in the European Community." *Journal of Common Market Studies* 24, no. 5 (1991).

———. *The Policy Challenge of Ethnic Diversity: Immigration Politics in France and Switzerland*. Cambridge: Harvard University Press, 1994.

Ishay, Micheline. *Internationalism and Its Betrayal*. Minneapolis: University of Minnesota Press, 1995.

Jay, John, Alexander Hamilton, and James Madison. *The Federalist Papers*. New York: Mentor, 1961.

Jefferson, Thomas. *Writings*. Ed. Merrill D. Peterson. New York: Library of America, 1984.

Jervis, Robert. *Perception and Misperception in International Politics*. Princeton: Princeton University Press, 1976.

Johnson, Loch. *America's Secret Power*. Oxford: Oxford University Press, 1989.

Joll, James. *The Origins of the First World War*. New York: Longman, 1984.

Jones, A. H. M. *Athenian Democracy*. Baltimore: Johns Hopkins University Press, 1986.

Judt, Tony. "Counsels on Foreign Relations." Review of William Bundy, *A Tangled Web: The Making of Foreign Policy*. *New York Review of Books*, May 24, 1998, 8.

Kagan, Donald. *The Archidamian War*. Ithaca: Cornell University Press, 1974.

Kaldor, Mary. "European Institutions, Nation-States, and Nationalism." In *Cosmopolitan Democracy: An Agenda for a New World Order*, ed. David Held and Daniele Archibugi. Cambridge: Polity Press, 1995.

Kan, Paul. "Realism and Its Discontents." *Journal of Public and International Affairs* 5 (spring 1994): 7–16.

Kant, Immanuel. *Political Writings*. Trans. H. B. Nisbet. Cambridge: Cambridge University Press, 1992.

Kant, Immanuel. *Zum Ewigen Frieden*. Bern: Scherz, n.d.

Kapur, Sudarshan. *Raising Up a Prophet: The African-American Encounter with Gandhi*. Boston: Beacon Press, 1992.

Kateb, George. "Nuclear Weapons and Individual Rights." *Dissent* 33, no. 2 (1986): 161–72.

Keen, Sam. *Faces of the Enemy*. New York: Harper and Row, 1991.

Kehr, Eckart. *Der Primat der Innenpolitik*. Berlin: E. Ebering, 1930.

Keller, William W. *The Liberals and J. Edgar Hoover: The Rise and Fall of a Domestic Intelligence State*. Princeton: Princeton University Press, 1989.

Kennan, George. *American Diplomacy*. Chicago: University of Chicago Press, 1984.

———. Foreword to *Making Europe Unconquerable: The Potential of Civilian-Based Deterrence and Defense*, by Gene Sharp. Cambridge, Mass.: Ballinger, 1986.

———. *Memoirs, 1925–1950*. Boston: Little, Brown, 1967.

———. "Morality and Foreign Policy." *Foreign Affairs* 63, no. 2 (1985).

Keohane, Robert O. *After Hegemony: Cooperation and Discord in World Political Economy*. Princeton: Princeton University Press, 1984.

Kissinger, Henry. *Diplomacy*. New York: Simon and Schuster, 1994.

———. "A Gentle Analyst of Power: Hans J. Morgenthau." *New Republic*, August 2–9, 1980, 12–14.

Klare, Michael T. "Pointing Fingers." *New York Times*. August 10, 1977.

———. *War without End*. New York: Knopf, 1972.

Kofsky, Frank. *Harry S. Truman and the War Scare of 1948*. New York: St. Martin's, 1993.

Kozol, Jonathan. *Amazing Grace*. New York: Crown, 1995.

Krasner, Stephen. "Compromising Westphalia." *International Security* 20, no. 3 (1995–96): 115–51.

———. *Defending the National Interest: Raw Materials Investment and U.S. Foreign Policy*. Princeton: Princeton University Press, 1978.

———. "Realism, Imperialism, and Democracy: A Reply to Alan Gilbert." *Political Theory* 20, no. 1 (1992): 38–52.

Kratochwil, Friedrich. *Rules, Norms, and Decisions: On the Conditions of Practical and Legal Reasoning in International Relations and Domestic Societies*. Cambridge: Cambridge University Press, 1989.

Kristeva, Julia. *Strangers to Ourselves*. New York: Columbia University Press, 1991.

Krugman, Paul. "The Wealth Gap Is Real and It's Growing." *New York Times*, August 21, 1995.

Kymlicka, Will. *Liberalism, Community, and Culture*. Oxford: Oxford University Press, 1989.

Lakatos, Imre. "Falsification and the Methodology of Scientific Research Programmes." In *Criticism and the Growth of Knowledge*, ed. Lakatos and Alan Musgrave. Cambridge: Cambridge University Press, 1970.

Lake, David. "Powerful Pacifists: Democratic States and War." *American Political Science Review* 86, no. 1 (1992): 24–37.

Lane, Charles. "The Tainted Sources of *The Bell Curve*." *New York Review of Books*, December 1, 1994.

Langer, William L. "The Origin of the Russo-Japanese War." In *Explorations in Crises*, ed. Langer. Cambridge: Harvard University Press, 1969.

Lappe, Francis Moore, and Joseph Collins. *World Hunger: Twelve Myths*. New York: Institute for Food and Development Policy, 1986.

Lappe, Francis Moore, Joseph Collins, and Rachel Danaher. *Betraying the National Interest*. New York: Grove Press, 1987.

Layne, Christopher. "Kant or Cant?" *International Security* 17, no. 2 (1994).

Lebow, Ned. "Declining Power and the Preventive Motivation for War." *World Politics* 40 (1987).

Lenin, V. I. *Collected Works*. 45 vols. Moscow: Foreign Languages Publishing House, 1974–.

Leplin, Jarrett, ed. *Scientific Realism*. Berkeley and Los Angeles: University of California Press, 1984.

Levertov, Denise. *The Freeing of the Dust*. New York: New Directions, 1975.

———. *Light Up the Cave*. New York: New Directions, 1981.

Levy, Jack S. "Domestic Politics and War." *Journal of Interdisciplinary History* 18, no. 4 (1988).

Lindblom, Charles. *Politics and Markets*. New York: Basic Books, 1977.

Locke, John. *Two Treatises of Government*. New York: Hafner, 1947.

Lüthy, Herbert. *France against Herself*. New York: Meridian, 1957.

Luttwak, Edward. "Paradoxes of Conflict." *Boston Review*, October–November 1997, 12.

MacPherson, C. B. *The Political Theory of Possessive Individualism: Hobbes to Locke*. Oxford: Oxford University Press, 1962.

Madison, James. *Writings*. Vol. 6. New York: Putnam, 1906.

Maoz, Zeev, and Bruce Russett. "Alliance, Contiguity, Wealth, and Political Stability: Is the Lack of Conflict between Democracies a Statistical Artifact?" *International Interactions* 17, no. 3 (1992): 245–68.

Marx, Karl. *Capital*. 3 vols. Trans. Samuel Moore and Edward Aveling. New York: International Publishers, 1967.

———. *Ireland and the Irish Question*. Ed. R. Dixon. New York: International Publishers, 1972.

———. *Letters to Dr. Kugelmann*. New York: International Publishers, 1934.

———. *On America and the Civil War*. Ed. Saul K. Padover. New York: McGraw-Hill, 1972.

———. *On Colonialism and Modernization*. Ed. Shlomo Avineri. Garden City, N.Y.: Doubleday, 1968.

———. *On the First International*. Ed. Saul K. Padover. New York: McGraw-Hill, 1973.

———. *Politische Schriften*. Ed. Hans-Joachin Lieber. 2 vols. Stuttgart: Cotta Verlag, 1960.

———. *The Poverty of Philosophy*. New York: International Publishers, 1963.

———. *The Revolution of 1848–49: Articles from the "Neue Rheinische Zeitung."* Trans. S. Ryazanskaya. Ed. Bernard Isaacs. New York: International Publishers, 1972.

Marx, Karl, and Friedrich Engels. *Selected Correspondence*. Trans. I. Lasker. Ed. S. Ryazanskaya. Moscow: Foreign Languages Publishing House, 1965.

Marx, Karl, and Friedrich Engels. *Selected Works*. 2 vols. Moscow: Foreign Languages Publishing House, 1962.

———. *Selected Works in One Volume*. New York: International Publishers, 1974.

———. *Werke*. 39 vols. Berlin: Dietz Verlag. 1959–.

Mayer, Arno J. "Domestic Causes of the First World War." In *The Responsibility of Power*, ed. Leonard Krieger and Fritz Stern. Garden City, N.Y.: Doubleday, 1967.

———. "Internal Causes and Purposes of War in Europe, 1870–1956: A Research Assignment." *Journal of Modern History* 41, no. 3 (1969): 291–303.

———. "Internal Crises and War since 1870." In *Revolutionary Situations in Europe, 1917–22: Germany, Italy, Austria-Hungary*, ed. Charles L. Bertrand. Montreal: Centre interuniversitaire d'études européennes, 1977.

Mayers, David. *George Kennan and the Dilemmas of US Foreign Policy*. Oxford: Oxford University Press, 1988.

McCamant, John "Intervention in Guatemala." *Comparative Political Studies* 17 (1984): 373–407.

McCoy, Alfred W. *The Politics of Heroin: CIA Complicity in the Global Drug Trade*. Expanded edition. New York: Lawrence Hill, 1991.

McGregor, Malcolm F. *The Athenians and Their Empire*. Vancouver: University of British Columbia Press, 1987.

McNamara, Robert, with Brian VanDeMark. *In Retrospect: The Tragedy and Lessons of Vietnam*. New York: Times Books, 1995.

Mearsheimer, John. "Back to the Future: Instability in Europe after the Cold War." *International Security* 15, no. 1 (1990).

Mee, Charles L., Jr. *The Marshall Plan: The Launching of the Pax Americana*. New York: Simon and Schuster, 1984.

Meier, Christian. *The Greek Discovery of Politics*. Trans. David McLintock. Oxford: Clarendon Press, 1990.

Meiggs, Russell. *The Athenian Empire*. Cambridge: Harvard University Press, 1972.

Miller, Adam. "Professors of Hate." *Rolling Stone*, October 20, 1994.

Miller, Jean Baker. *Toward a New Psychology of Women*. Boston: Beacon Press, 1976.

Miller, Jerome. *Search and Destroy: African-American Males in the Criminal Justice System*. Cambridge: Cambridge University Press, 1996.

Miller, Richard W. *Analyzing Marx*. Princeton: Princeton University Press, 1984.

———. *Fact and Method*. Princeton: Princeton University Press, 1987.

Mink, Gwendolyn. *Old Labor and New Immigrants*. Ithaca: Cornell University Press, 1986.

Montesquieu, Charles Louis de Secondat, Baron de la Brède et de. *De l'esprit des lois*. Ed. R. Derathé. 2 vols. Paris: Editions Gallimard, 1973.

———. *Oeuvres complètes*. Ed. Andre Masson. 3 vols. Paris: Editions Gallimard, 1950–55.

Moore, Barrington, Jr. *Social Origins of Dictatorship and Democracy*. Boston: Beacon Press, 1965.

Morgenthau, Hans J. "An Appreciation of Hannah Arendt (1906–1975)." *Political Theory* 4, no. 1 (1976): 5–8.

———. "Another 'Great Debate': The National Interest of the United States." *American Political Science Review* 46, no. 4 (1952): 961–88.

———. *The Decline of American Politics*. Vol. 1 of *Politics in the Twentieth Century*. Chicago: University of Chicago Press, 1962.

———. "Human Rights and Foreign Policy." In *Moral Dimensions of American Foreign Policy*, ed. Kenneth Thompson. New Brunswick, N.J.: Transaction Books, 1984.

———. *The Impasse of American Foreign Policy*. Vol. 2 of *Politics in the Twentieth Century*. Chicago: University of Chicago Press, 1962.

———. *In Defense of the National Interest*. New York: Knopf, 1952.

———. *Politics among Nations*. New York: Knopf, 1948.

———. *Politics among Nations*. 2d ed., revised. New York: Knopf, 1964.

———. *Politics among Nations*. 3d ed. New York: Knopf, 1960.

———. *Politics among Nations*. 4th ed. New York: Knopf, 1967.

———. *Politics among Nations*. 5th ed. New York: Knopf, 1973.

———. *The Purpose of American Politics*. New York: Knopf, 1960.

———. "Quisling Show." *New Republic*, December 21, 1959.

———. *The Restoration of American Politics*. Vol. 3 of *Politics in the Twentieth Century*. Chicago: University of Chicago Press, 1962.

———. *Scientific Man versus Power Politics*. Chicago: University of Chicago Press, 1946.

———. "The Shadow and Substance of Power." In *Vietnam and the United States*. Washington, D.C.: Public Affairs Press, 1965.

———. *Truth and Power: Essays of a Decade*. New York: Frederick Praeger, 1970.

Moyers, Bill D. *The Secret Government: The Constitution in Crisis*. Washington, D.C.: Seven Locks Press, 1988.

Murray, Charles A. *Losing Ground*. New York: Basic Books, 1984.

Nash, Gary B. *Race and Revolution*. Madison: Madison House, 1990.

Navasky, Victor S. *Naming Names*. Middlesex: Penguin, 1981.

Niebuhr, Reinhold. *Christianity and Power Politics*. New York: Charles Scribner's Sons, 1940.

———. *Moral Man and Immoral Society: A Study in Ethics and Politics*. New York: Charles Scribner's Sons, 1944.

———. *Reflections on the End of an Era*. New York: Charles Scribner's Sons, 1934.

———. *A Theologian of Public Life: Selected Writings of Reinhold Niebuhr*. Ed. Larry Rasmussen. Minneapolis: Fortress Press, 1991.

Oakeshott, Michael L. *Rationalism in Politics and Other Essays*. Ed. Timothy Fuller. Indianapolis: Liberty Press, 1995.

———. "Scientific Politics." In *Religion, Politics, and the Moral Life*, ed. Timothy Fuller. New Haven: Yale University Press, 1993.

Ober, Josiah. *Mass and Elite in Democratic Athens*. Princeton: Princeton University Press, 1989.

Orwin, Clifford. *The Humanity of Thucydides*. Princeton: Princeton University Press, 1994.

Paine, Suzanne. *Exporting Workers*. Cambridge: Cambridge University Press, 1974.

Parenti, Michael. "Is Nicaragua More Democratic Than the United States?" *Covert Action Information Bulletin* 26 (1986): 48–52.

Payer, Cheryl. *The Debt Trap*. New York: Monthly Review Press, 1974.

Phillips, Kevin P. *The Politics of Rich and Poor: Wealth and the American Electorate in the Reagan Aftermath*. New York: Random House, 1990.

Plato. *Apology*. In *The Dialogues of Plato*, trans. R. E. Allen. Vol. 1. New Haven: Yale University Press, 1984.

———. *Crito*. In *The Dialogues of Plato*, trans. R. E. Allen. Vol. 1. New Haven: Yale University Press, 1984.

———. *Gorgias*. Trans. Terence Irwin. Oxford: Clarendon Press, 1979.

———. *Republic*. Trans. Richard W. Sterling and William C. Scott. New York: Norton, 1985.

Pouncey, Peter. *The Necessities of War: A Study of Thucydides' Pessimism*. New York: Columbia University Press, 1980.

Proctor, Robert N. *Value-Free Science? Purity and Power in Modern Knowledge*. Cambridge: Harvard University Press, 1991.

Putnam, Hilary. "On the Corroboration of Theories." In *Collected Philosophical Papers*. Cambridge: Cambridge University Press, 1975.

Putnam, Robert D. "Diplomacy and Domestic Politics: The Logic of Two-Level Games." *International Organization* 42, no. 3 (1988): 427–60.

Raaflaub, Kurt. *Die Entdeckung der Freiheit: Zur historischen Semantik und Gesellschaftsgeschichte eines politischen Grundbegriffs des Griechen*. Munich: Beck, 1985.

Rasmussen, Larry. "Introduction: A Biographical Sketch." In *A Public Theologian: Selected Writings of Reinhold Niebuhr*, ed. Rasmussen. Minneapolis: Fortress Press, 1991.

Rawlings, Hunter R. *The Structure of Thucydides' History*. Princeton: Princeton University Press, 1981.

Rawls, John. "Justice as Fairness: Political Not Metaphysical." *Philosophy and Public Affairs* 14(1985): 223–51.

———. "The Law of Peoples." In *On Human Rights: The Oxford Amnesty Lectures*, ed. Stephen Shute and Susan Hurley. New York: Basic Books, 1993.

———. *Political Liberalism*. New York: Columbia University Press, 1993.

———. "The Priority of Right and Ideas of the Good." *Philosophy and Public Affairs* 17 (1988): 251–76.

———. *A Theory of Justice*. Cambridge: Harvard University Press, 1971.

Reich, Michael. "The Economics of Racism." In *The Capitalist System*, ed. Richard C. Edwards, Reich, and Thomas Weisskopf. Englewood Cliffs, N.J.: Prentice-Hall, 1972.

———. *Racial Inequality: A Political-Economic Analysis*. Princeton: Princeton University Press, 1981.

Rich, Adrienne. "For Ethel Rosenberg." In *A Wild Patience Has Taken Me This Far*. New York: Norton, 1981.

———. *What Is Found There: Notebooks on Poetry and Politics*. New York: Norton, 1993.

Roberts, Jennifer Tolbert. *Athens on Trial*. Princeton: Princeton University Press, 1994.

Robinson, William L. "Globalization, the World System, and 'Democracy Promotion' in U.S. Foreign Policy." *Theory and Society* 25, no. 5 (1996).

———. *Promoting Polyarchy*. Cambridge: Cambridge University Press, 1996.

Rogin, Michael Paul. *Ronald Reagan the Movie and Other Studies in American Political Demonology*. Berkeley and Los Angeles: University of California Press, 1987.

Rosecrance, Richard. *Action and Reaction in World Politics*. Boston: Little Brown, 1963.

Rousseau, Jean-Jacques. *Oeuvres complètes*. 3 vols. Paris: Editions Gallimard, 1964.

Ruchames, Louis, ed. *A John Brown Reader: The Story of John Brown in His Own Words and the Words of Those Who Knew Him*. New York: Abelard-Schuman, 1959.

Rummel, R. J. "Libertarianism and International Violence." *Journal of Conflict Resolution* 27, no. 1 (1983): 27–71.

———. "Libertarian Propositions on Violence within and between Nations." *Journal of Conflict Resolution* 27, no. 1 (1985): 419–55.

Russett, Bruce. *Controlling the Sword: The Democratic Governance of National Security*. Cambridge: Harvard University Press, 1991.

———. *Grasping the Democratic Peace: Principles for a Post–Cold War World*. Princeton: Princeton University Press, 1993.

Ryan, William. *Blaming the Victim*. New York: Vintage, 1976.

Sainte-Croix, G. E. M. de. *The Class Struggle in the Ancient Greek World: From the Archaic Age to the Arab Conquests*. Ithaca: Cornell University Press, 1981.

———. *The Origins of the Peloponnesian War*. Ithaca: Cornell University Press, 1972.

Saxton, Alexander. *The Indispensable Enemy*. Berkeley and Los Angeles: University of California Press, 1971.

Schelling, T. C. "The Global Dimension." In *Rethinking America's Security*, ed. Graham Allison and Gregory F. Treverton. New York: Norton, 1992.

Schorske, Carl E. *German Social Democracy: 1905–1917*. New York: Harper and Row, 1972.

Schrecker, Ellen. *No Ivory Tower*. New York: Oxford University Press, 1986.

Schulzinger, Robert. *The Making of the Diplomatic Mind*. Middletown, Conn.: Wesleyan University Press, 1975.

Schwartz, Joseph M. *The Permanence of the Political*. Princeton: Princeton University Press, 1995.

Scolnik, Joseph M., Jr. "An Appraisal of Studies of the Linkages between Domestic and International Conflict." *Comparative Political Studies* 6 (1974).

Scott, James. *The Moral Economy of the Peasant: Rebellion and Subsistence in Southeast Asia*. New Haven: Yale University Press, 1976.

Sen, Amartya. *Inequality Reexamined*. Cambridge: Harvard University Press, 1992.

Sen, Amartya, and Martha C. Nussbaum. "Capability and Wellbeing." In *The Quality of Life*, ed. Nussbaum and Sen. Oxford: Clarendon Paperbacks, 1993.

———. *The Quality of Life*. Oxford: Clarendon Paperbacks, 1993b.

Shapere, Dudley. *Reason and the Search for Knowledge*. Amsterdam: D. Reidel, 1984.

Sharma, Hari P. "The Green Revolution in India: Prelude to a Red One?" In *Imperialism and Revolution in South Asia*, ed. Hari P. Sharma and Kathleen Gough. New York: Monthly Review Press, 1973.

Sharp, Gene. *Making Europe Unconquerable: The Potential of Civilian-Based Deterrence and Defense*. Cambridge, Mass.: Ballinger, 1986.

Sharp, James Roger. *American Politics in the Early Republic: The Nation in Crisis*. New Haven: Yale University Press, 1993.

Singer, J. David. "The Levels-of-Analysis Problem in International Relations." In *The International System: Theoretical Essays*, ed. Klaus Knorr and Sidney Verba. Princeton: Princeton University Press, 1961.

Singer, Peter. "Famine, Affluence, and Morality." *Philosophy and Public Affairs* 1, no. 3 (1972).

Smith, James Morton. *Freedom's Fetters*. Ithaca: Cornell University Press, 1956.

Snyder, Glenn H., and Paul Diesing. *Conflicting Nations: Bargaining, Decision-Making, and System Structure*. Princeton: Princeton University Press, 1977.

Spero, Joan Edelman. *The Politics of International Economic Relations*. New York: St. Martin's, 1977.

Sunstein, Cass R. *Democracy and the Problem of Free Speech*. New York: Free Press, 1993.

Taylor, Charles. "Neutrality in Political Science." In *Philosophy, Politics, and Society*, ed. Peter Laslett. 3d series. New York: Barnes and Noble, 1964.

Thompson, Dennis, and Amy Gutmann. *Democracy and Disagreement*. Cambridge: Harvard University Press, 1996.

Thompson, E. P. *Beyond the Cold War*. New York: Pantheon, 1982.

Thoreau, Henry David. "The Last Days of John Brown." In *The Portable Thoreau*, ed. Carl Bode. New York: Penguin, 1982.

Thucydides. *History of the Peloponnesian War*. 4 vols. Loeb Classical Library, 1976.

———. *History of the Peloponnesian War*. Trans. Thomas Hobbes. Chicago: University of Chicago Press, 1989.

Tickner, J. Ann. "Hans Morgenthau's Principles of Political Realism." In *Gender and International Relations*, ed. Rebecca Grant and Kathleen Newland. Bloomington: Indiana University Press, 1991.

Tillich, Paul. *The Protestant Era*. Chicago: University of Chicago Press, 1948.

Todorov, Tzvetan. *The Conquest of America*. New York: Harper and Row, 1985.

Trelease, Allen W. *White Terror: The Ku Klux Klan Conspiracy and Southern Reconstruction*. New York: Harper and Row, 1971.

Tucker, Robert W. *The Inequality of Nations*. New York: Basic Books, 1977.

———. "Professor Morgenthau's Theory of Political Realism." *American Political Science Review* 46, no. 1 (1952): 214–24.

United States Civil Rights Congress. *We Charge Genocide*. Ed. William L. Patterson. New York: International Publishing, 1949.

United States Kerner Commission. *Report of the National Advisory Commission on Civil Disorders*. Washington, D.C.: U.S. Government Printing Office, 1968.

Van Evera, Stephen. "Primed for Peace: Europe after the Cold War." *International Security* (winter 1990–91).

Vazquez, John A. *The Power of Power Politics: A Critique*. New Brunswick, N.J.: Rutgers University Press, 1983.

———, ed. *Classics of International Relations*. 2d ed. Englewood Cliffs, N.J.: Prentice-Hall, 1990.

Walker, R. B. J. *Inside/Outside: International Relations as Political Theory*. Cambridge: Cambridge University Press, 1993.

Walker, R. B. J., and Saul Mendlovitz, eds. *Towards a Just World Peace: Perspectives from Social Movements*. London: Butterworths, 1987.

Waltz, Kenneth N. *Man, the State, and War*. New York: Columbia University Press, 1959.

———. *Theory of International Politics*. New York: McGraw-Hill, 1979.

Walzer, Michael L. *Just and Unjust Wars*. New York: Basic Books, 1977.

———. *Just and Unjust Wars*. 2d ed. New York: Basic Books, 1992.

———. "The Politics of Rescue." *Dissent* 42, no. 1 (1995): 35–41.

Weber, Max. *Economy and Society*. Trans. Gunther Roth and Claus Wittich. 3 vols. New York: Bedminister, 1968.

———. *From Max Weber: Essays in Sociology*. Ed. and trans. H. H. Gerth and C. Wright Mills. New York: Oxford University Press, 1958.

Westergaard, John, and Henrietta Resler. *Class in a Capitalist Society: A Study of Contemporary Britain*. New York: Basic Books, 1975.

Wilson, John. "'The Customary Meanings of Words Were Changed'—or Were They? A Note on Thucydides 3.82.4." *Classical Quarterly* 32, no. 1 (1982): 21–26.

Wolin, Sheldon. "Political Theory as a Vocation." In *Machiavelli and the Nature of Political Thought*, ed. Martin Fleisher. New York: Atheneum, 1972.

Woodhead, A. Geoffrey. *Thucydides on the Nature of Power*. Cambridge: Harvard University Press, 1970.

Woods, Randall Bennett. *J. William Fulbright, Vietnam, and the Search for a Cold War Foreign Policy*. Cambridge: Cambridge University Press, 1998.

Zolo, Danilo. *Cosmopolis: Prospects for World Government*. Trans. David McKie. Cambridge: Polity Press, 1997.